LOVE'S QUARRELS

A VOLUME IN THE SERIES

Massachusetts Studies in Early Modern Culture

EDITED BY

Arthur Kinney

LOVE'S QUARRELS

Reading Charity in Early Modern England

EVAN A. GURNEY

University of Massachusetts Press
Amherst and Boston

ISBN 978-1-62534-381-9 (paper); 380-2 (hardcover)

Designed by Jen Jackowitz
Set in Monotype Dante
Printed and bound by Maple Press, Inc.

Cover design by Milenda Nan Ok Lee
Cover art: Master of the Béguins, French or Flemish, active 1650–60
(possibly Abraham Willemsens, Flemish, active by 1627, died 1672).
Beggars at a Doorway, Purchase, 1871, Metropolitan Museum of Art.

Library of Congress Cataloging-in-Publication Data

Names: Gurney, Evan A., author.
Title: Love's quarrels : reading charity in early modern England / Evan A.
  Gurney.
Description: Amherst : University of Massachusetts Press, [2018] | Series:
  Massachusetts studies in early modern culture | Includes bibliographical
  references and index. |
Identifiers: LCCN 2018019146 (print) | LCCN 2018047109 (ebook) | ISBN
  9781613766286 (e-book) | ISBN 9781613766293 (e-book) | ISBN 9781625343802
  | ISBN 9781625343802?(hardcover) | ISBN 9781625343819?(paperback)
Subjects: LCSH: English literature—Early modern, 1500–1700—History and
  criticism. | Charity in literature.
Classification: LCC PR418.C33 (ebook) | LCC PR418.C33 G87 2018 (print) | DDC
  820.9/355—dc23
LC record available at https://lccn.loc.gov/2018019146

British Library Cataloguing-in-Publication Data

A catalog record for this book is available from the British Library.

An early version of chapter 1 appeared as "Thomas More and the Problem of
Charity" in *Renaissance Studies* 26, no. 2 (2012): 197–217, published by John Wiley &
Sons Ltd. Copyright © 2011 The Author. *Renaissance Studies* © 2011 The Society for
Renaissance Studies, Blackwell Publishing Ltd. An early and much truncated version
of chapter 2 appeared as "Spenser's 'May' Eclogue and Charitable Admonition," in
Spenser Studies: A Renaissance Poetry Annual 27 (2012): 193–219. Copyright © 2012 AMS
Press, Inc. I am grateful to the publishers of these journals for permission to reprint
this material.

CONTENTS

PREFACE AND ACKNOWLEDGMENTS

This book might have been a love story. Set in early modern England, it begins with two rivals, tells of a knight in dented armor who encounters Love personified, and ends (as some romances do) with divorce. But instead it is a story about love itself, and more specifically about charity—its shapes and forms, and the conflicts that emerged in response to its various demands. Despite its idealized role as the binding agent keeping society whole and in harmony, charity nevertheless is situated right in the middle of some of the fiercest disputes of the period, from the vexed inception of Reformation theologies and biblical translations in the 1520s to political and ideological controversies arriving in the midst of civil war.

Taking this contention as its starting point, *Love's Quarrels* examines the role of charity in shaping the negotiations of early modern writers who were responding to urgent social, religious, and political pressures. The book's title, taken from one of Margaret Cavendish's many remarkable verses in *Poems, or Fancies,* highlights the central premise of this study—that charity in fact generated quarrels of various kinds, that its call to love did not always bind together communities but sometimes fractured them. Cavendish, who published her poems in the first few years after the civil wars had ended in England, knew firsthand what violence could ensue from competing visions of love. In addition to underscoring the passionate intensity associated with charity, this book makes a second principal claim: charity, in nearly every context in which it emerged during the early modern period, is complicated by a range of interpretive demands. Charitable living, that is, required charitable reading, but this task was unsettled by a host of obstacles that threatened to undermine the project of moral, social, and textual interpretation.

Charity believes all things, so the apostle Paul tells us, and perhaps readers will think I have been uncharitably quick to see a problem or complication where there isn't one. It is true that scholars, especially those of us in literary studies, are motivated to find in texts a troubling complexity that needs unpacking. But in this case, quite simply, charity emerges near or among many of the most confounding issues of the period. For those living in early modern England, the biblical imperatives of charity—to love God and love your neighbor as yourself—sent them straight toward the most difficult and troubling aspects of human experience, producing vexing questions about poverty, morality, liberty, and religious devotion. These are topics worth debating, as writers such as Thomas More and John Milton knew well, and the shape and substance of those arguments are worth deciphering still.

Moreover, the contentious debates provoked by charity's demands remain with us even if they have taken on names of another kind—and so we continue in the twenty-first century to dispute the scope and sanction of human rights, the best policies to prevent or reduce unemployment, the right methods of health care provision, or the most reasonable and compassionate approaches to immigration. Our own disagreements often exhibit a belligerence similar to many of the controversies examined in this book, with each party or faction sure of its own righteousness. There are many lessons we can learn from the past, and this not least among them: our most passionate quarrels are often born of love, and our fiercest opponents often have charitable motives.

It is a hard but honorable task to acknowledge the charity of our enemies, but in my case it might be harder still to make sufficient note of all the charitable kindnesses I have received from friends and colleagues throughout the long duration of this project. First, the charitable institutions. I have been fortunate to spend nearly my entire academic career at two shining jewels of the University of North Carolina system—its schools in Chapel Hill and Asheville—where I have been given models of exemplary scholarship and inspiring teaching. During the research stage of this project, the patient staffs at the British Library, the Bodleian Library, Davis Library, the Folger Shakespeare Library, and Ramsey Library provided assistance. This project would never have been possible without support at UNC Asheville from the Dean of Humanities, Wiebke

Strehl; the University Research Council; and the Department of English. And my own learning has been sustained and invigorated by the spirit of curiosity modeled by my students at UNC Asheville.

It is appropriate, given its emphasis on charitable reading, that this book has been the recipient of careful attention and generous feedback from gracious readers. At its beginning, this project was shaped by conversations with the late Darryl Gless, a remarkable scholar and an even more remarkable person; in the manuscript's early stages, David Baker, Mary Floyd-Wilson, and Megan Matchinske provided clear-eyed recommendations for expansion and refinement; when I was caught in a thicket of doubt, Shayne Legassie helped me to believe in the project; Kirk Boyle offered thorough and helpful feedback during a crucial stage of revision; and near the end of this project, Will Revere provided invaluable suggestions for improvement. Alice Stanton's sharp eyes and expertise greatly enhanced the final manuscript. I am especially grateful to the two anonymous readers of the University of Massachusetts Press for their intelligent and meticulous feedback, and I am grateful too for the guidance and support provided by Mary Dougherty and Arthur Kinney at University of Massachusetts Press. Finally, I must single out two readers in particular for their tireless aid and practical wisdom: Reid Barbour and Jessica Wolfe guided my weaker wandering steps throughout this long journey. All of these readers are true alchemists; if there is gold in these pages, it is theirs; the lead is mine.

Since embarking on my academic career, I have been a caterpillar in a large commonwealth of charitable friends and colleagues. For their hospitality, provision, and support, I thank Erica Abrams Locklear, John Mark Adrian, Ben Aiken, Robert Erle Barham, Goodie and Jack Bell, Allison Bigelow, Eleanor and John Billington, Rick Chess, Michael Dowdy, Griff Gatewood, John Inazu, Belinda and Michael McFee, Dan Pierce, and Betsy and Allan Poole. This is to list just a few of those who have sustained me over the years.

Charity begins at home, they say, and in my case I was the beneficiary of much love and nurture from my family, enfolded in a wide circle of caring siblings, aunts and uncles and cousins, grandparents and children. My uncle Peter set me on this academic path long ago with his encouragement as well as his model of humility and integrity. I have been gifted with two loving parents, Pamela Graham and Michael Gurney, and then I had the good luck to find two more in Carl and Sue Steele.

To Rebecca, Charity herself, mother of our little brood, thank you for taking me by the hand and, each day, writing "love" more clearly for me to read.

LOVE'S QUARRELS

Of Charitie.

Of Charitie.

¶ *The fignification:*

AS many as intend to be pertakers with Chriſt & his Apoſtels
muſt vſe this worke of charitie, which is to fede the hungry,
to clothe the naked, to harbor the harbourles, & lodge the ſtran-
ger, to viſite the ſicke, and to relieue the priſoners and poore af-
flicted members of Chriſt, this is the dueties of all faithfull people.

D.ii.   tyme

FIGURE I. Stephen Batman, *A Christall Glasse of Christian Reformation* (London: 1569), sig. Oii. Beinecke
Rare Book and Manuscript Library, Yale University.

INTRODUCTION

CHARITABLE SIGNS AND TOKENS

On Christmas Eve in 1545 Henry VIII delivered an address to Parliament that culminated in an impressive panegyric to the virtues and necessities of charity. Occasioned by the successful passage of the Chantries Act, which authorized the king to dissolve specific chantries, colleges, and hospitals, and "ordre them to the glory of God, and the proffite of the common wealth," ostensibly preparing the way for the continued development of governmental distribution of poor relief, the speech has often been interpreted as a powerful exhortation to avoid the dangers of ecclesiastical unrest and as an early attempt to forge a middle way between religious extremes in England:

> Beholde then what loue and Charitie is emongest you, when the one calleth the other, Hereticke and Anabaptist, and he calleth hym again Papist, Ypocrite, and Pharisey. Be these tokens of charitie emongest you? Are these the signes of fraternall loue betwene you? No, no, I assure you, that this lacke of Charitie emongest your selfes, will bee the hynderaunce and asswagyng, of the feruent loue betwene vs, as I said before, except this wound be salued, and clerely made whole.[1]

An impassioned plea for his subjects to set aside their religious differences, the king's parliamentary address, perhaps Henry's "finest hour," nevertheless embodies the very problems it purports to lament.[2] After all, by abolishing chantries, which offered prayers for the dead and other services, the act would suppress a traditional and powerful expression of charitable love. It was political measures like this, as well as the dissolution of monasteries, that would encourage John Stow later to place Henry as the central figure presiding over a "declining time of charity" and Sir John Denham to depict the king as a defender of the faith but a destroyer of charity.[3]

Henry's fine sentiment, moreover, is complicated by a host of political, religious, and social tensions bound up in the concept of charity. Although the king's expressed intention echoes the claims voiced by Henry Brinklow and other contemporary advocates for poor relief, the act he is promoting was probably triggered by fiscal considerations in the wake of wars with Scotland and France.[4] Numerous influential members of court acquired private ownership of the confiscated lands and properties by sale, casting a decidedly equivocal shade over Henry's appeal to reforming the public good of the commonwealth. Likewise, even as he urges his subjects to reconcile their differences in behalf of charity, Henry explicitly asserts the Crown's own authority in matters of church governance, ordering his "lordes temporal" to bring accusations of clerical corruption to the throne: "Come and declare it to some of our Counsaill or to vs, to whom is committed by God the high aucthoritie to reforme and ordre such causes and behauiours."[5] Royal sovereignty hardly proved to be a stable guarantor of religious concord in England throughout the early modern period, and even in late 1545 the king's confident declaration of his supremacy in ecclesiastical reform belies the continued contemporary disputes over how and by whom the church should be ordered. Henry conveniently waited until the final ten days of Parliament, when the influential conservative bishops Cuthbert Tunstall and Stephen Gardiner were out of the country, to introduce his chantry legislation.[6] By gesturing, moreover, at the doubtful "signs" and "tokens" of charity, which seem to be somatic as well as semiotic given his image of a wounded body politic, Henry's speech underscores the complex interpretive work of reading charity in social and political contexts. Finally, the king appears to glance at the intractable differences between his Reformed and Roman Catholic constituencies by including a conjunction—"what loue and Charitie"—to acknowledge and join together the lexical commitments of both factions.

Henry appeals to charity as a means of stabilizing a vexatious commonwealth, but he fails to concede that charity was also one of the primary reasons for England's unrest. That is, the problem was not necessarily a "lacke of Charitie" but too much of it, or too many opinions about what it meant, and Henry, even as he exhorts his subjects to compromise, is staking his own royal claim to serve as the ultimate arbiter of charity. In attempting to reshape the definition and significance of charity for his own purposes, Henry's chantry speech provides a compelling illustration of this book's primary argument: charity in early modern England was as much a problem as it was a solution, a sure sign of trouble even when invoked in behalf of peace.

Love's Quarrels will examine some of the period's most contentious debates, which were the result of competing visions about charity's demands. Henry's speech implicates several of these thorny issues: the philological and interpretive commitments of rival theologies that drove Thomas More and William Tyndale into a debate over scriptural translation; the obligation to perform charitable admonition or fraternal correction, which was uncomfortably situated between conflicting imperatives of reconciliation and reform; the argument, specious or otherwise, that charity can negotiate the tremulous balance between private and public uses of wealth; and the manner in which charity can be used as a justification for communal bonds or individual liberties. All these disputes are complicated further by the task of reading charity—how to decipher the "tokens" of charity and interpret the "signs" of fraternal love. Many of these debates culminated with explosive force in the 1640s, and though the central questions about the proper role and function of charity remained unresolved, this decade of dynamic political and religious change provides a useful terminus for this study. In fact the book could just as well end where it begins: Henry's chantry speech was reprinted in 1642 as *A famous speech of King Henry the eighth*, its continued relevance captured in the publisher's choice of subtitle, which appears to admonish both king and Parliament just before the eruption of civil war: *Tending to charity and concord, and therefore necessary for men of these times.*[7]

"A Virtue of Vast Extent and Latitude": The Meanings of Charity

It is difficult to overestimate the power and scope of charity during the early modern period. Used to describe a state of general harmony—"the sweet cement, which in one sure band / Ties the whole frame," to invoke George Herbert's phrase from "The Church-floore"—the term "charity" encompasses questions about the roles of religion, law, politics, and commerce in forging, stabilizing, and reforming social relations, collective trust, and communal identity.[8] Precise meanings of charity varied among early modern contemporaries, but nearly every definition had at its foundation the biblical commands to love God and neighbor, two separate directives from the Old Testament (Deuteronomy 6:5 and Leviticus 19:18, respectively) that Jesus yokes together in the gospel narratives.[9] Because of these biblical prescriptions, almost everybody agreed that charity was crucial, that it was the primary force binding together any real or imagined community, and that it occupied an uneasy middle ground between the twin obligations to perform justice and mercy. But these shared beliefs merely added pressure to a vigorous debate, with those simple imperatives lending an urgency and power to complex questions about devotional practice, communal identity, political economy, and legal philosophy.

If charity was part of the cultural bedrock in early modern England, it was under immense tectonic pressure and consequently prone to rupture or fissure into conflict. Equally important, charity was available to all factions that might desire to convert or subvert the concept's already contested meanings and marshal its potent claims in support of their own vision of church and commonwealth. The concept of charity predictably found its way into apologies for the Church of England or Parliament, for example, but it was likewise a central force in shaping the rival claims of religious nonconformists like the Brownists and political dissenters like the Diggers. This book attempts to remain sensitive to the overlaps, intersections, and congruencies between these disparate voices and interests, rather than focusing merely on the conflict engendered by their mutual belief in the significance of charity.

One of the problems of charity for early modern contemporaries stems from the shared conviction that charity ought to govern, in one way or another, all social and spiritual relations. But this ubiquity creates a different kind of problem for scholars studying the period, who are confronted by a term that was deployed in a bewildering multiplicity of contexts. Charity is universal in its scope, linked as it is to a divine referent ("God is charity"); but so too is charity relative, circumstantial, local, worked out at the level of individual bodies and texts. A quick glance at the entry for "charitable" in the *Oxford English Dictionary* offers a helpful illustration of the dilemma: the adjective modifies and presumably confers dignity on subjects across a wide spectrum of vocabulary, describing religious belief or behavior ("charitable devotion"), specific social practices ("charitable hospitality" or "charitable almsgiving") and social institutions ("charitable houses" and "charitable hospitals"), an interpretive disposition ("charitable reading"), and even precise legal terminology ("charitable trusts" and "charitable uses").[10]

Although linked together by the general concept of charity, each of these definitions exists in its own semantic field of cultural particularities and meanings. This book will move swiftly among and between these contexts, but I will try to signal where I mean "charity" as a term, as a concept, or as an action. The challenge of terminology is exacerbated further by the diminishment in prominence afforded to charity by more recent generations in England and the United States, since the word, as Raymond Williams notes, "has become (except in special contexts, following the surviving legal definition of benevolent institutions) so compromised that modern governments have to advertise welfare benefits . . . as 'not a charity but a right.'"[11] The bulk of this transition, John Bossy suggests, had already occurred by 1700, when the word merely meant "an optimistic judgment about the good intentions of others; an act of benevolence towards the poor or needy; an institution erected as a result of such an act."[12] Bossy is probably overstating the case—in 1692 Edward Pelling could still refer to it as "a Virtue of vast Extent and Latitude"—but clearly our own cultural imagination struggles to conceive of charity as playing a crucial role in political governance or even, as Williams notes, in the distribution of aid.[13]

This semantic trajectory was hardly assured during the early modern period. If contemporaries were worried about charity's future diminution of significance and impact, the problem seemed to be one of dilation rather than contraction, with the apparent proliferation of meanings rendering the concept unintelligible. Samuel Collins, for example, notes that language itself has become distorted (in his view by a Puritan opposition) until "Charitie, modestie, puritie, they are but names," and Christopher Potter complains that for his Roman Catholic opponent "mere malice must passe for pure Charity."[14] Other writers pursued the issue with more delight than apprehension, interrogating the boundaries of this apparent moral subjectivity. In *The Jew of Malta,* Christopher Marlowe articulates with glee the situational relativism inherent to conventional Christian piety: "The meaning has a meaning; come let's in: / To undoe a Jew is charity, and not sinne."[15] And Shakespeare, too, explores similarly opportunistic distortions, as in Berowne's efforts in *Love's Labor's Lost* to negate the erotic premises of his perjury by invoking charitable love: "It is religion to be thus forsworn: / For charity itself fulfils the law, / And who can sever love from charity?"[16] Charity infiltrates every discourse of the period—even hatred, as Alexandra Walsham's brilliant study of toleration, *Charitable Hatred,* memorably heralds in its title. Numerous texts diagnose failures of some kind, an individual or a culture falling out of charity—"tell charity of coldness," as Ralegh would say—but these are rhetorical gestures that rely on the concept's cultural primacy. In other words, early modern writers were faced with a dilemma much different from charity's disappearance: it did not fall away, but the case was altered; the concept retained its forceful impact, but it meant different things to different people. This book traces the volatile translation, interpretation, and application of this crucial term in the moral vocabulary of the period.

This is not meant to dismiss or overlook important continuities between the medieval and early modern periods. The problems of understanding and responding to the imperatives of charity are hardly unique to the sixteenth and seventeenth centuries. Charity had been the source of intense debate among a range of reformist ideologies in England, Lollardy in particular, long before Martin Luther and others attacked the purgatorial doctrine and penitential machinery of the church. In fact, this native tradition of reform made London and other regions in the country receptive to certain strands of Protestant doctrine. Any reader of Langland or Chaucer knows that monks and friars could serve as ironic emblems of charity well in advance of the reforming projects of the sixteenth century. One can find, moreover, a host of writers in the rich literary landscape of late medieval England who dramatized various ethical postures that were under pressure from urgent social, political, and economic forces.[17] Social historians, meanwhile, have uncovered the complicated forms and developments of charitable giving in England during the Middle Ages, and in his classic study of medieval poor law, Brian Tierney highlights crucial ruptures and ambivalences that were hardwired into canon law, as evidenced by the differing attitudes toward discriminatory almsgiving among Chrysostom, Ambrose, and Augustine.[18] During the early modern period, on the other hand, the earlier rituals and beliefs associated with Roman Catholicism were entrenched so stubbornly in local communities that the Church of England and central government were never able to fully eradicate their influence, and recent scholarship has reminded us of the traditional forms of charity present in literature ranging from Shakespeare to Sidney.[19]

This book takes the late 1520s and early 1530s as its starting point because of several crucial developments during the Henrician regime—the rejection of papal supremacy and dissolution of monasteries, the expansion of poor relief and vagrancy suppression, and the scriptural translations performed by humanists like Tyndale, in addition to the upsurge of reformist theologies—that animated suddenly urgent questions about the specific powers and functions of charity. These debates exploded with even greater force during the subsequent century. This feature of early modern English culture is the subject of *Love's Quarrels*: how charity, ostensibly an idealized ethic governing all human and divine relationships, emerged at the center of so many of the era's most contentious disputes.

A range of scholars, of course, have engaged specific discourses within this larger trend: Walsham's work on toleration provides a crucial reminder of the paradoxes inherent to the concept of charity as well as its potential for violence; Debora Shuger has examined how charity was bound up in notions of censorship and the regulation of language more generally; Katrin Ettenhuber has traced John Donne's inventive appropriations of Augustine's hermeneutics of charity; and Reid Barbour's study of charity during the Caroline period uncovers a bewildering variety of applications of the concept, all of which contributed to a fractured religious and political culture.[20] That is just to name a few, and this work's debt to a number of other scholarly influences should be clear throughout the pages below. But *Love's Quarrels* aims for a broader and more synthetic approach that tries to make sense of these specific disputes, one that traces the interpretive discontent that often reveals itself when the imperative of charity is invoked during the period. To perform "charity" in whichever context—to read or give or live charitably—remained a crucial obligation, but its demands were fraught with confusion, controversy, and high stakes.

One can see these vexing features of charity perhaps most evidently in the reformist theologies that reimagined the role of charity in achieving salvation. When Martin Luther declared that Christians were justified—that is, made or deemed righteous by God—by faith alone (*sola fide*), he reframed theological discourse for at least a century of succeeding religious thinkers in England. Emerging in the wake of a complicated medieval dialectic of contrition and repentance prompted by divine grace, with differing conceptions of human merit, Luther's soteriology (or doctrine of salvation) drew an emphatic distinction between the justifying work of Christ and any kind of human response. This becomes a crucial point of difference between the theology of Roman Catholics, who considered the interior, regenerative impact of divine grace part of a longer process of justification, and Protestant reformers, nearly all of whom, though altering and refining Luther's work in various ways, conceived of justification as an event rather than process, a divine declaration of one's changed status rather than a product of any human endeavor, however limited. Protestant theology (following John Calvin) instead used the term "sanctification" to describe the process whereby a justified Christian begins to acquire the regenerative power to perform authentic good works. The distinctions were largely notional—justification was in fact inseparable from the beginning of sanctification, according to Protestants—but human acts of charity were in this case safely governed by divine authority.

The theological reforms of Luther and Calvin eliminated much of the intense anxiety associated with traditional discourses of piety and penitence, giving the early Protestant, in Thomas More's eyes, a "lewd lyghtnes of mynd & vayn gladnesse of harte, whyche he toke for spyrytuall consolacyon."[21] But in removing from charitable works any salvific power, Protestant reformers nevertheless invested them with hermeneutic significance: rather than effecting salvation, charity assumed the role of a text in which "ye may read your faith by your works," as Margaret Fell declares, taking a cue from Thomas Cranmer, whose "Homily on Faith" in *The Book of Common Prayer* instructs individuals to "mark the increase of love and charity" and so perceive theirs "to be a true lively faith."[22] Rather than resolving the problem of spiritual anxiety, sanctification involved its own troublesome process of reading and interpreting good works.

It is easy to see why, on account of the theological confusion between Roman Catholics and Protestants, religious polemicists often talked past each other on crucial points related to charity. Debates between the two sides typically reduced complicated questions about the sources of divine revelation and the transformative powers of grace into a simple dichotomy pitting Roman Catholic works against Protestant faith. Misunderstandings of this kind are on display in England throughout the period, from the fraught exchange between Thomas More and William Tyndale, contending over issues related to scriptural language and interpretation, to later debates sparked by various religious and political events, such as the arrival of Jesuit missionaries in the Elizabethan era, the Gunpowder Plot, the Oath of Allegiance, the potential Spanish Match during the Jacobean years, and efforts at toleration by Charles I and William Laud. Nor were Lutherans and Calvinists and Roman Catholics the only voices debating the precise salvific role of charity in England. The Family of Love, for example, gained an eminence among religious sects in the latter half of the sixteenth century when the work of German mystic Hendrik Niclaes (or H.N.) appeared in England and emphasized a kind of *imitatio Christi* that ascribed saving efficacy to the "service of love."[23] Later, in the early seventeenth century, members of the Church of England who were influenced by the doctrinal positions of Jacobus Arminius renewed discussion among English Protestants about the status and merit of charitable works. Other religious nonconformists added various nuances to the debate, contributing to the diverse theological texture of the period, which was muddled further by poets and dramatists who often appropriated and misconstrued these ideas, and, in some cases, deliberately mocked them. I have tried, as far as possible, to include a variety of confessional voices in this book to provide a fuller sense of charity in the period.

Although these theological issues generated radical change, the influence of charity was felt in similarly forceful but distinct ways at the level of ecclesiastical governance—that is, in the discipline rather than doctrine of the church. Historians have complicated our picture of the Church of England during the period, which was far from a neat and tidy *via media* jockeying between the extremes of Papism and Puritanism.[24] Instead there was a spectrum of competing and overlapping religious interests, all of which contributed to a vigorous debate about the proper forms of worship and identity. Charity assumed a central role in these disputes, which concerned church polity (whether or not to discard the episcopal superstructure inherited from Roman Catholicism for the more democratic Presbyterian system instituted in Geneva), church ritual (whether or not charity demanded or disbarred one from receiving communion, for example), and church identity (whether charity should tolerate sinful behavior or strip away the reprobate from the ecclesiastical community).

In these debates charity was supposed to govern and regulate language, modifying and softening the substance of admonition, aiming for amendment rather than abuse, thinking the best of people's intentions. This did not always happen in practice, of course. As the central imperative driving rival projects of communal purity and communal harmony, charity often incited more controversy than it subdued. Reformists might stress, with William Ames, that it was "the duty of justice, or charity . . . to admonish, chide, and punish an offender," while conformists would lament, with Richard Hooker, "the state of this present age wherein zeal has drowned charity."[25] Deriding Presbyterians and separatists, Gabriel Harvey sneered, "If they bee godly, God help Charity," and a later religious libel smeared Puritanism in similar terms: "A puritan is hee, is never known / To thinke on others good beside his owne / And all his doctrine is of hope and faith / For charitie 'tis poperie hee saith."[26] In the first sermon preached before Charles I, John Donne claimed that "Charitie is without all Controuersie," but in spite of its scriptural derivation, the statement comes across as a paradox, not least because Donne's sermon itself engages in controversy with Rome.[27]

Changes related to charity were not confined to matters of soteriology or ecclesiology, and perhaps the most profound shift occurred in the everyday experiences of people in the city and parish. A succession of government regimes experimented with poor relief schemes, at both the national and municipal levels, aimed at redistributing material resources to those in need of support, a project that was intensified by the dissolution of Catholic institutions of charitable giving such as monasteries and chantries.[28] These efforts to reform England's social infrastructure faced several obstacles, however. For one thing, political authorities often misunderstood the root causes of poverty. Perhaps more important, statutory legislation disrupted a complex web of social relations by proscribing informal gifts of alms or hospitality to sturdy beggars and vagrants, itinerant persons displaced from their native parish for a variety of benign or illicit causes. Vagrants were notorious for their capacity to induce or coerce gifts of charity from unsuspecting persons, and literary works throughout the early modern period betray an anxious fascination with these figures, exploring a variety of methods for identifying their ruses and disguises. Government authorities encouraged (and in some cases forced) individuals to avoid this kind of interpretive problem by directing their donations to churchwardens or Collectors of the Poor, leaving the task of distribution to officials who were supposedly better equipped to determine the status of the impoverished.

These developments emerged, however, in a social landscape that continued to privilege hospitality and informal giving. Charity of this kind, spontaneous and intimate, had long been considered among the most eminent forms of neighborly love, and statutory legislation could not fully diminish its cultural power. In many cases prospective givers of charitable aid had to negotiate between contradictory rules mandated by their ministers, who often celebrated charitable giving, and their parish officials and parliamentary legislators, who discouraged gifts to beggars. Keith Thomas, assessing Tudor statutes of poor relief, puts the case bluntly: "Nothing did more to make the moral duties of the householder ambiguous."[29] The interpretive demands of performing discriminate charity, which forced individuals or magistrates to scrutinize or "read" beggars for signs of authentic or feigned poverty, bear a similarity, as I will show, to the hermeneutics privileged by humanists like Desiderius Erasmus, who stressed the importance of reading a text with a consideration for historical context, textual economy, and authorial intention.[30] So, in a roundabout way, these material imperatives lead back to the problem of scriptural interpretation and theological controversy, linked by the interpretive demands of reading, broadly defined.

Throughout the period, then, a varied spectrum of religious adherents disputed the theological primacy of charity, interrogated the spiritual sanction of good works, and articulated radically new visions of church community. Humanists and biblical scholars reinvigorated a tradition of charitable reading, a hermeneutic that writers of the period, including polemicists and satirists, would repeatedly solicit from readers even as they refused to offer the same benefit to their opponents. Local and national governments, meanwhile, attempted to implement practical schemes of material charity to relieve the poor—charity that required overseers and magistrates to read and categorize their populace in various classes of need—in addition to providing legislation aimed at promoting and protecting the status of charitable gifts. The elusive ideals of loving God and neighbor produced similar complications in matters of commerce, medicine, and natural philosophy. This book maintains that these were not discrete developments or debates linked merely by superficial resemblances in the cultural lexicon. Instead the following chapters will show how charity—in particular its concomitant and demanding project of interpretation—informed, unsettled, and reshaped a number of apparently distinct modes of discourse.

These disputes placed pressure on a concept that already struggled under the weight of its idealism. As with any virtue, the interior space of moral principle and exterior sphere of moral conduct are fused together, but in charity the intersection between intention and action seems especially charged. Stephen Batman underscores this relationship, noting, "As many as intend to be pertakers with Christ & his Apostels must vse this worke of charitie," naming in succession the corporal works of mercy.[31] That is, the earnest workings of a faithful spirit ought to become visible (one might even say, ought to be "written") on the bodies of the poor, those without food, shelter, and other material exigencies. By highlighting the importance of use, or practice, in making real and efficacious one's intention, Batman (admittedly a moderate Protestant) is recycling a contentious piece of advice from the Epistle of James—"faith without works is dead"—but charity, precisely because it is alive and incarnate and performed, remains prone to hypocrisy and misinterpretation. This is true both of givers of charity, who might employ a benevolent exterior to cloak a malicious purpose (like Marlowe's Barabas or the Satan of *Paradise Regained*), and of recipients of good works, who might be considered undeserving of such precious commodities.

If charitable works were the "fruits of faith," there were plenty of bad apples ready to spoil the bunch, or so it seemed to the early modern English, who were deeply suspicious of men and women who might divert alms and other monies away from the proper channels of charitable distribution. Throughout the following chapters, various contexts in which charity appears—the realms of theology, law, marketplace, and medicine—are threatened by the destabilizing presence of heretics, vagrants, rogues, and mountebanks, real or imagined. Despite their marginalized status, this shadowy assortment of characters played a key role in shaping early modern conceptions of charity, exposing the potential for love to be unjust or for good intentions to produce bad results, and placing pressure on fundamental social and personal commitments.

Charity's protean nature, not merely a matter of appearance with its consequent problems of disguise, remains bound up in rhetorical deception as well. By attending to a range of circumstances and contexts, and by adapting to various audiences, charitable rhetoric acquires persuasive power but also invites accusations of casuistry and equivocation. As Ettenhuber notes of Donne's *Biathanatos*, charity can facilitate a movement "from argument and proof to dissimulation, concealment, and even deceit."[32] This charitable adaptability applies to beggars, too, as Sir Thomas Browne notes in *Religio Medici*, observing the interpretive skills of "Master Mendicants" who can read faces for physiognomic signs of mercy and thereby choose targets likely to offer charitable alms.[33] A more complicated problem underlying this issue involves the matter of reciprocity and exchange. By idealizing relations between oneself and neighbor (or text and reader), charity poses an interpretive drama: each constituent in the dynamic is challenged to think the best of the other, which makes them equally vulnerable to abuse. In his poem "Divinitie," Herbert aptly calls this reciprocal dynamic (one that involves a kind of exchange not merely between oneself and neighbor, but also human and God) a Gordian knot, which is precisely the image that Milton employs and aims to sever by deploying the "all-interpreting voice of charity" in the cause of individual liberty.

Never fully resolved or stabilized, these problematic features of charity produce anxious questions about its status and role, which early modern writers probe and examine and dramatize in different ways. Which biblical translation is more charitable: that which accommodates an individual encounter between scripture and spirit, or that which privileges the mediating power of church and tradition and common sense? Which is more crucial to social and ecclesiastical relations: charitable admonition intended to reform abuses to church and community, or a charitable recognition of mutual fallibility and sinfulness? Which traits of loving conduct best embody the spiritual and material imperatives of charity? Which is more productive of charitable use: immense stores of private wealth born of self-interest (which can be redirected toward charities) or a robust collective spirit that privileges the public good? Or in fact can these apparently contradictory postures coexist in a fruitful commonwealth? Which charitable prescription possesses more authority: the medical advice of learned physicians or the spiritual wisdom of learned divines? Does charity bind together or liberate otherwise tyrannized subjects, or can it accomplish both imperatives at once in its paradoxical economy?

Love's Quarrels: Methods and Contexts

These questions about charity are repeatedly taken up by, among others, Thomas More, Edmund Spenser, Ben Jonson, Thomas Browne, and John Milton, all of whom, though motivated by and responding to widely varying circumstances, nevertheless choose to appropriate the word "charity" and recuperate, reform, or even parody its significance. *Love's Quarrels* uses each of these writers as a locus to explore more expansive cultural discourses related to charity during the early modern period, placing central texts within a larger nexus of debates associated with the concept or term: the projects of charitable translation, charitable admonition, charitable allegory, charitable use, and charitable liberty. My intention is not to give a comprehensive survey of charity as a concept or practice, still less to provide a narrative of its evolution; instead this book studies several significant disputes that emerged in response to what was surely one of the most powerful forces at work in early modern England: a general (and, as I take it, largely genuine) desire to practice Christian love in the world.

Despite the range of generic material under consideration, this book privileges literary texts in its examination of charity. The fictive worlds of the poet and dramatist provided opportunities in early modern England to stage interpretive dilemmas of various kinds, to transport the textual domains of casuistry casebooks and biblical hermeneutics into the sphere of everyday experience. Consider, for example, a crucial scene in Shakespeare's *Measure for Measure,* when Angelo attempts to coerce Isabella into his bed by offering to free her imprisoned brother, baldly suggesting, "Might there not be a charity in sin / To save this brother's life?"[34] In this casuistic appeal, Shakespeare implicates a range of problematic discourses related to charity: its currency in amatory lyric as well as devotional practice; its Augustinian legacy of participating in political coercion of various kinds; its close proximity to the economic and legal margins of society, figured here in prisons such as Bridewell that housed men and women like Isabella's brother, Claudio; and its rhetorical power, which was appropriated by a multitude of early modern voices, many of whom were markedly dubious characters. A close reading of Angelo's threat in this scene points to a larger and persistent cultural anxiety that received similar expression in rogue literature, religious polemic, medical tracts, and statutory laws. Rhetorical analysis of this kind offers a productive mode of access into such a protean, conflicted, and often polemical concept.

It is in these two qualities—its principal focus on literary texts, and its contention that understandings of charity were unstable and amorphous—that *Love's Quarrels* departs from the model offered by Alexandra Walsham's study of providence, a similarly crucial and far-ranging concept in early modern religion and culture. Whereas Walsham stresses the continuity of providentialism throughout the period, a valuable corrective to assumptions that a Puritan minority monopolized such discourse, this book emphasizes the protean nature of charity, both as a term and concept, and its mutability and volatility during the period.[35] By placing literary works such as Spenser's *Faerie Queene* or Jonson's *Volpone* within a larger consideration of the discourse of charity in the period, and remaining sensitive to the ways in which charity intersects a number of contexts, *Love's Quarrels* reveals how several competing cultural obligations were united by the same concept, producing tension, disagreement, and confusion.

Given its emphasis on the tasks of charitable reading and its interpretive demands, this book assigns a foundational role to the Bible in shaping early modern constructions of charity. As Debora Shuger observes, the Bible "operated as a synthetic field, the site where the disciplines converge."[36] The impact of biblical texts, and their vexed interpretation and application, extended far beyond matters related to belief and worship, implicating a host of other debates that derived in part from specific passages in scripture and key remarks by patristic thinkers, to say nothing of the central biblical mandates to love God and neighbor. There were pragmatic social and political imperatives to provide material charity for the poor, for example, but these received further reinforcement and forceful expression in the Sermon on the Mount and other biblical exhortations to perform almsgiving, which influenced matters of taxation, criminal law, medical care, and work programs.

The role of charity in building and refining a church community, meanwhile, was interpreted through the prism of various Pauline epistles, but these scriptural passages had a hand in political disputes, communal reforms, and social engineering. Theories of scriptural hermeneutics—ruled in part by a charity posited by Augustine and refined by other theologians—surface in literary disputes over the role of satire, and, in the hands of such inventive and prodigious intellects as John Donne and John Milton, can be deployed to defend suicide or divorce, respectively. This last point is crucial in shaping the methods of this project, as my focus on scriptural interpretation provides a kind of metonymic function as well, standing in for the more general fixation in early modern England on reading texts of various kinds. As Henry observes in his chantry speech, the field of charity is one of signs and tokens: reading beggars and Bibles for signs of desert or idleness or heresy; reading admonitions for charitable intention or motives of malice; reading plays and reading wills for charitable use or for private interest; reading bodies for tokens of disease or schism or mercy; and reading relationships for signs of authentic marital union.

It is no coincidence, then, that this study of charity begins with biblical translation and interpretation. The first chapter examines the debate over the scriptural provenance and meaning of "charity" between Thomas More and William Tyndale, who sparred in the wake of Tyndale's unauthorized translation of the Bible. Much of this chapter is preoccupied by the contradictions of both positions. Tyndale employs a putatively charitable practice of translation in order to erase the word "charity" from scripture, whereas More, in defense of charity, refuses to afford Tyndale the benefit of charitable interpretation. But this otherwise scriptural controversy takes place in the context of contemporary developments of poor relief and vagrancy suppression, statutory laws and municipal policies that exhibit similar hermeneutic methods of distinguishing (and then punishing) a sturdy beggar much like a heretical translator. In other words, the modes of distributing material charity mirror in important ways the practices of biblical reading and interpretation.

The debate between More and Tyndale illustrates a larger problem, too, namely that charity—as a word and concept—is always being translated, always being interpreted, shifting its shape depending on the circumstances of the reader and his text. The overlaps in meaning within chapter 1 set the stage for the rest of the book by anticipating crucial preoccupations that persist throughout the period: the unabashedly punitive aspects of early modern charity, which might, depending on its recipient, administer alms or a whipping; the interpretive challenges posed by the textual and physical body; and, above all, the frantic urgency elicited by the concept, which was something worth fighting for, and even a weapon to use while fighting. Words like "charity," as Brian Cummings has shown, "were prone to ambiguous interpretation, and every ambiguity concealed a threat as well as a promise."[37]

The second chapter takes up two specific tasks of charity—how to build and reform the church, and how to protect the church and sustain its harmony—questions that posed equal amounts of hazard and opportunity for the generation immediately following the accession of Elizabeth to the throne in 1558. In the Admonition Controversy that dominated much of the religious conversation in England during the 1570s, these two approaches to charity converge, as so-called Puritans deployed charity as a galvanizing force of spiritual reform while defenders of the church establishment prioritized social, political, and religious concord. Motivated by charitable reform, Puritans were nevertheless accused of malice by their opponents; motivated by charitable harmony, conformist clergy were nonetheless charged with corruption by their antagonists. The failure of charitable admonition is not limited to ecclesial discourse, however, and a close reading of contemporary literature reveals similar ruptures that threaten to undermine the relationship between writer and reader. In Edmund Spenser's *May* eclogue, for example, the pastoral dialogue between Piers and Palinode participates in many of the same rhetorical failures as the Admonition Controversy, but by subjecting both perspectives to close ironic scrutiny, the eclogue achieves its own kind of charitable success. Meanwhile, in the aftermath of the Bishops' Ban of satire in 1599, the exchange of Whipper pamphlets presents a trio of satirists who debate how satire ought to be conducted, who can sanction such discourse, and who can explain why it matters to the larger community. In their dispute over the proper role and function of satire, John Weever, Nicholas Breton, and Everard Guilpin reproduce many of the arguments espoused by various writers during the Admonition Controversy, revealing crucial continuities in Elizabethan literary culture—in this case the imperative of moral reform—that link religious polemic to formal verse satire.

A number of the participants in the Admonition Controversy use the figure of the vagrant or rogue as an avatar of the supposedly hypocritical claims to charity made by their opponents. There was a general fear during this period that pretenses of charity masked a darker purpose. Perhaps on account of this anxiety, in an effort to clearly identify and define authentic manifestations of the virtue, a host of early modern writers attempt to allegorize charity, to give the abstract principle flesh and blood, but this project too remains unstable. If Spenser imagines charity as a chaste and fertile mother, Milton pictures a severe governess of belief, while Crashaw envisions a humble handmaid. If Sir Tobie Mathew, in his *Missive of Consolation*, figures forth the two poles of active and passive charity by reverently depicting the hands of the crucified Christ enveloping the whole world in a loving embrace, Thomas Floyd compares charity to "an euerturning spie, alwaies prouiding and labouring for him in whom she resteth."[38] These visions of charity descend to the level of affective passions, with charity typically conceived as a warming passion, but even in this case there were notable exceptions. George Gifford, for example, alludes to the earlier Marian regime's repression of Protestantism by burning heretics, when he claims in an imagined disputation with a Papist, "I confesse our charitie and yours are not al one, for the charitie of you papists, is a burning loue."[39] Thomas Browne, meanwhile, opposes a hot-blooded puritanical zeal for charitable reform with his own idealized charitable disposition that "best agrees with coldest natures."[40] Charity always seems to be shape-shifting, a phenomenon dramatized by the anonymous play *Pathomachia: Or, The Battell of Affections*, performed sometime in the 1610s and printed in 1630, which dresses up personified vices as virtues: "I will haue Selfe-loue transelementated into the shape of Charitie, for the Dunces say, Charitie begins at home."[41] In an apparently parodic embodiment of the Pauline maxim, charity in early modern England was in fact all things to all people.

Spenser confronts this issue at the outset of his allegorical project in *The Faerie Queene*, which is the subject of chapter 3. In his great poem Spenser takes for granted the interpretive dilemmas associated with charity and, in fact, makes its vexing materiality one of the thematic priorities of the poem's first book, which is focused on Redcrosse, the knight of holiness. By placing charity's agonized relationship between spiritual idealism and physical reality at the center of the narrative, and by dramatizing the easy slippage between *eros* and *agape* throughout Redcrosse's journey, Spenser tempts both knight and reader to confuse romantic love with charitable love. Redcrosse's eventual progress through the enigmatic House of Holinesse and his encounter with the embodied presence of Charissa,

Spenser's personification of charity, provides a lesson in the spiritual conduct required to stabilize the potential dangers of loving service. At the same time, however, this chapter uncovers and highlights Spenser's refusal to engage a separate problem for allegorists in early modern England: the bodies of the itinerant poor. These beggars, vagrants, and petty thieves stood as visual and physical embodiments of the Elizabethan state's failure to eradicate begging from its realm. Despite Spenser's preoccupation with such figures in his other works, he chooses in *The Faerie Queene* to remove the recipients of charitable giving from his allegorical purview, stabilizing the interpretive dilemma by focusing on the interior, spiritual motives of charity rather than its external, physical consequences.

The first three chapters of *Love's Quarrels* focus on charity in a variety of causal functions, as a motivating force for translation, a catalyst for reform, or an instructive emblem for moral discipline. But early modern contemporaries also considered charity to be a final product, the culminating work of earlier activity. In the case of commerce and trade, charity could even be the end that justifies certain avaricious means—or at least that is the premise of this book's fourth chapter, which examines the economic growth and mercantile expansion that took place during the early Jacobean era, when contemporary cultural norms were adapting to changes in the commercial behavior of early modern London and England more generally. In this context one can observe an emergent emphasis on the concept of charitable "use," a specific legal term refined by contemporary statutory legislation to encourage individual owners of private wealth to offer charitable donations, as well as an idealized concept supposed to govern the profit-making ventures of commercial exchange. The practice remained vulnerable, however, to abuse and exploitation. Charity, which offered a convenient and powerful concept to supporters as well as critics of mercantile growth, thus became implicated in the larger discourse of moneymaking and money-sharing.

The moral ambivalence associated with charitable use receives its fullest representation on the London stage, an emergent commercial enterprise in its own right, as Jacobean writers repeatedly dramatized ruptures in the charitable postures among entrepreneurs of various kinds. Ben Jonson's city comedies provide particularly fruitful case studies of this conflicted issue, betraying the playwright's own unease with literary as well as commercial exchange, and probing the charitable imperatives that sometimes marry private profit with public good and sometimes mar both. In *Volpone* and *The Alchemist*, moreover, Jonson attempts to negotiate the uneasy dialectic between professional playwright and commercial audience, testing the limits of charitable relations by dramatizing their vulnerability to criminal or roguish elements—including his own.

The first four chapters focus mainly on the manner in which charity negotiates vexed communal imperatives, but the final chapter examines two related efforts to achieve a centered self by means of what I am calling charitable singularity. In the increasingly polarized discourse of the 1630s and early 1640s, when Thomas Browne was writing and revising *Religio Medici,* charity had come to signal specific, entrenched political and religious commitments, but Browne's treatise manages to evade conventional markers of faction, despite its forthright claims, by refusing to indulge in what he calls "uncharitable Logicke." Instead he envisions a charity that accommodates not merely sympathy but also singularity, with its focus on personal liberty and individual experience. Browne's charitable singularity remains flexible enough to navigate various dispositions and make sense of apparent contradictions. Equally important, by deploying a vocabulary of learned physic that shifts between spiritual and affective conditions, and by expressing a reserved suspicion that religious disorders—heresy, schism, despair—might be discovered and cured by skilled diagnostics or experiment, *Religio Medici* offers an alternative discourse in which to perform a vigorous spiritual stocktaking.

Browne suggests that charity resides most fully in "coldest natures," but in Milton's *Doctrine and Discipline of Divorce,* a treatise the author revised and expanded for a second edition, and then supplemented with three additional tracts, there is more of Samson's "fiery virtue" than cool disposition. Like Browne, however, Milton deploys a flexibility in his manipulation of conventional figures of political and religious discourse, and charity plays a crucial role in this strategy, figuring in his efforts to refashion typical approaches to scriptural hermeneutics and Christian liberty, and adumbrating his future defenses of republicanism in his prose works. Milton's contemporaries found it difficult to reconcile his emphasis on charity with the subject endorsed by his treatise, divorce, but even if he marshals the virtue in behalf of domestic liberty, charity functions throughout the tracts as a kind of coupling agent, linking gospel prescription with natural law, right reason with the Holy Spirit, or good works with faith. Milton tasks charity with both "binding and loosening," as he phrases it: he employs a charitable hermeneutic that will free individuals from the strictures of a disaffected marriage (to a spouse or, presumably, to a sovereign), giving allowance for the potential that libertines might abuse such freedom, in order to provide the opportunity for a marriage born of authentic human companionship.

Browne and Milton both deploy charity in the cause of binding and loosening, but they approach the issue from opposite ends: Browne circles his sphere so he can be liberated within its boundaries, while Milton severs his bonds so that he can be joined in what he considers a more genuine union. Their dialectic adds an exclamation point to the primary argument of this book—that charity in early modern England was a source of powerful contention—and brings the project back to where it started: the troubling overlap between charity and the physical body, the competing obligations of spiritual devotion and communal sociability, and the challenges of charitable reading.

A brief pamphlet entitled *The True Character tending to Love* appeared in 1647, written by B.N., "a lover of charity" according to the title page, who felt compelled to write a short, simple treatise reminding readers just what charity entails. Expressing a conventional nostalgia for the communal solidarity of yesteryear, but with the added force of a civil war context, the work seems unremarkable but for a surprising admission in its preface: "Considering with my selfe of the benefit of love, together with the difficulty of it, which hath almost worne it out of use amongst Christians, I thought fit to afford some help to lead carefull Christians up this mount of love."[42] In the separate halves of his introductory clause, the anonymous writer underscores the two major premises of this study, that the benefits of charity were crucial to sixteenth- and seventeenth-century English culture but frustratingly difficult to achieve, a reminder that contemporaries were aware not only of charity's importance but also its troubling complexity. There is an echo here of Langland's Wille in *Piers Plowman*, who laments, even after receiving a disquisition on the concept from Anima that traverses an entire passus, "And yet I am in a were [perplexed by], what charitie is to meane."[43] Despite its apparent simplicity, charity was perplexing, hard to understand and harder still to perform, prompting writers throughout the period to take up its central imperatives, as well as its various shapes and possibilities, for investigation, experiment, and debate.

At last, after much reasonyng, when no reason would serue, although he deserued no death, hee was condemned by vertue of the Emperours decree made in the assemble at Ausbrough (as is before signified) and vpon the same, brought forth to the place of execution, was there tyed to the stake, and then strangled first by the hangman, and afterward with fire consumed in the mornyng at the towne of Filford, an. 1536. crying thus at the stake with a feruent zeale, & a loude voyce: *Lorde open the Kyng of Englandes eyes.*
DDD.iiij.   Such

FIGURE 2. John Foxe, *Actes and Monuments* (London: 1570), 1229. Woodcut. Houghton Library, Harvard University.

CHAPTER 1

CHARITABLE TRANSLATION

Thomas More, William Tyndale, and the Vagrant Text

This chapter starts with a problem of philology. "Charity," Thomas More claims in his *Dialogue Concerning Heresies* (1529), is one of the "thre wordes of grete weight" (the other two are "priest" and "church") that William Tyndale "hath mysse translated" in his unauthorized 1526 version of the New Testament. So begins an intense debate between More and Tyndale about the word "charity" itself, its linguistic provenance, its status in contemporary usage, and its suitability for scripture.[1] But their polemical exchange reveals other crucial differences in what they conceived to be charity's role in shaping their scholarly and spiritual commitments. Moving beyond specific questions of grammar and usage, much of this debate centers on competing notions of Christian community: where it begins and ends, how it is fashioned and by whom, and what is the proper means of protecting and invigorating that community with love. By adumbrating future disputes about how charity ought to inform the process of building, sustaining, and reforming the English church and commonwealth, the controversy between More and Tyndale sets the stage for a history of this concept during the entire early modern period.

The logic of charity circles back to itself. "Charity compels us to speak about charity," as Richard of St. Victor notes in a treatise on the subject, and this chapter is no different.[2] Each discussion of a problem related to charity unlocks another problem, like a nest of boxes: the translation of "charity" sets into sharp relief differing principles of interpretive charity, which are likewise deployed in the distribution of material charity, and each of these modes of charity often results in charitable correction or punitive discipline. The central question for More and Tyndale in this case stems from an argument over semantics and usage—is the best English equivalent for *agape* "love" or "charity"?—but it produces additional questions about scriptural hermeneutics and church governance. Brian Cummings's succinct diagnosis of the period applies here: "The humanist crisis of language in this way merges with the Reformation crisis of theology."[3] And so what begins as the province of humanist scholarship obtains a theological significance that is especially charged in the early days of the Reformation, and More and Tyndale, who would have likely been sympathetic to each other as humanists, were thrust into a religious debate that was impassioned and irreconcilable. Both authors are sensitive in their debate to the ethical and political impact of biblical translation, its inherent theological dynamism, how translation and interpretation are synonymous activities. Depending on the inflection of one's scriptural reading, for example, efforts to preserve or to reform a peaceful community might oblige a kind of charitable mercy or a kind of charitable violence. The respective positions of More and Tyndale testify to this ironic flexibility. One can remove charity from the Bible, as Tyndale does, to protect its sanctity; one can also deny a charitable reading to a potential heretic, as does More, who aims to protect the customs and traditions associated with charity.

Their controversy quickly shifts from lexical subtleties to more urgent questions about contemporary devotional practice. In the course of defending the philological verity of his translation, Tyndale appeals to the word behind the word, as it were, the original Greek term *agape* that animates and informs both Latin and English forms of love. This is partially the result of Tyndale's commitment to reading *ad fontes,* tracing scripture back to its original sources, and partially the result of the author's own peculiar rhythm and pitch of English vernacular. But it is possible for a translation to be correct and tendentious at the same time, and one suspects (as More does) that Tyndale is pleased to erase centuries of church tradition in the process. By rejecting the more conventional word "charity" in favor of "love," a term more general in meaning and less encumbered by Roman freight, Tyndale embeds within his biblical text a critique of

the contemporary church, suggesting that "charity" had become too sul-
lied by clerical vice to adequately describe the Christian love of God and
neighbor. His is an approach that considers scripture, rightly understood
by individual readers inspired by the Holy Spirit, to be the proper means
of establishing and reforming a godly community. More, on the other
hand, desires a translation that has been underwritten by church authorities. Privileging the *consensus fidelium*, which incorporates the common
customs and common sense of the universal church, More believes that
"charity," as a technical term employed by the church and widely accepted
by English readers, was the right word for the translation of *agape*. But one
nevertheless suspects (as Tyndale does) that More is pleased to consider
the process of scriptural translation so vexing that any vernacular edition
must remain perpetually out of reach to lay readers. His is an approach that
considers the church to be the only proper means of stabilizing the chaos of
unmediated access to scripture and its otherwise dangerous consequences.

It is fitting that a debate about the word "charity" becomes a catalyst for
probing complex scriptural and social problems in the period, as this tricky
linguistic sign, according to Augustine's work *On Christian Doctrine*, is also
the key principle governing the whole process of scriptural translation
and its subsequent interpretation. In outlining standard principles of biblical hermeneutics and describing the various dilemmas facing any reader
or translator of scripture, *On Christian Doctrine* offers a compelling corollary to the debate between More and Tyndale, especially since it seems
clear that they both read the work closely. Augustine emphasizes that a
proper interpretation must be grounded in an understanding of the whole
of scripture (which Tyndale demands from his lay readers) as well as a
firm foundation in the church's beliefs and practices (which More stresses
in the course of his argument). His most important criterion, however,
underscores the ethical and even charismatic dimensions of Augustinian
hermeneutics: biblical interpretation cannot be adequately performed by
any individual without a charitable or loving posture toward scripture,
itself the product of divine grace, as well as a desire to edify the larger
Christian community.[4]

The beginning and the end of interpretation must be charity, the
summa of scripture, the double love inscribed in Christ's commandment
to love God and neighbor. Augustine simplifies the assorted problems
facing an interpreter, who must negotiate the discrepancy between the

written word (*scriptum*) and the writer's intention (*voluntas*), the ambiguity and obscurity of various linguistic signs, the subtle distinctions between literal and figurative expressions, the competing intentions of writer and reader. Everything is reduced to a single dichotomy: one either reads with *caritas* or *cupiditas*, with rightly ordered or disordered love. This, of course, is precisely More's argument when he claims that Tyndale's translation displays a malicious intent to harm the church. In many ways, however, Augustine seems to support Tyndale's position, insofar as he is less concerned with the problem of understanding a figurative expression and its inevitable dilation of meanings than making the interpretation of scripture—*any* interpretation—useful and edifying. That is, if a reader misreads a text but does so with a charitable intention, there is little harm in it unless it becomes perverse habit, and even mistranslations can benefit the Christian community, although they ought to be corrected.[5] Elsewhere, in his *Confessions*, Augustine endorses a multiplicity of interpretations for an obscure scriptural word or phrase (he gives "heaven and earth" as an example), suggesting that there is truth enough for all if the aim is love.[6]

At the end of the second book of *On Christian Doctrine*, Augustine provides a description of *caritas*, as if to clear up the problem once and for all: the charitable interpreter possesses "a meek and humble heart, subjected easily to Christ with a burden that is light, established, rooted, and built up in charity so that knowledge cannot puff him up."[7] Augustine borrows heavily here from Paul's First Epistle to the Corinthians (and his Letter to the Ephesians), which likewise tasks the virtue of charity with negotiating the several imperatives of interpretation within a Christian community. But even if charity can stabilize the uncertain process of biblical translation for Augustine, it seems to be at best an anchor for the individual conscience. It does not resolve the interpretive trial for the larger Christian community: how can anyone be sure that the translator or exegete was motivated by *caritas* rather than *cupiditas*? What marks a loving or malicious translation? Moreover, as Katrin Ettenhuber notes, Augustinian hermeneutics "can accrue or divest themselves of polemical significance as the context requires, and can combine the heights of eschatological ascent with profoundly problematic acts of rhetorical aggression."[8] In fighting over the word "charity," for example, both More and Tyndale explicitly and implicitly invoke Pauline and Augustinian concepts to support their rival approaches to scripture. In either case it is impossible to fix their respective postures with a single intention, especially as their controversy was situated in a political and religious era of rising uncertainty. One can read charity *and* malice into the work of More, protector of the church or its resident bully, as well as the work of Tyndale, heretic or gifted translator.

If linguistic meanings have a tendency to wander abroad, if there remains a deep urge to fix them in a stable semantic field like the frozen words of Rabelais, a similar desire manifests in the municipal worlds of distributive justice during the Tudor period. The controversy between More and Tyndale took place when the administration of poor relief, or material charity, was undergoing significant alterations that would profoundly influence England's future efforts to reduce poverty. In the 1520s, London had implemented a badging scheme to identify authorized beggars, and during the following decade England's parliament was revising statutory laws related to poor relief and vagrancy at the same time that Tyndale's translation was receiving consideration by royal authorities. These efforts by Tudor governments were influenced in part by recent developments on the continent, where Martin Luther was instigating reform in poor relief in Germany, Ypres had adopted an innovative new scheme aimed at poor relief in 1525, and Juan Luis Vives (a friend of More's) published *De Subventione Pauperum*, a controversial theory of relief that drew criticism from the Sorbonne and other clerical authorities on account of its premise that charity be administered by secular rather than ecclesiastical mandate. Recent work by historians has shown that few of these were new developments in England: discriminate charity and selective giving were entrenched in English practices of social aid long before the arrival of Tudor statutes; hostility toward the vagrant poor can be traced back to the mid-fourteenth century; and some medieval villages even introduced methods of taxation to provide relief.[9] But the scope and intensity of poor relief schemes developed in the early sixteenth century signals a departure from the charitable giving that characterized the medieval period. In particular, Tudor legislation is marked by amplified efforts to acquire information concerning the recipients of aid as well an increased worry over potential fraudulence.

Indeed, these provisions for the poor arrived in tandem with more sophisticated and urgent efforts to suppress vagrancy. As early sixteenth-century poor laws demonstrate, the evaluative gaze of a reader could extend from the textual body of the Bible (and its inspired or heretical translator) to the body of the beggar, from the semiotic meanings of scriptural language to the somatic markings of the deserving poor. Just as clerical authorities feared the spread of heresy under the guise of "charitable" translation or scriptural commentary, all of these schemes worried over the capacity for vagrants or rogues to abuse the systems of poor relief. Both developments—biblical translations and the practical implementation of charitable aid—involved similar problems of interpretation, supervision, and disciplinary correction. Much like words and their meanings, bodies are easily fugitive and easily disguised, and as with scriptural translation, the principle designed to protect the integrity of material charity is itself a kind of charitable hermeneutic. These bureaucratic systems attempted to stabilize the interpretive dilemma, empowering municipal officers to discover the histories of impoverished subjects, their circumstances, their ability to perform labor, and their social status. Authorities, moreover, tried to make the interpretive process easier by insisting that the itinerant poor possess passports, by issuing licenses to beggars, and by making a vagrant's criminal history legible on the body by way of a brand or scourge. Applying a hermeneutic practice of reading beggars much as one would properly read a text, these schemes reveal a culture in England that desired to implement charity but remained anxious about its potential for misapplication. And the penalties for abusing these systems of relief, while not as severe as the punishments for heresy, were nevertheless extremely harsh.

The apparent obstacles disrupting the administration of poor relief mirror many of the preoccupations vexing church authorities during this period. In both cases the project of reading—haunted by the specters of vagrancy and heresy—was complicated by the text's potential as a site of disguise and fraud. The biblical text and the bodily text of a beggar were each fraught with the possibility of misinterpretation, but these difficulties seemed to promote rigor rather than elasticity in judgment. Perhaps the stakes were too high to treat things with indifference in the first decade of the Reformation and in an era of rising poverty, although this trend would be rehearsed in other contexts throughout the early modern period. In any case, if the motives of a translator or beggar were considered in violation of charity, they were *ipso facto* malicious and required punitive correction, which was considered a matter of charitable justice. Tudor poor laws, for example, typically heralded their charity by way of two con-joined enterprises, as in the 1547 *Acte for the Punishment of Vagabondes and for the Relief of the poore and impotent Parsons*. A century later the bishop Roger Manwaring reputedly claimed, "King Edward the sixth was as Charitable in granting Bridewell for the punishment of Sturdy Rogues, as in bestowing St. Thomas Hospital for the relief of the poor and helpless."[10] Charity does not remain abstract for long, resulting if not in corporal mercy then in corporal punishment: with stocks and whipping for vagrants and with fire for heretics—whether in the bonfires of heretical books or at the martyr's stake.

All of this factors into the debate between More and Tyndale. In More's two attacks on Tyndale, the *Dialogue* and his later *Confutation of Tyndale's Answere*, a massive tome that heaps up evidence as if to crush Tyndale and his translation beneath its weighty bulk, these entangled notions of charity become fully evident: the divergent responsibilities of a scriptural translator in shaping and responding to a spiritual community; the sharp distinctions between charity and malice; and the pressing claims of the body, with its assorted temptations to sloth, avarice, gluttony, and lust, which prove so importunate in casting suspicion on any expression of charity. Among other things, it becomes apparent why More, sparring in a debate partially motivated by Tyndale's decision to translate *agape* as "love" rather than "charity," seems so uncharitable. It has long been a commonplace among More's readers to note his unkind disposition toward Tyndale. Midway through the sixteenth century John Foxe observes that the characters in More's *Dialogue* "soon forget their charity, and fall a railing," and near the end of the twentieth century Alistair Fox's biography notes a pattern in the polemics whereby More's "charity is displaced by violence."[11] Tyndale is not much better in this regard. It is difficult not to be impressed by the remarkable intellect of each antagonist, as well as their memorable expressions of English vernacular, the subtle elasticity of More's *Dialogue* and downrightness of Tyndale's prose, but one nevertheless struggles to account for the vituperative tone that governs the exchange.

More and Tyndale's mutual derision is not an absence of charity, however, but the product of two rival visions of charity. Given their prior commitments, they are almost forced to read the other's project in terms of malice. In More's mind, for example, the mere act of vernacular translation already confirms Tyndale's heretical disposition, and he takes care in his *Dialogue* to show his readers that Tyndale's work does not merit a charitable reading:

> [Tyndale] laboureth of purpose to mynysshe the reuerent mynde that men bere to charyte / and therefore he chaungeth that name of holy virtuous affeccyon / in to the bare name of love comen to the virtuous love that man bereth to god / and to the lewde loue that is bytwene flecke & his make.[12]

In this passage More confidently attributes malicious intent to Tyndale, who "laboureth of purpose" to diminish among his readers a reverence for charity. Notice the modifier he uses to describe Tyndale's choice of word—"the bare name of love"—as if the translator had stripped charity naked for the leering eyes of the unlearned laity. Here More gestures at the biblical trope, stemming from I Peter, that characterizes charity as a cloak or veil covering a multitude of sins.[13] In this case, More implies, Tyndale has stifled the voice that cries out on his behalf, removing the cloak that would cover his translation's sins, now bared for "comen" readers to witness.

Skeptical of reformers who privilege an invisible church or internal conscience informed by the Holy Spirit, More presupposes the physical and bodily reality of Christian love, and, echoing Augustine's dichotomy between *caritas* and *cupiditas,* he can only see two alternatives: "holy virtuous affeccyon" and "lewde loue." There he finds an exceptionally flexible and pertinent adjective in contemporary usage, as "lewd" might describe a specific type of love among or for the laity (whom Tyndale was empowering) or an unlettered love (and More levies accusations of ignorance at Tyndale), but especially a kind of lascivious love, with Tyndale and Luther, the two translators of scripture into vernacular, as "flecke & his make."[14] Conflating translation with theological interpretation, certain that Tyndale deliberately altered scripture in such a way that would undercut the church's authority, More suggests that "love," a banal word possessing dangerous sexual connotations, would be the natural preference of someone in bed with Lutheran heresy. Tyndale, in *An Answere Vnto Sir Thomas Mores Dialoge,* responds in kind. After defending his translation, he indicts sundry clerical abuses in England and abroad, and rebukes

More's own carnal attitudes toward charity, claiming that he has betrayed the cause of Christian humanism for a monetary reward and misappropriated scriptural authority for the sake of earthly power.

All of this brings us back to the issue of hermeneutics. Much of the controversy, after all, was the result of interpretation, the search for a fixed intention hidden within words on a page. For his part, More treats Tyndale in the manner of a suspicious almsgiver who is approached by a false beggar; More's charity is not displaced by violence but affirmed by it. Meanwhile, Tyndale's efforts to reform the function of Christian love end up razing much of the church's scriptural edifice. This claim might seem like hyperbole given the pedantic matter of their quarrel. In assessing their predicament with a kind of exasperation, for example, C.S. Lewis reduces the greatest part of More's dispute with Tyndale to a quibble over diction: "One sees how tragically narrow is the boundary between Tyndale and his opponents, how nearly he means by faith what they mean by charity."[15] This is true. But it is also true that their respective commitments to "love" and "charity" signify entrenched differences in their spiritual and political imaginations, or as James Simpson notes, they both move from philological grounds "to prior, ideational texts, the text written on the heart."[16] In the word *agape* they each read distinct and rival forms of Christian duty. Tyndale and More were both dead by 1536, and after them it was difficult for an English writer to employ the word "charity" without adopting a conscious stance regarding some aspect of their dispute.

Agape: The Problems of Translation and Interpretation

The difficulties in translating biblical notions of love began long before More's dispute with Tyndale. When translating the assortment of Hebrew words used to describe "love," all of which were deployed throughout the Jewish scriptures in a variety of contexts, the Septuagint translators generally employed the single (and relatively obscure) Greek word *agapan,* which meant "to esteem" or "to prefer" or "to be grateful" in classical sources. In so doing they eschewed the more accessible and inclusive term *eros,* perhaps on account of its associations with libidinous sexual desire or its established place in Greek philosophy.[17] The translators occasionally adopted *philia* to describe filial or fraternal love (even then, rarely), but its implicit reciprocity—the mutual love shared by equals—must have seemed inadequate to describe the relationship between humans and the divine. Consequently, the word *agape* acquired new significance, deriving its central importance from the injunction of Deuteronomy 6:5 to "love the Lord thy God with all thine heart, and with all thy soul, and with all thy might," which prescribes the primary form of worship and obedience due to the God of Israel. Elsewhere, *agape* describes the love of God to his chosen people (Deut. 7:7–8), as well as an idealized social ethic commanding citizens to "love thy neighbour as thyself" (Lev. 19:18).

These loosely related figurations of a specifically religious *agape* receive further emphasis in the synoptic gospels, particularly given the manner in which Jesus links the commands of Deuteronomy 6:5 and Leviticus 19:18, implicitly aligning fraternal love with the traditional love of and obedience to God.[18] Luke, perhaps the most gifted Greek stylist of the gospel writers, demonstrates especially remarkable subtlety in his deployment of *agape* by developing these specifically Jewish and Christian meanings of a religious love alongside more traditional, classical senses of the word. So, for example, he uses *agape* to describe the centurion's esteem for the Jewish nation (Luke 7:5), a sinful woman's gratitude for Jesus's forgiveness (Luke 7:47), and even the preference of Pharisees for their own ostentatious displays of devotion (Luke 11:43).[19] Pauline epistles further complicate the word's legacy. While *agape* is most frequently deployed in its verb form in the Septuagint, gospels, and extra-biblical sources, which reflect the verb-oriented characteristics of the Greek and Hebrew languages, the word appears most often as a noun in the Pauline epistles, marking a profound lexical shift with serious implications for future translators. Paul generally employs *agape* to describe fraternal love between humans rather than a human response to God or Christ, which is usually figured as faith or *pistis,* but the alteration only expands the definition of *agape* rather than reducing its scope.[20] As a word that might mean divine love, religious devotion, or mutual love among humans, in addition to an already complicated secular legacy, *agape* places difficult demands on any biblical translator, who must be attuned to circumstance, tone, verbal context, and authorial idiosyncrasy.

This, then, was the predicament facing Jerome and other early translators of the New Testament.[21] What is more, no equivalent Latin term existed for *agape*. In order to convey the appropriate sense of each particular usage of the word, the Vulgate employs a combination of *dilectio* and *caritas* to convey the sense of higher love, and *cupiditas* or *concupiscentia* as a de-based form of self-love, with *amor* filling in the gaps. Jerome explains his theory of translation in Epistle 57 to Pammachius, declaring the primacy of translating for sense rather than literally *verbum e verbo*, although he does claim scripture requires additional consideration and caution before adjusting any literal word.[22] At the same time Jerome defends his principle of *ad fontes*, privileging original sources over potentially corrupt derivatives. Already he articulates an approach to translation that marries the original text (in its original language) to a contemporary context and usage, but Jerome also recognizes the inherent dangers of such a project, an acknowledgement authorities later used to justify banning vernacular translation. Indeed, Arundel's *Constitutions* (drafted in 1407 and issued in 1409), which outlawed biblical translation in England, specifically refers to Jerome's admission that "it is a perilous thing, as the Blessed Jerome testifies, to translate the text of Holy Scripture from one idiom into another."[23] Similarly unequipped to translate the precise meanings of *agape* into English, and evidencing perhaps more conservatism than authorities might have expected, Wycliffite versions of the Bible (followed by the Douay-Rheims) simply rendered *dilectio* as "love" and *caritas* as "charity," but there was no easy solution for translators.[24] Later, when Tyndale answers More's initial accusation, he acknowledges the particular dilemma confronting any translator of *agape*, and one might even observe a note of genuine exasperation in his tone: "Verily, charitie is no knowen Englishe, in that sence which *agape* requireth . . . Wherfore I must haue used this generall terme loue, in spite of myne hart oftentimes."[25] Regardless of polemical, theological, or interpretive considerations, charity poses difficulties to any translator of the Bible.

That frustrated qualification, "in spite of myne hart sometimes," voiced amid the heat of polemical assault, might suggest that Tyndale attempted to strike his own balance between his head and heart, between the letter and spirit of scripture, but this hesitancy hardly depicts Tyndale's initial self-assurance as a translator. The prologue to the 1525 Cologne fragment (interrupted after an informer alerted authorities), his first description of what would become his life's work, provides a more apt summation of his approach to translation:

I have here translated . . . the new Testament for your spiritual edifying, consolation, and solace: Exhorting instantly and beseeching those that are better seen in the tongues than I, and that have higher gifts of grace to interpret the sense of the scripture and meaning of the spirit, than I, to consider and ponder my labour, and that with the spirit of meekness. And if they perceive in any places that I have not attained the very sense of the tongue, or meaning of the scripture, or have not given the right English word, that they put to their hands to amend it, remembering that so is their duty to do.[26]

It is a command performance for someone beginning his career as a translator of scripture. Reading that first simple clause blazoned like fiat across the page, "I have here translated," it is easy to see how Stephen Greenblatt finds in Tyndale's work the "expression of a powerful *confidence.*"[27] There is an urgency here as well, one that immediately engages his readers, whom he instructs to "consider and ponder" his work with "meekness." By way of a humility topos spiced with an imperative tone, Tyndale attempts to manipulate the reception of his translation, exhorting his audience to take it seriously but also to read it charitably. His reference to "gifts of grace" suggests that he was consciously fashioning his vocation after the advice of Paul in 1 Corinthians 12–14, articulating a vision of personal labor where individual and communal interests intersect, fulfilling the pedagogical and pastoral responsibilities Paul asks of the congregation in Corinth. Furthermore, Tyndale reminds his readers of their own obligations to follow this scriptural imperative: "so is their duty to do." The declaration, a trumpet blast aimed at established English authorities of church and state, who continued to proscribe any vernacular translation, derives its full force from the most powerful exhortation to perform charity in the Pauline canon.

Tyndale's prologue declares that he was called to translate the Bible as an act of love to God and neighbor, and others should contribute their own particular gifts to the enterprise. The prologue to the Wycliffite Bible makes a similar assertion, claiming to "have translatid the bible out of Latyn into English" out of "comune charite to saue alle men in oure rewme."[28] Indeed, More was aggravated by the claims of Tyndale and others that "begynne theyr pystles in suche apostolycall fashyon that a man wold wene yt were wryten from saynt Paule himself."[29] The crucial factor of Tyndale's project, and what provoked such fierce opposition, was its inherent individualism at both the level of translator and reader, whose greatest interpretive aid according to Tyndale remains the interior revelation of the Holy Spirit. But this loose collection of individuals, linked through their shared experience of the scriptural word, was ostensibly oriented toward a communal good.

More was dubious of Tyndale's spiritual and scholarly intentions, of course, and he was equally concerned with a laity ill-equipped to interpret scripture correctly, but more generally he seemed skeptical of a project that was not underwritten by consensus. Indeed, Benedek Péter Tóta suggests that More derived his own theory of charitable hermeneutics from 1 Corinthians 14, in which he envisions charity as a speech-act, a performative utterance rooted in integrity and obliged to defend the truth from false interpreters and flatterers.[30] In this interpretation Paul's counsel begins with the communal order and culminates in his vision of a fully edified Christian congregation that will be empowered to encounter an individual unbeliever: "But and if all prophesy, and there come in one that believeth not, or one unlearned, he is rebuked of all men, and is judged of every man: and so are the secrets of his heart opened."[31] In the context of More and Tyndale's debate, the dynamic becomes all the more suggestive because Paul explicitly sets charity, with its collective emphasis, in opposition to knowledge that "puffeth up" individuals. Even as charity motivated Tyndale to begin a project of translation, the same virtue obliged More to halt its progress. Perhaps more to the point, More supported a notion of charity that obtained its sanction and power from the communal order rather than the other way around. So, which was Tyndale: the individual edifying the community by his gift in tongues or the unbeliever? The complexity that characterizes sixteenth- and seventeenth-century understandings of charity stems in large part from the concept's vexed scriptural foundation: charity might serve to validate an individual's contributions to a community or it might justify a congregation protecting itself from an outsider's potential threat of disruption to communal harmony. As Erasmus, in his *Diatribe*, reminds Luther during a similarly fraught controversy of the period, scripture and Spirit remain insufficient criteria for resolving theological disputations, as both sides have recourse to scriptural citation and claims of divine revelation.[32]

The implications for More's approach to charity and translation are profound. His primary contention, that Tyndale's "mistranslations" betray a desire to inculcate scripture with heretical doctrine, persisted throughout the controversy, but More's antipathy for Tyndale likewise stems from a simple difference in temperament. In the *Dialogue's* equivocal endorsement of a vernacular translation of scripture, More cites the difficulties of translation as reason for hesitation, restraint, and a conservative approach to such an endeavor, especially when salvation is at stake. How can one render, More asks, "well and lyvely the sentence of hys author / whyche is harde always to do so surely but that he shall somtyme mynyshe eyther of the sentence [form] or of the grace [meaning] that it bereth in the formare tonge."[33] Consequently, he favors "comen custome" rather than any sudden lexical shift, whatever its claims to accuracy might be, and he indicts Tyndale's failure to accord with the accepted usage of an English audience familiar with the term "charity." A profound skepticism of any solitary enterprise underlies this principle of translation, which insists that individual beliefs remain circumscribed by authority and consensus. A similar attitude toward scriptural interpretation can be found in More's *Responsio ad Lutherum,* which mocks Luther for relying on scripture to displace church authority, since the church, after all, has done the hard work of determining what is in fact scripture.[34] More was not adamantly opposed to scriptural translation by individuals; in 1515 he wrote to Martin Dorp defending Erasmus's *Novum Instrumentum,* a massive scholarly undertaking that would later be the foundation of Tyndale's own biblical project. But he clearly privileged the communal order first, and More believed fending off individual heretics like Tyndale—much like the unbeliever of 1 Corinthians 14—to be a vital function of charity.

More has specific philological complaints, too, in which scholarly, aesthetic, and moral principles all begin to overlap. He appears especially concerned that Tyndale's choice of "love" rather than "charity" effaces important distinctions between various types of love: "For though charyte be alway loue / yet is not ye wote well loue allway charyte."[35] More's argument echoes a comment made by Thomas Aquinas in *Summa Theologiae* 1a.2ae.26 when he attempts to distinguish between *amor* and *dilectio,* which follows a similar treatment of the matter by Augustine.[36] Much like More, both Augustine and Aquinas recognize that distinctions need to be made between *caritas* and *dilectio,* two specific forms of love, and *amor,* a general term that encompasses the former two in addition to love of friendship and love of concupiscence. *Caritas* is always *amor,* but *amor* is not always *caritas.*

Unlike More, however, neither Augustine nor Aquinas expresses much apprehension over the philological muddle; indeed, Augustine strenuously defends the scriptural sanction of *amor* against its detractors. More seems particularly worried by the erotic implications of "love," which will be discussed later, but implicit in his anxiety is the belief that a neutral term like "love" facilitates misprision and erodes centuries of church tradition that had clarified the nature of godly love. Nevertheless, the charges he levies at Tyndale's translation appear noticeably fastidious, especially in comparison to the more temperate positions of Augustine and Aquinas.

Tyndale does little better in response to More's critique. In *The Obedience of a Christian Man*, he boldly defends the English vernacular, claiming "the greke tonge agreeth moare with the English then with the latyne," but his initial rejoinder to More, as I mentioned, concentrates on the philological obstacles of translation—"Verily, charitie is no knowen Englishe, in that sence which *agape* requireth."[37] In comparison to his confident justifications of his choices to use "congregation" or "repent," the debate over "charity" elicits a relatively confused defense. He seems genuinely flustered, relying on a series of rhetorical questions:

> For when we say, geue youre almes in the worshepe of God and swete saint charite, and when the father teacheth his sonne to saye blissinge father for saint charite, what meane they? In good faith they wot not. Moreouer when we say, God helpe you, I haue done my charite for this day, do we not take it for almes?[38]

This hardly answers More's charges, beyond delivering a jab at the church's theology of meritorious almsgiving and associating charity with the supposed superstitions of intercessory prayer. If he were primarily concerned with refuting More's insinuations that Lutheran theology informs his translation, Tyndale chooses a poor strategy.

Although the rhetorical questions provide unconvincing support for his translation, Tyndale's repeated use of the stylistic device does emphasize the difficult choice facing the translator, and he begins asserting this point more forcefully:

> And the man is euer childing and out of charitie, and I beshrew him sauing my charitie, there we take it for patience. And when I say a

charitable man, it is taken for mercifull. And though mercifulnes be a good loue, or rather spring of a good loue, yet is not euery good loue mercifulnes. As when a woman loueth her husband godly, or a man his wife or his frende that is in none aduersitie, it is not alway mercifulnesse. Also we say not thys man hath a great charitie to god, but a great loue.

Here Tyndale, with his barrage of conjunctions, seems to gesture by way of polysyndeton at the dynamic complexity of Paul's message in 1 Corinthians 13: 4–7, when the apostle uses fifteen verbs to describe the different functions of *agape*.[39] (One can also hear in Tyndale's defense Erasmus's ironic ventriloquy of an academic theologian who complains that Paul's first letter to the Corinthians "neither divides nor defines [charity] according to the rules of dialectic."[40]) However, by describing the multiple significations of "charity," Tyndale actually provides a rationale for its inclusion, as the word clearly meant more than merely "giving alms" and yet its sense remained narrower than "love." What is more damning, perhaps, is Tyndale's use throughout the New Testament's epistles of "concupiscence," a latinate word more traditionally translated as "lust" and explicitly set in contrast to charity by Jerome, a polarity further reinforced by Augustine in much of his theological writing.[41] In his various apologies for privileging "love" in his translation, Tyndale claimed to be rebelling not against church and tradition but the entire latinate lexicon on which "charity" was founded; yet if "lust" need not consistently replace "concupiscence," why the discrepancy in the case of "charity"?

Tyndale's argument becomes plainer when he justifies an approach to translation that empowers readers to arrive at meaning after a consideration of context, as he explains in his preface to the New Testament: "Where the text seemeth at the first chop hard to be understood, yet the circumstances before and after, and often reading together, maketh it plain enough."[42] Articulating a rule of translation that aims for inclusivity when confronted by a philological dilemma such as *agape*, Tyndale suggests he can avoid potential inaccuracy by remaining general—"euery loue is not charitie . . . nor euery hope christen hope"—and allowing readers to interpret nuance from the passage's context: "The matter it selfe and the circumstaunces do declare what loue, what hope, and what fayth is spoken of."[43] This might bolster More's argument that relying solely on scripture is a vexed approach to theology, but as a principle of translation or hermeneutics, Tyndale's statement stands on relatively firm ground, safe behind the vanguard of humanists like Lorenzo Valla and Erasmus, both of whom championed biblical interpretation that privileged a consideration of style, context, and usage.

Noting the "humanist vocabulary" that Tyndale deploys ("the circumstances before and after" or "the matter it selfe and the circumstaunces"), Cummings shows how Tyndale was laboring "to justify English theological usage through an emerging philology of the English language."[44] Tyndale's decision to use "love" would perhaps have earned the approbation of Valla, whose own scriptural translations attempted, when possible, to render the Latin equivalents for Greek words in a consistent and predictable manner. Indeed, both Valla and Erasmus chastise the Vulgate for its frustrating vagaries of diction.[45] Meanwhile, even as he follows Jerome in warning against the dangers of word-for-word translation, Erasmus (More's own "derelynge" friend, as Tyndale notes gleefully) invests the translator of scripture with a great deal of discretionary power: his *Paraclesis*, which envisions the field hand singing the gospels at his plow, was likely the catalyst for Tyndale's vocation, and in the prefatory address of his 1522 *Paraphrase on Matthew*, he bluntly asks why clerical authorities have not made the gospels available to laymen in the English vernacular.[46]

Whereas Erasmus aims for clarity and consistency in scriptural translation as a means of stabilizing a dynamic and often obscure text, however, Tyndale expresses a much stronger belief in the clarity and transparency of the scriptures themselves, which he believed would explain themselves to each reader.[47] By limiting himself to a consistent word for *agape* in every instance, Tyndale was adhering to certain humanist principles and creating more relational immediacy between reader and text, distancing to some degree the interpretive impact of the translator. Nevertheless, it seems clear that Tyndale was also attempting to reinforce and reproduce in English what he believed to be the self-interpreting nature of the biblical text, a conventional belief among reformers who stressed the primacy of scripture. He did provide his own simplistic interpretive apparatus to accompany the New Testament, which several scholars have mentioned when questioning Tyndale's supposed confidence in biblical transparency. But as his career continued, even as he developed a more sophisticated understanding of Hebrew and a greater awareness of the Bible's complex lexical heritage, Tyndale reduced his marginal notes and glosses dramatically, which suggests a growing degree of confidence in his audience's ability to interpret scripture with the aid of the Holy Spirit.[48] Finally, Tyndale's choice of "love" also supported one of the key tenets of Luther's theology, which attempted to dismantle any kind of hierarchy of good works. Both Luther and Tyndale believed that each individual Christian, if motivated by an authentic faith, need not distinguish between various good works—different kinds of charity or love, if you will—because *anything* done out of faith in God (even picking up a straw, as Luther remarks in his treatise *On Good Works*) is an act of loving service.

Tyndale's translation, then, was equal parts Luther and Erasmus. As Henry Wansbrough puts the case, although clerical authorities "might legitimately claim that Tyndale's New Testament was 'naughtelie translated', it was also accurate."[49] More, deeply suspicious of what he considered to be a tendentious translation, remained unconvinced by Tyndale's argument, and in the *Confutation* he continues to accuse Tyndale of obscuring important distinctions between "holy virtuous affeccyon" and "lewde love." There might be occasions to translate in such a way that sacrifices precision for accuracy, he claims, but "charity" satisfies both requirements:

> Here maketh Tyndale a grete processe / and telleth vs that cheryte hath in englysshe speche dyuers sygnyfycacyons, somtyme loue, somtyme mercy, somtime pacyence. And what is all this to purpose? Sholde he therfore leue out cheryte where it may conueniently stande? . . . what nede was it to put the indyfferent worde loue in the place of the vndowted good worde cheryte, there as ye sentence well shewed that it sygnifyed neyther mercy nor pacyence but loue / and then the worde sygnyfyed that it ment good loue whych is expressed by cheryte.[50]

In this case More subtly privileges the Vulgate or conveniently forgets that *caritas* already served as a lexical compromise in translating *agape*, that there were no simple Latin or English equivalents for the Greek word, but his contention remains forceful. Tyndale's choice of "love" clearly possesses just as many diverse significations as "charity," so why not preserve the term more widely accepted by contemporaries? More argues further in behalf of decorum, dismissing the importance of what the language of an original text means to its contemporaries and claiming, "Tyndale muste nedys in hys englysshe translacyon use hys englysshe wordes in suche sygnyfycacyon as the people vseth them in hys owne tyme."[51] It is a slight exaggeration to claim, as Germain Marc'hadour and Thomas Lawler do, that "usage alone is the ground of More's rebuke," since More was obviously using this argument to support his primary accusation that Tyndale's translation amounted to Lutheran heresy, but More clearly considered Tyndale's lexical iconoclasm proof of the larger hazards involved when individuals sought to handle and disseminate the word of God.[52] Both men were excellent scholars of Greek, and their respective theories of translation were each founded in good humanist principles, but they remained unwilling to negotiate in the manner Jerome envisions necessary for any translation: Tyndale might have been too quick to dismiss a contemporary English equivalent for classical and scriptural *agape,* whereas More's shrill defense of church tradition and English usage would place impossible demands on any vernacular translation purporting to adhere to the original text.[53]

It is difficult to claim a victor in this particular aspect of the contest. But there is evidence Tyndale later recognized the dangers of his project, which placed an enormous amount of responsibility on the individual translator. In 1534 a fellow English reformer in exile, George Joye, oversaw the publication of a pirated edition of Tyndale's translation, in which Joye replaced the word "resurrection" with "life after this life," a change Tyndale feared might facilitate arguments in behalf of purgatory or other doctrines he felt were rooted in doubtful scripture.[54] In order to respond directly to the change, Tyndale appended a second note to his readers at the front of his revised edition of the New Testament, in which he accused Joye of failing to "walk after the rules of love and softness which Christ, and his disciples teach us."[55] Just as the prologue to the Cologne fragment figures his own translation as a charitable endeavor intended to edify and console, here Tyndale charges Joye with "[playing] boo peep with the translations" and violating fundamental precepts of Christian love by casting doubt on biblical certainty and endangering congregational harmony: "that were the next way to stablish all heresies and to destroy the ground wherewith we should improve them."[56] In this debate he ultimately ends up playing the role of Thomas More, defending catholic consensus and worrying over the injurious effects of ignorant or malicious translations of scripture.

Immediately after this assertion, Tyndale rests his evidence against Joye on the twin bedrock of scriptural and canonical authority, "according to the open and manifest scriptures and catholic faith."[57] If Joye's translation of resurrection is correct, Tyndale claims, "then must my translation be faulty in those places, and saint Jerome's, and all the translators that ever I heard of in what tongue soever it be."[58] It is a diplomatic tactic as well to align his work with that of the Vulgate (against which many detractors opposed his translation) and subsume his own theological views under the aegis of the church while maintaining the independent authority of the scriptures. Clearly Tyndale betrays an anxiety concerning the impact of mistranslation, recognizing its dangerous capacity to fracture the unified faith of the church, though he remains convinced of his own project's divine sanction. But also involved in his rebuke to Joye is a personal stake, a concern that his own name remain unassociated with suspect scholarship, just the sort of individualist ethic More decries in his critique of Tyndale's translation.

Meanwhile, More might have benefited from the instructive example of Thomas Lupset, whose *Treatise of Charitie,* written in 1529 and published four years later, offers a humane, measured, and incisive model of critique. Employing a dialogue much like More's, and comparably spiced with humor, Lupset offers a similar criticism of Tyndale's translation, which he considers insufficiently precise in its replacement of "charity" with "love." The tone of the criticism directed at Tyndale, however, is much different. Lupset's own description of charity fuses a type of Christian Stoicism with Neo-Platonism, requiring a contempt for worldly passion and bodily pleasure that gradually ascends to a rarefied form of love equivalent to dwelling in God: "This charitie is god, and God is this charitie."[59]

By studiously avoiding the specter of the body—much different, as we will see, from More and even Tyndale—Lupset's notion of charity remains detached, abstract, a product of deliberation, even if his philological argument is oversimplified:

> For trouthe it is, that all Charite is loue: but it is not trouth, that all loue is charite. In greke charite is *agape,* and loue is *eros,* as in latine loue is *amor,* and charitie *Chaeritas.* In al these thre tonges there is the same difference in the tone worde from the tother, that is a penne and

a quylle. . . . Likewyse loue is the common affecte of fauour: charitie is loue reduced into a due order towardes god and man, as to loue god alone for him self, and to loue man for goddes sake.⁶⁰

Lupset's dismissal of Tyndale's translation echoes the sentiments More published the same year in his *Dialogue,* but here no accusation is levied at Tyndale himself, merely at his preference for "love" instead of "charity." Influenced perhaps by Chrysostom's emphasis on indiscriminate charity (Lupset translated at least one of his sermons), he encourages a type of unconditional love to all people, friends and enemies alike. When asked by his sister what fault lies in Tyndale's choice of words, the brother responds: "The same defaulte I put in hym, yt you wold put in one, the whiche doth giue to you wiers for perles, or quilles for pennes. But sister, remembre, you wolde haue me be short."⁶¹ It is as if Lupset wishes to distance himself from the fray, desiring to enact that indifferent love he espoused earlier. The critique remains rational, even aesthetic, without devolving into ad hominem attacks or rumor-mongering. Obviously Lupset has his own distinct project in mind, but the work suggests an alternative to More's polemic, one in which a charitable reading is embodied in the actual discourse. Perhaps Lupset, a Christian humanist deeply involved in the political vicissitudes of Henry's court, wished to promote a constructive theological dialectic by aiming for his own positive description of charity without marshaling an offensive against Tyndale's opinions and beliefs.

In the decade that followed, once Tyndale's translations had received official sanction and royal imprimatur by way of the Great Bible of 1539, this debate over usage grew largely defunct: "Conservatives could no longer appeal to established English biblical usage against Tyndale's translations: Tyndale's English was becoming institutional."⁶² But charity—or love—remained a touchstone that revealed the confessional commitments of future translators. The reforming spirit of the Geneva Bible, for example, is signaled by its preference for "love," whereas the Rheims New Testament, published in 1582 for Catholic exiles and recusants living in England, preferred "charity." This history comes full circle with the Authorized Version in 1611, which returned "charity" to its privileged seat as the official translation of *agape* promoted by the Church of England.

The Order of Charity: Poor Relief and the Vagrant Text

In his defense of scriptural translation regulated by the common beliefs and traditions of the church, More, as I have claimed, evinces a temperamental distrust of Tyndale's individualism. But he also deploys a specific brand of communal rhetoric that links Tyndale, the heretic undermining the church's spiritual welfare, to another marginalized population supposedly threatening the material welfare of the commonwealth: vagrants. It is a subtle and effective strategy. Early in the *Dialogue* he takes care to emphasize Tyndale's shifting identities—"mayster Wyllyam Huchyn / otherwise called mayster Tyndall"—and he recycles the device in *The Apology,* calling Tyndale and his confederates "potheded postles . . . that wander about the realm into sundry shyres, of whom euery one hath in euery shyre a dyuerse name."[63] Such a tactic confirms Tyndale's status as outsider, whose travel merits the same suspicion accorded to vagabonds, figures who exploit material charity much as Tyndale's texts abuse the word "charity." In the preface to his *Confutation,* after explicitly associating recent occasions of dearth and increased poverty with the influx of heretical texts, More likens Tyndale and other reformers to vagrants who support themselves with misappropriated alms: "These felowes that naught had here, and therfore noughte caryed hense, nor nothynge fyndynge there to lyue vppon / be yet sustayned and mayntened wyth monye sent them by some euyll dysposed persones." More seems to expect his audience to have a similar attitude, adding, "We shall not need to dowte of what sort we shall reken the remanaunt."[64] The malicious deceit of both vagrants and heretics, marginal figures who put the community at risk, clearly justifies More's punitive response.

These might seem like throwaway lines, the kind of learned jocularity that characterizes much of More's work, but he is tapping into a deep cultural anxiety about the status of charitable giving and what constitutes a proper response to the problem of vagabonds. Such figures, variously described as "valiant" or "sturdy" or "able-bodied" beggars, were becoming more prominent in debates over the practical administration of discriminate alms as municipal authorities across Europe introduced a variety of poor relief schemes to cope with a sudden increase in poverty. Although the existence of vagabonds encouraged just as many arguments for religious reform as it stifled, More is able to accomplish several purposes by equating Tyndale's heresy with vagrancy. His comparison presents a specific and memorable figure that casts disrepute on Tyndale's translation; it also offers a defense of his own conduct during the controversy, since the prevailing logic of the early modern period demanded that vagrants receive a punitive response; finally, it gives a compelling rationale for More's conservative attitude toward translation. As with heretical texts, the process of determining whether or not a beggar was actually a disguised vagrant required a difficult interpretive task for individuals that could be stabilized and regulated by a reliable collective entity. Even though More was on the losing side in the case of scriptural translation (the vernacular Matthew's Bible would gain official sanction merely two years after his execution), his careful, communal approach to interpretation provides a neat and tidy analogue for contemporary poor relief. It also underscores a paradox that characterizes this period of history: even as Europe witnessed a dynamic and wide-reaching movement to facilitate intimate individual encounters with vernacular scripture, municipal schemes of poor relief were developing with similar speed in order to govern and mediate individual acts of charity.

Addressing the problem of vagrancy was hardly a new phenomenon in England, as local communities had already been adapting in response to the growing population of transient poor. The situation intensified in the 1520s and 1530s, when central authorities, influenced by the comprehensive reforms in poor relief sweeping across the continent, vigorously attempted to "heal" a commonwealth grown sick with vagrants.[65] In addition to new poor laws that were being implemented at both local and national levels, Juan Luis Vives published a treatise in 1526 devoted to the subject, *De Subventione Pauperum,* which he directed to his adopted city Bruges upon request by its prefect, Louis de Praet, ambassador to England for Charles V.[66] Meanwhile, the groundbreaking Ypres Ordinance, instituted in 1525, was translated by William Marshall and published in 1536, part of a more general effort to enact thoroughgoing reform. Even Tyndale, writing on the continent, was promoting improvements to poor relief. In his *Exposition of Matthew,* for example, during an otherwise steady denunciation of vainglorious works, he inserted a parenthetical statement that outlined "the right way" of distributing alms to the poor: "We should know in every parish all our poor, and have a common coffer for them; and that strangers should bring a letter of recommendation with them of their necessity, and that we had a common place to receive them into for the time."[67]

Historians of social welfare routinely note the inefficacy of early Tudor policies of poor relief—the Henrician statutes of 1531 and 1536, the Edwardian act of 1547, and even the Elizabethan acts of 1572 and 1576—all of which provided insufficient administrative machinery to ensure the proper execution of regulations, misunderstood the root causes of poverty, and remained overly preoccupied with the evils of idleness. But the statutes do demonstrate, however, a recognition among the English populace of the difficulties inherent in any charitable enterprise, which was vulnerable to misapplication or fraud. Equally relevant, these reforms set into sharp relief two important characteristics associated with charity in the period. First, contemporary developments in poor relief underscore the punitive discipline coursing through even the practical application of alms: the virtue of charity, as More and Tyndale and their contemporaries understood it, might require somebody to give money or food, especially in an occasion of need, but it might also oblige that person to give correction or punishment, which is why authorities insisted that "increased penalties for vagabonds were an act of charity, a necessary concomitant to increased poor relief."[68] Second, the poor relief schemes implicate crucial questions of scriptural translation and hermeneutics, or to put it in another manner, they demonstrate certain habits of reading that shed light on the debate between Tyndale and More. Charity demanded a complicated and constant program of reading. In one's relationships, one's devotional life, even in the practical realities of daily living, the process of administering charity required an array of interpretive strategies to negotiate its various complications, not least of which were its potential for abuse or exploitation. Such distrust is as plainly evident in contemporary poor relief as it is in More's defense of the traditional translation of "charity."

In addition to providing publicly funded outdoor relief for deserving poor, most of the new reforms were intended to suppress begging, enforce labor, and discipline the able-bodied poor by way of punitive measures. All of these practices, "gifts" of punishment as well as aid, were conceived in terms of Christ's mystical body joined by faith and charity, the most powerful and authentic expression of communal harmony available to municipalities.[69] As the town of Ypres declared in a defense of its innovative poor relief scheme instituted in 1525, the classical metaphor of the body politic neatly merged with Christ's mystical body into the predominant figuration of Christian community: "For than shall christen charite wytnesse / that we ar membres of one body and heed."[70] Language of this kind was commonplace, as Paul Slack notes, and here emerges another relation between heresy and vagrancy, since anything that endangered order was conceived as a sickness or sore that threatened to infect the commonwealth's body—"All kinds of mischief, heresy, and error were 'pestilent'"—while the laws that cleaned them away were considered medicinal purgatives.[71] In his *Supplication,* for example, More seems to conflate the conditions of vagrancy and heresy by way of this presiding conceit, condemning "bold presumptuouse beggars . . . hole & strong in body but weke & syk in soule / that haue theyr bodys clene fro skabbys and theyr soulys foule infect wyth vgly great pokkys & leprye."[72] England, in More's eyes, was sick with heresy and vagrancy. The overlaps between charity and medicine or physic are not limited to vocabulary, as Robert Burton and Thomas Browne later show, but here it is worth stressing the manner in which a somatic register persistently manifests in both the spiritual and material imperatives of charity.

The marriage of conflicting interests knit together in the mystical body was more complicated in practice than in theory. The Ypres Ordinance, which offers a grand promise of universal love and pity extended to all people, illustrates the difficulties of implementing such a charitable ideal:

Seeing that god approved no thinge more than kyndnesse towardes our neibour / for he that loveth his neibour fulfilleth the lawe: therefore we thinke that pity shuld be stretched to all pore peple on every syde, but yet in such manner that the ordre of charity saved / we preserve oure citizens whose persons and maners we knowe before strangers with whom we have none acquaintance.

After acknowledging the divine sanction of neighborly love and then reiterating its importance, the ordinance proceeds as if with a syllogism—"therefore we thinke"—suggesting that the following vision of generosity and abundance "stretched to all pore peple on every side" is at once necessary and natural. But the town inserts an important qualification, one that maintains the integrity of its project of pity but nevertheless insists on "the ordre of charity." Just in case the city's abundance is exhausted, merely as a matter of policy, Ypres will extend charitable aid first to its own citizens, "whose persons and maners we knowe."

The order of charity to which Ypres alludes had been developed in canon law with a great deal of sophisticated handwringing, as theologians attempted to establish classes of poverty by which they might prioritize their almsgiving.[73] Articulating the standard position of medieval canon lawyers, Ypres effects a compromise, preferring the careful distinctions in poverty made by Ambrose even as it professes the ultimate ideal of indifferent charity urged by Chrysostom, so long as supplies last. One reason for establishing categories of desert, interestingly, is the imperative of justice—"he that loveth his neibour fulfilleth the lawe"—as theologians had long considered charity to involve both the virtue of justice as well as mercy.[74] A relatively nuanced skepticism of the efficacy of alms likewise influenced the scheme; as the Ypres ordinance observes, following a precedent set by Augustine and others, ill-administered charity might facilitate injurious patterns of living, particularly among professional beggars: "To suche [counterfeit poor] beggynge shulde be forbidden that they shulde nat turne the goodenesse of good men into an evyll vse."[75] Finally, as Michel Mollat explains while noting the gradual inclusion of punitive measures for vagabonds among charitable schemes throughout Europe, the authorities were also prompted by mistrust and apprehension of poor strangers pouring into the city from rural provinces: "They no longer knew with whom they were dealing."[76]

Much of the new machinery of poor relief in England was intended as a means of acquiring more knowledge of the impoverished recipients of aid. Discriminate charity had existed previously in concept, but these new schemes instituted widespread categorization of the poor by local and national governments, which required a thorough interrogation of each beggar. As Tyndale observes, "We should know in every parish all our poor." So English authorities began compiling an altogether different kind of Domesday Book, as it were, focusing on those who *lacked* property. London implemented a badging scheme in 1524, and the 1531 vagrancy statute, 22 Henry VIII, c. 12, enacted a similar policy, requiring beggars to be examined, registered, and provided a license to beg for alms in a limited area. In addition, the statute offered a comprehensive illustration of the sturdy vagabonds who should be denied aid: "Any Man or Woman being hole & mighty in body & able to laboure . . . be vagarant & can gyve

none rekenyng howe he doth lefully gette his lyvyng."[77] Nor does the statute stop there. Officials were likewise expected to apprehend unauthorized scholars, erstwhile sailors, proctors and pardoners, quacks, "and all
other ydell personnes goynge aboute . . . usyng dyvers & subtyle craftye
& unlawfull games & playes."[78] Almost farcically meticulous, the statute's systematic inventory of vagrants and their various guises is intended
to combat the contemporary perception that members of the able-bodied
poor were developing greater capacities of disguise that threatened to derail any charitable enterprise. All of these statutes, which involve badging
or licensing worthy beggars and branding, imprisoning, and later earmarking fraudulent ones, endeavored to make the bodies of the poor more
legible. By instituting these "semiotic schemes," to borrow William C.
Carroll's term, authorities were attempting to alleviate the hermeneutic
burden inherent to material charity by stabilizing a vagrant text.[79]

The 1531 act reads like an addition to the burgeoning genre of rogue literature, popular pamphlets and poems trafficking in caricatures of vagrants
and petty criminals that were based largely on the late fifteenth-century
work *Liber Vagatorum*. Robert Copland's *Highway to the Spital-house*, for
example, excoriates "losels, myghty beggers, and vacabonds, / And tre-
wands that walke ouer the londs, / Mychers, hedge crepers, fylloks, and
luskes," as well as vagrants who wear the clothing of soldiers or lepers
"and so beggyng deceyue folke ouer all / . . . / And wyll abyde no laborous
subiection."[80] The similarities between the two texts reinforce the notion
that civic officers (and to a lesser extent charitable givers) were expected
to "read" strangers like a book.[81] Consider the detailed description of the
subprefect duties in the Ypres ordinance:

Their offyce was appoynted to them by the prefectes to visyte the
poore houses / shoppes / and cotages of the poore and nedy ons /
and to marke surely where / what / and howe moche helpe euery
one neded. Yea and ouer this by certayne tokens and coniectures to
get the knowledge of their condicyon / their helth / their homly and
secrete grefes / their maners / and (as nere as can be) theire merytes /
and to write these in a boke or tables ordeined for the same purpose.[82]

The language of the ordinance expressly compares the work of the
subprefects to biographers, and in this case the beggars of Ypres were

being written down so as to be read and comprehended by the magistrates. England would soon have similar municipal officers—Collectors or Overseers of the Poor—who would examine destitute inhabitants, providing begging licenses if necessary, and register their condition in churchwarden accounts. The bodies of beggars were unstable texts, however. In order to make a correct and informed decision, authorities desired to know a beggar's circumstances in full by evaluating his or her personal, familial, and professional contexts, even any "secrete grefes."

Many of the efforts at poor relief, then, relied during this period on a bureaucratic or administrative form of reading. These schemes, in their efforts to make the poor legible, mirrored the scriptural hermeneutics practiced by humanists, who considered a range of circumstantial details in reading the biblical text. This is not, perhaps, an especially radical observation given the prominence of humanist philosophy in shaping sixteenth-century poor relief, but it is worth explaining in more detail.[83] Kathy Eden notes how Erasmus and other humanists revived a venerable interpretive program that favored a thorough study of historical and textual context when reading a work, in addition to a consideration of the writer's intention and the work as a whole.[84] As Erasmus explains in his *Ratio Verae Theologiae*, readers of the Bible "should attend 'not only to what is said, but also by whom it is said, to whom, with what words, and on what time, on what occasion.'"[85] This approach derived in part from a recognition of the rhetorical nature of scripture, its capacity to teach and transform the reader, as well as an appreciation for the dynamic dialectic between reader and text. Indeed, this was the spirit of scripture Erasmus admired so deeply, and he linked its character of charity—again, what Augustine deemed the *summa* of scripture in *On Christian Doctrine*—to Christ, who accommodated his earthly audience by expressing divine truths in parables and stories, and was himself a means whereby God made his mystery known to humankind.[86] Much of the interpretive program Erasmus developed to accompany his biblical translation was intended to facilitate a recognition of the divine Word present in scriptural words, what Marjorie O'Rourke Boyle, in describing his rhetorical theology, calls "a lively faith in the real presence of Christ as text."[87] There emerges more generally in Erasmian hermeneutics and humanism a strong connection between pious living and pious reading, a rhetorical and ethical praxis that links together body and text.

Even as Erasmus derives his rhetorical theology from the charitable accommodations of Christ and Paul, he associates their capacity for disguise and adaptation with Proteus, an apt figure for the rhetorical dynamism of vagrant beggars as well.[88] In the reading practices of contemporaries there is a recognition that language itself is neutral matter, that it possesses the capacity to dress falsehood up as truth and vice versa. Just as interpretive sophistication can distinguish between an authentic or spurious work of Jerome, as Erasmus claims—he compares this process to recognizing the face of a friend—it can discover in a religious text the work of Christ or the work of a heretic, and can discern whether a beggar is needy or fake.[89] Erasmian hermeneutics, the consideration of context and intention and circumstantial details, are evident in the communal authorities who questioned beggars, in More's approach to Lutherans, and even in Tyndale's attitude toward conservative clerics. In order to determine Tyndale's heretical status, for example, More simultaneously traces his bodily and textual histories, repeatedly noting Tyndale's habitation in Germany, his place of publication, his repeated use of Luther's commentaries, and other contextual details. Meanwhile, as Ramie Targoff shows, Tyndale (with someone like More in mind) describes a similar set of interpretive strategies for recognizing hypocrisy, departing from Luther's model in his *Exposition of Matthew* by emphasizing the performative aspects of public prayer, which exposes the body as a site for interpreting inauthentic devotion.[90] In each of these cases, one can observe a pattern in which the written text and bodily text merge in semantic terms.

The need for these interpretive strategies highlights the dialectical tension involved in recovering a stable meaning from a text of any kind. Statutory laws only increased the pressures attendant on reading the signs of poverty. Individuals could no longer give alms with a glad and indifferent heart, since the 1531 statute prohibited anyone to "gyve any herborowe monye or lodgyng to any beggers beyng stronge & able" at the risk of being fined a discretionary sum, a figure that was raised in 1536 to ten times the amount of the alms given.[91] Charitable givers might choose to ignore these directives, of course, but they did so in defiance of statutory law. Compelled to interrogate the recipient and ensure the beggar possessed a license, donors were encouraged to give private alms only to members of their own parish and otherwise to direct all offerings to the common box in the parish church. The laws punished individuals who offered the wrong kind of charity, but the statutes were harsher yet on the recipients of such aid. Beggars found outside of their licensed limits were put in the stocks, and beggars without any license were whipped and then listed as "valiant" beggars. The 1536 statute instituted a milder punishment for "sturdy" vagabonds, the provision of forced labor, but second-time offenders were similarly whipped and lost their right ears, and any officials who refused to administer punishment would suffer a similar fate. England was by no means peculiar in this regard. Vives, for example, admitted the necessity of discipline in his plan for the city of Bruges: "Those who frequent gaming places and wine or beer taverns should be penalized. If one or two reprimands have no effect, they should be severely punished."[92] Likewise in the Ypres ordinance, at the end of a section listing the duties assigned to "prefects of the poor," a statement defending the imperative of municipal justice sanctioned the punitive measures involved in the scheme: "For iudges and lawes in Cyties were ordeyned for nothinge els but that such as dyd amysse shulde be punysshed accordynge to iustyce."[93]

Note how explicitly these schemes of poor relief, endorsed by each writer as a fulfillment of the scriptural injunction to act with mercy, remain attached to a notion of justice. The precedents for such an attitude are both classical and Christian. Thomas Elyot, in his 1531 treatise *The Boke Named the Governour,* channels the wisdom of Seneca's *De Clementia* when he cautions the magistrate about exercising "vayne pitie, wherin is conteyned neyther iustice nor yet commendable charytie."[94] The obligation to perform fraternal correction, meanwhile, was a theological commonplace in this era, buttressed by Augustine and Aquinas and others who expressed sentiments similar to those set forth in *Dives et Pauper,* whose author claimed, "If he forfete and do ayenste charyte / it is charite to chastysyn hym and punshyn hym tyl he wele amendyn hym for sauacion of his soule and example of othere."[95] This concept of charity animates the Admonition Controversy of the 1570s, when the Church of England struggled to accommodate rival projects of reform and consensus, but it remains crucial too in providing a link between vagrancy and heresy. As Brian Tierney notes in his history of medieval poor law, there was an explicit (if accidental) link between the coercive charity Augustine promotes in order to suppress heresy—"It is better to love with severity than to deceive with lenience"—and theories of poor relief that excluded the undeserving.[96] This association only expanded further in the early sixteenth century, when the relentless program of charitable reading, which encouraged interplay between the body of a text and the bodies of beggars and nonconformists, offered writers and readers of the period numerous opportunities to deploy charity as a tool of punishment.

Eros and "Belly-Love": The Charity of Polemic

It is no surprise that the hermeneutics associated with material charity produced some kind of material consequence—beggars would receive alms or discipline—but the process of reading nonconformist religious works often led to bodily punishment as well. Indeed, following the spread of John Wycliffe's views and the emergence of Lollardy in the late fourteenth century, heresy in England was associated with book production and literacy. *De Heretico Comburendo*, the 1401 statute that established the official policy of burning heretics to death (which Thomas More cites approvingly in his *Dialogue*), identifies the writing of books as a specific marker of heresy. The Arundel *Constitutions* of 1407, which proscribed biblical translation into the vernacular, reinforced the link between unauthorized texts and heretical opinions, and placed in an especially dubious position any theological commentary written in English.[97] The legislation used, unsuccessfully, to extirpate Lollardy in the early fifteenth century was invoked by authorities to repress Lutheranism a century later. Just as the punitive machinery of England's poor laws increased the pressure on prospective almsgivers, who were now legally obligated to correctly identify a beggar's tokens of authentic poverty, penalties for heresy amplified the interpretive anxiety associated with contemporary works of religious controversy.

These fears are evident in Simon Fish's 1529 tract *A Supplicacyon for the Beggers*, which expresses a legitimate terror among laymen who dreaded a clergy empowered to accuse any man of heretical views:

> Lyke wyse saie they [the reformers] of all the hole sort of the spiritueltie that if they will not pray for no man but for theim that gyue theim money they are tyraunts and lakke charite, and suffer those

soules to be punisshed and payned vncheritably for lacke of theyre prayers. These sorte of folkes they [the clergy] call heretikes, these they burne, these they rage ageinst, put to open shame and make theim bere fagottes.[98]

Religious reformers, according to Fish, who have merely observed the uncharitable opportunism of clerics using purgatory for commercial gain, are consequently threatened with heresy and fire. In Fish's perspective, the response by church authorities is wildly incongruous. Of course, by accusing the clergy of sedition (among other things) elsewhere in his text, recommending that the king abolish ecclesiastical offices, and reanimating the specific critiques of church property and income made by the Lollard *Disendowment Bill* from 1410, Fish is participating in the movement that was exciting such violent responses from clerical authorities.[99] And by using beggars to ventriloquize his reformist arguments, Fish becomes a religious stand-in for the disguised vagrant or rogue who was plaguing administrators of poor relief, which More emphasizes in his response, *The Supplication of Souls*. As More claims, Fish begins "wyth a cloke of charyte" but "doth by and by no lesse dysclose hys hatered and malice." More seems to believe of heretical texts what Tyndale declares of the Bible—a self-interpreting nature—but his observation also acknowledges the chameleon nature of love or the "great face of charyte," which affords heretics (or false beggars) a convenient cloak in which to disguise themselves.[100] As the movement for reform gathered momentum and the church became more entrenched in its defense, the rhetoric from both sides polarized and intensified.

In addition to Tyndale's translations and native Lollard pamphlets, and in spite of attempts by officials to suppress unauthorized tracts, texts promulgating Lutheran doctrines and denouncing the ecclesiastical authorities arrived in London from the continent in considerable numbers throughout the early stages of the Reformation, creating a doubtful religious environment in which the orthodoxy of any English man or woman plucky enough to advocate clerical reform was questioned.[101] Meanwhile, Henry VIII's ambivalent conduct during the period added an element of political intrigue and distrust to the movement of religious reform. English writers were beginning to experiment with the potential of new print technology to reach widespread audiences and cultivate new communities, and the instability of textual exchange encouraged a radicalized dialectic in which polemic's verbal violence and ideological certainty thrived.[102] Just as magistrates attempting to dispense alms "no longer knew with whom they were dealing," ecclesiastical authorities struggled to ascertain whether writers were simply encouraging traditional reform or explicitly spreading heresy.

In this charged and uncertain atmosphere, More was given a commission by Cuthbert Tunstall, Bishop of London, to "show to simple and unlearned men the cunning malice of the heretics."[103] That is, he was charged with uncloaking heretics like Fish and displaying the malicious reality underneath their charitable guises. To this purpose More wrote the *Dialogue Concerning Heresies,* a text that bears an initial resemblance to *Utopia's* elaborate and playful structure. Now, however, he exchanges the pervasive irony and Latin language of his earlier work, which effects an irenic distance from the turbulence of contemporary political realities, for a more straightforward vernacular better suited to confront heresy and expose its fraudulence. Ostensibly presented as a conversation between "the author" and a "messenger" with Lutheran sympathies, the *Dialogue* conveys with remarkable verisimilitude the impression of an intimate but potentially terrifying scene for any reformer: More, at home and every bit the "Mayster Chauncellour," engages in a merry and digressive dialogue with a rather naïve religious ingénue who, as More blithely asserts the logical necessity of committing heretics to the fire, slowly comes to grips with the vulnerability of his position. When More's persona grows increasingly vitriolic (and the messenger appropriately acquiescent in response), contemporary readers must have perceived the overlap between his inflammatory rhetoric and the actual violence written on the bodies of heretics.[104] His writing intentionally deploys vivid corporeal imagery in order to give substance to the doctrines of his opponents. Tyndale's heretical malice is thus embodied in the text and then chastised or cured by More's suitably severe rhetoric, which functions as a kind of charitable surgery. Indeed, More's polemics can often seem "terrifying in their virulence and lack of restraint," as David Loewenstein has put it recently.[105] Consider More's response to *The Ymage of Love,* for example, a treatise published in 1525 by the friar John Ryckes, which includes some fairly benign satire of clerical practices, suggesting that authentic charity should prompt men and women to perform actual deeds of love rather than purchasing images or other church ornaments. More initiates his revised version of the *Dialogue* by dismissing Ryckes's treatise as the work of a heretic with a "malycyous mynde / to mynysshe & quenche mennes deuocyons."[106] One can hear in this passage an echo of his accusation that Tyndale "laboureth of purpose to mynysshe the reuerent mynde that men bere to charyte." Underlying these statements is a deep concern that the forces of charity are being marshaled against its rightful defenders.

The religious culture in the 1520s and '30s afforded few opportunities for deliberation or authentic conversation, and the situation was further exacerbated by the generic mode of controversial writing. Beyond the somewhat pedantic aspects of their disagreement, reading the debate between More and Tyndale can be a frustrating experience, since they so often seem to be talking past one another. Both writers simultaneously employ two separate registers throughout their dispute: in one way they are conducting a sophisticated philological debate about the proper method of scriptural translation and interpretation, as I have discussed; but in another way they are both trying to reach and persuade audiences who occupied a tenuous middle ground between orthodoxy and reform. Consequently, the argument between More and Tyndale could never remain solely focused on philological or even theological minutiae. It was intensely rhetorical. Much of the persuasive labor exerted by both writers centered on convincing their audience of their opponent's malice. Their exchange consequently provides a valuable opportunity to examine the different shapes of charity that emerge amid the rigors of polemical rhetoric.

In particular, their vituperative language takes advantage of the incarnational character of charity, its close associations with the body. This chapter has shown the overlaps between material charity and charitable hermeneutics, how municipal officers imported textual skills of interpretation to their task of distributing discriminate alms, but the trajectory could move in reverse as well. In what would become a typical strategy in sixteenth- and seventeenth-century religious polemic, both More and Tyndale exploit the worldly and bodily sphere of charity in order to accuse the other of malice, self-interest, and lust of one kind or another. It is

a rhetorical tactic to smear the ethical integrity of one's combatant by way
of *ad hominem,* but the ploy is still bound up in the profound theological
and hermeneutic implications of charity. So, when Tyndale attempts to
reinvest *agape* with its scriptural and spiritual intention, More claims the
translation is merely an attempt to sanction lewd love. Tyndale, meanwhile, responds to More's defense of the church by implicating him in
the clerical machinery that he believed had perverted authentic Christian
charity in order to turn a profit, calling it "belly-love." Indeed, the most
persistent characteristic of charity in this debate is its association with the
body. Whether or not his opponent lusted for flesh or mammon, worship-
ing the rival demons of Luther or pope, each writer employs images of the
body to cast doubt on the other's charitable intentions.

More's *Dialogue* uses the body's erotic potential to dramatize problematic questions of charitable hermeneutics that show the insidious effects of
heresy, its "cunning malice" in appropriating charity for fraudulent ends.
Given his expressed preference for distinct categories of love on account
of the perilous traffic between *eros* and *agape,* one might expect More to
spend great length distinguishing the positive characteristics of "charity"
from "love," but he seems to do the opposite. When the topic of Tyndale's
"mistranslation" of charity arises, More's messenger (who finds Tyndale's
ideas attractive) immediately acquiesces: there is no debate over philological verity; "charity" is clearly the better word.

Of more interest both to More and us, however, is the manner in which
sex and charity, both made manifest by physical interaction, begin to overlap and what that means for interpretation. The topic provides occasion
for one of More's "merry tales":

> The more pytye by my fayth quod your frende that euer loue was
> synne. And yet yt wold not be so moche so taken yf the worlde were no
> more suspycyous than they say that good saynt Frauncys was / whiche
> whan he saw a yong man kys a gyrle ones in way of good company /
> kneled downe and held vp hys handys into heuen / hyghly thankynge
> god that charyte was not yet gone out of this wretched worlde.[107]

The diverting anecdote, strategically important in a potentially tedious
discussion of translation, captures the lay reader's attention, to be sure,

but the story also implicates charity in the sexual act, a notion reinforced by More's response and the messenger's quick rejoinder:

> He had quod I a good mynde and did lyke a good man / that demed all thynge to the best.
> So say I to quod he. But howe far be folke fallen from the good mynde now. Men be now adayes waxen so full of mystruste / that some man wolde in fayth wene his wyfe were nought / yf he shold but fynde her in bed with a pore frere.
> Forsothe ye be a wanton quod I.

In some ways the episode undermines More's agenda, his erotic jokes puncturing the honor he intends to accord the word "charity." Invoking one of the traditional rules of charitable hermeneutics—deeming "all thynge to the best"—in order to bring the interpretive principle close to the edge of bathos, More and his messenger mock the innocent misunderstanding of St. Francis and wryly condemn the distrust of a husband who finds his wife in bed with a friar. Suddenly the *Dialogue* smacks of fabliaux.

Although the messenger is the true "wanton" here, and More's persona shows dignified restraint, one nevertheless wonders why the author chooses to link charity to sex so explicitly. Perhaps More wishes to demonstrate charity's ability to transform potential sexual sin into the rarefied air of Christian love, but given the anecdote's context, and how the episode demonstrates the dangerous capacity for *eros* to pull charity down into the sexual morass, it seems most likely that More intends to place limits on charitable hermeneutics. Indeed, returning to the matter of Tyndale's translation, the messenger laments the growing mistrust of contemporaries and purports to "play saynt Frauncys parte and iudge the man [Tyndale] no worse than the matter requyreth." But More takes great pains to show that the mistrust is deserved in this particular anecdote. This, of course, is likely the point, that More (and the messenger) *should* be mistrustful of Tyndale, who is in bed with Luther, and that charitable hermeneutics should not apply to heretics.

With this interlude More prepares his readers for the culmination of his assault on Tyndale's translation, which deliberately associates Tyndale and Luther as collaborators in a joint heresy: "For now it is to be considered that at the tyme of this translacyon Hychens [Tyndale] was with

luther in Wyttenberge." More's procedure here is similar to an Ypres subprefect or an English overseer examining the poor "by certayne tokens
and coniectures." The circumstantial evidence More has gathered leads
to the natural conclusion that Tyndale's translation and Luther's heresy
are "flecke and make," partners in their unholy attitudes toward charity:

> But nowe the cause why he chaunged the name of charyte / and of the
> chyrche / and of presthed / is no very grete dyffyculte to perceyue.
> For syth Luther and his felowes among other theyr damnable her-
> esyes haue one / that all our saluacyon standeth in faythe alone / and
> towarde our salvation nothynge force of good workes / therefore it
> semeth that he laboureth of purpose to mynysshe the reuerent mynde
> that men bere to charyte / and therefore he chaungeth that name of
> holy virtuous affeccyon / in to the bare name of love comen to the
> virtuous love that man bereth to god / and to the lewde loue that is
> bytwene flecke & his make.

The passage provides a forceful example of the author's method in reading heretical texts. Characterizing Tyndale's translation as something that
turns gold to lead and charity to "lewd love," More suggests that for a
translator so irreverent and devoid of virtue, someone who "laboureth
of purpose to mynysshe" the rarefied place of Christian charity, the very
rules of charity do not apply, or at least should manifest themselves in an
altered fashion. More's own "wanton" wordplay now appears less curious. Recasting himself in the role of St. Francis but revising the story,
More imagines Luther and Tyndale—"flecke and make," a man and his
paramour—kissing in the streets of Wittenberg, and he will not make the
same mistake: this is not charity but lewd love. The expression is apt. For
his part More believed that the reformers' assault on church authority,
especially their disregard for good works, betrayed a desire to indulge in
Manichean sinfulness, and he felt his allegation was substantiated by the
damning evidence of Luther's marriage, an abomination "Tyndall himself (which thing is worse then the deede doing) mayntaineth in hys boke
their dede for well done."[108] This, More stresses, is precisely what happens
when charity gives place to love. Indeed, in his *Confutation*, he even suggests that Tyndale's "love" serves as a convenient translation of charity
given his adversary's approval of priests marrying.

Having performed his own kind of charitable hermeneutics to sniff out Tyndale's heresy, More subsequently focuses on his obligation as Lord Chancellor to perform justice, which requires him to "cure and hele well those that are all redy infected / so harde is that carbuncle catchynge onys a core . . . or yf it happely be incurable, then to the clene cuttynge out the parte for infeccyon of the remanaunt."[109] His very confutation of Tyndale is conceived as a sort of violent surgery, one intended to be so incredibly painful it might dissuade others from contracting the malady. More justifies his approach in the *Dialogue* by citing Augustine's method of chastising Donatists and heretics with imperial force to "fere them with bodyly punyshment," and, as Alexandra Walsham has shown, More derives his validation of corporal discipline as a means of Christian correction from a rich theological legacy.[110] Aligning an ostensibly malicious project—verbal violence intended to inflict pain and promote fear—with the theological imperative of charity, he manages to accord scriptural sanction to his polemical writing. Much like the sturdy vagabonds who were whipped for jeopardizing the spirit and practice of communal charity, Tyndale, having not begged for but mistranslated charity, merits a figurative lashing from More's pen.

Tyndale appears in his *Answere* especially exercised by More's accusation of Lutheran heresy, claiming, "When he sayth *Tyndall was confederate with Luther,* that is not truth."[111] Tyndale's theological positions are in fact difficult to categorize definitively, in part because theology remains secondary to his central projects of translation and polemic. Certainly he prioritizes faith before charity at the apparent expense of good works in a number of treatises (particularly in *The Parable of the Wicked Mammon*), but even More, near the beginning of his *Confutation*, suggests with a hint of distaste that there exists common ground between Tyndale's theology and his own with regard to charity.[112] Nevertheless, More had good reason to suspect Tyndale's translation, which included introductions to the gospels and epistles that demonstrated an unmistakable acquaintance with Luther's doctrine and in many cases were a direct translation of his work. Despite his disingenuous claim of *sola translata,* Tyndale was clearly invested in ecclesiastical reform, intentionally changing several key words in his translation that had long served as the scriptural foundation of various church practices.[113] The Bible was no static manuscript for Tyndale but the dynamic word of God, and he never apologizes for brandishing scriptural translation as a kind of ecclesiastical scalpel meant to cut away corrupt clerical practices like so many gangrenous limbs. While he may not have fully discounted the efficacy of charity, Tyndale clearly wished to strike from good works their supposed papal depravity and recast their scriptural sanction in more spiritually acceptable terms.

Before he could offer any positive reformulation of love or charity, however, Tyndale needed to refute More's assertion that reformed theology—and by extension his own vernacular translation—was suffused with a latent eroticism. The frequency and hyperbole with which More indicts Luther's marriage as well as any other reformers who reject celibacy are strategic; the constant refrain follows the reader throughout his *Dialogue* and *Confutation* like the howl of a single-minded fury. Initially Tyndale appears less enthusiastic about engaging in this kind of flyting match, and he has less to gain by doing so, but his eventual rejoinders decrying the exaggerated sexual misconduct of orthodox priests give his *Answere* the feel of a Chaucerian romp: following the example of their pope, he claims, priests steal from the poor, take the parish tithes, and run to Rome in order to "dwell by a stues or to carye a stewes with him / or to corrupte other mennes wiues."[114] Both writers risk such farcical asides in order to emphasize the carnal love of the other and demonstrate its injurious effect on authentic charity.

But Tyndale exercises a remarkable about-face when he shifts from the attack to defend priests who choose to marry, declaring authentic charity as the sole mitigating factor that might sanction such carnal love. Given the inexorable flow of Tyndale's energetic rhetoric and style, his relentless progress in disproving one accusation after another by More, it is easy to overlook the magnitude of such an assertion. Employing a hermeneutic of charity to justify oath-breaking, something Bellarmine would later do in behalf of recusant Catholics in Protestant England, Tyndale claims that if a priest burns with such passion as to seriously jeopardize his chastity, he should abjure his monastic vows and marry:

> No power amonge them that professe the trouth / maye bynd where god lowseth / saue only where loue and my neybours necessite requireth it of me . . . So that this law / loue thy neyboure / to helpe him as thou woldest be holpe / must interpret all mans laws.[115]

Here Tyndale is redeploying the famous scriptural commission of Matthew 16:19 that was traditionally used to uphold papal prerogative. Valla employed a similar strategy in his *Donation of Constantine*, claiming that the papal power of binding and loosing remains circumscribed by divine and natural law, and Tyndale also might have been influenced by Luther's comment concerning marriage that "charity above all things has absolutely no need of laws."[116] But Tyndale's reference here acquires grander scope, adumbrating the radical arguments that would be made over a century later by John Milton, who used the same scriptural reference of binding and loosening—indeed, much the same logic as well, that charity interprets all other human laws—to advocate no-fault divorce. Here too Tyndale suggests that More is focused on the wrong kind of sensuality. The urge to make these vows, as far as Tyndale is concerned, springs from a wrongful confidence in works, imposing on God the necessity of contractual obligation.

Tyndale is just as careful to associate More with his own kind of carnality. Rather than levying accusations of sexual transgression, however, Tyndale portrays More as an avaricious traitor who has succumbed to "belly-love." Despite no real evidence to support his claims, Tyndale considers More's honesty compromised by a desire for wealth, repeatedly linking his antagonist to Balaam, a false prophet who purposefully misled Israel, and Judas, the archetypal biblical figure of betrayal: "But charitably I exhort him in christe to take hede for though Judas were wilier then his felowes to get lucre / yet he proved not most wise at the last ende."[117] The reader finds this assertion sprinkled throughout Tyndale's *Answere* nearly as often as More makes mention of Luther's marriage, a rhetorical coup de grâce usually expressed by Tyndale in the guise of merciful advice— "charitably I exhort him in christe to take hede"—as he smears More's reputation out of feigned goodwill. According to Tyndale, More's refusal to endorse a vernacular translation has less to do with Tyndale's own potentially heretical views than More's prior commitment to base carnality. "Worldely & fleshly minded," More is unable to be charitable rather than purposefully refusing to be so, having already exchanged his charity to God and neighbor for lucre:

For he vnderstandeth the Greke, and he knew them long yer I. But so
blynd is couetousnesse & dronken desire of honour. Giftes blind the
eyes of the seyng and peruert the wordes of the righteous [Deut. Xvii]
When couetousnes findeth vauntage in seruyng falsehead, it riseth vp
into an ornate malice agaynst the truth.[118]

Essentially Tyndale accuses More of betraying the cause of Christian humanism for his thirty pieces of silver, claiming the church has purchased
the services of More's mercenary pen.

It is at this point, when England's first great humanist scholar and
first great biblical translator of the early modern period have accused
each other of lust and avarice, respectively—when they have done this,
moreover, in behalf of charity—that readers might wish to cry out, as
Louis Schuster has done, in a lament for the polemical mode, its peculiar
capacity to warp any charitable hermeneutic into one of malice.[119] The
exchange between More and Tyndale offers a picture of the contemporary intellectual and theological landscape, one in which the steep chasm
between opposing camps afforded little middle ground for nuance or
compromise. Despite their rival commitments, however, the dispute likewise shows that the importance attached to charity was one of the few
things shared by both sides, although this agreement generated conflict
rather than consensus. Translating charity from the biblical text and into
the social world of England was a dynamic and unsettled project, and the
controversy between More and Tyndale offers an opportunity to track its
provenance and impact at the start of the early modern period, from lexical to literary to legal principles, from matters of scripture and theology
to basic material imperatives, from the rhetorical violence written on the
page to the disciplinary violence written on the body.

SIONS
CHARITY
TOWARDS HER
Foes in misery,

I N

A DIALOGVE BE-
tweene a Citizen of LONDON,
and a Country-Gentleman, concerning the Offenders of these times.

Mat.7.1. *Iudge not, that ye be not Iudged.*
1 Cor.13.6. *Charity reioyceth not in iniquity, but reioyceth in the truth.*

London Printed by *R.H.* for *I.D.* 1641.

FIGURE 3. *Sions Charity* (London: 1641). RB 482837, The Huntington Library, San Marino, California.

CHAPTER 2

CHARITABLE ADMONITION

Moral Reform in Elizabethan Polemic and Satire

This chapter begins where it ends, with a passage from *The Whipping of the Satyre* (1601) by John Weever, a poem that is remarkable for a number of reasons, not least its attempt to reform by way of satire a select group of reform-minded satirists:

> Come on your ways, I'le ye no more reproue,
> But what your friends bad, that perfourme I must,
> Correct ye sharply, not for hate, but loue.[1]

Although he uses the same means as his rivals—satire—to perform the same function—moral correction—Weever expresses confidence that his opponents' verse deserves reprehension whereas his own ought to be lauded. In making this paradoxical claim, Weever identifies two crucial distinctions between the respective forms of satire. The first is political or institutional. The poet explains that his own satirical correction is sanctioned by the allegorical sisters Church and State, collective entities far more reliable than the individual moral authority claimed by his adversaries. The second distinction is one of purpose. Accusing his opponents of malicious speech, he declares that his own verses of correction are intended "not for hate, but love." Although they superficially resemble each other in content and mode, Weever claims, the respective satires have been composed with different moral aims in mind.

Weever's poem initiated a literary skirmish (collectively called the Whipper pamphlets) that emerged in response to the Bishops' Ban of 1599, which formally proscribed the publication of satires and epigrams, but larger problems related to language and love figure prominently in the debate.[2] Charity serves as the hinge whereby Weever manages to position himself as someone who is sanctioned to defend communal authorities from malicious expression and, consequently, licensed to respond in kind. Thus a single poem manages to embody one of the most vexing paradoxes related to charity during the period. Weever's opponents were required by charity to remain silent, whereas Weever was required by charity to correct them. In the complicated moral dialectic of *The Whipping of the Satyre* and its larger context, charity becomes at once the instrument and obstacle of moral reform, even as it is the bulwark of communal authority and one of its greatest threats.

If charity as a central Christian concept galvanized More's and Tyndale's rival epistemologies of language and translation—on the one side, a charity understood best in the context of rational institutions and governed by ecclesiastical consensus, and on the other, a charity originating in the individual's communion with divinely revealed scripture—the concept fueled a similarly problematic distinction with regard to the ethical domain of language. Charity was implicated in cultural speech norms that can often seem contradictory. As the previous chapter explained, early modern conceptions of charity were flexible enough to allow for severe discipline, and Tudor poor relief schemes simultaneously distributed alms to deserving poor and whippings to able-bodied beggars. Appropriately administered, the gifts and punishments were both understood as expressions of charity. A similarly rigorous imperative governed charitable social relations, which compelled neighbors to provide fraternal correction as a means of rectifying immoral behavior. Consider Edmund Bonner's "Homelie of Christian Love and Charitie," published in 1547 in the book of homilies prescribed to churches throughout England, which articulates the two offices of charity as a twin task of encouraging the godly and chastising sinners:

And such evil persons, that be so great offenders of God and the commonweal, charity requireth to be cut off from the body of the commonweal, lest they corrupt other good and honest persons; like as a
good surgeon cutteth away a rotten and festered member for love he
hath to the whole body, lest it infect other members adjoining to it.[3]

Church authorities bore a great deal of this responsibility in wielding coercive powers to bring about repentance, but charitable correction was an
essential duty for every member of the community, "an ordinance of God
whereby christian men are to recouer their brethren from their sinnes," as
William Perkins notes, or a "common worke belonging to all *Christians,*
especially being bound to it . . . in charitie to our Brethren," as Phineas
Fletcher puts it.[4] Admonition of this kind was considered essential to the
spiritual life of the individual and corporate Christian body.

But this created its own peculiar dilemma. Charity, because of its pride
of place among cultural values, was also invoked by contemporary laws
and social norms as a guarantor of one's good name, functioning as one
of the core legal and moral principles intended to protect individuals from
defamation and serving more generally as a stabilizing force undergird-
ing communal harmony. Debora Shuger's magisterial study of censorship
underscores this role of charity in contemporary regulation of language,
or what she (following John Weever's Whipper pamphlet) calls the "law
of all civility."[5] Members of a community were obligated to observe decorum in their language to preserve a neighbor's reputation from scandal.
Efforts at fraternal correction were supposed to occur in private, particularly in the case of public figures of authority, as Thomas Aquinas lays out
in great detail in his *Summa Theologiae,* though he allows for public rebuke
"where there is real danger to the faith."[6]

The truth or falsity of public assertions was often irrelevant, as Shuger
clearly shows, since the priority of charity outweighed claims to verity,
a position that was later bolstered by legal principle (and explicitly stated
by Sir Edward Coke) during the 1606 Star Chamber case of *De Libellis
Famosis.*[7] In 1583 the wardens of the Stationers' Company articulated their
role in the governance of language in similar terms, noting the "charitable
ordynaunces" that had been instituted "to avoide the disordered behauior
of prynters and suche troubles that mighte growe by printing."[8] Several

of the occasional poems responding to the 1628 assassination of George Villiers, Duke of Buckingham attest to this powerful role of charity in silencing critique out of respect for reputation and order: "What! Shall I say now George is dead / That hee's in hell? Charitie forbidd." Meanwhile in Owen Felltham's response to the assassination, a poem otherwise notable for its ambivalent posture toward Buckingham, the obligation to remain charitably silent emerges as the single moral certainty: "If thou hadd'st a falt / My Charitie shall leave it in thy vault / There for thyne owne accompting: 'tis undue / To speake ill of the dead, thoughe it be true." This ethical responsibility of charity, as Shuger demonstrates, was applicable not merely because Buckingham was dead but also because he was a figure of public authority, and any libelous statements might make a scandal of government.

The cultural prominence of charitable decorum during the Elizabethan period posed a vexing challenge to members of the Church of England who felt compelled to discharge their own charitable obligations by articulating the need for continued reform. They needed to convince others that their strident truth-telling should be preferred to a sociable restraint. Their task was further complicated by an episcopal government with most of its entrenched hierarchies and coercive powers intact. In many ways this problem reaches back to the late medieval era of Wycliffite writings and other forms of clerical satire, as Edwin Craun has ably explored, when reformist voices developed strategies for using "fraternal correction as a tool to redistribute power in institutional life."[9] A process of rigorous self-examination was central to this tradition of reform. It required the resolving of one's own charitable will before correcting others, which served a rhetorical as well as moral function, since defenders of the church establishment often accused dissenting voices of envying clerical power and property. William Perkins identifies additional rhetorical demands involved in any project of admonition, noting that "Christian wisdom" was required, a consideration of circumstance, since "all times and places serue not to this purpose," and he adds that corrective language acquires more power if it uses scriptural precept and is spoken in a "spirit of meeknesse."[10]

Despite these careful strictures, expressions of fraternal correction remained vulnerable to accusations of envy and malice. In the ideal scenario a charitable audience would recognize the admonisher's charitable intent, but a different kind of reciprocity was more likely to emerge in the polemical and satirical discourse of the period: a supposition of malice generally provoked a malicious (or defensive) reading and perpetuated the divisions separating both sides. "Most mischievous foul sin, in chiding sin," as Duke Senior would say in *As You Like It,* or as an anonymous pamphlet in 1641 puts it, books of this kind "have in them much of provocation, and nothing of edification" and "doe but exasperate them, or harden them, and rather keep them from repentance."[11] Public discourse was dynamic and unstable, and the line distinguishing charitable admonition from uncharitable slander was difficult to perceive. Those who offered moral correction were often accused of violating the social ethic, charity, which motivated their utterance in the first place.

This chapter traces the contours of that phenomenon, focusing on the manner in which various understandings of charity contributed to the contentious ecclesiastical debates of the Elizabethan era, especially insofar as they were examined and interrogated at the height of what would be known as the Admonition Controversy during the 1570s. In addition to discussing key participants such as Thomas Cartwright and John Whitgift, this chapter includes among the strident chorus an ironic and perhaps unexpected interlocutor, the Protestant poet and satirist Edmund Spenser. In his *Shepheardes Calender* (1579), a collection of eclogues published shortly after the polemical exchange between Cartwright and Whitgift, Spenser uses the pastoral dialogue of *May* to dramatize the conflicting views that threatened to undermine contemporary religious discourse. The eclogue's two characters, Piers and Palinode, articulate differing attitudes toward the role of charitable admonition in building and sustaining a reformed community, and, in voicing the principles underlying their respective positions (including their limitations), Spenser playfully replicates many of the rhetorical failures of the Admonition Controversy. Placed in the context of contemporary theological and ecclesiastical polemic, his poetry can seem like a resolute evasion of the ferocious certainty with which other writers regularly deploy charity. Ultimately the eclogue offers few answers to the dilemma of charitable admonition, but in the figure of material charity, which is threatened by the presence of Papist vagrants and Puritan parsimony, Spenser discovers an apt metaphor for the challenges of his own poetic and even satiric vocation.

Spenser's *May* eclogue, composed and published during a period of intense ecclesiastical debate, is a natural vehicle for dramatizing the problems of charitable admonition and interpretation. It is more surprising to find similar preoccupations surfacing later in the 1590s and early 1600s among Elizabethan satirists, whose models were more consciously classical and whose targets were less obviously related to religious controversy. But if Piers and Palinode illustrate for Spenser the problems of envious (as opposed to charitable) reading, satirists such as Joseph Hall and Thomas Middleton likewise rail against Envy to begin *Virgidemiarum* and *Microcynicon*, respectively, and John Marston scorns Detraction in favor of "true judgment" at the outset of *The Scourge of Villanie*. If Spenser uses almsgiving as a metaphor that links charitable giving with charitable reading, so too does Ingenioso, at the end of *The Second Part of the Return from Parnassus*, indict the cold charity of any unappreciative audience members.

It is clear that many of the principles motivating participants in the Admonition Controversy are echoed by satirists of the subsequent generation, and this chapter ends by examining the problem of charitable admonition in the Whipper pamphlets, which serve as a metonymic stand-in for Elizabethan and early Jacobean satire more generally. Indeed, the link between charitable admonition and satire continued to find purchase decades later, when Martin Parker responded to critics with a "demy Satir" that mixed "mercy with revenge":

> My muse hates Railing, as shee Scornes to Flatter,
> Though Justice hold her scales with equall poyse,
> Charity sways the beame; she none destroys,
> Some shee will check, and tell them of their deeds,
> From which rebuke if happily proceeds,
> Any amendment, she'll be like the nurse,
> That whipps a child whom she loves ne'r the worse.[12]

Notice how Parker's charity aims to negotiate the tenuous balance between separate imperatives that Donne would have called "kinde pitty" and "brave scorn." In this vision corrective language can be painful, comparable to whipping, but it also remains lovingly restrained by charity, which "sways the beame" of justice and "none destroys."

This is not to suggest that the features of satirical literature are equivalent to religious discourse, however much Francis Bacon worried in 1589 that the Martin Marprelate controversy, a series of unauthorized Puritan pamphlets satirizing church government in 1588 and 1589, would "turne religion into a Comedy or Satyr."[13] But the invocation of charity in an otherwise literary or social context signals an attention to comparable anxieties in explicitly religious polemic, a fretful energy that conventional genealogies of Elizabethan satire often ignore. One might say that much of the moral purpose of Puritans like Martin Marprelate (and some of their irascibility) is inherited or appropriated by rough-tongued satirists in the 1590s, who adopt similarly inventive strategies of verbal abuse and complaint, even as they multiply and broaden the conventional targets of charitable admonition. However new seem their experiments with linguistic and marginal play, from the Marprelate and anti-Martinist tracts to later satires and epigrams by John Donne, Joseph Hall, John Marston, and others, many of the same fundamental problems and paradoxes remain: How to distinguish between the motives of charity and envy? How to reconcile the projects of purity or harmony? Or, as Donne, a figure who bridges both these discourses, asks in "Satyre 3," "Can railing, then, cure these worn maladies?"[14] Although these questions are not resolved by the Bishops' Ban of 1599 or the Whipper pamphlets that followed, this brief but intense conversation about the proper role of the satirist in the commonwealth offers a satisfactory endpoint to this examination of charitable admonition. In this way we can observe how religious admonition adumbrates more general problems related to literary exchange, and how charity and all its concomitant imperatives continued to inform these fraught communal negotiations.

The Admonition Controversy

During the early 1570s, the Church of England still struggled to define itself as a political and ecclesiastical institution. Attempting to accommodate a number of disparate religious groups as it clumsily framed a supposed middle ground between religious extremes, the English church faced vexatious unrest, not merely from Anabaptists and a resilient Roman Catholic population composed of recusants and church papists, but from so-called Puritan detractors as well.[15] Nor was the political and religious establishment that governed the Church of England comprised of a single or coherent identity but instead consisted of "an uneasy partnership of court bishops, prominent politicians, civil lawyers, divines and the more important heads of house at the universities working, directly or indirectly, with the monarch."[16]

Given this insecure ecclesiastical structure and amalgam of ideologies and interests, it is no surprise that charity, which was supposed to foster concord, figured so prominently in debates over church government. In fact most disputes drew matter and energy from a fundamental disagreement about how charity ought to shape the Church of England. Puritans exhorting the political and ecclesiastical authorities to reform the carnal practices of a religious state still mired in Roman Catholicism would invoke Paul's First Epistle to the Corinthians, which underscores the role of charity in establishing a godly community of Christian believers. Conformists would cite the same scriptural passages to plead in behalf of the establishment and levy a critique of reformers unwilling to compromise for the sake of unity. This debate over church reform thus mirrors the scriptural dilemma that placed More and Tyndale at odds with one another.

These tensions received full expression in the Admonition Controversy of the 1570s. After a decade and a half of Elizabeth's reign, a number of Puritan reformers had grown increasingly dismayed by the lack of reformation made by the Church of England, frustrated by vestiges of "Papism" that remained entrenched in the episcopal infrastructure and ritualistic formalism of ecclesiastical worship. Much of the dissent was concentrated among adherents of Presbyterian discipline who wished to model the English church explicitly after Geneva's polity. In 1572 these demands for further reform reached the public forum when John Field and Thomas Wilcox published *An Admonition to the Parliament*, which outlined the various problems plaguing the church and posited Presbyterian polity as an obvious and easy solution. In the controversy that followed, church authorities and religious reformers debated aspects of church discipline, but they also argued over the role and sanction of charitable admonition.

Historians have convincingly demonstrated that Puritans differed from conformists in degree rather than kind, as "the hotter sort of protestants,"[17] and this amplified temperature applies to charity as well. Puritans agreed with conformists that charity lay at the heart of any effort to build and shape a Christian church, but they placed a stricter emphasis on the ethical responsibilities of charitable conduct, which reinforced their stringent criteria for church membership. This led to inevitable conflict. Should charity serve as the "the knot of all Christian society" in an inclusive vision of the visible church, as conformists believed, encouraging reconciliation and mutual recognition of sinfulness? Or should it be clearly evident in the refining of the church body by the good and right conduct of the godly, an instrument with which the church actively opposes any vestige of papal carnality? More to the point in the contemporary debate, does charity justify the continued use of the ceremonies, traditions, and "furniture" inherited from the Roman Catholic Church, maintained by Elizabeth, and generally agreed to be *adiaphora*—things indifferent, neither injurious nor obligatory for personal salvation? Or should charity be extended to those whose consciences are somewhat more precise, whose notion of "Christian liberty" would not countenance worldly state-building that does not conform to their vision of a godly church? Finally, should charitable brethren avoid engaging in controversy altogether, or does the scriptural injunction to edify others require such controversy in the ongoing process of reforming the church? In the polemical exchanges between Puritans and conformists, notions of charity remain unstable, adapted to suit context and circumstance. Both sides appropriate the concept in order to defend a more inclusive vision of church discipline (suggesting that the opposition lacks fraternal affection) or use it to sanction an exclusive vision of the church and excommunication (suggesting that the other's charity is too carnal or too malicious for a reformed church).

Puritan adherents of Presbyterian discipline claimed that their vision of charity was motivated not by exclusivity, however, but by edification, a Christian imperative that receives particular emphasis throughout the Pauline epistles:

But let vs followe the trueth in loue, and in all things growe vp into him, which is the head, that is Christ, / By whome all the bodie being coupled and knit together by euerie ioynt, for the furniture therof (according to the effectual power, which is in the measure of euerie parte) receiueth increase of the bodie, vnto the edifying of itselfe in loue.[18]

John Coolidge notes how Elizabethan Puritans traced this Pauline metaphor back through a rich scriptural legacy that conceived of the communal order in living, organic terms, a direct contrast to the lifeless edifices privileged by the world.[19] Charity was the transformative principle by which such communal glory could be achieved ("knowledge puffeth up, but love edifieth"). Coolidge observes how this subtler, more dynamic understanding of the term "edification" encouraged Puritans to demand an active opposition to the temporal priorities of Elizabethan politics, which placed civic harmony before spiritual perfection. Conformists flattened the definition of "edify" to mean transmitting information or preaching doctrine, which, in the context of this particular debate, one could not do without submitting to ecclesiastical regulations and wearing the vestments ordered by Queen Elizabeth. But Puritans conceived of God's living temple in more emphatic terms—anything that was not done precisely for the health of the community contributed to its destruction. In their eyes, any priest who wore vestments in order to edify had chosen to clothe himself in "the garments of Balamites, of popish priestes, enemies to God and all Christians."[20]

The *Admonition,* in broaching the topic of vestments and other aspects of church discipline, lays bare this fundamental difference in emphasis among contemporary interpretations of Pauline charity. By incorporating ceremonies and vestments into worship, the pamphlet claims, the English church was operating under a false notion of charity and building a hollow spiritual edifice: "These were the meanes and instrumentes to foster and cherishe riotousnesse, to neglecte true charitie, and to be shorte, to bring in folish and stagelike furniture."[21] Conformists might invoke the spirit of charity to justify ecclesiastical compromise, but Puritans claimed such an approach neglected true charity, which ought to assume a more active role in shaping and reforming the congregational body. Indeed, in his *Replye to an answere made of M. Doctor Whitgifte,* Thomas Cartwright defends the ecclesiastical function of elders by declaring their role integral to the "offices of charity," which involved the supervision and private exhortation of congregational members to conduct themselves in godly behavior under the threat of excommunication:

> That the principal offices of charity cannot be exercised without this order of ancients it may appear for that he which hath faulted and amended not after he be admonished once privately and then before one witness or two cannot further be proceeded against according to the commandment of our Saviour Christ.[22]

A decade later John Udall would articulate demands for Presbyterian discipline with even more force: "Without admonition by the Eldershipp, all duties of charitie cannot be exercised towards sinners."[23]

Both Cartwright and Udall envision a community of Christian believers who demonstrate continued spiritual reformation in a process of discipline carefully governed by elders, while the reprobate would be progressively lopped off the congregational body, "to cut them cleane from the church, as rotten and infected members," as William Fulke recommends.[24] This was the "principal office" of charity, its most important function, one that was essential to its role as "the glewe of mutuall concord."[25] And just as elders reproached sinners at the congregational level, spiritual leaders sometimes needed to rebuke political authorities. Thus Cartwright and others, most notably Walter Travers, emulated the model of John Field and Thomas Wilcox, who were fulfilling their charitable obligations by admonishing Church, Parliament, and Queen for a wrongheaded approach to religious governance.

The *Admonition* authors were promptly imprisoned for their pains, a coercive response by authorities that seemed to Puritans to stem from either misunderstanding or malice. Subsequent pamphlets reminded ecclesiastical authorities that such inflammatory rhetoric was merely a form of tough love motivated by a concern for the spiritual community, a curative discipline they were attempting to administer to a group of overly sensitive patients. The writer of *An exhortation to the byshops to deale brotherly with theyr brethren*, for instance, opens his pamphlet with a gesture of apostolic charm:

> We have in charity framed ourselves to be come all things unto all men, that at the least we mighte winne some to Christ; and have

therfore thought meete to publishe this small woorke, wherein the
bishops and prelates of this realm (much like to galled horsses, that
cannot abide to be rubbed) are frendly admonished of their duetie
towards God, and of love towardes their brethren.[26]

According to the logic of charity, such chastisement could be conceived as a
good and loving act, a "frendly" admonishment to reform church government. It was important to frame the polemic as fraternal correction rather
than malicious abuse for legal and ethical reasons, but in this case the function of charity was not merely rhetorical—it was driving the spirit of the
whole enterprise. The words of Revelation 3:19 stand in for this cultural
commonplace, one that was especially powerful for Puritans: "As many
as I love, I rebuke and chasten." Marprelate, for example, repeatedly—and
earnestly it seems—claims that his tracts are motivated by "the love of a
Christian church, prince and state."[27] And later, in a misguided attempt
to insert himself in theological controversy on the continent, James I (no
friend to Puritans) uses the same imperative to justify his remonstrance of
the theologian Conrad Vorstius: "Besides, the charitie, which Wee beare
to the said States Our neighbors and Confederates, professing the same
Religion that we do, did enforce Vs to admonish them, to eschew and
preuent in time so dangerous a contagion."[28]

It was the conception of charity as a spiritual force edifying the godly
community that buttressed the Puritans' furious appraisal of what they
deemed to be ecclesiastical neglect, but their role as spiritual gadflies was
already sanctioned, at least to a moderate degree, by the Elizabethan 1559
Injunctions that galled so many reformers. The injunction against slander
appears to license a process of charitable rebuke:

Item, because in all alterations, and specially in rites and ceremonies,
there happen discords amongst the people, and thereupon slanderous
words and railings, whereby charity, the knot of all Christian society, is loosed; the queen's majesty being most desirous of all other
earthly things, that her people should live in charity both towards
God and man, and therein abound in good works, wills and straitly
commands all manner her subjects to forbear all vain and contentious

disputations in matters of religion, and not to use in despite or rebuke of any person these convicious words, papist or papistical heretic, schis-matic or sacramentary, or any suchlike words of reproach. But if any manner of person shall deserve the accusation of any such, that first he be charitably admonished thereof; and if that shall not amend him, then to denounce the offender to the ordinary, or to some higher power having authority to correct the same.[29]

Intended to uphold charity and maintain the bonds of civil society, the injunction demonstrates how conventional was the Puritan approach to charitable admonition. In order to facilitate moderate reform, the injunction endorses a process of amendment similar to the role afforded to elders in Presbyterian discipline. Puritans and conformists might have differed in specific aspects of application—many Puritan communities exceeded the rubric provided by the Prayer Book in proceeding with excommunication[30]—but both sides in this dispute agreed on the important and contentious role of charity in shaping a community. The political orientation between conformists and reformers was reversed, however, illustrating the loggerheads at which both sides had arrived: Elizabethan government invoked charity as a means of protecting the established order by forbearing "all vain and contentious disputations in matters of religion"; Puritans believed that charitable edification involved just such active participation in the life of a church community, and that order would follow by virtue of that edification.[31]

The injunction also shows how the polemical exchange initiated by Puritans, however charitable in its intention, nevertheless ignored the officially prescribed method of admonition. Puritans preferred to enact their own censure outside the established channels of justice, a tactic born of expedience since the injunction ordered that Cartwright and other reformers bring their objections to the very people—the ecclesiastical ordinaries—about whom they were complaining. Whitgift's response to the *Admonition* does not ignore the causes of Puritan dissent, but he reminds his opponents to adhere to contemporary standards of charitable privacy: "Charitie doth not so couer open and manifest sinnes, that it suffereth them to be vnreprehended, but it remitteth priuate offences, it doth not publish secret sinnes at the first: neither doth it disclose all things that it knoweth to the defamation of a brother, when he may be otherwise reformed."[32] It is as much a matter of process as principle.

Other conformists were more extreme in their defense of clerical authorities. Conceiving of charity as a hermeneutic that willfully ignored errors, what Richard Hooker calls a "charity which is unwilling to behold anything that duty bindeth it to reprove,"[33] they employed the biblical trope of charity as a cloak or veil—from 1 Peter 4, which is citing Proverbs 10:12 but also gesturing at the sons of Noah—either to encourage polemicists to cease their rhetorical violence or to persuade readers to disregard potential calumnies or slanders. Henry Howard uses the trope to emphasize Puritan hypocrisy: "A mote cannot escape their censure in their neighbours eye, & yet great beames & rafters lie couered vnder their owne. I maruayle what is become lately of charitie, *Quae operit multitudinem peccatorum: which couereth the multitude of sinnes.*"[34] Later, in his *Admonition to the people of England*, Thomas Cooper underscores the divisive nature of Presbyterian discipline, with its fault-finding and formal admonishment, reminding his audience that "christian charitie will hide the blemishes and faultes of their brethren, and specially of the preachers of the gospell sincerely teaching Gods trueth."[35]

Precisely because Puritan admonition was disregarded or even suppressed, the more disruptive voice of Martin Marprelate emerged in the 1580s as an alternative vehicle of dissent. In *Hay any Worke for Cooper*, Marprelate brilliantly lampoons Cooper's (and other conformists') position that charity ought to suppress censure of any kind:

> For you do, as though a thief should say to a true man, I must needs have thy purse, thou must bear with me, it is my nature, I must needs play the thief. But yet thou dealest uncharitably with me if thou blazest it abroad: for though I make an occupation of theft, yet charity would cover it."[36]

Marprelate's persona and work was later revived during the 1640s, when similar debates over the rectitude and efficacy of admonition acquired equal urgency. Witness the polemical exchange between Joseph Hall and John Milton, which echoed, seven decades later, many of the same concerns voiced by Whitgift and Cartwright. In *A Defence of the Humble Remonstrance,* Hall reminds critics of the bishopric, "Brethren, whiles you desire to seem godly, learne to be lesse malicious. In the meane time, God blesse all good men from such charity," a comment that exercises Milton greatly in his *Animadversions:* "Your charity is much to your fellow-offendors, but nothing to the numberlesse soules that have beene lost by their false feeding; use not therefore so sillily the name of Charity."[37]

Conformists generally marshaled charity in behalf of an irenic plea for decorum and moderation. Many bishops were sympathetic to the arguments of nonconformists, who were still recognized as valued, albeit troublesome members of the English church, but this was also a deliberate strategy to characterize their opponents as irrational extremists. There is rhetorical value in deploying a pretense of charity in polemic, investing the writer with scriptural authority and conditioning the audience to interpret favorably the writer's supposedly benevolent argument.[38] Moreover, by emphasizing charity's role as the spiritual and material bond unifying the church, conformists implicated Puritans as inhospitable promoters of disorder, or even as potential separatists. They would employ logical arguments to oppose the content of Puritan polemic and then invoke charity to censure the mode or manner of Puritan disputation. Regarding *adiaphora,* conformists such as John Bridges flipped on their head the arguments of Puritans, claiming that Puritans were neglecting true charity by nurturing dissent and condemning rituals in corporate worship: "Without concord, they are vtterly no Churches at all: for which cause, if we will haue good regard to the safety of the Church, we must wholy with diligence looke to that which Paule commaundeth, that all things be decently done, and according to order."[39]

Puritans, of course, were voicing dissent expressly in behalf of church order. The conformists' deliberate refusal to see anything amiss—to cover their multitude of sins in behalf of charity—struck reformers as irresponsible. It is a relatively safe generalization to remark that Puritans desired to use charity as an instrument for making the godliness of both individuals and communities more visible, thereby establishing clearly demarcated boundaries between the devout and the impious. Rather than ignoring the errors of ecclesiastical officials, Puritans believed clerics should be held to even more stringent ethical standards. Cartwright seems to be responding directly to the Whitgift's use of charity as a cloak in his *Replye*, in which he attacks a false notion of Christian love: "Abuse not his graces in devising cloakes to cover their disorders / but that they would set before them the love of Christ."[40] Henry Barrow, in *A brief discoverie of the false church*, partially justifies his separatist movement by observing that the charity of conformists contributes to a false sense of concord. Because it obscures the spiritual condition of the church and its individual members, Barrow claims, "Charitie had need haue a good ground in these high matters, & not walke by rote, least yt destroy both them & yt self."[41] A similar anxiety, exacerbated by political insecurities and the threat of Rome, motivated Puritans to worry that charity, as understood by conformist clergy, would destroy the Church of England.[42]

I have attempted to trace general trends among the Puritans and conformists in the Admonition Controversy, but both approaches to charity were too inflexible to survive the exigencies of polemical exchange. Conformists occasionally mirrored the combative rhetoric of Puritans, for example, invoking charity to articulate a powerful and even painful defense of the church body. Rather than use the transformative power of charity to create and edify a godly church as Puritans wished, conformists considered charity an instrument to protect and defend an orderly church that had already been established. They were not upset with the disciplinary underpinnings of Puritan charity, just opposed to its specific application to their own church governance. Conformists could employ this approach with even more efficacy than Puritans because the metaphorical discipline present in their polemic was reinforced by the threat of real violence by the magistrate.

Consider, for example, John Whitgift's reply to Cartwright, when he apologizes for the severe discipline of charity:

> I whet the sworde no otherwise agaynst you, than Christian charitie and the state of the Church requireth. It is neither the sworde that taketh away life, nor fire that consumeth the body, which I moue vnto, but it is the sworde of correction and discipline, which may by sundrie other meanes be drawne out, than by shedding of bloud.[43]

Whitgift emphasizes the figurative nature of his violence, which he claims is at once justified and rendered obligatory by charity. But he reminds readers likewise of the "sundrie other meanes" by which a Christian magistrate might enforce conformity, an implicit reference to England's continued, albeit restrained policy of combating heresy with "fire that consumeth the body."[44] Like Thomas More and the earlier generation of English ecclesiastical conservatives who defended the Roman Church against Protestant reformers, and just as Laudians like Richard Montagu and Edward Boughen would do several decades later in the 1630s, Whitgift aligns Christian charity with the "state of the Church." That is, by situating the precedence of ecclesiastical unity and claiming that the church defines charity rather than the other way around, he suggests that adherents of ecclesiastical reform are motivated by a perverse kind of anti-charity. Thus Whitgift was embodying the very office Cartwright wished to invest in elders, admonishing the Puritans and tacitly threatening excommunication. Whitgift and other figures in the religious establishment were perfectly content to justify coercion based on a communal imperative, even as they exhorted Puritans to soften their censure in behalf of Christian love.

Puritans noticed this hypocrisy. Frustrated by this charitable rebuke, they suggested that conformists intentionally misinterpreted their efforts at fostering concord, practicing a "cunning" that "savoureth more of a Spanish inquisition than a Christian charity."[45] Cartwright—who elsewhere emphasizes the crucial role of excommunication in safeguarding the church—castigates Whitgift for levying accusations of heresy and schism. In his *Replye*, Cartwright underscores the communal project of reform-minded brethren:

> But as our knowledge and love is imperfect here in this world / so is our agreement and consent of judgment unperfect. And yet all these hard speaches of yours or uncharitable suspicions of papism, anabaptism, catharisme, donatisme etc whereby you do as much (as lieth in you) to cut us clean of from you / shal not be able so to estrange us or seperate us from you.[46]

It is a remarkable passage. The main thrust of Cartwright's argument is clear—that Whitgift's "uncharitable suspicions" are slanderous—but he adds a tempering note of skepticism. Tracing political and ecclesiastical dissent back to the fallibility of human love and judgment, invoking and modifying 1 Corinthians 13, Cartwright suggests that the church community will always fall short of its ideals. Finally, his words offer an important reminder that Puritan dissent during Elizabeth's reign, even in its most radical form, was in fact motivated by a desire for church unity rather than religious separatism.

Despite its well-intentioned premise, the Admonition Controversy remained a disappointment for Puritans, failing to initiate any immediate reform and prompting the religious establishment to entrench itself against vocal opposition. It was a rhetorical failure too, and for both sides. Despite the animadversions practiced by both Whitgift and Cartwright, a technique that placed both writers within close proximity on the page, a sense of absurd distance pervades the entire polemical exchange. Unable or unwilling to recognize the good intentions of the other side, the two authors completely miss each other. In assessing the controversy, Bacon likewise overlooks the primary problem when he dismisses both sides by claiming that "a character of love is more proper for debates of this nature than that of zeal": this was not a matter of zeal on the one hand and love on the other, but a problem of too much zealous love among both.[47] The Puritans, keen to use charity for admonishment, remained unwilling to receive their own admonishment from ecclesiastical superiors; and conformists, desirous of charitable interpretation that would "cover a multitude of sins," were reluctant to offer that service to dissenters. This tension helps situate the strange behavior of the two shepherds in Spenser's *May* eclogue, to which I will now turn. Here, Piers repeatedly engages Palinode in behalf of reform despite being rebuffed by the supposedly affable shepherd, but the shepherds' dialogue, much like the Admonition Controversy, stalls on account of their limited perspectives.

Spenser's *May* Eclogue and Charitable Admonition

From its very inception, Spenser's *May* eclogue in *The Shepheardes Calender* has been understood as a representation of contemporary ecclesiastical disputes in Elizabethan England. According to the confident gloss of E.K., whose annotations appear throughout the original edition and were likely written by Spenser himself (and certainly with his consent), the "moral" eclogue is framed as a debate between two pastors, a Protestant with a satirical pedigree named Piers (Plowman) and a "Catholique" named Palinode, "whose chiefe talke standeth in reasoning, whether the life of the one must be like the other."[48] E.K.'s easy dichotomy, accompanied by the implicit supposition that Piers represents an authoritative Spenserian voice, has propped up most scholarly examinations of the piece.[49] Summing up the conventional approach to reading the *May* eclogue, Harry Berger, Jr., notes, with the slightest hint of irony, "For most commentators the ecclesiastical allegory makes the debate coherent."[50] Berger's remark subtly calls attention to the fact that a separate camp of readers exists, who, setting E.K.'s tidy allegory to the side, find the eclogue unstable and its pastoral dialogue often illegible, as Piers and Palinode resolutely defy the simple roles E.K. assigns to them. Why does Piers, for example, who "list none accordaunce make / With shepheard, that does the right way forsake" (164–65), disregard his own austere principles, leave his flock, and sit down with a troublesome interlocutor to tell a fable? Moreover, as Berger himself observes, the two shepherds employ radically different allegorical registers, essentially talking past each other for the entire eclogue, and several scholars have identified other complicated dynamics present in the poem.[51] Readings of this kind, in which both Palinode and Piers are joint recipients of Spenser's critique, generally ignore the ecclesiastical context entirely and focus on the failure of dialogue when perspectives "confront each other as two separate, incommensurate poetic discourses."[52]

The following reading of the eclogue combines both approaches by locating the problematic aspects of Spenser's dialogue within the context of contemporary religious debate. Rather than using the ecclesiastical allegory to make Spenser's pastoral debate coherent, I try to make sense of its incoherence by way of the ecclesiastical allegory. Spenser, after all, was a student at Cambridge when Whitgift relieved Cartwright from the Lady Margaret chair on account of Cartwright's inflammatory lectures on the primitive church and episcopacy, and *The Shepheardes Calender* was published only two years after Cartwright's *Rest of Second Replie* in 1577, when the polemical artillery of Cartwright and Whitgift finally fell silent.[53] Moreover, there are striking similarities between the eclogue's conversation and larger contemporary discussions of ecclesiastical polity, as others have noted, and Piers articulates persuasive arguments for church reform that Palinode's rejoinders only partially blunt.

Rather than valorizing one camp or the other, however, Spenser writes an eclogue of rhetorical failure, dramatizing the respective challenges of voicing and receiving charitable admonition. In doing so he creates a dynamic and unsettled conversation between two characters who resist simple categories, although at first glance they seem easily defined. Indeed, even if readers debate just how much Spenser intends to critique Palinode, there is a consensus that he represents a kind of communal instinct, a desire for friendship, a celebration of springtime ritual, and a weakness "of felowship" (172) for hearing fables and tales from his companions. One might call him a caricatured conformist. Piers, meanwhile, whether or not one considers him a frosty malcontent or a courageous champion of clerical piety, apparently adopts the iconoclastic pose of a solitary reformer who "list none accordaunce make" (164) with disreputable shepherds. After all, as Piers declares, "Who touches Pitch mought needs be defiled" (74). Note that I include quotations to support these characterizations, as the text itself repeatedly substantiates them. Spenser has constructed a problematic dialogue between two different ethics of concord: one, Palinode's, which refuses to acknowledge that which "may not be mended" and thus avoids "conteck," and another that envisions a community in which careful governance and sober conduct are clearly visible and safe from "such faitors, when their false harts bene hidde" (170).

Or so it seems. The larger narrative offers a slightly different story. Palinode, the friendly voice of fellowship, almost immediately assumes a defensive posture and curtly dismisses Piers's efforts at reform. He spends most of the eclogue accusing Piers of faultfinding, calling him names, and deriding his "fooles talke" (141). Why is Palinode, whose emblem declares "that who doth mistrust is most false," so gruff, so mistrustful? What motivates his sensitive response? And Piers, who finds no "fayth . . . there in the faythlesse," who prefers a world of clear divisions between bad and good, persistently engages a companion who possesses dubious pastoral credentials and proves a recalcitrant interlocutor.[54] Moreover, he shrouds his own ethics in the murky world of poetic fable-making, despite his desire for stable guarantors marking his reformed community. The dialogue seems unlikely from the start. But it makes more sense if we keep in mind the contradictions evident in the Admonition Controversy, and though Piers and Palinode do not serve merely as mimes for Cartwright and Whitgift, aping their exchange under a pastoral sky, the shepherds dramatize a similar moral and religious conflict. Treating both sides with ironic understanding, Spenser simultaneously participates in and comments on the problematic tension that threatened to derail contemporary church-building and communal reform.

E.K. does not invoke the Admonition Controversy in his argument but instead frames the eclogue as a debate between "two formes of pastoures or Ministers, or the protestant and the Catholique: whose chiefe talke standeth in reasoning, whether the life of the one must be like the other." The binary does not hold up, nor does it seem meant to. Later in the *Calender*, Palinode appears by proxy in *June*, when Thomalin (the more distinctly Protestant shepherd in this later exchange) paraphrases Palinode's condemnation of Roman Catholic ecclesiology after taking a trip to Rome. Even E.K.'s attitude toward Palinode seems inconsistent, as his glosses regularly treat the shepherd as a relatively benign if misinformed figure. Obviously the paratext is dubious at best, and early modern readers of the *Calender* would probably be conditioned to receive E.K.'s commentary with some degree of skepticism.[55] But E.K.'s description of the shepherds serves at least two purposes for Spenser. By identifying the exchange as a debate between Protestantism and Roman Catholicism, E.K. distances the anonymous poet from a sensitive religious controversy within the Church of England. He might be reductive, but E.K. helps defuse some of the potential hazards involved in Spenser's project, especially given its obvious topicality. More important, E.K.'s dichotomy introduces and reinforces the ecclesiastical polarities arresting contemporary religious debate. In a manner similar to the practice condemned by Elizabeth's injunctions, E.K. smears Palinode with the "convicious" word of "Catholique" before the exchange is even under way, prejudicing readers against Palinode's opinions and dramatizing the problems of interpreting pastoral allegory. Thus E.K.'s argument, which prepares readers for the shepherds' mutual failure to generate constructive dialogue, participates in the larger failures of ecclesiastical discourse in England.

The eclogue starts out favorably enough, in spite of E.K.'s paratext, with Palinode delivering an opening paean to the "mery moneth of May."

Looking for affirmation from his companion, he asks, "Bene not thy teeth on edge, to thinke, / How great sport they gaynen with little swinck?" (89). Despite its festive spirit and colloquial irony—which might not be as innocent as it appears—Palinode's question elicits a jarring response from Piers: "Perdie so farre am I from enuie, / That their fondnesse inly I pitie. / Those faytours little regarden their charge" (37–39). Piers takes the question so seriously that he worries over the moral implications of his answer, immediately introducing the ethical conditions of his response. By insisting that his ensuing rebuke stems from a virtuous disposition, motivated by pity rather than envy, Piers intends to circumscribe his critique within the sanction of Christian admonition. Imagining a spectrum of ethical responses to the revelry (channeling his inner Aristotle), Piers introduces two important poles—"so farre am I from enuie, / That their fondnesse inly I pitie"—which help him navigate the complicated act of interpretation or judgment and likewise establish the parameters of his moral discourse.

Piers is concerned about accusations of envy, a vice conventionally considered in opposition to communal fellowship on account of its willfully malicious misinterpretation, and often invoked by poets like Spenser's Immeritô, whose prefatory poem "To His Booke" warns the newly penned *Calender* to be prepared lest "Envie barke at thee, / As sure it will" (5–6). Moreover, an envious disposition might imply some kind of virtue among the hireling shepherds Piers derides, as Thomas Rogers notes, quoting Cicero, "I haue always bine of this minde, that I haue thought enuie gotten by vertue, to be no obscuring of my name, but an illustrating of the same."[56] Instead, Piers frames his critique in terms of charitable rebuke, employing pity—with all its valences of Christian love, mercy, and piety—to achieve a moral equilibrium. Piers wants his statement to fall within the purview of fraternal correction, a safeguard that would transform his critique into a genuine admonition concerned for the communal well-being and distinct from mere detraction. And his actual rebuke justifies that stance to a degree. Decrying the abuses of nonresident clergy who held multiple benefices was a fairly moderate position of reform, one that garnered sympathy even from a number of conformists, and it was often linked to the charitable imperative of poor relief.

Piers's remark nevertheless fails completely. Any declaration of pity typically sounds hollow and disingenuous when followed by relentless scornful derision, as occurs here and throughout the eclogue when Piers hurls insults at clerics. More notably, however, his fairly simplistic framework remains incapable of stabilizing the discourse. The entire premise of his admonition is vulnerable to the interpretation of his interlocutor, Palinode, who promptly accuses Piers of the envious disposition he had just disclaimed:

> Sicker now I see thou speakest of spight,
> All for thou lackest somedele their delight.
> I (as I am) would rather be envied,
> All were it of my foe, then fonly pitied:
> And yet if neede were, pitied would be,
> Rather, then other should scorne at me:
> For pittied is misshape, that nas remedie,
> But scorned bene dedes of fond foolerie. (55–62)

Recent scholarship has emphasized the failures of the dialogue by diagnosing the shepherds' different poetic registers: each simply misses what the other is saying. But in this case Palinode does not retract the careful interpretive criterion employed by Piers; instead he inflects it through his own field of preference. There is a hypersensitivity in his reply, a tension that strains the debate, as Palinode tacitly acknowledges that his own behavior, much like those May-gaming shepherds, is under review. That self-referential position buried in a parenthesis—"I (as I am)"—might remind the reader of E.K.'s warning, that Palinode's is the voice of an equivocating "Catholique" priest, but the statement also suggests a defensive posture: feeling the withering glance of his companion, he (as he is) "would rather be envied" by such as Piers. Lacing his response with ironic conditionals—"All were it of my foe" and "yet if neede were"—Palinode launches a complicated assault on Piers's judgment: although I suspect you are speaking out of envy, he declares, even your claims of pity are foolish ("fonly pitied") and consequently merit this scornful reply, since "scorned bene dedes of fond foolerie." Later Palinode rebuffs Piers again in similar terms, claiming his didactic carping is mere "fooles talke" (141). If Piers offers pity, Palinode wants none of it. Spenser adds to the ironic texture here, since Palinode seems to be the pastor who follows most closely the wisdom of E.K., who declares in the eclogue's argument that "it is daungerous to mainteine any felowship, or giue too much credit to their colourable and feyned goodwill."

This friction governs the entire exchange. Piers invokes the conventional nostalgia of satirists (as well as Presbyterians like Field and Wilcox), longing for a simpler society, a pastoral golden age, something akin to the earliest Christian communities when spiritual leadership was plainly better: "Well ywis was it with shepheardes thoe: / Nought having, nought feared they to forgoe" (109–10). Rather than critiquing the impracticality of such pastoral idealism, Palinode chooses to highlight Piers's malice, much like a conformist defending the church establishment. As opposed to deeming all things to the best, Piers "findest faulte, where nys to be found," he "buildest strong warke upon a weake ground," and he "raylest on right withouten reason" (144–46). Here Palinode combines his defense of the communal interest with something of a personal validation: "Nay sayd I thereto, by my deare borrowe, / If I may rest, I nill live in sorrowe" (150–51). This is an authentic palinode or retraction, inverting the final rhyme Piers used earlier to express his dire view of contemporary religion: "This was the first sourse of shepheards sorowe, / That now nill be quitt with baile, nor borrowe" (130–31). Of Palinode's "borrowe" E.K. remarks, "that is our Saviour, the commen pledge of all men's debts to death," but the word was also used to denote a loan or pledge of surety, or even an elaborate agreement among ten neighbors—a tithing—to hold themselves jointly accountable before the law.[57] He makes his oath in the language of economic and social community in order to dismiss Piers's troublemaking. Indeed, Palinode later asks to "borrow" the fable for Sir John to use in church.

The difference in attitude between the shepherds seems clear: whereas a suspicious Piers, worried about "wolves, full of fraud and guile," rejects the efficacy of borrowing, Palinode is more confident in the positive aspects of community:

> And sooth to sayne, nought seemeth sike strife,
> That shepheardes so witen ech others life,
> And layen her faults the world before,
> The while their foes done eache of hem scorne.

Let none mislike of that may not be mended:
So conteck soone by concord mought be ended. (158–63)

Like Whitgift and other conformists, Palinode wants peace and concord, an end to strife, a general fellow-feeling that relies on trust, whereas Piers "list none accordaunce make / With Shepheard, that does the right way forsake" (164–65).

And yet there clearly is an ironic undercurrent, a recognizable gap between Palinode's ideals and his practice, as he himself refuses to interpret Piers's critique in a positive manner. There is a persuasive force to Patrick Cullen's suggestion that Palinode's "petulant unwillingness to accept Piers's frosty rigidity . . . represents human nature, with its natural desires and limitations," but something more is at work than mere petulance.[58] Readers genuinely sympathize with Palinode, whose springtime encomium meets a frigid reception, but one also senses that he has exploited the terms of verbal exchange in this dialogue by refusing to offer Piers any legitimacy. He articulates communal priorities—"by my deare borrowe"—only to stifle a contrarian perspective. He is not a stupid interlocutor but an oversensitive one who feels all too keenly the implications of Piers's remarks, and he does a masterful job of appropriating the rules of charitable interpretation in his own behalf, refusing Piers the sanction of well-meaning admonition. Such behavior declines to "touch pitch" after its own fashion.

Just when the eclogue appears to reach an impasse, Piers revises his strategy, telling the truth but telling it slant by way of a beast fable: an ill-fated kid, left alone by his mother, and motivated by some combination of pity, self-love, and stupidity, opens his doors to a begging fox who destroys him. Piers's earlier discussion of irresponsible clergy becomes allegorized here into a scene of actual experience. Presumably Piers intends for the fable to reiterate his earlier message and convince Palinode of the real dangers plaguing the Church of England, but the story complicates any easy dichotomy between right and wrong, importing the previous interpretive criteria of Piers and Palinode—envy and pity—into a more complex social situation. If pity worked as a corrective to envy for Piers in his criticism of absentee "shepherds," the passion remains prone to misapplication, especially in the context of foxes who disguise themselves as

members of the deserving poor. Recall, from the last chapter, Thomas
Elyot's caution against "vayne pitie," a commonplace of the period. The
"inly" pity Piers advertised earlier will get the kid into trouble when he encounters the fox and, "pittying hys heavinesse" (259), lets in his destroyer.
Much like Elizabethan authorities, Piers desires a clear world reduced to
binary oppositions, but the real perils of hypocrisy and misrepresentation
cloud his own vision.

On the other hand, this shift in tactics signals a change in Piers, a recognition of rhetorical contingency that could enable him to adapt his
moral to any type of audience. Gregory Kneidel reminds us that Puritan
reformers emphasized the importance of educating a ministry that could
adapt to circumstance: "Spenser's very mode of allegorical fabulistic ar-
gumentation coyly allies his poetic project with the preaching that pru-
dently accommodates the intellectual capacities of various audiences."[59]
In this way Piers is a convincing Puritan. Like Cartwright and Travers and
others, moreover, Piers is not simply an iconoclast, and his advocacy for
more precise standards of godly conduct within the church stems from a
communal imperative rather than a separatist agenda. Finally, in using
vagrancy as an image of ecclesiastical disorder, Piers follows the model of
Puritan complaint during the 1570s, when Parliament introduced substantial revisions to poor relief intended to organize parish administration
more efficiently. Travers, for example, compared the owners of multiple
benefices to actual beggars, presumably because they, like rogues and
vagabonds, were not attached to a specific church: these nonresident
clergy "in the meane tyme eyther do nothinge / or ells goe about as they
list in all the realme as roges and masterles servantes seekinge some mayster that will hyre them and use ther Labor."[60] Field and Wilcox deployed
a similar metaphor in the *View of Popishe Abuses* that was annexed to the
Admonition, excoriating absentee clergy who "get benefices by friendship
or money, or flattery, where they can catch them: or to conclude, if al these
faile, that they may go vp & down like beggers, and fal to many follies."[61]
Just as More linked heresy to vagrancy, smearing Tyndale with a double
brush, Piers links absentee clerics to false beggars, suggesting that their
vestments are merely a disguise used for material advantage: "Such faitors, when their false harts bene hidde, / Will doe, as did the Foxe by the
Kidde" (170–71).

But the episode also provides a reminder of why fables, parables, and allegories are unreliable. Piers intends for his fable to warn Palinode against prioritizing harmony before righteous conduct, but his apparent moral lesson sabotages his own enterprise. That is, Piers must disguise his message in order to receive a charitable reading from Palinode, but he complicates his own lesson by dramatizing in his fable the actual dangers of a charitable reading. It is impossible to know, when Palinode rebuffs his companion a final time at the eclogue's conclusion, whether Piers fails outright or is merely a victim of his rhetorical success. That the fatuous and possibly Papist "Sir John" will acquire the fable gives this paradox a further humorous edge. Spenser clearly delights in the ironic ambiguity of the moment, which suggests that he remains more interested in highlighting the situation's hermeneutic instability than in promoting any partisan doctrine or discipline. And by including the fable and its consequent failure, Spenser closely aligns the functions of poet and priest, dramatizing the limitations of discourses available to both pastors and pastorals.

Spenser also underscores the problematic aspects of storytelling by indicating that Piers is complicit in the danger he describes. Much like the kid's mother, Piers abandons his own flock to potential foxes as he tells Palinode his fable. In fact, the eclogue's woodcut suggestively portrays the kid's demise occurring right under Piers's nose. This paradox bears a resemblance to the accusations Whitgift levies at Puritans who he claims have abandoned their ministerial responsibilities because of mere *adiaphora*. Moreover, Piers obviously relishes the art of entertaining. Berger is right to note the sheer poetic delight coursing through the shepherd's description of the fox, an energetic display much "closer to the playful or impious spirit of popular beast fable than to the reform voice"[62]:

> Then at the dore he cast me downe hys pack,
> And layd him downe, and groned, Alack, Alack.
> Ah deare Lord, and sweete Saint Charitee,
> That some good body woulde once pitie mee. (245–48)

Note the elaborate alliteration and assonance, and the lively sarcasm—Piers is having fun playing the poet. It is therefore no surprise to find Piers later in *October* participating in a protracted dialogue examining the purpose and power of verse. His description of the fox suggests that he is no stranger to rhetorical disguise, that he is manipulating Palinode after his own fashion (which recalls, appropriately, the alliterative tradition of Langland). At one point, when the anaphora and other repetitions build a momentum that culminates in that pathetic cry of the fox—"Ah deare Lord, and sweete Saint Charitee, / That some good body woulde once pitie mee"—the speech of Piers and the fox seem to blend together, united by a shared personal pronoun. There remains a hint of irony, a tacit acknowledgement of complicity in the deception, when Piers employs his own poetic agency to indict the fox, who "can chat, / And tell many lesings of this, and that" (284–85). Piers, who intends to capture Palinode's sympathies, vilifies the fox for engaging in the same kind of artful deception. As Piers describes the persuasive rhetoric of the fox, Spenser's readers face an interpretive conundrum, one that demonstrates how poetry participates in the fictive spectacle that enables the fox to capture the kid.

The fable itself is a failure, at least as far as Piers is concerned, and Palinode remains unconvinced. Palinode revises the performance of the kid, refusing to fall victim to the foxy rhetoric of his fellow shepherd; he seems to have grasped the fable's intended lesson but directed its force against Piers. After hearing the story to its conclusion, he ridicules his companion—"Truly *Piers,* thou art beside thy wit, / Furthest fro the marke, weening it to hit" (306–7)—and proceeds to appropriate the story in behalf of "Sir John," precisely the type of unlearned priest Piers derides. Note that Palinode excuses his local priest's ignorance by emphasizing just the sort of charitable intent—"For well he meanes" (317)—that he refuses to ascribe to Piers. At the poem's conclusion what appears to preserve the shepherds' friendship is silence, as Piers mutters to himself, before they both head back home under the evening sky, "Of their falshode more could I recount" (314). The narrative's moral works against itself, and one wonders if Piers ultimately represents the kid, fallen victim to his own conception of pastoral heroism. Indeed, Richard Chamberlain reads the poem as a commentary on the limitations of a particular brand of totalizing allegorical criticism, arguing that instead of reinforcing the authority of E.K. or underwriting the ascetic impulse of Piers, "the work is produced by a fellowship of interpretation and text"—that is, the poem plays a joke on both Piers and E.K., and supports Palinode's optimism in human fellowship.[63] Such a reading probably valorizes Palinode and his reductive notions of community more than Spenser himself intended, but it underscores the instability of allegorical interpretation as well as the eclogue's failure to provide a resolution to the conflict it dramatizes.

Perhaps the eclogue itself does not *fail* as much as circumscribe its aims. Much of my argument has labored to suggest that the Admonition Controversy offered Spenser a model of unsuccessful dialogue between two irreconcilable sides, one aptly summarized by the final pair of emblems in the eclogue: "Who doth most mistrust is most false"; "What fayth then is there in the faythlesse."[64] And in terms of rhetorical success, Piers accomplishes little more than Cartwright does in the face of intractable opposition from Palinode and Whitgift. Spenser may be sympathetic to arguments for church reform—Piers is the eclogue's central speaker, after all—but he seems content merely to dramatize the mutual responsibility of both parties in the ongoing conflict. Rather than praising or blaming either Piers or Palinode, Spenser seems most interested in the dilemma itself, an immediate predicament facing the Church of England but also linked to Spenser's own vocation, with its fragile dialectic between poet and audience.

The *May* eclogue provides Spenser an opportunity to stage important issues of charitable interpretation that were immediately relevant to contemporary church discipline, but these questions preoccupied him throughout his career. Even as he developed a more sophisticated allegorical poetics, he continued to explore the complicated relationship between mutually competing truths and virtues—the inevitable clash of temperance and militant chastity, for example. And his paradoxical treatment of a highly charged ecclesiastical controversy anticipates the rich, complex, and sometimes contradictory engagement of theology and biblical imagery in *The Faerie Queene*. Finally, if Spenser treated the inadequacies of polemical discourse with an ironic understanding, it was probably because he recognized the limitations of his own poetic discourse, acknowledging the likelihood that his fables would not merely meet the ridicule of Palinode but also suffer the "venomous despite" of the *Faerie Queene*'s Blatant Beast.

Elizabethan Satire: "A course of little charitie"

Just over two decades after publication of *The Shepheardes Calender,*
Nicholas Breton recycles the pitch-and-tar conceit that Piers employs in
May to critique conservative clerics, but Breton directs its force against
satirical poets, who compromise their message (he claims) by using a defective medium:

> Who toucheth pitch and tarre cannot be cleane.
> A wilfull wit doth worke it selfe much woe.
> In euery course tis good to keepe a meane:
> And being well, to liue contented so. (631–34)

Breton's language in *No Whippinge, nor tripping* echoes Piers, but his project is far different. Rather than championing church reform and opposing the prelacy, he celebrates Whitgift and Bancroft's act of censorship
in 1599, the Bishops' Ban of satirical and erotic verse, expressing the ideal
conformist stance: leave moral reform to church authorities. Although
Breton's comments appear among the Whipper pamphlets, a literary debate focused on the relative merits of satirical verse, the exchange gives
voice to larger questions of communal reform and the proper sphere of
charitable admonition that surfaced throughout the Elizabethan era. As
with the Admonition Controversy and Spenser's *Shepheardes Calender,* a
problematic tension emerges in the Whipper pamphlets between charitable correction and charitable decorum. Debora Shuger has already examined how the Whipper exchange centers on "the theological basis of
privacy—its felt relation to charity norms," how charitable sociability typically suppressed public castigation, but I want to complement Shuger's
analysis by considering how charity also functions as a moral imperative
motivating the composition and publication of satire.[65] In the Whipper
pamphlets we can find, yet again, competing visions of charity's role in
governing admonition.

By including the Whipper pamphlets in a larger discussion of ecclesiastical reform, I am aligning satirists rather uncomfortably with various
types of religious nonconformists of the period, Puritans in particular,
but the association was made explicitly by contemporaries as well: "How

euer chiden by the Puritanist, the Humorist, or the Satyrist yet in mine experience I found it more charitable then the Countrie Vulgarist."[66] Elizabethan formal verse satire, though consciously classical in its generic conventions, offers a literary analogue for religious admonition on account of its similar enterprise of moral reform. Robert Hayman notes the ethical kinship between the two discursive modes in his book of satirical epigrams, declaring that "Sermons and Epigrams haue a like end, / To improue, to reproue, and to amend."[67] One persuasive reading of the Bishops' Ban has suggested that ecclesiastical authorities worried that satirists were consciously displacing the more traditional literature of moral exempla.[68] Perhaps it should be no surprise that so many satirists later took clerical orders, as Donne, Hall, and John Marston did, for example. In fact, Richard McCabe finds in Hall's career a continuity of purpose, tracing his satirical vocation back to a Puritan upbringing that emphasized fraternal castigation, and observing that his later sermons repeatedly "echo, restate, and develop the complaints" of his satires in *Virgidemiarum*.[69]

Both satirists and religious nonconformists of the period produced works marked by a desire for intention and action to align, as well as by a thoroughgoing repugnance for hypocrisy. Samuel Rowlands attempts to valorize the truth-telling function of satire, but he echoes the voices of Puritan reform from the 1570s and 1580s when he lambastes those who claim to "Haue charitie, auoyde contentious strife, / Oft he speakes thus, that nere did good in's life."[70] Since the Whipper exchange was a response to a ban on satire made by episcopal mandate and known generally as the *Bishops' Ban*, signed moreover by Whitgift and Bancroft, both of whom played prominent roles in combating Puritan dissent, it is predictable that specific vestiges of the Admonition Controversy appear throughout the exchange. Numerous religious references suggest that both satirists and their opponents recognized and exploited the similarities between satirical discourse and ecclesiastical controversies that remained relevant to the Church of England at the turn of the century.

Much like Field and Cartwright and other Puritans, the Elizabethan satirist can sometimes seem like an optimistic or even naive writer, apparently assured of his vocation's righteousness. But Elizabethan satirists also demonstrated an almost obsessive concern for reader response (again, much like those Puritans), anxiously anticipating the prospect of a malicious reception, which was typically confirmed. As Spenser drama-tizes in the *May* eclogue, there is a kind of reflexivity inherent to charita-ble admonition—those who offer a critique are themselves dependent on the recipient's interpretation of charitable intent—and the only successful encounter of this kind requires what might be called charity to the sec-ond degree, an ideal relationship between writer and reader. Elizabethan satirists performed a variety of rhetorical gymnastics in order to defend their work against potential accusations of malicious writing, and in fact the defiance of envious readers became a satirical set-piece, practiced by Joseph Hall, Thomas Middleton, and Ben Jonson among others. By virtue of these and other defenses constructed by satirists, a supposedly mali-cious interpretation simultaneously authenticated the satire (by reinforc-ing the viciousness of the age) and invalidated the critique of satire (by suggesting that envy prompted the accuser).

By adopting these strategies, satirists consciously fashioned their work for readers with the problem of charitable interpretation as one of its core preoccupations. Lawrence Manley, who observes an urgency in the post-scripts and proems of verse satire similar to the prologues and epilogues of comical satire in the theater, suggests that the satirist was attempting (and failing) to shape a complicated cultural aesthetic, noting "a genuine inability to define a stable style or to substantiate the satirist's judgment by appeal to a sustaining social terrain."[71] Manley's remark gestures at the larger problem plaguing satirists, who were at once appealing to con-servative social and moral norms but also defying those norms by way of their transgressive discourse. Recent scholarship on censorship dur-ing the period emphasizes the complex intersection between public and private social values that produced so much tension for both writers and readers. Shuger notes that early modern authorities were primarily con-cerned with the manner in which transgressive language incited violence among aggrieved parties, which accords with Cyndia Susan Clegg's ob-servation that the inconsistent theories of licensing and rare occasions of censorship during this period were motivated more by circumstance and self-interest than ideology.[72] Writers, then, had to be centrally concerned with the social and relational consequences of their work. The satirical mode in late Elizabethan England was not merely fascinated by reader reception—it relied on it.

Satirists often signaled their good intentions by associating their work with the tradition of fraternal correction. Richard Niccols's prefatory epigram "Ad lectorem" at the beginning of his collection of satirical epigrams is wholly conventional, reminding readers, "If thou be faultie, let it not offend thee, / Heere to untrusse; this whipping may amend thee."[73] Typically the satirical voice positions itself as a loving teacher, or parent, providing severe discipline, striving, as Marston puts it, "to scourge poluting beastliness" and whip vice from the body of the commonweal.[74] Thomas Lodge describes his satirical project as one that aims to "dissuade by fatherly admonishment, / Schoole, and correct, advertise, and prevent: / Make him by government, and perfect zeal, / A happier member of his common weale."[75] Framing his satire as a medicinal purgative, Thomas Drant fuses together in *A Medicinable Morall* the legacies of Horace and Jeremiah, and other writers baptize the Juvenalian dictum that it is difficult not to write satire, nodding toward the prophetic voices of ancient Israel. Donne memorably begins "Satyre 5" by aligning his theme with "Charity and liberty" in combatting wretchedness and wickedness.[76] Samuel Rowlands embeds his satire within a larger network of amicable social obligations, since "A Man may tell his friend his fault in kindnes, / To wincke at folly, is a foolish blindnes."[77] Others invoke the genre of speculum literature, presenting a textual "glass" to readers who might recognize their own sinful misbehavior and thereby accuse themselves.

Like their contemporaries, all three participants in the Whipper exchange describe satire as an extension of fraternal correction—in fact, it is one of the few things on which they all agree—setting into sharp relief the resemblances between religious polemic and satirical literature. Their responses to the Bishops' Ban illustrate how fully Elizabethan satire was committed to a project of charitable admonition but also how vulnerable such claims were to receiving their own moral rebuke.

The Whipper Pamphlets

The Whipper pamphlets are by no means the most sophisticated examples of verse satire during the Elizabethan period, but their value consists in the distinctive responses to the Bishops' Ban of 1599 expressed by the participants in the exchange, each of whom represents a different attitude toward satire more generally. Weever's work, *The Whipping of the Satyre*, which initiated the exchange by attacking the satirist (presumably John Marston), the epigrammatist (possibly Everard Guilpin), and the humourist (almost certainly Ben Jonson), attempts to carve out a particular space for state-sponsored satire that places fraternal admonition under the aegis of public authority. That is, Weever recognizes the important role satire can perform in effecting moral reform, but he likewise acknowledges its capacity for violence if practiced by the wrong individual. Nicholas Breton's *No Whippinge,* on the other hand, indicts all satirists—and that includes Weever—for usurping the role of religious and political authorities, and he exhorts poets to ignore the topic of vice altogether, which is better left to the priesthood (one might call this a conformist stance). Guilpin's stance in *The Whipper of the Satyre his Pennance* is less consistent. At times he seems to concede Weever's position that uncharitable expression is dangerous and immoral, though he asserts, in the rough, obscure style characteristic of Elizabethan satire, that satirists actually perform a crucial type of fraternal or even parental correction. But Guilpin never maintains this stance for long, always returning to an idealistic position that associates satire with a kind of *furor poeticus,* a vatic privilege based on the satirist's access to Truth, which supersedes any communal obligations related to charitable conduct. (In this prophetic spirit he uses as his immediate model Joseph Hall, who claims that his satires were "Begot long since of Trueth and holy Rage."[78])

So, the short-lived Whipper controversy yielded three distinct responses by poets to the Bishops' Ban: one that attempted to sanctify and empower the satirist as poet-prophet; another that proscribed satire altogether on account of its antisocial aggression and misappropriation of moral authority; and a third that envisioned a compromise between those extremes, a privileged version of satire practiced only by an artistic elite who received sanction from the political and religious orders.

Breton, who of the three authors expresses the most adamant disapproval of satire, seems especially concerned by the literary mode's impact on a tenuous social fabric. Perhaps that is why so much of his work feels passive, like an elaborate apology, just the sort of model charitable reproof that might receive its own charitable reading. (The poem's subtitle, after all, announces that it will forgo whipping and instead provide *"a kinde friendly Snipping."*) Desiring a kind of negative reciprocity—you ignore my faults and I will ignore yours—Breton's prefatory epistle in *No Whippinge* carefully distances his work from the fray: "Now for my selfe, I proteste that humor of Charitie, that I wish to finde at all their handes that see and will reproque my folly: for I am none of the seauen wise men, and for the eight, I knowe not where to seeke him" (4). Breton's stylistic sophistication is a real advantage—his rhyme royal stanza, with an initial envelope rhyme that eventually resolves itself in couplets, embodies a progressive move toward harmony. But *No Whippinge* struggles to contend with the strident voices of Weever and Guilpin, who employ matching stanzaic structures in the tradition of flyting contests or answer poems. Breton comes across less like a participant in the agonistic exchange than like a detached observer. Whereas the other two attempt to shrink the distance between writer and reader, ultimately concluding their works by depicting a physical skirmish, Breton's decorous verse maintains a cool distance that is ultimately ineffectual. The submissive attitude endorsed by *No Whippinge,* which gestures at a political quietism even Whitgift might hesitate to endorse, illustrates the problematic alternative to satire or admonition. It seems wholly appropriate that the publication of Breton's poem immediately preceded the most heated phase of the Poets' War (a skirmish between Jonson, Marston, Thomas Dekker, and perhaps Shakespeare) as well as Guilpin's inflammatory response to Weever: he reforms no one.

Nevertheless, Breton's cautious verse admirably captures some of the specific problems plaguing any discourse of reformation:

> It is a course of little charitie,
> To find out faults, and fall vpon them so;
> And tis a wit of singularitie,
> That perfect wisedom doth but little show:
> Which thinks it giues the foole the ouer-throw,
> And might haue bene farre better exercised,
> Then in the folly that it hath suprized. (281–87)

The careful tone of moderation is announced by the litotes in the stanza's first line, which the fourth verse reinforces, aligning charity and wisdom in a policy of restraint that neither finds out faults nor shows them. Note, by way of contrast, the contestatory spirit inherent to the "wit of singularitie," which, in its opposition to the communal solidarity of charity, falls on folly in an ambush and overthrows it. Even this assertion, however, is diluted by the diplomatic conditional of the final couplet, and here Breton probably is responding tactfully to Weever's more aggressive writing, which exercises the same folly—satire—it intends to overthrow. Breton offers little argument about the presence of vice in England and the need for reform, but he claims the process needs to occur within the scope and sanction of established communal norms. The poem refuses to allege whether or not church authorities will be able to effect reform, but it states unequivocally that no other entity should make the attempt:

> The Preachers charge is but to chide for sinne,
> While Poets steppes are short of such a state:
> And who an others office enters in,
> May hope of loue, but shalbe sure of hate.
> 'Tis not a time offences to relate. (43–47)

Breton notes the important distinction between correction meted out by public authorities and fraternal or private admonition, but he is also responding to the Bishops' Ban—"'tis not a time offences to relate"—recognizing the political contingency of the moment. This is a pragmatic statement acknowledging the futility of the entire satirical enterprise, but also a failed rhetorical strategy, alienating the audience it intends to reform.

If Breton resists the idea of using violence to end violence, the anonymous writer of a commendatory poem prefacing Weever's *Whippinge* explicitly celebrates that same conundrum, ignoring Weever's apparent hypocrisy: "Then view him well, that with impartiall eye, / Dares scourge the Scourger of base villany." The poem apparently considers Weever's testimony uncomplicated by its participation in the very literary mode he purports to condemn. That is, the poet recognizes that Weever employs satire to attack the satirist for doing exactly what Weever intends to do, whip "base villany." Placing to the side biographical concerns, since Weever—if he is the Whipper—wrote his own share of satirical literature (as well as epigrams), the inherent hypocrisy of Weever's enterprise neither illegitimates his project nor obscures his message. Instead, the paradox of using satire to attack satire underscores the currency of charitable admonition in early modern England and demonstrates how much the Elizabethan satiric mode borrows from religious discourse. Indeed, Weever places the concept of charitable admonition at the center of his allegorical narrative, as Church exhorts her sister Commonwealth to punish the satirist, who threatens communal stability: "Dutie enioyn's me to ioyne in with you; / For they are blest, that labour to represse / the course of sinne, and curse of sinfulnesse" (112–14). With sophisticated parison and internal rhyme, Weever frames his work in terms of dutiful conformity to state policy and religion. He invokes the same charitable imperative, which obliges an individual to respond to sinful behavior with loving discipline, expressed by Roman Catholic polemicists and Presbyterian elders alike throughout the sixteenth century.

In fact Weever uses essentially the same argument as satirists like Guilpin to legitimize his own project, carefully styling his critique as fraternal admonition. In the following stanza, for example, Weever draws the epigrammatist and humourist to him, creates an atmosphere of intimate friendship, and reminds them to receive his speech in the same loving terms with which it was supposedly fashioned:

> Come hither now, friend Epigrammatist,
> And doe not wring my words to wrong my speech,
> Harken thou likewise, captious Humourist,
> And heare that mildly, what I friendly teach:
> For those that speake in loue and charitie,
> Should both beleeued and beloued be. (619–24)

This, just before the speaker lays on with his rod "not for hate, but loue" (993). How different then is Weever's satirist, speaking in love and charity, from Guilpin's defense in *The Whipper Whipped*, which claims that the "friendly Satyrist" merely provides parental correction:

> Doth one amisse, or doth the Child offend?
> Shall not the Fathers care correct that Child,
> First by perswasions kindly to amende,

> And gentle speeches, wordes with fauour milde?
> Will not this do, and shall he spare the body
> Of that faire Stripling? Go to, you are a noddy. (61–66)

Both poets suggest they are following common sense, performing an accepted method of discipline inherited from social custom. Guilpin, who underscores the rationality of his enterprise, articulates the very process of admonition that Travers envisions for congregational elders, who initiate the process of reform with private persuasion and, if the misbehavior continues, amplify the punishment.

Anticipating the satirist's claim to be writing for the public good, Weever notes that such fraternal correction (aside from his own) should remain in the private sphere:

> Want ye not loue, that with malignant spight,
> Vncouer'd all the fraile infirmities
> Of your weake brethren, to the wide worlds sight?
> Want ye not loue, that all men do despise,
> And would extort from others open shame,
> Your famous glorie and your glorious fame? (805–10)

During the Admonition Controversy and other debates over *adiaphora*, Puritan arguments often appropriated this scriptural commonplace, claiming that ceremonial aspects of church discipline threaten communal harmony by unduly testing the consciences of "weake brethren," but in a secular context the passage comes perilously close to accommodating moral delinquency. Rather than supporting stringent moral criteria, charity is enlisted to suppress any moral voice at all. Of course, Weever does not want to stifle all moral claims, just those that are not state-sponsored.

The real distinction between Weever's verse and the satire it critiques, then, is less a matter of method than it is of political authority. He suggests as much when, at the heart of his poem, he appeals to the statutory laws and royal prerogative as evidence of satire's misappropriation of power:

> Our noble Princesse (Lord preserue her Grace)
> Made godly laws to guide this Common-weale,

And hath appointed Officers in place,
By those her Lawes with each offence to deale:
Well look the rowles, no office ouerskippe,
And see if you can find the Satyrshippe. (577–82)

The stanza's final word could easily be misread as eldership, which would
fit the meter, and it seems relevant, as Weever's political conceit gestures
at Puritan dissent. He tacitly suggests that satirists threaten the alliance
between church and state knit together by "our noble Princesse," whose
royal prerogative underwrites the episcopal superstructure and ought
to stifle complaint (there is no mention of Parliament here). Of course,
Weever has already obtained the Satyrship for himself. Earlier in the poem
he asserts the primacy of state authority but only as a vehicle to legitimize
his own satiric function, which he claims for himself by way of ambivalent
syntax, when Church and Commonwealth "both assign'd, and bade me
streight prouide, / To take vp Satyre, and take down his pride" (149–50).
Does the Whipper apprehend (and take up) the *figure* of Satyre and humble
him, or does the Whipper assume (and take up) the *office* of Satyre in order
to humble him? It is difficult to tell. The fantasy of serving as state-licensed
satirist may seem far-fetched in the wake of the Marprelate controversy,
but perhaps no contemporary artist other than Jonson—who was busy
writing *Cynthia's Revels* and *Poetaster* at this time—is so audacious in associating his own satirical project with court sanction. Indeed, Weever,
supposedly an advocate for Puritan reform, goes further than Jonson by
suggesting that he speaks for the Church of England as well.[79]

Weever's ambition is not lost on Guilpin, who accuses his opponent of careerism, employing arguments similar to those levied at Jonson by Marston
and Dekker near the end of the Poet's War. What is fascinating, however,
is the manner in which that assumed careerism manifests itself. Guilpin
portrays Weever in the ceremonial accoutrement of the episcopacy, wearing a vestment, one of Elizabethan England's most incendiary topics of
the previous half-century: "And thus I argue, holding argument / Against
the proud aspiring insolent / Apparreld in an imbry vestament, / As if
within obliuions continent (38–41). Guilpin casts doubt on the integrity of
Weever's enterprise, portraying the Whipper as an ambitious, avaricious
establishment figure whose own political credentials are suspect, since

his previous offenses (presumably Weever's own satires and epigrams) require "oblivion" or legal amnesty. Lastly, "imbry," a phonetic misuse of almory or aumbry, which were church rooms or cupboards where charitable alms and sacramental vessels were stored, suggests that Weever is misappropriating funds that should be distributed to the poor.[80] Using a metaphor that evokes the problems of almsgiving as well as ecclesiastical pomp and circumstance, Guilpin insinuates that Weever is monopolizing charitable readings (as opposed to providing charitable relief) from within the church establishment to further his own private glory.

The charge is not an arbitrary one. In *The Whippinge*, Weever disparages the satirist's method as "the naked beggary of a thred-bare wit, / To get an almes of commendations by: / For each should earne the price of praise indeed, / And doing so, not one should need to need" (789–92). Weever states that satire should not rely on charity for its success, but rather should earn the reader's respect in the literary marketplace. So Guilpin responds in kind, interpreting Weever's corrective discipline as a type of currency for which he must offer a reciprocal exchange: "What so you chaunce to lend without request, / I will repay't with double interest" (239–40). Elsewhere Guilpin castigates Weever's role as a beadle, a menial parish official associated with the disciplinary features of poor relief:

> If this will then force a reformation,
> Why shall I feare to say a knaue's a knaue?
> What shall I stand in dread of coniuration,
> Because Vntrusse hath from his duskie Caue
>> Sent a leane writhen Beadle all in haste,
>> To lay the mantion of the Satyres waste. (217–22)

Here is the incredible optimism of a satirist who believes he can "force a reformation"; here too is the inherent violence of his method, which does not hesitate to hurl insults if they are truthful. "This" presumably refers to satire, since Guilpin has just dramatized a scene in which an erstwhile malefactor experiences a moral alteration after encountering the satirist. But Guilpin's message is clear: when it comes to reformation, the ends justify the means.

So, in this discourse about the proper method of charitable admonition, Breton argues that *who* articulates the need for reform—namely, the clergy—matters more than how it is expressed. Guilpin, after a nominal gesture toward charitable norms, eventually focuses solely on whether or not reformation occurs as a consequence. Neither writer fully engages the most forceful claims of Weever, who, despite his self-aggrandizing project, seems to recognize the complex issues at stake even if cogent expression sometimes escapes him. Weever critiques the satirist's intention (which he claims is glory rather than reform), attacks the satirist's method (which he claims is maliciously violent), and censures the satirist's inefficacy (since he claims that sin still exists). But all these claims are undercut by a pervasive irony. Weever's own intention is almost unapologetically ambitious, and his method of reform violently exposes private individuals to public shame. Given the prompt replies from Breton and Guilpin, the success of his reforming project remains dubious. Whether or not the irony is conscious seems inconsequential to the larger point: by participating in the phenomenon he critiques, Weever dramatizes the difficulty of balancing professional literary aspirations with entrenched social and political imperatives, as his satire simultaneously asserts and attempts to constrain the impact of published satire. He tries to fashion a paradigm in which the inventive self-promotion and caustic social critique inherent to Elizabethan satire might coexist comfortably within a communal framework, even if he must portray the imagined "Satyreship" as a dream vision. Consequently, the state authorities Weever purports to protect function more as an imposition, a constant reminder of the complicated negotiations involved in charitable norms.

FIGURE 4. Frans Floris, *Caritas with Children* (c. 1560). Panel, 156 × 107 cm. The State Hermitage Museum, St. Petersburg, Russia. Photograph © The State Hermitage Museum. Photo by Svetlana Suetova.

CHAPTER 3

CHARITABLE ALLEGORY

Figures of Love in Spenser's *Faerie Queene*

Thomas Churchyard composed a poetic treatise near the end of his long life entitled *Churchyards Charitie* that was, among other things, an elaborate plea by a destitute writer for charitable alms—not just charity *of* or *by* Churchyard but *for* him too. In general the poem is a study in clumsiness, which reaches its apogee in the prefatory epistle to Elizabeth, when the poet delivers what is surely one of the least elegant similes addressed to the queen during her rule:

> For as the hen, hir chickens keeps from kite
> So charitie, doth save hir children all
> From common plagues, and wicked worlds despite
> And all the wrath, that from the clouds can fall.
> She spreds hir wings, to keepe hir birds from cold
> And learns poor chicks, to picke vp grains of gold.
> This charitie, so checkles ore hir broode
> She scrapes the earth, to make hir young ones feed
> And freely from, hir selfe doth spare them foode
> She takes in hart, such care for those that neede.[1]

Shortly before this stanza Churchyard addresses the monarch directly, marking her as a figure of loving maternal rule and thus making the analogy explicit: just as the mother hen offers to the world an image of Charity personified, so too does Elizabeth. There is nothing wrong with the comparison as far as it goes, but certainly no one would confuse its scope and tone with the majesty of Milton's Spirit brooding dove-like on the abyss in *Paradise Lost*. One wonders, since Churchyard received his "grains of gold" in the form of a second pension in 1597, what exactly Elizabeth thought of being compared to a chicken, however charitable its feathers.[2]

Regardless of its blunders, Churchyard's effort is on point in one respect. From her inception as queen, Elizabeth had been understood in iconographic terms, as Astraea, for example, or Hope, as she was prominently displayed on the title page of the 1568 Bishops' Bible, with various royal stars in an allegorical constellation. This symbolic program originated with Elizabeth's 1559 coronation entry: during her procession from the Tower of London to Westminster, the queen encountered a series of elaborate pageants that constructed (quite literally) a spiritual and political apparatus by which she and everyone else were to understand her monarchy. These lessons culminated in a show of charitable mercy, when the queen encountered a young representative of Christ's Hospital standing at St. Dunstan's church. In Richard Mulcaster's account of the progress, the queen "did cast up her eyes to Heaven, as who should say 'I here see this merciful work toward the poor, whom I must in the midst of my royalty needs remember.'"[3] The moment is clearly significant to Mulcaster in revealing something intrinsic to the queen's character—he takes care to repeat the anecdote several pages later—and in his account Elizabeth's decorous attention prompts the child to recite a speech that declares the intertwined civic and royal legacies of London's hospitals:

> This one spectacle yet rested and remained, which was the everlasting spectacle of mercy unto the poor members of almighty God, furthered by that famous and most noble prince Henry the Eighth, her Grace's father, erected by the City of London, and advanced by the most godly, virtuous and gracious prince King Edward VI . . . doubting nothing of the mercy of the Queen's most gracious clemency by the which they may not only be relieved and helped, but also stayed and defended.[4]

Mulcaster and the pageant scenarists, aided by Elizabeth's own histri-
onic power, are writing for the queen a role in this "spectacle of mercy"
that mediates between heaven and earth, between city and court. In her
charismatic response to the poor, Elizabeth becomes a personification of
Charity, and as the heir to the Tudor throne she becomes patroness of the
city's charitable foundations, most fully figured in the poor children of
Christ's Hospital. Mary Tudor's conspicuous absence in this royal geneal-
ogy of Christ's Hospital's sponsorship might have been a pointed reference to her own accession day, when she notably snubbed the children,
but it offers as well the powerful lesson that charitable provision relies on
a reformed spirituality.[5] Elizabeth plays her part perfectly—and in fact she
later dispenses alms "toward the relief and comfort of the most poorest
persons within the city's hospitals"—but her symbolic gestures, looking
up to the heavens for instance, are governed by Mulcaster's interpretive
control, which he exerts throughout the textual narrative.[6] Mulcaster, in
other words, was not merely one of the authors of the pageant but also
its most significant reader, imparting from his privileged seat the inmost
thoughts that prompted Elizabeth's conduct, ensuring that the episode's
potent allegory remained orderly and legible.

A far different allegorical mode governed the 1606 entertainment at
Theobalds celebrating the royal visit by Christian IV of Denmark, brother-
in-law of King James, who arrived in England for a four-week stay over the
summer. After progressing from one royal residence to another, the two
kings eventually arrived at Theobalds, the home of Robert Cecil, Earl of
Salisbury. James Sutton provides a detailed examination of the monarchs'
four-day sojourn at Theobalds, noting in particular the complicated negotiations of Salisbury, soon to be dispossessed of his residence by the very
king he hosts, in struggling to honor the "expansive agency" of James by
establishing an appropriate tone of decorous welcome.[7] Featuring artistic
productions by Inigo Jones and Ben Jonson among others, Salisbury's entertainment attempted to underscore the impressive liberality of all the
important participants within a framework of sophisticated refinement,
establishing an atmosphere of extravagant abundance that remained carefully modulated by artistic control and well-mannered civility. But if love,
as contemporary observer John Savile notes, provided one of the central
themes of the revelry—love between kings and between brothers, a host's

love for his guests, a subject's love for his king, and the love of a king for his people—it also proved difficult to control.[8] The event is a compelling demonstration of the instability and dynamism of allegorical representation.

A final evening of revelry culminated in a lavish banquet to be accompanied by a masque or entertainment. The show, derived from 1 Kings 10, began with a presentation of gifts to the kings by the Queen of Sheba, intended to highlight the Solomonic image James had fashioned for himself, in addition to celebrating the international alliances present in Salisbury's residence and knit together by familial bonds of love. This sophisticated emblematic program was to be subsequently reinforced by the staged appearance of the theological virtues and concluded by a celebration featuring Peace and Victory. Something went wrong, however, as we know from Sir John Harington's famous anecdote of the occasion, written in a letter to Secretary Barlow. The first problem was Queen Anne's absence, since, as Sutton notes, the role of Queen of Sheba was intended for her as a public reintroduction to court after giving birth to her daughter Sophia, and a gesture of shared union with brother and husband.[9] The baby died almost immediately after being delivered, though, and Anne remained in a period of mourning. Her presence might have ensured decorum and deflated the erotic potential of the exchange. Instead the performer unceremoniously fell into the King of Denmark's lap, spilling an array of beverages and cakes and creams in the process. The physical intimacy of the uncontrolled encounter seemed to prompt a kind of sexual response from the Danish king, who scrambled to his feet for a dance with the Queen of Sheba but ended up merely joining her in tumbling to the floor, after which he was carried back to his room. All of this left James alone on his throne without wife or brother-in-law, and the masque continued to slip further into the morass:

> The Entertainment and show went forward, and most of the Presenters went back ward, or fell down; wine did so occupy their upper chambers. Now did appear, in rich dress, Hope, Faith, and Charity; Hope did assay to speak, but wine rendered her endeavours so feeble that she withdrew, and hoped the King would excuse her brevity. Faith was then all alone, for I am certain she was not joyned with Good Works, and left the Court in a staggering condition. Charity came

to the King's feet, and seemed to cover the multitude of sins her sisters had committed; in some sorte she made obeysance and brought giftes, but said she would return home again, as there was no gift which Heaven had not already given his Majesty. She then returned to Hope and Faith, who were both sick and spewing in the lower hall.

What ought to have been an orderly iconographic display of power and virtue erupts into farce, prompting Harington to remark, "I neer did see such lack of good order, discretion and sobriety."[10]

It is difficult to imagine a finer burlesque. There is reason to doubt the veracity of Harington's account, of course, but the report's authenticity seems less relevant than the satirical opportunity presented by staging the theological virtues in the first place.[11] The respective personifications give material life to complex abstractions, but in this case their meaning swerves in the wrong direction, complicated by the vagaries of courtly behavior. Consider how much Harington is able to accomplish merely by associating traditional Christian emblems with the "rich dress" and dissolute behavior of the court. Suddenly the entertainment's erstwhile allegory has the look of satire; the theological virtues have been compromised by their political and spiritual guarantors. As if to emphasize the incongruous alliance, Harington observes a paradoxical progress that involves presenters who "went back ward, or fell down" in order for the entertainment to go forward, dragging heavenly ideals down into the courtly cesspool. A simple pun reinforces the travesty—Hope, hopelessly drunk, hopes to be excused.[12]

Hope's ignominious exit provides occasion to make a brief but incisive religious commentary about faith and works, perhaps an allusion to James 2:20 ("Faith without works is dead") and certainly a curt mockery of reformed religion. The scriptural parody continues as Charity arrives at the feet of James, covering "the multitude of sins her sisters had committed" (and conjuring up 1 Peter 4:8) while placing the physical and figurative space of King James at the center of this spectacle: the throne is a mess, soiled by the Queen of Sheba's spill and additionally graced, perhaps, by the vomit of Hope and Faith, who have retired in sickness to the lower hall. These gifts, scattered across the floor on which she kneels to make obeisance, provide the context of Charity's short speech, which locates

Heaven's full bounty in the person of the monarch. The entire spectacle succinctly and spectacularly lampoons the presumed divinity of kingship. James seems to recognize the implications of this debauched exhibition, since he subsequently refuses to accept the climactic gift of Victory's sword, limiting his participation in the whole affair.

Both of these dramatic shows—Elizabeth's coronation entry and the spectacle at Theobold's—are layered with allegories in several senses of the word. Each deploys the compositional strategy or rhetorical device of *allegoria*—speaking *other* for some purpose—by using conventional iconographic representations of the virtues in an exemplary function, offering an embodied illustration of psychic or otherwise abstract principles. And each becomes a "continued Allegory, or darke conceit," as Spenser would call it, or a catalytic allegory to use Linda Gregerson's phrase, insofar as their narratives produce secondary meanings beyond their own specific histories, each character moving in a landscape fraught with significances.[13] Thus Elizabeth, in the city of London's heuristic program, becomes a living image of the English throne's merciful attention to the poor, while James, in his passive seat of authority, transforms into an involuntary lord of misrule. In both Mulcaster's and Harington's texts, meaning shuttles between the interior world—of texts and persons, of doctrinal beliefs and moral dispositions—and the external fields of religious, political, and social history. If Elizabeth's coronation entry demonstrates the symbolic power enacted by such ritual scenes of allegory, the drunken episode at Theobalds illustrates its dangers.

The early modern English were accustomed to constructing allegories of interpretation, performing various kinds of *allegoresis,* reading texts for a mystical significance, reading bodies for signs of virtue or vice, or reading astrological events for providential tokens of divine favor. But the interpretive process was often unruly, its meanings contested. As George Puttenham notes in *The Arte of English Poesy,* an allegory is incomplete by definition, its implications "left at large to the reader's judgment and conjecture."[14] For Elizabethan writers this device served several rhetorical purposes, prompting the reader to look for hidden figural meanings that evaded a simple logic of equation, and protecting the text from censure or scandal with its inherent obscurantism. But the practice also left writers and their texts vulnerable to the whims of an unpredictable reader. This is likely why Mulcaster chooses to wield such exegetical control in his account, mediating the reader's engagement with the performance and interpreting the figurative import behind each action, whereas Harington seems to derive pleasure in a matter-of-fact narration that gives his reader flexibility of interpretation. However exemplary its purpose, the production of allegory always threatens to commit as much parody as it does praise, particularly when its meanings are partially constructed by an unreliable interpreter. In the case of Theobalds, for example, the sloppy acting can stand in for similarly disordered reading, providing its own allegory of the problem of allegory, which is imperiled by the performances of malicious or maladroit readers negotiating the interpretive distance between literal and abstract worlds.

Depictions of the theological virtues were vulnerable to complications of this kind, and this chapter will focus on two points of tension associated with allegories of charity: the problems of sex and poverty, respectively. The concept of charity, involving both the love of God and the love of neighbor, proved troublesome to allegorize because of its dynamism. "Charity is not a symbolical precept," as Pascal observes, it must be doing to be itself, making the virtue more resistant to static iconography than most abstractions.[15] Love will not sit still—think of how Sidney's *New Arcadia* describes Urania ministering to a lamb in the picture captured by Phalantus, or how Bunyan's Mercy is "always busying of herself in doing"[16]—and every new action complicates the potential allegory. Actions, moreover, can be simulated by figures like Pope-Holy in *The Romaunt of the Rose*, who "semede to be ful ententyf / To gode werkis," and the threat of hypocrisy troubles representations of charity throughout the late medieval and early modern periods.[17] In *Piers Plowman*, Wille asks Anima where he might find Charity, but the advice he receives is disconcertingly obscure, complicated by false semblances. The authentic Charity is seen among various folk, moreover, wearing a range of clothes, but "by colour ne by cleargy, know shalt ye never / Nether through works or words, but throughe will one [only]."[18] For Langland, it seems, charity can be known only by personal experience. In *Pathomachia*, an allegorical play of the early Stuart period in which personified virtues, vices, and passions vie for ascendancy, Charity leaves the city to help the poor (since, as Justice observes, charity is never idle), but his absence allows Self-love to slip in and impersonate him. Justice sniffs out the ruse quickly, but the drama raises the question of whether a less perspicacious reader might confuse one for the other.

This reliance on embodied expression often pushed allegories of charity into the realm of erotic discourse. Two specific but related legacies that were influenced by Christian Neo-platonism are worth examining here on account of their emphasis on the female body. The first is an exegetical tradition developed and refined throughout the medieval period as a solution to the potential scandal of the Bible's Song of Songs, which describes in explicit detail the yearning for erotic union between two lovers. "Let him kiss me with the kisses of his mouth" the first line proclaims in the Geneva version. For medieval clerics a literal understanding of the Song threatened to tempt the reader into sexual arousal, whereas allegorical interpretations of the biblical text revealed the mysteries of divine love. Bernard insisted that such scriptural nourishment ("nuptial union with the divine partner") was not for "the novices, the immature, those but recently converted from a worldly life," echoing a concern of Origen, who worried that the uninitiated reader "turns everything he hears from its inner to its outer and bodily meaning and feeds in himself the desires of the flesh."[19] But an ascetic impulse, as Denys Turner notes, cannot explain the pervasive enthusiasm among medieval exegetes (or early modern readers) for the erotic imagery of the Song of Songs. Allegorizing the sexual imagery was not merely a solution to the song's explicit eroticism; rather, the sensual details forcibly convey the spiritual message of divine love in a way few other biblical texts could equal.[20] In William Baldwin's 1549 *Canticles, or Balades of Salomon*, for instance, the woman's breasts are clearly essential to the entire vision as a vehicle of charity: "Howe fayre thy Dugges, thy charitie is my Spouse, / My syster swete, more fayre they are than wyne"[21]

Meanwhile, the vexed iconographical tradition of personified charity (typically identified as Caritas), which evolved throughout the medieval and early modern periods, fused together secular and sacred representations of love. The conventional figure of Caritas that emerged by the time Cesare Ripa published his *Iconologia* in 1593, "a Woman all in red, a flame on the Crown of her Head, with an Infant sucking, in her left Arm, and two other standing up, one of which is embrac'd with the right," borrowed heavily from portrayals of Venus, which likewise involve a flaming torch and a suckling child.[22] These depictions of the theological virtue, which flourished throughout the Renaissance, gestured at the Song of Songs by featuring lactating breasts and often a kiss between mother and child. But visual representations of charity, which relied on the female body for symbolic power, were quick to assimilate classical Venusian imagery as well, even if these details sometimes produced a slight unease or tension. Caecilie Weissert has observed an emphasis on beauty rather than maternity among a number of Caritas paintings in the sixteenth century, noting (among several others) a work by Frans Floris, whose personified virtue is nearly fully nude, draped just barely in translucent yellow fabric with a red robe nearby, gesturing by way of color at both sacred and secular legacies; there are the three children of tradition, but none of them are nursing and each wears a chain that calls to mind the *vinculum amoris* or chain of love; and what appears to be a nuptial torch casts a dim light over the lush pillows of her bed.[23] Similarly composite representations of love are evident throughout the period in such various texts as *Hypnerotomachia Poliphili*, Ficino's *De Amore*, or, as we will see, Spenser's *Faerie Queene*. Both the exegetical and iconographical traditions illustrate the central role of the female body in allegories of charity: on the one hand, erotic imagery can be read as an earthly representation of divine love, and on the other, sensuous details can make visible the abstract qualities of charity.

These tensions between erotic and divine forms of love emerge throughout the early modern period in numerous depictions of charity, from Herbert's "quick-eyed Love" to Crashaw's "Flaming Heart." Consider an early moment in Sidney's *New Arcadia*, when Kalander escorts Musidorus, disguised as Palladius, into his pleasure garden, which features a statue of Venus nursing the baby Aeneas. The statue announces its classical origins even as it gestures at the traditional Marian iconography of *Virgo lactans* or of Charity nursing her several children. But the typical scene of Christian maternity is disrupted by the child's preference "to look upon her fair eyes which smiled at the babe's folly, the mean while the breast running," as if the young Aeneas has made a choice to prefer erotic enjoyment rather than divine nourishment, the earthly Venus rather than her celestial counterpart.[24]

Thomas Adams tries to baptize his portrait's eroticism by linking its iconography to the Song of Songs, fusing the two traditions mentioned

FIGURE 5. Cesare Ripa, *Iconologia: Or, Moral Emblems* (London: 1709). Fig. 46: Carita. The Rare Book &
Manuscript Library, University of Illinois at Urbana-Champaign.

above, which only intensifies the problem of *eros* even as it signals the need for allegorical interpretation: "Charity is a louely vertue, little innocents hang at her brests, Angels kisse her cheekes; *Her lips are like a threed of scarlet, and her speech is comely, her Temples are like a Pomegranate within her looks.*"[25] Robert Herrick, on the other hand, in "Upon Sibilla," transforms the image into a titillating rural scene featuring a bathing milkmaid:

> With paste of Almonds, *Syb* her hands doth scoure;
> Then gives it to the children to devoure.
> In Cream she bathes her thighs (more soft then silk)
> Then to the poore she freely gives the milke.[26]

The power of erotic imagery to symbolize a transcendent union with the divine could easily be literalized into a scene of sexual arousal. But the embodied feminine features that made these allegories susceptible to erotic interpretation were also a source of power, giving the transcendent features of divine love real flesh and blood.

Images of neighborly love, particularly almsgiving or other merciful gifts, proved to be equally fertile matter for writers of amatory verse. In Fulke Greville's lyric riff on an old jestbook tradition, Scoggins is cuckolded by a noble lord, "who nobly pitying this poor woman's hap, / Gave alms both to relieve, and to delight, / And made the golden shower fall on her lap."[27] Mistress Low-water, in Thomas Middleton's *No Wit, No Help Like a Woman's*, calls gifts of this kind "such hot charity, which indeed is lust," and John Webster characterizes Brachiano's sexual advances in *The White Devil* with similar irony.[28] Richard Niccols includes in one of his epigrams the "Charitie" of a gentleman who gives "almes" to the adulterous wives of elderly men, and so "the horne of plentie growes."[29] Richard Lovelace plays on this theme as well in "The Faire Begger," declaring to his potential pauper-cum-mistress, "So both our wants supplied shall be, / You'l give for love, I, Charity." Later he takes advantage of a familiar scriptural formula from 1 Peter 4:8—charity's capacity to cover a multitude of sins—to extend the parody further: "Ill cover thee with mine owne selfe."[30] The image of charity as a knot that binds communities together could be sexualized too, turned into a knot of coupling. This parodic impulse becomes such a commonplace that "charity" has earned its own entry in a scholarly dictionary of sexual language from the period.[31]

The confusion of charity and sex provided writers with an opportunity for moral commentary or satire. The entertainment at Theobalds, for example, is complicated and intensified by its eroticism, which expresses by way of allegory Harington's more general political critique. In religious polemic, meanwhile, charity could serve as an ironic token of hypocrisy, avarice, or lust, and sometimes all three at once, as in the satirical poems by John Cleveland and Henry Tubbe that gleefully depict Puritan ministers receiving "provision" from "the common of the female charity" and "woemens charitie," respectively.[32] Richard Brathwaite describes "many zealous sempring sister[s]" who show how they "loue their brother, from their heart iffaith / For it is charity, as scripture saith" by visiting the beds of their Puritan "brothers."[33] Strategies of this kind, which had their origins in medieval anticlerical satire, had been honed to a fine edge in anti-Catholic polemic before they were applied to nonconformists.

For all its propagandistic control, Mulcaster's text, with its focus on charitable giving, is not as simple as it would seem either, particularly when read through the retrospective lens of history. Elizabeth's explicit association with Christ's Hospital, which seems to give the institution representative status in her larger magistracy, places a great deal of stress on the hospital's functional efficacy. Because the Reformation had dissolved many of England's traditional sources of hospitality and almsgiving, the charitable works performed or imagined by either Protestants or Catholics acquired inescapably polemical resonances, placing additional pressures on available expressions of piety. The various civic innovations in poor relief initiated by reformers, London's hospitals in particular, were promoted as emblems of a reformed church, signaling its proper devotion to the "relief, comfort and helping of the poor and impotent people . . . and not to the maintenance of canons, priests and monks, to live in pleasure; nothing regarding the miserable people lying in every street."[34] In *Actes and Monuments*, John Foxe includes a farewell letter from Nicholas Ridley, written shortly before he was burned during the Marian regime, which celebrates London's recent provision for the poor, praising (with ironic emphasis) "the erection and setting up of Christ's holy hospitals, and truly religious houses," calling them a "perfect spectacle of true charity and godliness unto all Christendom."[35] By displacing Catholic monasteries and chantries—Christ's Hospital, for example, was a repurposing of the suppressed Greyfriars building—the London hospitals heralded a new Protestant approach to poor relief. Note how they function in Ridley's phrase not merely as a site of provision but also as an object of display, a spectacle, serving a representative as well as distributive role in the reformed project of charity.

Poverty would nevertheless prove an administrative bugbear throughout Elizabeth's reign, putting in doubt the corporate sanctity of Protestant England. In continuing to refine earlier Tudor efforts at discriminate poor relief, the statutory policies enacted by a string of Elizabethan parliaments did their best to ensure that neither the queen nor anybody else would be addressed again in oratory by members of the able-bodied poor, and in fact the Poor Act of 1598 tried to do away with begging altogether. But the statutes were relatively ineffective at mitigating the effects of population growth, economic stagnation, and periodic crises of plague and dearth. The apparent increase in vagrants, sturdy beggars, ex-soldiers, peddlers, and other members of the itinerant poor proved a scandal to the commonweal, according to moralists and social critics, in part because they seemed to embody evidence of divine disfavor—with episcopacy, with Protestantism, or with England in general. If a well-functioning hospital could function as an institutional allegory for the charitable provision of the English monarch, vagrant bodies throughout the country undermined the allegorical power of the English hospital and the English nation.

So, while Thomas Cranmer sneered at Roman Catholic charitable practices, which favored, at the expense of the poor, "pardons, pilgrimages, trentals, decking of images, offering of candles, giving to friars and upon other like blind devotions," the Jesuit Robert Persons mocked the reformers' "new fownde charitie of a new fownd gospel," which he believed was incapable of maintaining "that hospitalitie for the poore, whiche was wont."[36] William Allen, too, used the putative absence of charity to cast doubt on England's communal aspirations to achieve a godly state: "Say but then vnto them by the words of S. Iames. Maister Protestaunt, let me haue a sight of your onely faith, with out good workes: and here lo, beholde mine and spare not, by my good workes."[37] It is no surprise, then, that William Fulke's rebuttal of Allen invokes the recent poor laws of 1572 and 1576 as evidence of England's sanctified credentials:

> Shew me M. *Allen* if thou canst for thy gutts, or name me any city in the world, where popery preuayleth, that hath made such prouision for the fatherlesse children and widowes and all other kind of poore, as is in the noble city of London and in diuers other cities and townes of this land, and by publike law appoynted to be throughout all the realme of England.[38]

Whether or not England was a nation of committed and godly Calvinists, it certainly intended to justify itself by charitable works, or at least, as Fulke continues, "to iustifie our profession against the Papistes." Thomas Adams similarly declares, in rebuking recusant Catholics, "Impudence it selfe cannot denie, but our Charitie is greater than theirs."[39]

Other Church of England divines, less blithe about the status of charitable giving among Protestants, worried that Catholics might "grind the face of our Religion, to say Religion and Charitie were at one time thrust out of this Kingdome."[40] These apologies for English charity—and the attacks that spawned them—continued to characterize religious polemic between English Protestants and Roman Catholics throughout the succeeding generations, from Andrew Willet's determined efforts to record all of England's charitable gifts in *Synopsis papismi* to the scornful dismissal of England's hospitals, especially in comparison to the Annunziata in Naples or the Hospital of San Spirito in Rome, by the Jesuit Matthew Wilson (alias Edward Knott) in *Mercy and Truth. Or Charity Maintayned by Catholics*.[41] For both Roman Catholics and Protestants, institutional forms of charity and their specific material gifts became emblems of the larger commonwealth's collective piety.

A similarly fraught interpretive movement between the literal and spiritual planes of charity occurred among private persons in England, or at least its Protestant subjects, who had become the privileged interpreters not merely of scripture but of their own pious actions as well. Reformed doctrine mitigated the role of charitable works in acquiring salvation, which was reserved for the justifying power of Christ's atonement, but in practical terms, Protestant theology displaced the salvific power of charity with a hermeneutic responsibility—charity no longer effected salvation but instead allowed individual believers to *read* their elect status. In a Reformed tradition that was "soft on assurance," as Paul Cefalu notes, English Protestants were encouraged to find comfort by "diligence and study" of their own virtuous behavior.[42] Thomas Cranmer's "Homily on Faith" in *The Book of Common Prayer*, for example, exhorts the individual Christian to find in his or her piety a signifier of faith: "Be sure of your faith, try it by your living, look upon the fruits that cometh of it, mark the increase of love and charity by it towards God and your neighbor, and so shall you perceive it to be a true lively faith."[43] Here Cranmer deploys an image Tyndale, John Frith, and other early reformers appropriated from scripture—the tree known by its good or bad fruits from Matthew 12 and Luke 7—to explain his theology of justification. John Foxe memorably highlights the subject in *Actes and Monuments* by including "Patrick's Places," some brief notes by the early reformer Patrick Hamilton that treat good works as if they were the middle term of a syllogism: "Faith maketh the good tree, and incredulity the evil tree: such a tree, such fruit; such a man, such works."[44] In another example of the practical syllogism privileged by reformers, Theodore Beza reminds his readers, "Trew faith is geven to the chosen sort onely, Ergo onely the elect doo repent and geve themselves to good workes."[45]

In these discussions of assurance, charitable works function by way of synecdoche, standing in for the entire body of a faithful life. But they also assume an allegorical status, as material signs gesturing at what would otherwise remain a veiled abstraction, providing embodied evidence of divine election. Like Elizabeth's gift to the poor, each charitable work becomes an emblematic action in what amounts to "a spectator view of morality."[46] Indeed, this is for William Perkins "one of the chiefest uses of good woorkes, that by them, not as by causes, but as by effects of predestination and Faith, both we, and also our neighbours, are certified of our election, and of our salvation."[47] Perkins is careful not to ascribe any causal power to good works, but it is easy to see how charity of this kind, such a key feature of Protestant doctrine, can slip easily into the very sort of instrumentalism Protestants abhorred in works theology. In fact Puritans, who often accused conformists of Papist ritualism, were sometimes forced to defend themselves against charges of Papism—or "merit-mongering"—as a result of their emphasis on practical piety.[48] Protestant good works could quickly metamorphose from allegorical emblem into blasphemous idol, depending on one's perspective.

Charity, in other words, was bound up in all sorts of vexed relations between the body and soul, a spiritual condition that could easily be eroticized and satirized, as well as a material action that could be invested with (or emptied of) spiritual significance. Like translation and admonition, as discussed in previous chapters, these allegorical treatments of charity highlight the problems of reading. The fruits of charity were easy to mistake, prone to hypocrisy, located in close proximity to erotic desire, and always vulnerable to spiritual and political instrumentalism. As Francis Quarles notes several decades later, charity is constantly shuttling between the dual imperatives of faith and love—its "nature doth confound / And mixe the former two"—and as a consequence struggles to "move / In proper motion."[49] This had always been the case with charity, of course, but the religious landscape in Elizabethan England raised the stakes, demanding that some kind of interpretive claim be attached to each vision of charity even as the meanings of the concept became less stable, more unruly.

Visions of Charity in *The Faerie Queene*

These two different kinds of troubled allegories of charity form a diptych that will govern the rest of this chapter's discussion of *The Faerie Queene*. In Book 1, Canto 10, of the epic poem, the wearied and troubled knight Redcrosse is guided by his companion Una to the House of Holinesse, so that he might recover his spiritual purpose and prepare for his ensuing apocalyptic battle with the Dragon. In this allegorical space, Edmund Spenser, much like the city of London, erects a "holy Hospitall," which has as its "founderesse" Charissa, a beautiful woman in a gleaming tiara who bears a resemblance to Elizabeth.[50] By choosing to personify and institutionalize charity in his legend of holiness, and by doing so in a manner that calls attention to the contemporary political and social landscape, Spenser confronts two simultaneous threats to allegorical representations of charity: its potential association with erotic desire and its tacit reminder of the failures among English institutions to relieve the poor. But he responds to these pressures in different ways. The problem of Charissa's body, described in sumptuous detail, is deferred until Redcrosse experiences a comprehensive penitential regimen that cures his body and spirit, just as those untutored monks had to postpone reading the Song of Songs until they had demonstrated a requisite mastery of biblical exegesis. Spenser's engagement with poor relief, meanwhile, ignores contemporary Protestant shibboleths, moving back to a sphere of loving action broad enough to accommodate potentially even a works theology.

These pressures from the material world are intrinsically linked to Redcrosse's own allegorical identity as the personification of holiness, which must be lived out in the realm of experience with all its concomitant dangers. As Joseph Campana has aptly noted, "Redcrosse's virtue is not his struggle against the flesh but his struggle to be flesh and not an empty allegorical body: an emblem of righteousness."[51] But early on in his career fleshly bodies persistently confound the knight, who often confuses or overrates bodily identity, power, and desire. Redcrosse seems predisposed to invest the flesh with the wrong kind of meaning and power. In the House of Holinesse, Charissa's insistent embodiment reminds the reader of these earlier trials that flummox Redcrosse: the attraction of romance, the dangers of self-justifying merit, the easy slippage into error, and the desire for erotic union. If her sisters are best allegorized by accessory symbols, by what they are holding (e.g., a serpent or anchor), Charissa's primary symbolic weight is borne by her body itself, her interaction with the material world signified by her fertility, the reality of her generative sexuality.

Charissa's physical beauty and maternal generosity is a matter of convention, of course, but Spenser folds this legacy into an allegorical romance during which the putative hero repeatedly falls victim to trials of the flesh, and the poet notably delays Redcrosse's encounter with a woman "of wondrous beauty . . . goodly grace and comely personage" (1.10.30). Even when he offers a positive allegory of charity, Spenser reminds readers of her perverse cousins elsewhere in the work, Errour and Duessa in particular, underscoring how closely the actions of self-love and lust mirror a life of authentic holiness. The likeness between Charissa and her demonic analogues, in other words, represents the possibility of loving in the wrong fashion, confusing erotic for agapic love. Spenser's

treatment of Charissa, as well as his depiction of Redcrosse's erotic temptations throughout Book 1, emphasizes the need to adopt a "carefull" posture in reading or performing charitable works, which Spenser repeatedly
frames as "dear love."

A different kind of challenge confronts readers of Charissa's holy hospital, who are tempted to link the material giving depicted in this episode
to a kind of spiritual instrumentalism. By framing charitable works as a
"ready path" (1.10.33) to heaven, and by apparently associating mercy with
supererogatory merit, Spenser invites readers to make the same accusation Envie levies at almsgivers earlier in the House of Pride, that charity
often serves as a salvific replacement for faith rather than an organic out-
growth of its presence. Envie is a malicious reader who inverts the conventional theological formula practiced by Protestants: an act of charity,
far from embodying the fruits of faith, actually signifies faith's absence.
If Spenser's treatment of Charissa registers his discomfort with the erotic
trials of romance, the holy hospital acknowledges that religious polemic
might pose an equally hazardous obstacle to charity by threatening to
undermine or warp good works of any kind. The poet's vision of institu-
tionalized giving gestures at theological controversies of the period, but
he purposely obscures the confessional differences between Protestant
and Roman Catholic approaches to charity, using the operative functions
of Charissa, Mercie, and the "seuen Bead-men" (1.10.36) to demonstrate
that a rich and fruitful life of holiness forces even a rigorous Protestant
into uncomfortable proximity with Roman Catholicism, thus making the
charitable giver vulnerable to accusations of Papism.

Spenser invites this association by including obvious traces of medieval
monasticism throughout the House of Holinesse, which has generated
a great deal of scholarly consternation about the dubious role of charity
in the episode and its residual hints of Catholicism. It seems odd, for example, that Spenser chooses a type of monastic piety as the primary distinguishing characteristic of the house's presiding matron, Cælia:

> Whose onely ioy was to relieue the needs
> Of wretched soules, and helpe the helpelesse pore:
> All night she spent in bidding of her bedes,
> And all the day in doing good and godly deedes. (1.10.3)

For many readers Cælia bears an uncomfortable likeness to a Roman Catholic abbess, and the description of Redcrosse's progress through her house encourages this sort of reading: he endures ashes and sackcloth from Patience, as well as fierce corporal discipline from Amendment and Penance, and after he encounters the seven beadsmen of Charissa's hospital, whose personification of the corporal works of mercy gestures at a meritorious works theology, Redcrosse converses with an ascetic hermit. However much readers wish to assign these characteristics merely allegorical status, as C.S. Lewis does when he declares that "all allegories whatever are likely to seem Catholic to the general reader," there they are, confronting the reader one way or the other.[52] James Kearney offers a more nuanced approach by contending that Spenser employs an iconoclastic poetics here, reclaiming and repurposing the language and forms of English history, employing "the Catholic associations of these old forms precisely in order to mislead his readers," who need to purify their devotional habits.[53] In Kearney's reading, the House of Holinesse becomes less a spiritual oasis than an additional temptation for Redcrosse and the reader, and the charitable works the knight receives and performs become an additional interpretive trial of the canto and ostensibly a potential threat to holiness.

This chapter offers a slightly different reading of the House of Holinesse and its vision of charity. The canto's explicit references to Catholicism cannot be explained away by merely noting their allegorical status; Kearney is surely right to find in Spenser's allegory an uneasiness with its own mode of representation, which calls attention to the dangers of idolatrous reading. But Kearney might be too ready to find in Spenser a desire for transcendence. Spenser does not merely "[tarry] with the letter in order to transcend it," but rather returns again and again to the necessary work of material action.[54] As Patrick Cullen has observed of the House of Holinesse, steeping oneself in otherworldly virtues like faith and hope offers its own kind of temptation, one that is countered "only by rooting them in the worldly virtue of charity."[55] The canto dramatizes a constant process of recalibration: Redcrosse's initial progress through the House trains him to read textual bodies in a spiritual register, to reorient his understanding of love; but after he encounters Charissa, the knight of holiness is redirected back to the world of material giving, and in the process, back into the contentious sphere of religious politics. This "godly worke of Almes and charitee" (1.10.45) facilitates a revelatory experience on the Mount of Contemplation, at which point he is sent down to struggle again in performing the task of holiness.

Charity, in Spenser's vision, perpetually cycles between spiritual and material realities, a movement that is especially imperiled earlier in the legend of holiness. By resembling warped forms of love that threatened earlier to disrupt Redcrosse's quest for holiness, Charissa and her holy hospital offer important correctives to related but distinct problems of interpretation: the expression of spiritual faith by way of material gifts and bodies can easily be confused with erotic desire or accused of hypocrisy. The problem of charity, moreover, sets into sharper relief the task that confronts an allegorical project aimed at producing ethical reform among its readers. Reliant on symbolic narrative in which bodies stand in for complex ideas, *The Faerie Queene*'s depiction of charity reminds us that the earthly realm of flesh and blood might need to be redeemed and reformed, but it cannot be left behind. This challenge is perhaps all the more pressing for a Protestant allegorist participating in a tradition that had replaced much of the church's sacramental life, whereby signs effected what they signified, with a scriptural focus that made reading one of the primary modes of spiritual transformation.

We are still learning how to interpret Spenser's allegorical poetics, how to read such a textured, multivalent, self-referential, conflicted text. But Spenser, of course, knew quite well "how doubtfully all Allegories may be construed," how readers might find his meanings, "clowdily enwrapped in Allegorical deuices," obscure or downright "displeasant" (714–16). As Kenneth Gross notes, Spenser foregrounds the vulnerability of his own text, acknowledging that "the necessary hiddenness of meaning in the poem is the very thing that leaves it open to the threat of violation by willful or slanderous misinterpreters."[56] The poet reinforces this danger by introducing Errour as the first threat encountered by the reader in the *Faerie Queene*. Spenser knew, moreover, or he seemed to know—if we take seriously his depiction of Archimago as a kind of allegorist, or image-maker, as well as a vagrant or "faytor false" (1.12.35)—that his own compositional method, with its capacity for disguise, invites skepticism or even antagonism. In other words, Spenser took seriously the weaknesses of his own project, even as he understood the challenges posed by allegory to be essential for reforming moral behavior, or for fashioning a noble person "in vertuous or gentle discipline" (714). By facilitating movement between letter and figure, shuttling between body and spirit, allegory itself embodies that crucial but complex enterprise of charity, linking faithful purpose with loving action and investing material gifts with spiritual devotion. This is "endlesse worke" (4.12.1) indeed.

Charissa and the Chain of Theological Virtues

Readers, shortly after they have reached the tenth canto of Spenser's first book, might be tempted to ask the same question Una poses early on in the episode: where is Charissa? One would expect to encounter in the House of Holinesse all three theological virtues of faith, hope, and charity together. Instead, Redcrosse, still recovering from a harrowing encounter with Despair and escorted by an attentive Una to and through the House, meets only Fidelia and Speranza, whose initial entry is marked by a shared purpose and commonality:

> Loe two most goodly virgins came in place,
> Ylinked arme in arme in louely wise,
> With countenance demure, and modest grace,
> They numbred euen steps and equall pace. (1.10.12)

The virgins, walking in perfect harmony with their arms linked together, suggest that a comprehensive unity exists between the two theological virtues, recalling the opening stanza of Canto 9 and its "goodly golden chayne, wherewith yfere / The vertues linked are in lovely wize." Note that a charitable affection links the two together "in louely wise"—that is, in a loving manner, or even in loving wisely—but when Una asks after their sister Charissa (Is she unwell? Is she busy?), they reply in unison:

> Ah no, said they, but forth she may not come:
> For she of late is lightned of her wombe,
> And hath encreast the world with one sonne more,
> That her to see should be but troublesome. (1.10.16)

Why does Spenser remove Charissa from the episode, postponing Redcrosse's encounter with charity in its fleshed-out allegorical form? What about charity is "troublesome"?

From a doctrinal perspective, a Church of England adherent would naturally promote the precedence of faith, as John King notes in his succinct explanation for Spenser's odd formulation: "Fidelia's seniority as the eldest sister exemplifies the subordination of charity to faith in line with the dictum in the *Book of Homilies* that 'true faith doth give life to the works.'"[57] But surely this could easily have been handled in a manner that placed Charissa among the sisters, or at least in one that called less attention to her detachment from the entire scene.

This is in fact a startling departure from contemporary Protestant depictions of the three theological virtues, which emphasized their inseparability and consequently allowed faith to prompt and govern all virtuous Christian action. Patrick Hamilton, so Foxe tells us in *Actes and Monuments,* was martyred by Roman authorities in Scotland for (among other articles) the heresy that "faith, hope, and charity be so linked together, that one of them cannot be without another in one man, in this life."[58] More than a century later an anxious Lettice Cary, Vi-Countess Falkland, still presumed this linkage to be an essential feature of the theological virtues, noting that "they are all links of one chain, if any one link be taken off, the chain is quite broken."[59] Moreover, by claiming that the virtues "are so knytte togither, that by no meanes they may bee separated," as Heinrich Bullinger insists, Protestants could rebut Catholics who accused them of abandoning charity altogether.[60] Separating the virtues, on the other hand, was an occasional Roman Catholic tactic in contemporary religious debates about justification theologies. In the published disputation between the imprisoned Jesuit Edmund Campion and various Church of England divines, a debate over justification *sola fide* hinges on the Protestant insistence that all three theological virtues are inseparable, or as John Walker claims in Spenserian language, "that fayth, hope, and charitie are coupled and lincked together."[61] Campion, on the other hand, assents to justification by faith but claims that hope and charity are equal and "distinct giftes" of divine grace, and consequently causes of justification as well. This is the sort of theological opportunism or "sleight" (as William Charke notes of Campion) associated with Jesuit casuistry that the archdeacon George Withers vilifies in *A view of the marginal notes of the popish Testament,* in which he responds to a note from Galatians 3:7: "So when it may serue your turne, things inseparable as true faith, hope, and charitie must be separated."[62]

Far from ensuring an orthodox Protestant reading, then, Spenser's separation of Charissa from her sister virtues leaves open the possibility that charity's operative sphere remains distinct from the justifying work of faith. Perhaps this explains why so many scholars have argued that Spenser gestures at a merit-based works theology in the latter half of Canto 10. Other scholars, who assume (quite plausibly) that Redcrosse is in fact Charissa's newborn child, invite additional theological complications by suggesting that the knight's spiritual regeneration has in fact been initiated by charity.[63] Charitable works had always proved "troublesome" to Protestant theology, but as many of Spenser's contemporaries would have observed, it is easier to subordinate charity to faith if the two virtues exist in close proximity. This is one reason why Tyndale and Frith and other reformers use the scriptural image of a tree, rooted in faith with fruits of charity, to reconcile and bind together the two concepts. Richard Younge, not content with a single biblical metaphor, offers a list of conjoined items that might represent the inseparability of faith and love, from fire and heat to the sun and its light.[64] Spenser, on the other hand, seems intent on separating charity from her sister virtues, ostensibly breaking the adamantine Protestant chain linking charity to faith and hope, even at the risk of associating his exposition of holiness with Roman Catholicism.

I mention these theological issues to underscore how Charissa's separation from her sisters threatens to disrupt the canto's allegorical program, how the strategy invites as much controversy as it dispels. But Spenser's choice to delay Redcrosse's encounter with Charissa makes more sense if we focus on the project of allegorical reading. Holy living requires holy reading, as Spenser makes clear by assigning Errour to the first canto, but at this point in the narrative Redcrosse remains mired in a hermeneutic of the flesh. And as Spenser explicitly states later in the poem, figures of love seem especially vulnerable to misinterpretation: "the baser wit, whose idle thoughts always / Are wont to cleaue vnto the lowly clay, / It stirreth vp to sensuall desire, / And in lewd slouth to wast his carelesse day" (3.5.1). For Redcrosse, who has yet to become "chaste in work and will" (1.10.30), it would be "troublesome" indeed to encounter a fully fleshed vision of personified charity, whose features by tradition are associated with erotic imagery. By insisting on the realities of pregnancy, Spenser brings Charissa's embodied presence to the foreground even as he confines her to a different allegorical space, one marked by a threshold Redcrosse cannot cross until he has been purged by Patience of "Inward corruption . . . / . . . Close creeping twixt the marow and the skin" (1.10.25).

This penitential sequence acquires even greater importance when Spenser finally introduces Charissa in a stanza that foregrounds her sensuality:

> She was a woman in her freshest age,
> Of wondrous beauty, and of bountie rare,
> With goodly grace and comely personage,
> That was on earth not easie to compare.
> Full of great loue, but *Cupids* wanton snare
> As hell she hated, chaste in worke and will;
> Her necke and brests were euer open bare,
> That ay thereof her babes might sucke their fill;
> The rest was all in yellow robes arrayed still. (1.10.30)

Unlike the ethereal Cælia or safely virginal sisters Fidelia and Speranza, Charissa is a fertile, procreative woman, and there is an openness about her, a physical frankness. She bears more than a superficial resemblance to Duessa—note even the similarity of their names—and both are described as wearing sumptuous apparel. They both possess a "comely personage," too, a phrase taken from the Geneva Bible's translation of 1 Corinthians 13 but deeply ambivalent in the Spenserian lexicon.[65] Spenser is aware of the dangers in characterizing charity in this manner. Charissa's erotic potential is bound within the protected sanction of marriage, a typical Protestant strategy, although the spouse (presumably Christ) remains anonymous and absent. When the poet declares that Charissa is "full of great love," he immediately reminds readers that "Cupid's wanton snare / as hell she hated," but Spenser's anxiety over Charissa's relative chastity belies the legacies he has chosen to deploy. Indeed, as Robert Reid observes, the House of Holinesse possesses more than a superficial likeness to medieval courts of love, and Charissa's antipathy for Cupid merely reinforces the comparison, which James Nohrnberg states precisely: "Even though she hates Cupid's snare as she hates hell, she fosters in her progeny the Christian form of that emotion which she otherwise reprehends."[66] Moreover, as Kathryn Walls notes, Spenser's reference to Redcrosse as Charissa's "vnacquainted guest" gestures in heavily sexualized language "to his contrasting 'acquaintedness' (cf. vna-cquainted) with Una."[67] Spenser not only engages the erotic implications of charity but makes them a central feature of his allegory.[68]

Certainly not all readers will agree with this assessment. Sheila Cavanagh, for example, claims that Spenser keeps Charissa "distanced from sexuality," and Gail Kern Paster remains equivocal, observing that Spenser "allows Charissa's breasts to be beautiful, and maternal, and perhaps even erotic."[69] Maybe I am overstating the case. But Spenser was participating in an iconographical tradition that acknowledged its own latent eroticism and that offered a powerful figure of the virtue's fruitful powers even as it posed challenges to Christian readers. Spenser's purposeful separation of Charissa from her sisters nods at Bernard's and Origen's admonitions to uninitiated readers of the Song of Songs, underscoring the requisite caution needed before engaging personified charity.

With this perspective in mind, consider Redcrosse's introduction to Charissa:

> [Redcrosse] they to *Vna* brought:
> Who ioyous of his cured conscience,
> Him dearely kist, and fairely eke besought
> Himselfe to chearish, and consuming thought
> To put away out of his carefull brest.
> By this *Charissa*, late in child-bed brought,
> Was waxen strong, and left her fruitfull nest;
> To her fayre *Vna* brought this vnacquainted guest. (1.10.29)

When readers encounter that simple prepositional phrase Spenser casually inserts as a transitional device—"By this Charissa"—they are encouraged to fill out the line by inserting the word "time," assuming it possesses a temporal function: "By this *time* Charissa . . . was waxen strong."[70] The previous stanzas, which detailed the long and painful penitential regimen Redcrosse endured, encourage this interpretation. But the explicit meaning suggests that the preposition refers to agency or means, that Charissa "was waxen strong" (as opposed to waxing cold) *by* Una's dear kisses and her fair remarks, which persuade her knight "himselfe to chearish," and more generally by Redcrosse's "cured conscience."[71] This reading ascribes a kind of causality to the work of Fidelia and Speranza, too, bringing the sisters into a closer Protestant embrace, but more generally the stanza emphasizes the importance of careful process.

Note, for instance, Redcrosse's newly "carefull brest." After the knight's spiritual amendment, readers are tempted to imagine him subsequently living free of care, having salved his anguished conscience and ensured his sanctified credentials. Aside from Scudamour's memorable predicament later in the house of Care, however, Spenser places more value in being full of care than being free of it. The lewd dream that interrupts Redcrosse's "carelesse sleepe" at the end of Canto 1 is instructive here, as is his lascivious encounter with Duessa at the start of Canto 7, "Both carelesse of his health, and of his fame" (1.7.6). Duessa herself falls into a "careless swowne" after Redcrosse defeats Sansfoy, and elsewhere in the poem the behavior of Idleness, Cymochles, Phaedria, and Blandamour are linked to the modifier. Perhaps the greatest apologist for carelessness in Book 1, Despair counters Redcrosse's fierce invocation of justice by claiming the superior obligations of mercy, observing that he offers errant knights a beneficent euthanasia based on a travesty of Epicureanism: "let him die of ease" (1.9.38), free of perturbation or care. Meanwhile a range of positive characters in Book 1 are described as "carefull," among them the faithful dwarf, Una, Satyrane, Arthur, and, tellingly, both Charissa and Mercie. Perkins, highlighting the crucial role of care in his discussion of conscience, notes that in a newly repentant Christian "there must follow watchfulnesse, and a carefull circumspection ouer all his waies."[72] Before he encounters the comely personage of Charissa, Redcrosse needs to cultivate more careful habits of reading, a preference for spiritual truths before fleshly temptations, and the patience to look for allegorical meanings beyond the superfice.

The distinction between "carelesse" and "carefull" behavior plays a similarly important role in a later episode of *The Faerie Queene*, one that involves another maternal figure who represents divine or human love. In Book 4, Canto 2, Spenser introduces the "fay" Agape, using the Greek term to signal her allegorical status as a personification of Christian love, which is reinforced by the trinitarian love embodied by her triad of sons. The episode is remarkably perplexing, an interpretive trial that stands out even among the other labyrinthine allegories of Book 4, but attention to "care" helps to clarify Spenser's project. Agape's children are the product of a violent rape by a wandering knight that occurs when the fay "sate carelesse by a cristall flood" (4.2.45). Likely intended as an allegory of productive strife, the sudden erotic violence in an otherwise tightly structured etiology of agapic love is unsettling, and it is further complicated by the implicit suggestion that the fay's carelessness invited the assault.[73] Once Agape becomes a mother, however, she intervenes with the Fates, pleading for an extended life for her sons, and she wins a kind of compromise by having them grant a concession whereby each son's life is transferred to the next. Agape's new maternal role is marked by a change in modifier; "carelesse" no longer, "then that carefull Fay / Departed thence with full contented mynd" (4.2.53). Returning home, she commands her sons to "loue each other deare" (4.2.53). There is a close connection between careful living and dear loving.

Surprisingly, Agape's loving behavior receives a stern rebuke from the narrator, which makes the episode all the more confounding, but there are significant overlaps between her actions and the posture of Charissa and her "carefull Nourse" Mercie. Like Agape, "carefull" Mercie is presented as an advocate who appears "before the maiestie diuine, / And his auenging wrath to clemencie incline" (1.10.51), although her intervention receives the unqualified approbation of Contemplation. In the case of Charissa, Spenser circumscribes her eroticism even as he calls attention to it, enacting his own "carefull" engagement with charity and clarifying for Redcrosse the sort of honor to which his love should aspire during his quest to fulfill "that royal maides bequeathed care" (1.10.63). In each of these situations, "care" seems necessary to the enterprise of loving responsibly, a difficult endeavor that involves a host of complications, not least the human capacity to mistake love and lust.

Recuperating Dearness

When Redcrosse and Una are reunited after the knight's penitential regimen in the House of Holinesse, Spenser places Una's "dear" kisses, reminiscent of the Song of Songs, in close proximity to Redcrosse's "care-full" breast, calling attention to the compatibility of these two words. By associating both actions with the emergence of Charissa, moreover, Spenser brings nearly to a close Redcrosse's long and troubled history with "dear love." Spenser is an heir of Tyndale's scriptural lexicon insofar as he prefers the word "love" to "charity," but one way to read Redcrosse's charitable conduct in Book I, as well as Spenser's own evaluation of the concept, is by tracing the relative impact in the narrative of the modifier "dear," an anglicized synonym for the Latin root of charity, *carus*. Thomas Norton's translation of Alexander Nowell's *Catechism* employs the phrase "dear love" in the place of *caritas*, for example, and Milton, a close reader of Spenser, likewise emphasizes the etymological link between "charity" and "dearness."[74]

The word "dear" carries with it, however, the inextricable link between charity and its erotic cousin, romantic affection, as it came to signify sexual as well as spiritual esteem, and both are tied up in the language of economic valuation or *quid pro quo* contract, though Spenserian charity often suggests a transcendence of mere price. The romantic manifestation of "dear love," what Tyndale might call "carnal" love, can be associated with an overemphasis on pity, both in its role as a physical, affective response (traditionally seated in the bowels) and in its original relation to piety, especially a kind of outward, self-congratulatory piety. Spenser uses the close proximity between the two meanings to dramatize the difficulties associated with restoring the spirit and sanction of "dear love," maintaining its physical and economic realities but striking from it associations of eroticism and self-interest. This becomes one of the central preoccupations in Book I—indeed, one that courses throughout the entire *Faerie Queene* and the *Amoretti* as well (e.g., Sonnet 68)—but Spenser takes pains to demonstrate the neutrality of the term, its problematic slippage between various affections, and the potential for any Christian knight to make the wrong kind of "dear pledge," a problem that perplexes Redcrosse until he visits the House of Holinesse.

From the outset a pledge of this sort identifies Redcrosse, whose breast bears "the deare remembrance of his dying Lord" (I.I.2), but the knight quickly falls into a crucial misunderstanding of "dearness" that is complicated by pride and lust. At the end of the first canto, asleep in Archimago's hermitage and victimized by false visions and sprites, Redcrosse dreams that Una, escorted by Venus, has been transformed into "a loose Leman to vile seruice bound: / And eke the Graces seemed all to sing, / Hymen io Hymen, dauncing all around, / Whilst freshest Flora her with Yuie girlond crownd" (1.1.48). Already he is in danger of confusing the nature of Christian charity, as well as his rightful relationship to Una, by reducing her spiritual love to mere physical lust. This initiates a paradoxical motif that associates loose voluptuousness with constraining chains—"a loose Leman to vile seruice bound"—one that reaches its climax in Canto 7 when Redcrosse, "pourd out in looseness" with Duessa, is made Orgoglio's "eternall bondslave" (1.7.7–14). In his *Divine Comedy* Dante uses similar imagery to depict the bonds of sin, portraying the souls in purgatory "solvendo il nodo," as they unloosen "the knot of their debt."[75] Here the language of contract participates in a debased economy of flesh, supported by a warped vision of the Graces, whose allegorical gift exchange "seemed" to idealize mere physical pleasure.

This is not the last vision of the Graces that Spenser will include in his poem; in Book 6, Calidore too will be transfixed by their "goodly band" (6.10.14) as they dance around a mysterious female. If the similarities between these episodes provide a reminder of how easy it is to mistake earthly and divine love, the differences are instructive: whereas Redcrosse's diabolical vision invites him to participate in "loues and lustfull play" (1.1.47), the Graces and their whole train disperse at the approach of Calidore, who seems to be experiencing his own erotic response, rising out of desire "to know" them (6.10.17). Their sudden departure underscores the fleeting transcendence and fierce chastity of "loues deare sight" (6.10.29).

Spenser's notion of Christian liberty operates in a similar but distinct paradox, described throughout the Pauline epistles but especially in Galatians 5. In the first verse of this chapter, Paul exhorts his audience to "Stand fast therefore in the libertie wherewith Christ hath made vs free, and be not intangled againe with the yoke of bondage," and later, in Gal. 5:13, this liberty enables authentic service: "For brethren, ye haue bene called vnto libertie: onely vse not your libertie as an occasion vnto the flesh, but by loue serue one another."[76] In *Amoretti* 67 Spenser dramatizes a similarly complicated vision of marriage, one that Milton will emphasize in his divorce tracts, in which a spouse's submission must be voluntary, "fyrmely tyde" by "goodwill." Whereas erotic love and desire employ a "loose" freedom that binds oneself to a contract of flesh, genuine Christian liberty results in the bonds of charity. Spenser further complicates this interpretive puzzle by regularly employing concatenatory poetic devices—anaphora, epanalepsis, and most often a chiasmus—to figure forth both kinds of "dear love."

Redcrosse misunderstands the one paradox for the other. Archimago's nymph, the false Una, exacerbates the knight's confusion, explaining to Redcrosse "in wemens pitteous wise" (1.1.50) her seductive posture in his bedchamber by rewriting the origins of Redcrosse's quest as a romantic narrative: "Your owne deare sake forst me at first to leaue / My Fathers kingdome" (1.1.52). The sprite employs a phrase that gestures at selfless love—"your owne deare sake"—but as mere pretext for asserting her claims to his service, using "sake" in its original litigious sense and ultimately suggesting that Redcrosse owes her something in return.[77] A stanza later she adds, in language that resembles Errour's "wicked bands" that "constraine" (1.1.19): "Loue of your selfe, she said, and deare constraint / Lets me not sleepe, but wast the wearie night / In secret anguish and vnpittied plaint" (1.1.53). The bonds of love have been twisted into the service of sexual fantasy.

Although Redcrosse avoids the immediate temptation—that is, he resists succumbing to the vision that has just been dancing through his head—his response, which echoes much of the sprite's language, indicates that his understanding of "dearness" remains perilously limited:

> Deare dame I rew,
> That for my sake vnknowne such griefe vnto you grew.
>
> Assure your selfe, it fell not all to ground;
> For all so deare as life is to my hart,
> I deeme your loue, and hold me to you bound. (1.1.53–54)

Redcrosse does not deny the sprite's romantic framework, retaining an implicit reciprocity in his schema and merely postponing the moment of erotic fulfillment until "his owne deare sake" is better known by his deeds (or good works). Shortly thereafter, wasting his own weary night in the throes of lust, dreaming of "Ladies deare delight" (1.1.55), the knight awakes to find that Archimago's sprites "Have knit themselues in *Venus* shamefull chaine" (1.2.4), aping in apparent flesh his own misguided dream of loving service. Scholars have often noted Redcrosse's generic confusion here at the outset of his journey, how he mistakes his role as Christian knight for a knight errant proper to medieval romance, but his abandonment of Una is often described as a lack of faith—a reading Spenser encourages by placing Sansfoy in the next scene. In addition to his infidelity, however, Redcrosse demonstrates a lack of charity, by misinterpreting Una's conduct and also by focusing on the wrong kind of "dear love," which confuses his attempts at holy conduct.

By the beginning of the second canto, then, "dearness" has already been appropriated by desire, associated with constraint and service, embodied by mere physical reciprocity, and ultimately will be ascribed to Duessa in place of Una. Indeed, Redcrosse echoes his earlier comment to Archimago's sprite during his first encounter with Duessa, offering a kind of self-congratulatory pity: "Deare dame, your suddein ouerthrow / Much rueth me" (1.2.21). Questions of affective pity and physical desire are explored more fully when Spenser turns to Guyon and temperance, but the paradox of "dear love" continues to govern the narrative of Book I, as erotic freedom eventually results in binding constriction. The phenomenon often relates to economic currency, as if the lover has bought something at a high price in a contract. Fradubio, for example, sums up his predicament in simple economic terms, lamenting, "my deare loue, / O too deare loue, loue bought with death too deare" (1.2.31). With its monosyllables artfully set off by a caesura, Spenser's tight chiasmic verse reinforces Fradubio's constraint, which is more obviously embodied by his transfiguration into a tree. The pattern is reiterated in the House of Pride, where, "mortgaging their liues to Couetise," men and women are "condemned to that Dongeon mercilesse" (1.5.46), until finally Redcrosse himself is imprisoned by Orgoglio, who accepts Duessa as his leman: "From that day forth Duessa was his deare" (1.7.16).

Clearly "dear love," a term associated with the rival affections of spiritual holiness and sexual wantonness, can easily go wrong. Spenser forces the reader to participate in Redcrosse's confusion by using comparable language and rhetorical figures to describe positive as well as debased forms of love. When Arthur describes his encounter with Gloriana, for example, he employs a chiasmus that depicts their relationship in contractual terms similar to those of Fradubio: "Most goodly glee and louely blandishment / She to me made, and bad me loue her deare, / For dearely sure her loue was to me bent . . ." (1.9.14). Although the "dear love" phrase recuperates some of its positive values in this context, it nevertheless demonstrates the challenge Redcrosse faces elsewhere in distinguishing between both planes of love. Much of Canto 9, in fact, is governed by bonds of one kind or another, heralded by the first stanza's invocation of the golden chain of virtues, "wherewith yfere / The vertues linked are in lovely wize" (1.9.1), and reinforced shortly thereafter when Redcrosse and Arthur participate in a gift exchange aimed at "fast frendship for to bynd" (1.9.18).[78] But these positive images of cooperative exchange turn grim when the knight encounters Despaire and, apparently motivated by pity and zeal for the dead knight he sees, demands "thine owne bloud to price his bloud" (1.9.37). The hellish figure, a "master [manipulator] of the golden chain," as Jessica Wolfe aptly puts it, redirects Redcrosse's own contractual economy of justice inward, bringing the knight to the point of suicide: "Is not his law, Let euery sinner die: / Die shall all flesh? What then must needs be donne, / Is it not better to doe willingly" (1.9.47).[79]

Charissa is associated with a number of bonds, too, but her maternal posture provides an implicit corrective to the coercive reciprocity of Despaire as well as the enclosed system of Errour, the other mother of Book 1. Whereas Errour's interiority leads to a binding constraint between mother and child that becomes mutually self-destructive, Charissa's pattern of movement continues to develop the paradoxical logic of "dear love": "A multitude of babes about her hung / . . . / Whom still she fed whilst they were weak and young / But thrust them forth still as they waxed old" (1.10.31).[80] After spending much of the previous nine cantos describing the perils of mistaking one kind of love for another, or loving the wrong object entirely (Duessa instead of Una, martial prowess instead of holiness, etcetera), Spenser merges spiritual and romantic union into a single image of "dear love" in Canto 10: "But faire Charissa to a lovely fere / Was lincked, and by him had many pledges dere" (1.10.4).

Identified as both a spouse and a mother, Charissa's character acquires scriptural and political resonances that far surpass a simple iconographic or doctrinal treatment of charity, as Caroline McManus succinctly summarizes: "Charissa, for example, can be read politically as another image of Elizabeth I (described by John Jewel as "the only nurse and mother" of the English church), iconographically as an image of *caritas*, and theologically as the Church, wisdom, or word of God (the Church, according to Leonard Wright, 'hath nursed you with her breasts, and brought you up in the knowledge of the truth')."[81] As McManus notes, Charissa's implicit role as the bride of Christ (the "louely fere"), a role traditionally assigned to the church, adds an even stronger political-historical dimension to the allegory. Charity becomes a crucial vehicle of accommodation reconciling the various and sometimes conflicting obligations during a life of holiness: the humanist vision of state-building, the ecclesial knot that binds together a spiritual body, a hermeneutic that harmonizes the scriptural canon, as well as a crucial ethical posture in communal and even romantic relations. Spenser takes care not to efface the problems attendant to his allegorical enterprise, but once Redcrosse recalibrates his understanding of love, Spenser's charity becomes a nexus between individual and corporate identities, "the ready path" (1.10.33) that leads not only to a solitary hermitage of contemplation but also to a vision of the heavenly city.

Following the House of Holinesse episode, the opening stanza of Canto 11 signals Redcrosse's recovery of "dear love," as Una confidently declares the redemption of his dearness: "Deare knight, as deare, as euer knight was deare, / That all these sorrowes suffer for my sake, / High heauen behold the tedious toyle, ye for me take" (1.11.1).[82] The chiasmic structure of that first verse, its repetition of "dear," and the intense alliteration and caesurae all raise the poetic register to a high pitch, preparing the reader as well as Redcrosse (to a partial degree) for his final encounter with the dragon. In many ways this episode recycles the language of "dearness" traced throughout the book, even employing a phrase reminiscent of the false Una's midnight confession, but it transforms typical romantic sentiment into a genuine spiritual experience. With heaven as a witness—a context made all the more poignant after Redcrosse's recent vision of new Hierusalem—Una frames the heroic actions of Redcrosse so as to transcend the logic of mere exchange. The hyperbole is functional here, gesturing at a divine mystery of selfless love. Una's knight is not merely dear but "as deare, as euer knight was deare"; rather than the empty words of Archimago's sprite, lamenting physical pain in order to intensify erotic feeling, the pairing of "for my sake / for me take" reinforces Redcrosse's tribulations without attempting to assert or explain their value, gesturing at heavenly reward without demanding it. And the last line is so pregnant with meaning that an alexandrine cannot contain it: readers must elide two syllables (presumably "heaven" and "tedious") in order to keep the verse from swelling into a venerable fourteener.

The Holy Hospital: "Godly worke of Almes and charitee"

If Charissa requires a sanctified form of reading that interprets the body in spiritual terms, Redcrosse's visit to the holy hospital poses a different kind of interpretive challenge, pivoting back to the world of material charity. But the poet includes a number of startling elements in his depiction of the corporal works of mercy, prompting what is now a longstanding debate among scholars over the relative orthodoxy of Spenser's Protestant credentials. Some of these readings seem one-sided, even polemical: Father Thomas Nelan delivers a heavy-handed discussion of Spenser's reliance on traditional Roman Catholic positions, while Frederick Padelford (joined by Anthea Hume) confidently declares the holy hospital to be representative of Calvinism.[83] Recently, a number of scholars have accepted as incontrovertible (by and large) the holy hospital's apparently Popish elements, and proceed to explain the existence of this problem through a variety of compelling arguments. (To borrow C.S. Lewis's observation of allegory, mentioned earlier, perhaps all good works are likely to seem Catholic to the general reader.) James Schiavoni claims that Spenser, in situating Calvinist doctrine next to Roman Catholic imagery, fuses together conflicting legacies of Augustine, whose complex work had been co-opted in the sixteenth century by both supporters and opponents of free will. Darryl Gless notes how Spenser's multivalent poetics accommodate readings of either persuasion, though he suggests that the episode is best read in the context of Protestant sanctification. Carol Kaske adds considerable nuance to the discussion by noting that the self-contestatory nature of this episode is actually biblical in origin, and she identifies numerous medieval and Renaissance commentators who had developed a style of scriptural reading to reconcile such contradictions.[84]

Scholars are taking their cue, in many ways, from the spiritual value assigned by polemicists to material charity in the sixteenth and seventeenth

centuries, when religious controversialists fiercely debated the sanction and efficacy of their particular charitable institutions. Given that
Protestant and Roman Catholic apologists consciously traced the shape of
their respective charities back to a doctrinal source, these institutions possessed their own allegorical significance, representing for contemporaries
a sign of civic reform and providential favor. On the ground in Ireland,
hospitals and erstwhile monastic properties were further politicized
on account of England's colonial project and the entrenched opposition
among Irish and Old English Catholics.[85] Sixteenth-century developments in poor relief pushed a different form of dichotomizing logic to the
foreground by laboring to distinguish between the deserving and undeserving poor. Impoverished or destitute members of the parish community were interviewed, their circumstances sifted and recorded by local
Collectors or Overseers of the Poor who determined whether they quali-
fied for charitable monies.[86] As for vagrants, rogues, and other members
of the itinerant poor, Tudor authorities attempted to regain "control of
the signifying systems," as William Carroll puts it, clarifying and stabilizing their status by branding, earmarking, or imprisoning fraudulent
beggars.[87] These individuals, too, were evaluated in spiritual and social
terms, with poor relief functioning as a marker of the church's boundaries. The author of the Second Admonition to Parliament referred to vagrants
simply as "the other swine," and Thomas Wilson acquiesced to the "lewd-
ness of the times" in defending the measures to repress vagrancy in the
1572 Act, when he claimed that "it was no charity to give to such a one as
we know not."[88] Material charity, in other words, involved a complicated
process of reading that moved in both directions, revealing among both
givers and recipients their corporate and personal identities.

Given this vexed landscape, Isabel MacCaffrey's reading of Canto 10,
which notes the "innocent simplicity about the method" and "perfect vis-
ibility of meaning," can sound like a paradox.[89] But her summary captures, I think, the spirit of Spenser's allegorical program in the latter half
of the canto. In the House of Holinesse, Spenser stabilizes the hermeneutics of charitable giving by removing the recipient from the scope of
his interest, endorsing in this particular episode an indiscriminate form
of giving. Such an approach to charity places enormous emphasis on a
"cured conscience"—hence Redcrosse's protracted regime of penitential
discipline—but also reduces the fraught complications associated with

discriminatory giving. As for doctrinal politics, Spenser seems to purposely obscure the confessional underpinnings of this episode, ameliorating the polemical thrust of charitable giving by describing, as Rosamond Tuve puts it, "what is supposed to happen constantly in the life of any Christian."[90] Given the equivocal tone of the canto, moreover, as well as the vein of satire that seems to course throughout, I think Spenser means to suggest that neither Roman Catholics nor Protestants have taken enough care in producing charitable institutions or cultivating charitable behavior in England.

It is surprising that Spenser refuses in this episode to give any celebratory nod to model charitable institutions in England. His chosen metaphor of hospital gestures toward a centralized municipal mechanism of giving and service, such as the Tudor poor laws or the hospitals of London, but it fails to resemble anything that English Protestants heralded as emblems of their collective charity: not St. Bartholomew's, not Christ's Hospital, and certainly not Bridewell.[91] (Nor does it resemble the Catholic alms-houses, chantries, and hospitals that functioned as the charitable institutions of the earlier half of the sixteenth century.) If Protestant doctrine managed to safely emphasize the regenerative power of performing charitable works under the umbrella of sanctification, the institutions of charity were shaped by humanist principles that prioritized transforming the recipients of aid. So the Elizabethan hospital was not a stable repository of beadsmen, but a teeming mass of human clay the community intended to mold into a better image of God. Christ's Hospital was not merely an orphanage, for example; it was an educational institution aimed at cultivating productive citizens of London, just as the many Bridewells emerging in England put the able-bodied poor to work, supposedly inculcating a positive ethos of labor among the vagrant population. Thomas Dekker captures the primary aim of Bridewell in *The Honest Whore*, Part 2, when the hospital's master says of its inmates, "As Iron, on the Anvill are they laid, / Not to take blowes alone, but to be made / And fashioned to some Charitable vse."[92] The corrective elements of the House of Holinesse arrive before the knight reaches the hospital, on the other hand, and they are focused on Redcrosse's own internal moral trajectory. There is little of such activity in the holy hospital.

In the ten stanzas that elaborate the various pursuits of these beadsmen, moreover, there is no mention of the pesky vagabonds and false beggars who appear in so many other contemporary literary works, sermons, and statutes. In other works, including *The Shepheardes Calender*, *Mother Hubberds Tale*, and even *A View of the Present State of Ireland*, Spenser himself consistently expresses concern for vagrants, but here he consciously avoids the topic.[93] Instead he presents an uncomplicated vision of giving. Cælia helps only the "helplesse poor," but otherwise the narrative remains unconcerned with sturdy beggars or rogues. There is no discussion of how to determine if someone has wrongfully asked for charity and what to do in that scenario, despite ample instructions and warnings in the recent poor laws of 1572 and 1576, in spital sermons, in contemporary treatises on giving, as well as in the advice offered by purveyors of rogue literature like Thomas Harman. Here Spenser rejects the contemporary practice of discriminate almsgiving, which evaluated the recipient and then swung as if on a hinge, offering either corrective discipline or charitable relief, and instead offers a more capacious program of giving: "Their gates to all were open euermore" (1.10.36).

Spenser seems equally intent on folding confessional factions beneath his larger umbrella of giving. Consider stanza 38, which is often cited as evidence of Spenser's support of traditional Catholic notions of grace, works-righteous theology, and even supererogatory merit. Notwithstanding the doctrinal complications that have been lucidly explored by a range of scholars, Kaske in particular, the poet's focus here seems directed toward the everyday, domestic concerns that interfere with charitable obligations:

> The second was as Almner of the place,
> His office was, the hungry for to feed,
> And thristy giue to drinke, a worke of grace:
> He feard not once him selfe to be in need,
> Ne car'd to hoord for those, whom he did breede:
> The grace of God he layd vp still in store,
> Which as a stocke he left vnto his seede;
> He had enough, what need him care for more?
> And had he lesse, yet some he would giue to the pore.

For all his supererogatory potential, the beadsman appears more anxious that self-interest would not corrupt the traditional "order of charity," which privileged the needs of kin before strangers, a doctrine associated with Protestants and Roman Catholics alike and often justified by the adage "Charity begins at home." The two lines that Kaske cites as works-righteous—"The grace of God he layd vp still in store, / Which as a stocke he left vnto his seede"—are framed by repeated mentions of the beadsman's trust that God will provide for him and his family. Here Spenser recycles a sentiment uttered by Piers in the *May* eclogue, when he associates familial inheritance with a corresponding distrust in divine providence:

> The sonne of his loines why should he regard
> To leaue enriched with that he hath spard?
> Should not thilke God, that gaue him that good,
> Eke cherish his child, if in his wayes he stood?[94]

Whether or not Spenser intends for "the grace of God" to be meant as salvation or material provision (and I think he is deliberately ambiguous), it seems clear that the beadsman is primarily concerned with the responsibilities of his office rather than its rewards.

The dominant biblical reference in stanza 38, as Naseeb Shaheen notes, is Matthew 6:19: "Hoorde not vp for your selues, treasures vpon earth, where the moth and rust doth corrupt, and where theeues breake through, and steale," as the Bishops' Bible puts it. Protestants willingly included this text in most discussions of material giving and occasionally paired it with the corporal works of mercy described in Matthew 25.[95] The passage was sometimes cited by reformers to oppose the ecclesial pomp and circumstance associated with the Roman Mass or purgatorial doctrines—what Hugh Latimer called "wylworkes" as opposed to "the workes of mercy"[96]—especially among English controversialists of the 1550s and '60s such as John Bradford, John Bale, and Thomas Becon. Others found the text useful as a means of framing a middle way between the justifying works of supposed Popish hypocrites and the pleasure-seeking idleness of sensual Epicures. More often, however, Protestant preachers stressed the notion of hoarding treasures in heaven in a pastoral context, as a means of orienting one's behavior toward the divine will.[97] It was a convenient text for Protestants who wished to emphasize Christian ethics without leaning overmuch toward a works-righteous theology. All of this lends support to Kaske's central thesis, which claims that Spenser purposely evades a clear answer regarding the justificatory power of good works, either as an imitation of scriptural equivocation or as an irenic posture toward diverse confessional audiences. Spenser's holy hospital is a remarkably ecumenical site of charitable works, especially in comparison to contemporary religious controversy.

Stanza 38's reference to Matthew 6:19 and its caution against thieves gestures back to an earlier discussion of charitable giving in Book 1, when Una encounters Kirkrapine, who was "Wont to robbe Churches of their ornaments, / And poore mens boxes of their due reliefe, / Which given was to them for good intents" (1.3.17). Here too the text is noncommittal in assigning specific blame. Conventionally read as a figure of anti-Romanist satire, Kirkrapine clearly embodies some form of Presbyterianism too, given his Scottish name and iconoclastic behavior, which involves disrobing "The holy Saints of their rich vestiments" (1.3.17) among other things. His fornication with Abessa (absent), meanwhile, could represent the spiritual and material vacuum in the Church of England among nonresident clergy. During the 1570s and '80s, partisans of every ecclesiastical faction censured their opponents for engaging in a kind of church-robbery, but the episode conveys Spenser's more general posture of skepticism toward the institutions that were mediating the distribution of material aid.[98] Note also that Spenser's focus is on Kirkrapine's disruption of the "good intents" of givers and the "due reliefe" of recipients, rather than the relative deserts of the poor and what precise relief they ought to receive. Regarding the misappropriation of charitable goods, Spenser expresses far more concern for the failures of church ministers and parish officers than for any members of the itinerant poor.

This attitude characterizes the entire episode of the House of Holinesse. Rather than describing the recipients of aid, Spenser devotes more energy to a critique of the social elite. Nearly every stanza related to a corporal work of mercy receives its own qualification, as a vein of satire courses throughout. The first beadsman, who bears only a superficial resemblance to the porter of Robert Copland's *Highway to the Spitalhouse,* offers entertainment to all except those who can reciprocate. The third beadsman offers clothing but manages also to censure those who wear "garments gay, / The plumes of pride, and wings of vanitie" (1.10.39), a sumptuary critique that was conventional in contemporary spital sermons as well. Prisoners without exception are relieved, with no distinctions based on their respective crimes (so this includes, one presumes, the imprisoned Jesuits who had arrived in England to reconvert the populace), and a discussion of sick people and Christian burial emphasizes the shared mortality of all that bear "Gods owne mould" (1.10.42), democratizing the experience of sickness and death. The final beadsman looks after the orphans and widows, but his primary responsibility seems to be defending them from "the power of mighty men" who intend "their rightfull causes downe to tread" (1.10.43), which glances at corruption in the Court of Orphans.

This is not quite estates satire or even clerical satire, but it is clearly rooted in a rich English poetic tradition of advocating for the poor. Rather than serving merely an exemplary function, then, the episode acquires a hortatory character too; and instead of illustrating England's redeemed credentials, or even demonstrating the habits of an elect Protestant, Mercie and her associates offer a powerful reminder of duties that are often ignored or abused. By following the narrative to its conclusion, when Redcrosse's charitable service opens up "that painfull way" to the hill of Contemplation and his invocation of Saint George, the reader has the sense that Spenser believes a stronger commitment to reforming its charitable institutions would help England discover its truest identity.

"To frame / In holy righteousnesse": Reading and Writing Good Works

At the culmination of Spenser's description of material charity, Redcrosse is instructed "in euery good behest / And godly worke of Almes and charitee" until he is perfect "from the first vnto the last degree" (1.10.45). Here the knight is associated with scriptural language that is typically reserved for God or Christ and consistently figures in scenes of divine judgment. But even in this rapturous description of holiness, Spenser reserves an ironic hollow space: "His mortall life he learned had to frame / In holy righteousnesse, without rebuke or blame." It seems a curious litotes, a grand neutral, and bizarrely self-conscious too, as if the height of holy living amounted to the absence of blame. The utterance calls to mind an earlier moment in the narrative, during Redcrosse's sojourn in the House of Pride, where the knight encounters (among the other deadly vices) Enuie, who possesses an equal antipathy for poetic and charitable works:

He hated all good workes and vertuous deeds,
And him no lesse, that any like did vse,
And who with gracious bread the hungry feeds,
His almes for want of faith he doth accuse;
So euery good to bad he doth abuse:
And eke the verse of famous Poets witt
He does backbite, and spightfull poison spues
From leprous mouth on all, that euer writt:
Such one vile Enuie was, that fifte in row did sitt. (1.4.32)

Casting envy as the symbolic combatant of charity is typical in religious iconography, as Giotto's frescoes in the Arena Chapel memorably illustrate, but Spenser's conflation of alms and poetry reveals an anxiety peculiar to his own project. Situated in an uneasy balance at the beginning and end of the stanza, both kinds of "good workes" receive mistreatment from the vice, whose posture toward virtue of any sort is comprehensive: "So euery good to bad he doth abuse." By placing the resources of material aid and language under simultaneous attack, the vice constitutes one of the more powerful threats to Spenser's larger project.

Enuie's brief appearance serves as a corrective to readers who might be tempted to sever the traffic between spiritual and bodily imperatives altogether and to focus instead solely on matters of faith. If the specter of Papist doctrine looms throughout the House of Pride, most fully embodied by Lucifera's Roman trappings and Idleness's monkish habit, there is a peculiar whiff of Protestantism about the person of Enuie. Although reformers often used the vice to illustrate Rome's interference with the spread of the Gospel, here Enuie suggestively resembles the worst kind of Protestant reader, one who willfully misinterprets the good works of charitable givers, whose "almes for want of faith he doth accuse."[99] English preachers often lamented seeing "olde charitie accused of heresie" among Protestant faithful, whose reformed zeal, much like Enuie, sometimes refused to acknowledge any redeeming quality in almsgiving and disparaged any emphasis on good works as a sign of Popish superstition.[100] This attitude was enough of a commonplace for Thomas Cooper, two decades later, to claim it as one of the eight enemies to charity: "A fift Policie, whereby Sathan keepes men from charity and true bounty, is a foolish feare that they may be esteemed Papists."[101] Spenser's irenic use of hyperbole—"all good works" and "euery good"—maintains that envy is a universal problem, but Protestant theology, with its insistence that charitable works were not in themselves meritorious, was especially vulnerable to postures of this kind.

Enuie's episode reinforces the link between charitable giving and charitable reading. Charitable actions were themselves texts to be read, of course—by the parish overseer or churchwarden, perhaps, or by the individual conscience searching for proof of election—and Enuie's posture offers a template for misreading good works of any kind. With this in mind, the potential censure Redcrosse might receive for his almsgiving makes more sense. Throughout Book 1 and elsewhere in *The Faerie Queene,* righteous behavior nearly always incurs rebuke and blame: we have just seen how the arid skepticism of Envie will accuse almsgivers of wanting faith; a few cantos later Archimago will interrupt Redcrosse's nuptials with an accusation of infidelity; Occasion will revile Guyon's temperate restraint; Ate will reproach Britomart for betrayal; Sclaunder will accuse Arthur and Amoret of lascivious behavior; Detraction and Enuy will charge lawgivers like Artegal with cruelty; and the Blatant Beast will rend "the gentle Poets rime" (6.12.40). This scene's insistence that Redcrosse behaves "without rebuke or blame" points to the illusory desire motivating such an utterance, an ironic reminder that the spectral presence of Enuie continues to hover over any representation of good works.

This includes Spenser's own "good work." The same verb used to describe a righteous life, "frame," governs his larger poetic project as well: in his letter to Ralegh, an epistle he wrote specifically "for auoyding of gealous opinions and misconstructions," he claimed, "I may be perhaps encouraged, to frame the other part of politicke vertues" (714–15). Spenser's preoccupation with the status of poetry emerges repeatedly throughout *The Faerie Queene.* "Enuies false surmise" (1.5.46) resurfaces elsewhere as Sclaunder or the Blatant Beast, as well as Detraction, the sister-hag of Enuy in Book 5, who can "misconstrue of a mans intent, / And turne to ill the thing, that well was ment" (5.12.34). The various representations of the threat to charitable reading reflect Spenser's ongoing concern with the reception of his work. Embedded in Enuie's portrait, moreover, is a truth that Spenser depicts elsewhere: some verse is bad indeed. Spenser illustrates how rhetorical power can be misappropriated, for example, by Archimago, an insidious doppelganger of the charitable rhetorician, who (like Proteus and Paul) can adapt to any circumstance on behalf of civil concord.[102] The injurious power of language, its ability to erode as well as edify communities, remains a problem throughout the entire work, one that is never fully resolved—think of Bon/Malfont, for example, or those writers Spenser invokes in Book 4's proem "that haue abused" the discourse of love (4.proem.2). Spenser seems to acknowledge the potential for his own verse to contribute to this abuse.[103]

Much of *The Faerie Queene* dramatizes the perils of reading, and in particular the challenge of negotiating between spiritual and physical truths. In this way it is an allegory about the problems of allegory. But Enuie's joint accusation against almsgiving and poetry, which aims to pervert the traffic between literal and figurative spheres, presents one of the greatest threats to Spenser's enterprise. Enuie wants to evacuate material or embodied actions—feeding the hungry, for example—of any kind of spiritual significance, to make almsgiving into an absent referent, and in the process to move allegorical narrative into simple literalism. The link between these two different "good workes" is not an arbitrary one, as both charitable reading and charitable giving are intertwined in Spenser's mind as crucial but vexed sites of interpretive difficulty, and the poet urges the reader not to deploy an envious hermeneutic in either instance.

In the House of Holinesse, Spenser constructs a complicated allegory that accomplishes several aims at once. In his careful recuperation of "dear love," he underscores the importance of reforming one's "entent" in order to shore up the vulnerabilities inherent to any charitable dialectic—between a giver and receiver or between a text and its reader. But Spenser also privileges a simplified and capacious program of charitable giving that insists on returning from the world of figure and symbol to the demands of the flesh: even as Redcrosse makes his own ascent to a life of pure contemplation, he is sent back down into the world to embody holiness as best he can. By invoking charity throughout the House of Holinesse, and indeed throughout the entirety of Book 1, Spenser attempts to shape the interpretive postures of his readers. In the sophisticated allegories of *The Faerie Queene*, Spenser is thinking about his own poetry while constructing images of material charity. He is asking for charity from readers even as he depicts it.

Expetendæ opes vt dignis largiamur.

Riches are to be defired, that wee may giue to thofe that deferue.

I haue heard that famous noble man, Lord Mathew Balbanus of Lucquois, reporte many times of himfelfe, that he praied God daily to grant him no exceffe or abundance of riches,

A a   except

FIGURE 6. Claude Paradin, *The heroicall devises of M. Claudius Paradin*, trans. William Kearney (London, 1591), 371. Emblem: "Riches are to be desired, that wee may giue to those that deserue." The Rare Book & Manuscript Library, University of Illinois at Urbana-Champaign.

CHAPTER 4

CHARITABLE USE

Ben Jonson, City Comedy, and Commercial Charity

When Francis Bacon published *The Advancement of Learning* in 1605, publicly launching his program of intellectual reform, he anticipated critiques from learned divines and others who would denounce the very premise of his treatise. Whatever their resistance to its particular claims, they would likely judge, as Bacon foresaw, that such a project would disrupt humanity's respect for and reliance on the divine works of creation. Bacon dismisses their potential worries over pride and ambition with a simple caveat:

> To conclude therefore, let no man vppon a weake conceite of sobrietie, or an ill applyed moderation thinke or maintaine, that a man can search too farre, or bee too well studied in the Booke of Gods word, or in the Booke of Gods workes; Diuinitie or Philosophie; but rather let men endeauour an endlesse progresse or proficience in both: only let men beware that they apply both to Charitie, and not to swelling; to vse, and not to ostentation; and againe, that they doe not vnwisely mingle or confound these learnings together.[1]

Just before this statement he invokes the Pauline maxim that knowledge puffs one up in pride and vanity, *scientia inflat*, in order to defuse its power, declaring that learning only becomes impious when severed from its moral guarantor: "This corrective spice, the mixture whereof maketh knowledge so soueraigne, is Charitie, which the Apostle imediately addeth to the former clause, for so he sayth, *Knowledge bloweth up, but Charitie buildeth up.*"[2] And later, in describing the greatest error perpetrated by those participating in the pursuit of knowledge, he warns against divesting learning from its authentic purpose, "the benefite and vse of men."[3]

Bacon knew he was picking a fight in the *Advancement*—with theologians and natural philosophers, with powerbrokers at court and at the universities—and it is clear he intended to draft the concept of charity into his own intellectual armament before his opponents could do the same. Certainly Bacon, who was tutored by John Whitgift at Trinity College, Cambridge, during the height of the Admonition Controversy, would have had an intimate vantage point from which to observe the concept's polemical power. For him to ally his project to Pauline wisdom is particularly expedient given the apparent perils of learning, since charity is the sole virtue that remains secure from excess, and he deploys multiple references to vain learning from Ecclesiastes, a nod to the Solomonic image purveyed by James I, the prospective benefactor of his ambitious project. All of these biblical allusions recast the debate in terms of prideful versus charitable learning, setting the vanity of knowledge in opposition to its utility, prioritizing civic undertakings before private commitments.

Bacon recalibrates the scriptural orientation of knowledge in order to undertake a more dynamic and productive stocktaking of its potential abuses and benefits. Such a tactic, Jeffrey Cordell has shown, owes a great deal to the model provided by an earlier generation of humanists, including Thomas More and especially Juan Luis Vives, who appropriated Pauline charity in behalf of learning.[4] If Bacon is worried in the *Advancement* and elsewhere about Aristotelian teleology disrupting or obscuring the process of generating knowledge, he nevertheless requires his own charitable purpose to govern the project: learning must be useful, and that utility must be charitable. He states the premise even more baldly in the preface to his *Instauratio Magna*:

Finally, we want all and everyone to be advised to reflect on the true ends of knowledge: not to seek it for amusement or for dispute, or to look down on others, or for profit or for fame or for power or any such inferior ends, but for the uses and benefits of life, and to improve it and conduct it in charity.[5]

In addition to its ethical aim there is an epistemological thrust to Bacon's charity, its active role in the making of knowledge underscored by the verb it governs, *regere*, to "conduct" or guide or rule. Earlier in the preface Bacon uses a verb with comparable regulatory powers to demonstrate the methodological import of charity: "And finally we pray that when we have extracted from knowledge the poison infused by the serpent which swells and inflates the human mind, we may not be wise with too high or too great a wisdom, but may cultivate the truth in all charity."[6]

Similar to its role as a corrective spice in the *Advancement,* where it keeps the body of human knowledge and power in a healthy, balanced constitution, charity here is essential to the process or cultivation of learning, not merely its purpose. It serves as a check to human error and ambition, its collective emphasis ensuring humility among practitioners. Epistemological reform is its own kind of devotional practice, moreover, "an effectuall inducement to the exaltation of the glory of God," replacing the worship of idols with a more profound piety grounded in the book of nature, one that cannot attain perfect knowledge but leads instead to "wonder, which is broken knowledge."[7] Things circle round in Bacon's encyclopedic program: charitable use stabilizes the inductive process and transforms learning into a kind of scientific almsgiving, but right-minded experiment and observation form their own kind of charitable devotion to a loving deity.

Indeed, it is difficult to overstate the importance of charity to Bacon's project, which hoped to find in knowledge "a rich store house, for the glory of the Creator and the relief of man's estate," a phrase that Michael Kiernan suggests could "stand as a rubric for his entire venture."[8] The concept of charity is explored earlier in Bacon's *Valerius Terminus,* is refined and expanded in his *De augmentis scientiarum* and given prominence elsewhere in his *Novum Organum,* and serves as the central principle organizing his utopian vision of Salomon's House in *The New Atlantis.* The author glances at charity in his Accession Day entertainment for Elizabeth, in *Wisdom of the*

Ancients, and throughout his essays and *Sacrae Meditationes.* Charity allows Bacon to marry the contemplative and active lives, since "in religion we are warned to show our faith by works, so in philosophy by the same rule the system should be judged of by its fruits."[9] And if the concept knits together theory and praxis, so too does it link the individual with a larger community, functioning for Bacon in part as a necessary concomitant in the transition of natural philosophy from the province of exceptional minds (the mage) who increase in moral perfection by way of wisdom to the communal advancement of learning that benefits society at large. Charity might be the single thread that runs throughout his entire career.[10]

Many scholars nevertheless dismiss Bacon's anthem of charity out of hand, insisting that his repeated invocations of the term are just so many "juristic tricks and shrewd twists of hallowed arguments."[11] This is the most persistent argument, that Bacon's use of "charity" is simply a rhetorical smokescreen, a theological token intended to convey his project past the turnstile of a benighted religious culture, mere doctrinal pretext "to consecrate the mastery of nature."[12] Others have accused Bacon of being something like a Volpone, appropriating Christian values as "a culturally acceptable justification for a preoccupation with luxury and materialism."[13] Sometimes this posture derives from a scholarly agenda to find in Bacon's work a philosophy of secular humanism that can be severed wholly from religion. Whatever their purpose, arguments of this kind misunderstand early modern notions of charity by limiting the term's provenance to a particular sphere of religious discourse, but they do set into sharp relief the central claim of this book—that charity is always a site of contestation, a concept that is persistently reinterpreted and reimagined and reformed.

I bring up Bacon's project and his scholarly reception to underscore the cultural power aligned with charitable use during the early seventeenth century, as well as the scrutiny such claims invite. Whether or not it is genuine (and I think it is), Bacon's invocation of charity signals his attention to contemporary misgivings regarding the acquisition of knowledge, as well as his confidence that charity is a forceful response to these reservations. Meanwhile, in their skeptical posture toward Bacon's emphasis on charitable utility, scholars mirror a cultural commonplace of the Jacobean period, when the relationship between charitable gifts and the market economy became a subject for close inspection. As markets and trade expanded and grew more sophisticated at the start of the seventeenth century, a sea change occurred in the funding, designation, and monitoring of charitable uses, trusts or endowments that established fixed incomes for benevolent institutions like hospitals and schools. Charitable giving of this kind was enmeshed in London's mercantile culture, a fact that was often celebrated but also suspected.

If some scholars look askance at Bacon's call for charity to stabilize the acquisition of knowledge, many Jacobean dramatists were likewise skeptical of claims made by supporters of commercial enterprise who often used charity to justify the acquisition of wealth. In this chapter I will examine two of Ben Jonson's city comedies, *Volpone* and *The Alchemist,* which stage similarly parodic fantasies of charitable use, probing the ruptures that threatened to undermine the marriage between profit-making and public good. As with the advancement of learning, so too with commerce: in both cases the concept of charity provided one of the important frameworks in which the process of acquisition (of money or knowledge) was measured and understood in terms of utility. But the system remained fragile, prone to suspicion and abuse.

Charitable Uses and Charitable Commerce in Jacobean England

I will refer throughout this chapter to the phrase "charitable use" in its specific legal sense, as a special kind of deed entrusted to feoffees, or trustees, who were obliged to manage the property of the benefactor, typically with the aim of producing profits that would be regularly distributed according to the charitable intentions of the donor.[14] But the concept of charitable use was complicated by a range of other contexts that are worth noting. It was bound up in theological discourse, for example, ever since Augustine distinguished between *uti* and *frui* in the *magna quæstio* of *On Christian Doctrine,* debating whether one should use or enjoy one's neighbor, or do both. Luther, celebrated by Bacon in the *Novum Organum* as the central figure in the project of reforming scriptural exegesis, reminds his

Christian readers to "use" the world, and Calvin, too, strenuously encouraged useful labor.[15] Such a posture requires difficult negotiations of what constitutes worldly or godly use, as Spenser dramatizes throughout *The Faerie Queene*. Moreover, Augustine's apparently distinct concepts of *usus*, which emphasizes the transitive status of property, and *fructus*, which gestures at an end or culmination, were actually fraught with confounding overlaps, as Linda Gregerson reminds us: "So greatly do the two concepts tend toward overlapping meanings that they are sometimes treated as cognates and are even, in the legal terminology governing property rights, conflated to a compound: *ususfructus*."[16]

Exerting its own semantic influence is a lexical cousin, another definition of "use" that described the process of lending money at interest, better known as "usury," which, though widely practiced by contemporaries, was often condemned and specifically opposed to charity—"If Usurie be established," one writer notes simply, "Charitie is banished."[17] The two legal concepts were actually quite close at the operative level, as both used property to generate more property, but "charitable uses" distributed the funds to pious causes. In this way "use," which also possessed a strong sexual connotation, became a lexical intersection of sorts, where purportedly antithetical practices met on neutral ground. Thus the phrase "charitable uses," which acquired unmistakable currency at the beginning of the seventeenth century, embodies many of the tensions examined throughout this chapter.[18]

Although all of these various inflections of charity and use remain pertinent in Bacon's *Advancement*, I suspect he has the legal designation specifically in mind. The Elizabethan parliaments of 1598 and 1601 had recently introduced legislative reforms to regulate the arena of charitable giving, initiating an unprecedented degree of litigious inquiry related to charitable uses. Three months before Bacon published his *Advancement*, James I had publicly admonished the trustees of any charitable uses falling outside the statute's jurisdiction—most notably the nation's "colledges, halles, and houses of learning"—reminding them that neglect or misemployment of "the devout, godly, and charitable intents of the said founders and givers" would incur his royal displeasure.[19] Addressing university professors and officers in particular, James offered a reminder that learning was a communal good and that charity ought to be the central principle governing their institutional conduct. By underscoring the charitable use of his own project, one that aimed to reform the pedagogies and philosophical principles of Oxford and Cambridge Universities among others, Bacon was appropriating a phrase of contemporary social and legal significance.

James's proclamation made specific reference to the Statute of Charitable Uses of 1601 (43 Eliz. I c. 6), an improved version of a similar statute passed in 1597–98, both of which were pragmatic laws aimed chiefly at oversight, intended above all to encourage potential donors to contribute property to charitable causes without fear of fraud or legal complications disrupting the flow of monies. The legal process of enforcing a charitable gift traditionally had been consigned to the Court of Chancery, but the procedure was tedious, costly, and unreliable, which discouraged potential petitioners from seeking legal redress. In order to remedy the complications inherent to Chancery procedure, and to encourage and protect charitable giving more generally, the statutes of 1597–98 and 1601 emphasized speed and simplicity in supervising the application of charitable uses.

These new laws authorized the Lord Chancellor to establish a commission, which consisted of the bishop of the diocese, his chancellor, and other persons "of good and sounde behavior," to inquire whether or not a charitable use had suffered from "Abuses Breaches of Trustes Negligences Mysimploimentes, not imployinge concealinge defraudinge misconvertinge or misgovernemente," and to rectify any problem they discovered.[20] A significant amount of power was given to the commission to ensure that applicable uses were performed to the intent of the donor: a feoffee could be ordered to repay money wrongfully withheld from charitable uses, and was often charged at a high rate of interest; leases or conveyances of property designated to charitable uses that were not bona fide purchases could be ruled void; land could be transferred from a dishonest feoffee to someone better suited for maintaining the charitable use; defective wills, which might otherwise compromise the charitable use, could be cured; and other powers were generally "as extensive as the evil demanded."[21]

The 1597–98 statute expressly acknowledges the problem of corruption in its preamble, which appears just after the parliamentary overhaul of poor relief, observing that charitable monies "have bene and are still like to be most unlawfully and uncharitably converted to the lucre and gayne of some fewe greedy and covetous persons, contrary to the true intente and meaning of the givers and disposers thereof."[22] Similar sentiment can be found in a wide range of contemporary literature. In his satire "On Vanity," for example, George Wither excoriates "guiftes of Charity / . . . done for shew and with hypocrisy," but he quickly moves on to the parasites who hijack charitable uses:

> For publike Guifts are turn'd to priuate vses,
> Faire Colledges are ful of foule Abuses.
> And their Reuenues I account as vaine,
> Because they lazy Dunces do maintaine.
> . . .
> Good Founders dreaming not of these Abuses,
> Gaue them at first to charitable vses;
> But we find now all alter'd, and the dues,
> The which by right vpon desert ensues,
> Like Offices in Court, are bought and sould,
> And places may be had, but how? for gold.[23]

Twice linking the rhyme "use" with "abuse," Wither depicts a process of charity intercepted by self-interest, as pious uses transform into mere profiteering. He appears particularly exercised by the corruption of schools designed to support orphans or disadvantaged students, although the description is general enough to apply to any number of charitable uses warped by abusive executors. Lewis Bayly expresses similar skepticism in his manual of godly living, *The Practice of Pietie*, urging potential donors to exercise a pragmatic independence when endowing gifts to charitable uses, and suggesting they refrain from placing these gifts in the trust of others:

> If thou hast no children, and the Lord haue blessed thee with a great portion of the goods of this world; and if thou meane to bestow them vpon any charitable or pious vses: put not ouer that good worke to the trust of others; seeing thou seest how most of other mens Executors, prooue almost Executioners.[24]

Robert Burton sums up the general attitude toward charitable uses, claiming, "most part there is *simulatum quid* a deale of hypocrisie in this kinde, much default and defect."[25]

Contributing to this prejudice, undoubtedly, were contemporary anecdotes that demonstrated the untrustworthy behavior of executors. There was also a cultural emphasis on performing good works while living, one that clearly informed Bayly's advice. Burton's skepticism toward charitable deeds, meanwhile, was probably strengthened by Calvinist theology, which emphasized the ineluctable sin that accompanies every charitable action. Consider the remarkable analogy John Donne uses in *Pseudo-Martyr* to emphasize the distinction between Protestant and Roman Catholic justification theologies: "And lastly, we can do no perfit good work; for originall sin hath poisoned the fountaines, our hearts: and those degrees and approaches, which we seeme to make towards good workes, are as if a condemned man would make a large will, to charitable vses."[26] Clearly the Statute of Charitable Uses reflected a more general attitude in the culture that was sensitive to the various threats posed to the public good by private desire.

Perhaps the most pronounced impact of the statute was its startling efficiency. From the first statute of 1597–98 to the death of James, more than one thousand rulings related to charitable uses were made, nearly twenty times the rate of inquiry during the two previous centuries, when only two rulings of this kind were made each year on average.[27] As Gareth Jones notes, however, the successful efficiency of the commission was not a product of its legal procedure but rather of the culture in which it functioned: "The commission was a potentially ponderous instrument of investigation and supervision: commissioners and jurors had to be found to serve and give freely of their time; parish administration had to remain efficient and parishioners enthusiastic . . . As long as society appreciated the urgency of the charity commissioners' task, the statutory procedure would flourish."[28] Indeed, though procedural obstacles associated with Chancery undoubtedly contributed to the scarcity of petitions in the earlier century, the dramatic increase of inquiries into charitable uses after enactment of the new statutes illustrates their vital role in distributing monies to the needy. Social historians have noted that endowed charities were a crucial source of poor relief, which was merely supplemented by the recently instituted national poor rate, a compulsory parish tax to relieve the poor.[29] As Steve Hindle remarks of the increased inquiries, "Litigation on this scale would hardly have been necessary had not endowments been regarded as so beneficial to the poor and vital to the political culture of the parishes in which they were administered."[30]

The 1601 statute itself points to an increased focus on—and obvious support of—charitable uses themselves. Indeed, the document reads like a catalog of potential charities:

> Some for Releife of aged impotent and poore people, some for Maintenance of sicke and maimed Souldiers and Marriners, Schooles of Learninge, Free Schooles and Schollers in Universities, some for Repaire of Bridges Portes Havens Causwaies Churches Seabankes and Highewaies, some for Educacion and prefermente of Orphans, some for or towards Reliefe Stocke or Maintenance for Howses of Correccion, some for Mariages of poore Maides, some for Supportacion Ayde and Helpe of younge Tradesmen, Handiecraftesmen and persons decayed, and others for reliefe or redemption of Prisoners or Captives, and for aide or ease of any poore Inhabitants concerninge paymente of Fifteenes, setting out of Souldiers and other Taxes.[31]

A decade later, Andrew Willet *did* construct a catalog of charitable works performed during the reigns of Edward, Elizabeth, and James. Willet's exhaustive record of good works is obviously an anti-Roman polemical work, "to stop their slanderous mouthes," and demonstrates the opportunity such charitable endowments presented to the monarch, church authorities, and city officials for propagandistic mythmaking, but it also illustrates more broadly how essential these charitable deeds were to the social fabric of London and England.[32] Charitable uses were heavily regulated and accompanied by suspicion because they were so important.

Charitable Commerce and Jacobean Theatre

Such scrutiny of charitable uses, and the refinement of legal machinery instituted to enforce them, reflects an increasing unease in early modern

England about the entire process of generating, exchanging, maintaining, and distributing wealth for charitable causes. Few contemporaries viewed merchant profits with mere antipathy or considered them socially destructive, but there was a kind of general anxiety about the moral status and communal value of moneymaking. Canon law had always had a troubled relationship with private property, not merely due to moral concern but also in terms of natural law and social justice, and these Christian preoccupations were augmented by classical *sententiae* inherited from Cicero, Seneca, and others, resulting in such cultural commonplaces as Bacon's view of wealth: "Of great Riches there is no reall use, except it bee in the distribution: the rest is but conceit."[33] Samuel Daniel, in his remarkable poem "To His Booke," juxtaposes "publique good" with "private heapes," and notes that any kind of fortune is measured by "having what it hath in use."[34] Philip Massinger, meanwhile, dramatizes the alternative posture in *The City Madam*, when the newly rich Luke expresses a liking for predatory gain, declaring his commercial interests by renouncing his moral obligations: "Religion, conscience, charity, farewell! / To me you are words only, and no more; / All human happiness consists in store."[35] If the flow of monies was often depicted in terms of "use," which was deemed socially acceptable, Massinger's work gives voice to the culture's persistent worry that monetary traffic might be intercepted by private interests, as well as its sense of relief when profits were redirected toward a larger network of social relations.

An earlier generation of economic and social historians located the origin of dissolving communal bonds within the rise of an acquisitive mercantile culture during the period, but these assumptions have been revised by current scholars like Craig Muldrew, who suggests that early modern England's economy continued to rely on cooperative notions of credit and obligation, mutual reciprocity, and charitable dealings.[36] A merchant's primary currency or commodity was credit, which was largely based on abstract notions of reputation, honor, and trust. That is, the language of the marketplace, even as it began to encourage or reinforce an individualistic and acquisitive economic model, clearly overlapped with traditional religious and social principles, despite awkward tensions between the imperatives of profit-making and profit-sharing. A number of fascinating

studies have mapped this economic discourse onto early modern literature, and Jacobean theater, immersed as it was in the commercial fabric
of London, seems particularly fertile ground for research of this kind.[37]

A focus on charity offers a unique perspective in charting contemporary responses to economic growth during this period, especially since
the concept, at once powerful but malleable, was reacting to, benefiting
from, and even participating in the mercantile behavior of early modern
London. For example, England had long conceived of work as an important disciplinary feature of charitable poor relief—hence the development
of Bridewells and other labor schemes throughout the country—but soon
the concept was invoked in terms of potential commercial enterprise, as
Thomas Mun does when he essentially equates jobs with charity in his
response to critics of the East India Company: "So that when all the other
doores of charitie are shut, the East India gates stand wide open to re-
ceiue the needy and the poore, giuing them good entertainment with two
Moneths wages before hand to make their neeedfull prouisions for the
voyage."[38] Published the same year, Michael Sparke's *Greevous Grones for
the Poore* characterizes the Virginia Company in even more lavish terms
of charity, despite its policy of shipping vagrants overseas as indentured
servants. In the introduction to his monumental history of trade and cir-
cumnavigation, Samuel Purchas imagines global trade as an expression
of charity: "The chiefest charitie is that which is most common; nor is
there any more common then this of Nauigation, where one man is not
good to another man, but so many Nations as so many persons hold commerce and intercourse of amitie withal."[39] Whatever the intentions of
François Rabelais in penning Panurge's encomium to debt, which culminates in a vision of a new golden age where everyone lends, everyone owes, and "Charity alone reigns, governs, dominates, triumphs," his
work is not merely a fantasy: an anonymous London pamphlet from 1622,
decrying imprisonment for debt, envisions a utopian market in which
lending transactions would be encouraged by reducing the bodily punishment imposed on debtors, declaring, "Free borrowing and lending
would cause and encrease charity and Christian amity amongst men, and
knit them together in stronger bonds of love, society, and friendship."[40]
Perhaps most remarkable is a comment by Thomas Milles, who suggests

that money itself, rather than the charity that might find expression by way of that money, is the "medium between Subjects and their Kings, and Exchange the very Cement that glues them both together."[41] In these visions of commerce, which seem to anticipate the moral and economic philosophies of Bernard Mandeville a century later, the marketplace overlaps so fully with charitable relations as to render any distinctions practically negligible.

Other depictions of early modern English merchants are fraught with ambivalence. Consider for example Nicholas Breton's *Characters*, which takes for granted the moral neutrality of the mercantile profession but notes that there are both worthy and unworthy types. Meanwhile, Thomas Gainsford, who observes how private commodity augments the public good and presents an otherwise positive depiction of the merchant, nevertheless expresses reservation about the means by which the profession acquires its profit:

> Merchant is onely traduced in this, that the hope of wealth is his principall obiect whereby profite may arise, which is not vsually attained without corruption of heart, deceitfull protestations, vaine promises, idle oathes, paltry lyes, pedling deceit, simple denials, palpable leauing his friend, and in famous abuse of charitie.[42]

Even among merchants themselves, as Laura Caroline Stevenson observes, there was resentment toward elite merchant adventurers, although "the wealth and charity of the great tycoons in city government were also sources of civic pride."[43] Early modern England's merchants might sometimes "abuse" charity, and they certainly might refuse to offer it, but they were still operating in a social paradigm that understood itself as a construct of charity. Merchants could not (and typically would not) isolate themselves from the communal ethos that governed early modern relations, complicating any distinctions between money-making and money-sharing.

One can detect a similar ambivalence in John Stow's 1603 *Survey of London,* with its curiously nostalgic celebration of civic virtue in London and resolute silence toward a number of important urban achievements related to charitable uses. Commenting on Stow's dismay in chronicling the gradual dissolution of civic bonds and communal values, a phenomenon supposedly effected by the city's rising commercialism, Ian Archer offers an important reminder of Stow's unreliability regarding these concerns: if certain rituals like the Midsummer watch were discontinued, "the corollary of this fragmentation of sociability was the increasing articulation of the social bond through the exercise of charity."[44] Archer's more thorough examination of Elizabethan London's social relations demonstrates that the city's burgeoning mercantile professions were not engaged in a zero-sum competition with the city's charitable institutions for material resources or other "capital," but actually galvanized a number of crucial developments in poor relief and other charitable works.[45]

Yet even if Stow's historical presentation of London lacks holistic accuracy, his work does register a crucial moment in the perceived role and function of merchants in the city. He clearly prefers to recognize communal or institutional expressions of charity, and his *Survey* articulates a reserved skepticism of charitable works performed by individuals who amassed private wealth. Anthony Munday's revision of Stow's *Survey* in 1618 provides a useful counterpoint in the manner it revises some of Stow's implicit accusations. Whereas Stow's original *Survey* ends with a list of churches and hospitals, as Helen Moore observes, Munday's replaces it with the order of the Lord Mayor, the Aldermen, and the Sheriffs: "One form of communal endeavor—charity for the poor and sick—is thereby replaced with the mercantile and ritual performances of the London companies."[46] Moore carefully notes that Munday does not, like Milles or Purchas, replace charity with trade—indeed, references to charitable works performed by Londoners actually increase in his text—but the difference in corporate emphasis underscores the shifting attitudes toward charity, as well as London's changing machinery in distributing gifts to the poor.

Munday's sanguine posture toward London's mercantile culture is reflected by Lord Mayor's Shows and other contemporary civic pageants that participated in the city's mythmaking, a milieu in which Munday himself was active.[47] These pageants, while insisting on the charitable deeds of various guild members and city officials, nevertheless reveal an implicit concern with the use of mercantile profit. Lord Mayor's Shows invariably reference the charitable works of previous city officials as an incentive or spur, challenging the newly sceptered mayor to ensure that he receive his own future blazon recording the various good deeds performed during his reign. Put another way, the celebrations attempted to place London's consumer culture safely within a moral universe governed by charity.

Munday's 1611 Lord Mayor's Show *Chruso-thriambos*, for example, ostensibly intended to honor the goldsmith Sir James Pemberton, culminates in a set of instructions from Nicholas Faringdon, who was four times Lord Mayor:

> You are a Gold-Smith, Golden be
> Your daily deedes of Charitie.
> Golden your hearing poore mens cases,
> Free from partiall bribes embraces.
> And let no rich or mighty man
> Injure the poore, if helpe you can.[48]

Gail Kern Paster notes that city pageants borrowed elements from court masques, but whereas masques circumscribed themselves by concluding with the fulfillment of virtue and heroism, embodied by the monarch in particular, "The pageant on the other hand insists on the open-endedness of its traditions in order to suggest to the Lord Mayor that his significance at the investiture is mostly potential."[49] Thomas Dekker's 1612 pageant, *Troia-Nova Triumphans*, employs an elaborate morality structure, reaching a climax in Virtue's triumph over Envy by way of good deeds, and concluding with Justice addressing the Lord Mayor, reminding him, "the Rich and Poore must lye / In one euen Scale," "Let not Oppression wash his hands ith' Teares / Of Widowes, or of Orphans," and, finally, "That Collar (which about thy Necke is worne) / Of Golden Esses, bids thee so to knit / Mens hearts in Loue."[50] The typical pageant, then, was not merely a celebration but a reminder of the ideal principles by which the city operated, a dramatic production that would only conclude after the Lord Mayor's annual reign had ended, when his performance could be assessed retrospectively.

But who was actually watching the pageant itself? Probably just the merchants, and maybe only the Lord Mayor's own company, which financed the annual pageant. Or, as Theodore Leinwand observes, "Lord Mayors' shows represent an attempt to confirm the honor and probity of 'the merchant,' but the merchant elite's message was relayed almost exclusively to its own kind."[51] In some ways, though, this seems to be precisely the point—the merchants themselves were celebrating their own importance in the life of the city and commonwealth. Consider Middleton's elaborate 1613 pageant, *The Triumphs of Truth*, in which London rises from a triumphal mount, surrounded by a number of virtues that support her:

> On her left side sits Perfect Love, his proper seat being nearest the heart, wearing upon his head a wreath of white and red roses mingled together, the ancient witness of peace, love and union, wherein consists the happiness of this land, his right hand holding a sphere, where in a circle of gold is contained all the twelve companies' arms, and therefore called the Sphere of true Brotherhood, or *Annulus Amoris*, the Ring of Love. Upon his left hand stand two billing turtles, expressing thereby the happy condition of mutual love and society: on either side of this mount are displayed the charitable and religious works of London—especially the worthy company of Grocers—in giving maintenance to scholars, soldiers, widows, orphans, and the like, where are placed one of each number.[52]

A cynical reader might note how London's impoverished citizens are categorized and reduced here to single, emblematic entities, thrust into iconographic representation by the merchant companies and justifying, as it were, the "floud of gold" that flowed earlier from London's allegorized Liberality, the sister spirit of Perfect Love. This sort of pageantry was enacted annually during the week of Easter when the children of Christ's Hospital paraded up to St. Mary's Spital and sat to the east side of the pulpit as the Lord Mayor, aldermen, and sheriffs of London gathered to hear the spital sermons of the Easter holy days.[53] In the case of Middleton's pageant, as Leinwand notes, the primary audience ("especially the worthy Company of Grocers") did not need to be convinced of the merchant's integrity. More likely, Middleton intended the pageant to show—to merchants and for merchants—their proper role in the commonwealth, how private gain could only be understood in the context of public good, that commercial enterprise and charity should walk hand in hand, however clumsily.

But these celebrations of charitable endowments acquire a more ironic edge when they are depicted on the London stage, placing the process of mercantile acquisition under a great deal of pressure. In Thomas Heywood's *If You Know Not Me, Part II*, for example, prominent city officials are treated to an iconic display of charity, as Bishop Nowell exhorts Sir Thomas Gresham and others to stare in admiration at the "pictures" of charitable deeds performed by various Lord Mayors throughout history. Heywood likely takes his cue from Stow's *Survey of London* here, and the scene seems intended to defuse the contestatory spirit inherent to the mercantile profession, to offer a powerful reminder that people should be privileged before abstract measurements attached to money, and, ultimately, to direct the flowing monies to their proper charitable uses. Ceri Sullivan suggests that the charity is enough to alleviate tensions introduced elsewhere in the narrative, but Jean Howard, referring specifically to William Rowley's *A New Wonder: A Woman Never Vext*, offers an incisive commentary that applies to the nostalgic depictions of charity in any of the sentimental city comedies of the period: "The overinsistence on charity flags a problem, a lack, in the social structure. If charity will not miraculously cure prodigality, incite reformation, and protect against economic ruin, it nonetheless marks the longing for social structures that could perform such work."[54]

In both Heywood's and Rowley's works, the repeated gesture toward charitable endowments—some of them as fanciful as Panurge's vision, as in Stephen Foster's plan to tear down the debtor's prison, Ludgate, and rebuild it as a charitable house—raises questions about the ethics of high-profit and high-risk business. In fact there was popular sentiment that charitable endowments often signaled uncharitable business practices. Andrew Willet uses mercantile exchange as a figure of unlawful dissimulation, "when as one dissembleth to anothers hurt . . . in the breach of charity, as Merchants in buying and selling," and Francis Quarles, too, rebukes hypocritical benefactors:

> They that, in life, oppress, and then bequeath
> Their Goods to pious uses at their death,

> Are like those Drunkards, being layd to sleepe,
> That belch and vomit what they cannot keepe.[55]

Robert Hayman declares in one of his epigrams, "What thou hast got by craft, and Usury, / Thou wilt bequeath in deeds of Charity," and later Samuel Butler glibly mentions, "That which is wickedly gotten may be disposed to pious uses."[56]

Clearly, early modern England struggled to reconcile apparently contradictory imperatives that emphasized mutual concord and mercantile contract, giving and selling, receiving and buying, and the London stage was a site in which these cultural tensions were given particular scrutiny. The problematic relationship between charity and commerce—in addition to the performative aspect of any charitable work—became a thematic fixation of sorts for Jacobean theater, itself a major catalyst in the uneasy transition from a literary system of courtly patronage and manuscript exchange to one that centered on commercialism and printed works. From their onset, theaters were considered a threat to poor relief, since plays encouraged "vnthriftye waste of the moneye of the poore," and because wealthier playgoers, in the commonwealth's theoretical zero sum game, chose to spend money on supposedly idle recreation rather than offering charitable gifts: "It is a woeful sight to see two hundred proud players get in their silks, where five hundred poor people starve in the streets."[57] It was general policy by the year 1600 for local municipalities to impose taxes on playhouses that were specifically devoted to charitable uses (hospitals in particular), and some form of weekly contribution to poor relief was often stipulated in the playhouse's license.[58]

Thus, in *The Alchemist*, when Face directs charitable funds to Bedlam and then plans to appropriate them for his own use, Jonson is importing contemporary accusations against the theater into the performance at Blackfriars' (where his play was staged), transforming forceful complaint into comedy. John Fletcher provides a similarly ironic conflation of charitable giving and the commercial world of the theater when Cacafogo, in *Rule a Wife and Have a Wife*, declares of his wealth, "Put it to pious uses, / Buy Wine and Wenches, and undo young Coxcombs."[59] Meanwhile, both parts of *The Honest Whore* make charitable institutions, Bedlam and Bridewell respectively, crucial settings of dramatic and moral climax, as does (in its own way) *Eastward, Ho!*. Other plays make charitable giving and endowments a central feature of the narrative machinery, as in *The Family of Love*, *Wit at Several Weapons*, and *More Dissemblers Besides Women*, probing and interrogating the role and efficacy of these social customs and institutions. In fact, Ken Jackson's observation of Middleton and Rowley—"exposing the false uses of charity... was, in fact, something of a thematic habit"—could stand in for many of their contemporaries as well.[60]

Ben Jonson is not always included in that group, but his city comedies *Volpone* (1606) and *The Alchemist* (1610), to which I will turn shortly, provide intimate portrayals of an urban world in which the imperatives of charity and commercialism are thoroughly and problematically intertwined. Jonson is willing enough to celebrate the positive impact of trade on the poor, as he does in *The Speeches at Prince Henry's Barriers*, for example, when he chooses to ignore martial exploits and instead congratulate Edward III's civil accomplishments, "the trade of clothing, by which art were nursed / Whole millions to his service, and relieved / So many poor" (187–89).[61] And in *The Magnetick Lady*, he provides a portrait of a rich merchant, the deceased Mr. Steel, who "did stand condemn'd / With that vain World, till, as 'twas prov'd, after / He left almost as much more to good uses" (1.4.58–9), although these were left in the trust of a usurer. But the playwright seems uncomfortable with any suggestion that commercial exchange was equivalent with charitable giving. This discomfort is apparent in *The Entertainment at Britain's Burse*, which Jonson composed after being commissioned by Robert Cecil to provide suitable entertainment for the opening of the New Exchange, an aristocratic marketplace developed by Cecil as a commercial rival to the Royal Exchange. The work, which features the Master extolling the virtues of a whole catalog of exotic items, ends up echoing the mountebank scene in *Volpone* (eventually certain objects are "given" away to the King, Queen, and prince, respectively) or, as has been mentioned by several scholars, Mrs. Otter's china house in *Epicoene*, which is really just a brothel. That is, Jonson—who is a pen for hire in this case—is clearly uncomfortable with the commodification of gifts, with the pretense that "All other places give for money, here all is given for love," as the Exchange's banner reputedly declared. At the very least he takes no trouble to conceal the problematic overlaps between charitable and commercial modes of reciprocity.[62]

In *Britain's Burse* and elsewhere in his work, Jonson zeroes in on the desire among his contemporaries to justify their commercial gain with a sense of charitable utility, an impulse he often censures on account of its inherent hypocrisy. But Jonson also recognizes his own involvement in this tenuous dynamic, as *Volpone's* Don Scoto vignette and *The Alchemist's* epilogue illustrate, not to mention his nod to Bedlam shows in *Epicoene.* These playful but ambivalent episodes signal the playwright's unease with his own dramatic enterprise. Jonson seems to acknowledge that his participation in commercial theater, justified to a degree by a project of moral reform, might be yet another fantasy of charitable use.

Volpone and the Commodification of Gifts

It is worth restating several of the principal roles of charity in the mercantile world of early modern England, and London in particular: contemporaries recognized charity as an important condition for the marketplace and more generally as a paradigmatic virtue knitting together society; charity was also its own currency of a kind, a source of good credit, which participated in and facilitated mercantile exchange; and finally charity was the proper end of business, the final product in the process of profit-making that was marked out by its "use." A sharper vision of this landscape helps clarify Jonson's moral project in *Volpone.* The play does not merely satirize acquisitive individuals whose profit-seeking ventures dissolve fraternal bonds, although he certainly targets the sort of destructive greed that transforms various Venetian citizens into caricatures of beast fable. Jonson condemns avarice to be sure, and luxury too, but he spends equal amounts of energy attacking affectations of charity, and in particular charitable "use," a term and concept that Volpone, Mosca, and others exploit throughout the narrative.

Jonson makes it clear in *Volpone's* first scene, immediately after the title character addresses his gold in a famously inspired travesty of prayer, that he is not censuring the actual London marketplace. Instead he satirizes the pretenses of a mercantile world that is commercializing the charitable uses of wealth. Notice how Volpone and Mosca explicitly distance their enterprise from the supposedly sordid realities of commercialism, emphasizing instead a method of acquisition that appears benign:

> Yet I glory
> More in the cunning purchase of my wealth
> Than in the glad possession, since I gain
> No common way: I use no trade, no venture;
> I wound no earth with ploughshares; fat no beasts
> To feed the shambles; have no mills for iron,
> Oil, corn, or men, to grind 'em into powder;
> I blow no subtle glass; expose no ships
> To threat'nings of the furrow-facèd sea;
> I turn no moneys in the public bank,
> Nor usure private. (1.1.30–39)

Volpone provides a catalog of human vocations, which proceeds from a primitive agrarian subsistence to various mercantile endeavors that slowly acquire greater sophistication, as simple merchandise gives way to more exotic products like glass, and on to monetary exchange in public banks, culminating in the practice of usury. By contrasting traditional methods of gain with his own "no common way," a description that blends aristocratic privilege with innovative experimentation, Volpone taps into a prevalent anxiety about the potentially uncharitable practices of any kind of commercial exchange intended to generate profit. John Marston dramatized with similar irony the same apprehension the year before in *The Dutch Courtesan*, in which Cocledemoy delivers an encomium to the "merciful gain" and "righteous income" of prostitutes.[63] Volpone does the bawd one better by circumventing the problem of trade altogether. He deliberately avoids the manufacturing process that grinds men as well as commodities, refuses to profit from the human vanity that fuels the glass-blowing industry, and resists the possible return on global trade because it risks human capital and currency.

This is made clearer in Johnson's play when Mosca picks up where Volpone leaves off, categorizing the various methods of acquisition that directly impinge on traditional notions of charity, and observing their careful avoidance of such malicious behavior:

> No sir, nor devour
> Soft prodigals. You shall ha' some will swallow

> A melting heir as glibly as your Dutch
> Will pills of butter, and ne'er purge for't;
> Tear forth the fathers of poor families
> Out of their beds, and coffin them alive
> In some kind, clasping prison, where their bones
> May be forthcoming when the flesh is rotten.
> But your sweet nature doth abhor these courses;
> You loathe the widow's or the orphan's tears
> Should wash your pavements, or their piteous cries
> Ring in your roofs and beat the air for vengeance. (1.1.40–51)

Mosca's monologue seems like an ironic nod toward the corporal works of mercy. But note how this is all framed in the negative, by the actions he and Volpone do *not* perform, as if the two rogues could distance themselves from the suffering of humanity altogether. There is a double edge to this critique: Mosca obviously glances at the various professions profiting from activities that should be circumscribed by charity, but the passage also satirizes any misguided attempt to perform the substance of mercantile exchange without its commercial shadow. If Volpone's "purchase" of wealth manages to avoid the potential harm effected by traditional commercial practices, he does not contribute to society in any fashion either. He will not get his hands dirty by wounding the earth, and, consequently, his sterile world will not feed anyone or anything but his own gaping vault. Volpone avoids the stigma of usury precisely because he does not loan money out, choosing only to receive money at no interest. But even usury was often understood to be essential to commercial life, if prone to mismanagement, as Bacon notes in his essay on the topic, observing, "If the *Usurer*, either call in, or keepe backe his Money, there will ensue presently a great Stand of Trade."[64] Volpone's posture betrays a refusal to participate in the fraternal bonds that knit together a community.

Or perhaps that is not the best way to put it, since Volpone capitalizes from communal bonds of precisely this sort. His interlude as the mountebank Scoto, for example, demonstrates a subtle understanding of the affective powers underpinning the marketplace. He understands how to manipulate an exchange by not fixing a price on the commodity he is selling. There is an obvious element of gamesmanship in his performance as Scoto, and his progressive devaluation of the medicine on offer is clearly an expected feature of the ritual, but the scene also registers a contempt for traditional practices of exchange. Instead, Volpone seems to prefer something less material as he drops the price from six crowns to six pence: "Well, I am in a humour, at this time, to make a present of the small quantity my coffer contains—to the rich in courtesy, and to the poor for God's sake . . . I will have, only, a pledge of your loves, to carry something from amongst you to show I am not contemned by you" (2.2.175–83). Volpone sells his medicine, itself the product of alchemical fantasy and a metaphor representing any kind of self-delusion, for something that seems immaterial: a pledge of love.[65] But his vault is filled with such pledges, illustrating the lucrative potency of his merchandise and the genius of his style of exchange. He has found a different kind of market, as it were. More to the point, the foundation of his entire policy is facilitated by the desires of various men and women about town who hope to inherit his wealth, and who thus "counterwork, the one unto the other, / Contend in gifts, as they would seem in love" (1.1.83–84).[66] Everyone *seems* to be making pledges of love, especially Volpone and his "beloved Mosca," who both rely on the pretense of charity in order to maintain their common purpose. When they finally engage in commercial partnership by way of informal contract ("I cannot now / Afford it you so cheap" [5.12.69–70]), the negotiations break down and result in their mutual ruin.

Until the eventual dissolution of their partnership, Volpone and Mosca turn people into gold—think of the description of Celia, "Bright as your gold, and lovely as your gold!" (1.5.114)—and they turn charity into gold like the alchemical fantasy later peddled by Subtle and Face. Using the lure of his money to exploit otherwise sacrosanct relationships, Volpone transforms his house into an "anti-hospital," to use Robert Wiltenburg's phrase, a kind of warped version of Spenser's holy hospital, infecting the proper relationships between Voltore and the public good, Corbaccio and his obedient son, Corvino and a faithful wife.[67] By framing himself as a worthwhile recipient of charity, old and ill and bereft of family, Volpone's theatrical acumen—and Mosca's subtle psychology—provides just enough justification for less sophisticated mercenaries to cloak their investments as charity. Indeed, this is precisely how Corvino explains his pandering to Celia, encouraging her to think of her imminent prostitution as "a pious work, mere charity, for physic, / And honest polity to assure mine own" (3.7.65–66).[68] In Jonson's phrasing, note that the appositive link between pious works and mere charity is joined by a coordinating conjunction that brings policy into the description: this is, Corvino claims, charitable work *and* good policy. His assertion, though obviously ridiculous in context, demonstrates the partnership between both concepts.

The two options were not mutually exclusive in early modern England. There is delicious irony, then, when Mosca refuses to return Corvino's gifts after Volpone's feigned death, linking his items of material charity with the deliberate prostitution of his wife:

> Hear you: do not you know, I know you an ass?
> And that you would most fain have been a wittol,
> If fortune would have let you? That you are
> A declared cuckold, on good terms? This pearl,
> You'll say, was yours? Right. This diamond?
> I'll not deny't, but thank you. Much here else?
> It may be so. Why, think that these good works
> May help to hide your bad. I'll not betray you,
> Although you be but extraordinary,
> And have it only in title, it sufficeth. (5.3.50–59)

Mosca treats Corvino's gifts just as the merchant described them, as honest policy, but Mosca alters the policy's directive, construing them in the context of preserving social reputation, as a means of disguising bad works as good rather than turning a mercantile profit. A commodity's use, in other words, can be manipulated. Mosca, moreover, can keep the gifts precisely because they were charitable rather than contractual, which allows him to determine their purpose and manipulate the exchange. Apparently he considers the various presents to be worth his silence where Corvino's cuckoldry is concerned, a lucrative gift in itself, since Mosca was poised to ruin the reputation of honor and credit on which an early modern merchant relied.

Because Volpone and Mosca manipulate the awkward relationship between charity and commerce, exploiting in particular the undetermined use of Volpone's riches as a means of generating more riches, the recent developments regarding charitable uses during this time period seem especially relevant. Jonson draws attention to the importance and misapplication of the term "use" throughout the play, and in the very first scene he highlights Volpone's abuse of the concept by way of spectacular parody: Mosca (echoing Horace's Ode 2.2) asserts to his patron, "You know the use of riches and dare give, now, / From that bright heap, to me, your poor observer" (1.1.62–63), who acknowledges the parasite's veracity by offering a reward. Alison Scott has taken the word "use" here as a starting point for investigating the problems of luxurious extravagance in *Volpone,* but Jonson is gesturing at a misapplication of charitable uses as well, directly referencing Volpone's maintenance of various figures who remain in a subordinate capacity, from Mosca to his dwarf and eunuch, and also providing a burlesque scene in which the rich give to the poor.[69]

Elsewhere Jonson emphasizes the conflation of sex and use during an otherwise innocuous scene involving Peregrine and Lady Politic-would-be, who attempts to recover a charitable rapport with the gentleman by suggestively offering her body as a gesture of goodwill:

> *Lady.*   If you stay
> In Venice here, please you to use me, sir—
> *Mosca.*   Will you go, madam?
> *Lady.*   Pray you, sir, use me. In faith.
> The more you use me, the more I shall conceive
> You have forgot our quarrel. (4.3.15–19)

Jonson plays with similar erotic implications during the scene of attempted rape, when Celia is ordered to "use thy fortune well, / With secrecy and pleasure" (3.7.186–87). Although it is backed by a long tradition of amatory lyric that gains erotic frisson by publicizing private pleasures, the imperative here seems poorly calculated rhetorically, at least in terms of its specific audience, who seems impervious to this kind of temptation. Indeed, one wonders if Celia's reputation for posterity might have improved if

Jonson had included a bit more dramatic tension, if she had had to wrestle with a more complicated ethical proposition, such as the "equal poise of sin and charity" Shakespeare poses in *Measure for Measure,* when Angelo offers to spare Isabella's life if she will sleep with him.[70] Instead Jonson's primary focus here is on Volpone, whose rapturous monologue is a projection of his own hedonism—the use of wealth he offers is purely private fantasy, a secret means of facilitating luxurious pleasure. In similar fashion Sir Politic-would-be stores up observations and general notions, "For mine own private use" (2.1.104), which he plans to employ as capital for various moneymaking schemes, and in the courtroom Voltore conspires to "use his vehement figures . . . Out of pure love, no hope of gain" (5.2.51–53). When Volpone initiates his plan to mock the various suitors by naming Mosca his heir, he urges his parasite to "use them scurvily" (5.2.75). With apologies to Falstaff, Volpone is not only perverse in the uses of his own wealth, but he is the cause that perverts the uses of other men's gifts.

Of course, as I have explained, the cultural expectation, underwritten by statutory law and celebrated by city pageant, would have been that the majority of Volpone's riches were designated for charitable uses, and in fact Volpone encourages this pretense, crying out in his supposed death throes to Mosca and Corvino: "Marry, my state is hopeless. / Will him to pray for me, and t'use his fortune / With reverence when he comes to it" (3.7.87–89). Consequently, this story of avaricious legacy hunters, which otherwise seems a product of Jonson's conscious classicism, acquires a contemporary resonance, as various potential executors threaten to appropriate enormous sums of wealth for private use. *Volpone* dramatizes a pervasive concern of society in early modern England, which fretted over any potential disruptions to the uneasy balance between accumulation and distribution of money. Robert Evans has examined the curious resemblance Volpone bears to Thomas Sutton, the renowned moneylender and eventual founder of Charterhouse School, a detail that did not escape the notice of several contemporaries. Evans notes that Jonson's long prefatory letter to *Volpone,* which centers on the problem of defamation, suggests that the playwright must have realized his audience would look to apply his work to specific individuals like Sutton: "Any implied criticism could have been read as having been designed . . . to spur the old man to use his wealth well, to finalize and implement the charitable designs he had long ago set down."[71]

Whether or not Jonson intended the play as personal libel, the contemporary perception demonstrates that *Volpone* was partially understood as a commentary on the charitable uses of wealth, and offers more fascinating evidence of a culture that considered the private wealth of individuals to be a communal concern. (Sir John Harington, for example, attempted to coerce Sutton into naming Prince Henry his heir.) A manuscript defending the memory of Sutton does nothing to contradict the assumption that Sutton's wealth was of public interest but instead states that Jonson merely targeted the wrong man: "Johnson lived to correct his mistake of [Sutton] out of a passage in Cicero twice translated by him . . . it appeared that [he] sought not soe much a prey for his covetousness to enjoy, as instrument for his goodnesse to bestow; who knew that of great riches there is noe reall use but distribution."[72] Using riches by distributing them was a cultural commonplace of the period, as I have mentioned, but *Volpone* perverts a custom that was accepted and practiced by the wealthiest entrepreneurs of the era. Instead Volpone defers distribution indefinitely while enjoying the pleasures of money in private.

Ultimately Volpone's wealth is not designated for an institution like Charterhouse School, "the Master-peice of Protestant English Charity,"[73] but rather confiscated by state authorities and directed to a hospital of incurable fools:

> *Avocatori.*   But our judgement on thee
> Is that thy substance all be straight confiscate
> To the hospital of the *Incurabili;*
> And since the most was gotten by imposture,
> By feigning lame, gout, palsy, and such diseases,
> Thou art to lie in prison, cramped with irons,
> Till thou be'st sick and lame indeed.–Remove him.
> *Volpone.*   This is called mortifying of a fox. (5.12.118–25)

It probably would be a mistake to consider the 1601 Statute of Charitable Uses of more topical significance than Edward Blount's 1600 translation of Tomaso Garzoni's *Hospital of Incurable Fools,* given the obvious allegorical texture of Jonson's satire, as well as Volpone's own declaration that "to be a fool born is a disease incurable" (2.2.163).[74] But the Avocatori's legal prerogative here gestures at the recent statute's power to shape and redirect charitable bequests, in addition to dramatizing the general desire among contemporaries to set right any potential misappropriation of funds that should be delegated to charitable causes, and to ensure the continued relationship between private profit and public good. Moreover, the reference to a hospital, however figurative in description, evokes the specific landscape of London poor relief, and Bedlam in particular, which attracted Jonson's attention before and after he composed *Volpone.* This would lend more texture to Volpone's final, provocative phrase, since the term "mortification," possessing a relatively obscure meaning derived from Scottish law, describes the distribution of property for charitable uses.[75]

The Alchemist: "Dear charity, / Now grown a prodigy"

Unlike *Volpone,* the illicit wealth amassed by tricksters in *The Alchemist* never reaches the public sphere but is diverted instead to the private use of Lovewit, the master of the house, who, discovering the fraudulent activities of his servant Face and cronies Subtle and Doll Common, demonstrates a shrewd opportunism in capitalizing on their schemes at the play's conclusion. The play's ending thus brings full circle its warped inversion of the proper relationship between commerce and charity: whereas London's model form of mercantile behavior, if we take the Lord Mayor's Shows as representative, suggests that individual commercial success should be redistributed in the form of charitable uses as a means of celebrating the communal order, material charity in *The Alchemist* serves instead as the capital that drives private commercial schemes, the starting point rather than end. This is the magic of alchemy, it seems, which transforms charity into private use, or at least monopolizes its material for personal pleasure.[76]

Jonson signals his interest in this dynamic by including repeated references to charity throughout the play. In fact, though the partnership between Face, Subtle, and Doll Common is explicitly depicted as a shared business venture, albeit one that is partly burlesque and obviously strained, Jonson nevertheless takes pains to frame their project in terms of charity. Doll Common, as her name befits her, makes several compelling arguments in behalf of communal purpose, exhorting both her partners to subordinate private interest to the collective good: "The venture tripartite? All things in common? / Without priority? 'Sdeath, you perpetual curs, / Fall to your couples again and cozen kindly / And heartily and lovingly, as you should" (1.1.135–38). Jonson probably means to parody Erasmus's introductory (and much celebrated) adage, *Amicorum communia omnia* ("Friends hold all things in common"), and the exhortation, spoken by a prostitute, possesses an ironic sexual resonance as well. But the tone does not fully undercut the classical and Christian notions of shared society that Jonson uses to introduce his tricksters, and in fact the episode appears to gesture at ecclesiastical controversy and charitable admonition when Doll commands Subtle, "Leave your faction, sir. / And labour kindly in the common work" (1.1.155–56). Appropriately, after promising to "conform" himself, Subtle invokes a conventional image of charitable society, claiming, "The knot / Shall grow the stronger for this breach" (1.1.152–62). Much like *Volpone*, Jonson seems to be satirizing a certain kind of charitable pretense—this commonality is all a masquerade, of course, and the partnership later dissolves into rivalry.

The perverse overlap between charitable and commercial desire, which courses throughout the play, is most fully embodied by Sir Epicure Mammon, whose urge to perform pious works sets into sharper relief his more comprehensive lust. An alchemical devotee and one of the work's primary satirical targets, Mammon desires the philosopher's stone for both private and public purposes, intending to distribute riches that are almost as immeasurable as the wealth he acquires. But the extravagance of his vision is unnatural, and in fact Mammon is introduced to the audience at the conclusion of the first act, in Subtle's mock dream vision, as a reformer of Nature itself:

> Methinks I see him entering ordinaries
> Dispensing for the pox, and plaguy-houses,
> Reaching his dose, walking Moorfields for lepers,
> And offering citizens' wives pomander bracelets

> As his preservative made of the elixir,
> Searching the spital to make old bawds young
> And the highways for beggars to make rich.
> I see no end of his labours. He will make
> Nature ashamed of her long sleep, when art,
> Who's but a stepdame, shall do more than she,
> In her best love to mankind, ever could.
> If his dream last, he'll turn the age to gold. (1.4.18–29)

This is, of course, Subtle's version of Mammon, a warped picture of the knight as painted by his own provocateur, and Subtle emphasizes the characteristics that make Mammon peculiarly vulnerable to the alchemist's machinations. It does not seem quite right to claim that Mammon is merely covering his lechery with the cloak of charity, as some scholars are tempted to do, since the knight's desires appear genuine enough to attract Subtle's predatory instinct.[77] He is clearly generous, wishing to cure leprosy and plague; he is also clearly lascivious, wishing to cure the pox (conveyed perhaps by certain "citizens-wives"). He desires urban renewal, reforming the hospitals and highways; so too he desires sexual renewal, and "to make old bawds young." But it is a worthwhile question to consider why Jonson chooses to dramatize these two traits as complements—a "voluptuous mind" (4.5.74), as Mammon later grieves, and a charitable instinct—*eros* and *agape* together in their most ludicrous dimensions. There is something seductive about both transcendent signifiers, in that each presents transformative power like alchemy itself, offering Mammon the apparent opportunity to enact his desire to imitate Godhead.[78] "Be rich," he declares to Surly in a parody of divine fiat, "And unto thee I speak it first: 'Be rich'" (2.1.24).

Subtle is not far off, it seems, in describing Mammon's dream of the Golden Age, itself an archetypal vision of natural bliss that the knight turns into something more like the myth of the Midas touch, which eventually reaches sexual climax: "She shall feel gold, taste gold, hear gold, sleep gold; / Nay, we will *concumbere* gold" (4.1.29–30). Mammon attempts to rival or surpass nature, to "do more than she, / In her best love to mankind, ever could." Consequently, his charitable and erotic visions remain unnatural, artificial, even monstrous. Later Subtle will describe "dear charity" to be "Now grown a prodigy with men" (2.3.17–18), and he means, presumably, that fraternal love is all too rare and marvelous, but Jonson also suggests that the virtue acquires a freakish aspect when practiced by men like Mammon. This prodigious form of love replaces the humble expression of daily charity that binds together communities, bleeding into Mammon's otherwise laudable desire to embody "the citizen-hero code of social conduct"[79]:

> I shall employ it all in pious uses:
> Founding of colleges and grammar schools,
> Marrying young virgins, building hospitals,
> And now and then a church. (2.3.49–52)

That last reference to a church, its climactic finality superbly deflated— "and now and then"—is merely an end to the beginning of Mammon's fantasy, since he intends to buy the roofs off churches to supply his alchemical project.

Marrying private monies and public works, Mammon hopes to join the ranks of other great Jacobean philanthropists like Thomas Sutton, it seems, endowing colleges and building hospitals and providing dowries. But these gifts, ostensibly directed toward charitable purposes, are merely manifestations of power. It remains unclear whether Jonson purposefully satirizes the charitable ethos of London's merchant community, or whether he employs the principles advertised in so many Lord Mayor's Shows to emphasize how far Mammon falls short of the mark. I think Jonson probably intends, with careful irony, to demonstrate how charitable gifts are often motivated by erotic desire, how the public good often walks hand in hand with private aspirations to fame and power. Mammon's fantasies certainly blur the distinction between erotic perversion and charitable giving (notice his excited reference to young virgins), and his future pious uses revolve around their own kind of pleasure principle, much like his sexualized vision of Doll Common: "But this form / Was not intended to so dark a use" (4.1.96–97).

Jonson uses Mammon's erotic imagination to pull down charity into the material sphere, where it becomes merely another exotic commodity he can acquire and consume. He explains to Surly that his "base affections" will not compromise the alchemical production because his involvement is merely a matter of consumer exchange:

> *Surly.*   Why, I have heard he must be *homo frugi*,
> A pious, holy, and religious man,
> One free from mortal sin, a very virgin.
> *Mammon.* That makes it, sir, he is so. But I buy it.
> My venture brings it me. (2.2.97–101)

Mammon's distinction between production and consumption, or labor and capital, bears suggestive resemblance to capitalist discourse.[80] But the knight's projection—aside from his plan to distribute elixir "at the rate" (2.1.75)—aims to explode notions of profit by rendering labor and exchange unnecessary. (It is worth noting, however, that his utopian vision will remain hierarchical, with Mammon as the king of his own commonwealth, much like Gonzalo in *The Tempest*.) Indeed, there is particular irony in Subtle's earlier description of Mammon, "I see no end of his labours," since the knight attempts to remove labor from both moral and material economies.[81] His aim is not to eradicate labor (or death) in the primitive sense, as in a prelapsarian paradise, but rather to obviate the process by virtue of unlimited purchasing power. It seems like a vision of charity and commerce participating in a mutual endeavor, exerting their own capacities, but each in a limited sphere: so, the alchemist's not-for-profit charity produces the philosopher's stone, which is purchased by Mammon and then used in an array of commercial and charitable schemes. Such a conception of charity reduces the virtue from a general social principle to a specific action that can be applied when convenient.

The religious separatists, Ananias and Tribulation Wholesome, express similar conceptions of charity as something to be employed only in select circumstances. Ananias, for example, asks Subtle whether or not the materials they plan to buy and invest in alchemy are owned by orphans whose parents had been "sincere professors," in which case they would be obliged to make a fair exchange:

> *Subtle.*   Good. I have
> Some orphans' goods to come here.

Ananias. Of what kind, sir?

Subtle.   Pewter and brass, andirons, and kitchenware,

Metals that we must use our med'cine on,

Wherein the brethren may have a penn'orth,

For ready money.

Ananias. Were the orphans' parents

Sincere professors?

Subtle.   Why do you ask?

Ananias. Because

We then are to deal justly, and give (in truth)

Their utmost value.

Subtle.   'Slid, you'd cozen else,

And if their parents were not of the faithful?

I will not trust you, now I think on't,

Till I ha' talked with your pastor. (2.5.51–62)

This is slightly different from the hypocrisy of Zeal-of-the-land Busy ("rich by being made feoffee in trust to deceased Brethren" [5.2.55]) and Dame Purecraft ("a devourer, instead of a distributor, of alms" [5.2.46]), both of whom will be integrated into Jonson's festive community at the end of *Bartholomew Fair.* Instead, Ananias articulates a perverse kind of situational ethics that reserves charitable dealing for specific religious adherents and tacitly condones the exploitation of others. Jonson was probably appropriating (and misrepresenting) specific economic tenets of various religious sects derived from their marginalized status, especially certain exclusivist principles espoused by H.N. and other Familists. The hyperbole serves to underline real tensions that existed in the local Blackfriars community, and especially between the theater (which might represent the performative aspects of religious conformity) and its neighboring Puritan population.[82]

Although he presents Ananias as an Amsterdam separatist and thus avoids engaging London Puritans directly, Jonson dramatizes a characteristically Puritan dilemma: how can the morally scrupulous survive London on their own terms? Even members of the separatist community cannot agree, it seems, as Tribulation demonstrates in his efforts to convince Ananias of temporizing, a posture that Jonson explicitly links to

Puritan notions of church reform, including the "hope of rooting out the bishops" (2.5.82). Jonson's critique of separatism and Puritanism centers on hypocrisy, to be sure, but he also attacks their specific policies. Much like Mammon's perversely mercantile vision of alchemy, the separatists treat commerce and charity as mutually exclusive projects that depend on the person involved in the exchange, rather than using charity as an *a priori* condition for ethical economic conduct. Jonson adds ironic depth and texture to his treatment of charitable commerce by expressing the normative social vision, one in which charity governs the entire process of economic exchange, through the person of Subtle, perhaps the least reliable character in the play:

> Has he a competent sum there i'the bag
> To buy the goods within? I am made guardian
> And must, for charity and conscience' sake,
> Now see the most be made for my poor orphans,
> Though I desire the brethren, too, good gainers. (3.2.115–19)

Here Subtle pretends to act as the intermediary in a mutually beneficial exchange that is governed by charity and conscience, but in this case charity has become the leverage Subtle uses to facilitate additional profit.

Subtle and Face are particularly adept at exploiting the language and material of charity. As Quicksilver notes in *Eastward, Ho!* of the London marketplace and its economic machinations, "If virtue be us'd, 'tis but as a scrap to the net of villainy" (2.2.18–19). The two rogues educate Mammon, for example, and encourage him to consider the alchemical process as something extra-commercial. Eventually the knight learns that he cannot merely "buy" the alchemical product of Subtle's so-called charity, and the process whereby he intends to acquire and distribute wealth requires something more participatory in its ethical demands:

> *Face.*   Ay, and repent at home, sir. It may be,
> For some good penance, you may ha' it yet:
> A hundred pound to the box at Bedlam–
> *Mammon.* Yes.
> *Face.*   For the restoring such as ha' their wits.

Mammon.   I'll do't.

Face.   I'll send one to you to receive it. (4.5.84–88)

This dialogue merely continues Jonson's fascinating portrayal of charity as an investment aimed at material rather than heavenly rewards, but he casually inserts a theological dimension to the episode. The play's commercial metaphors remain at the forefront, complicating Face's depiction of almsgiving as a meritorious exchange, but Jonson offers a confessional equilibrium between the Protestant "repent" and Roman Catholic "penance," between the active reason and volition involved in Mammon's purification process and the mysterious, providential results framed in the conditional: the charity of either faith is good enough to be gulled by, apparently. Face, witty enough to express a double entendre here of "restoring such as ha' their wits," will no doubt be happy to receive the Bedlam charity and bring it back home to his own vault. As a butler who sells the house's dole beer (1.1.53), Face is already comfortable commodifying traditional forms of charitable giving. The particular reference to Bedlam acquires added meaning since the hospital, which displayed its patients to visitors in order to stimulate charitable donations, had become a popular stop for citizens who wished to make a stylish tour "through London to th'Exchange, / Bedlam, the China-houses" (4.4.47–88).[83] As a site where public performances of charity merge with the private acquisition of social credit and fashion, Bedlam also bears a likeness to contemporary playhouses like the Blackfriars theater. There is an additional suggestion, of course, that Bedlam is the proper home for Mammon himself.

Near the play's conclusion, Face, who possesses an intimate understanding of his victims' respective psychologies, calls attention to the sensual fantasies that inform Mammon's notion of charity, which remains limited in its utility for all its hyperbole, a perpetual dish of cream for "tits and tomboys":

Lovewit.   What a great loss in hope have you sustained!

Mammon.   Not I, the commonwealth has.

Face.   Aye, he would ha' built

The city new, and made a ditch about it

Of silver, should have run with Cream from Hoxton;

> That every Sunday in Moorfields the younkers
> And tits and tomboys should have fed on, gratis. (5.5.75–80)

There is real humor in puncturing the knight's pretensions, although as Alan Dessen notes, the commonwealth *has* been the greatest loser in all of this, and Mammon consequently becomes "a symbolic embodiment of the failure of social obligation and personal responsibility in a world dominated by gold."[84] But the knight still has the opportunity to benefit the commonwealth, even after his dreams have dissolved. Willing to return Mammon's private property, Lovewit merely requires him to accept "public means" of humbling himself in a legal and performative ritual that recalls Quicksilver's spectacle of contrition at the conclusion of *Eastward, Ho!*. Mammon refuses to participate, however. By declining to submit his own pride to the public good and serve as a moral to others, he fails the test of charity and loses his private property in the process. He will only give in a posture of superiority.

In the end Mammon is little different from his friend Surly. Mammon is willing to indulge his charitable fantasies if he remains in possession of the philosopher's stone, to administer material goods without ever experiencing loss. But whereas he attempts to circumvent labor and production by engaging in a sophisticated marketplace that can buy or sell virtue, Surly will not participate in any kind of investment whatsoever:

> *Mammon.* This gent'man you must bear withal.
> I told you he had no faith.
> *Surly.*   And little hope, sir,
> But much less charity, should I gull my self. (2.3.122–24)

Of course, Surly really does lack charity, as Jonson makes clear. If the parable of the talents is indeed the governing conceit of *The Alchemist*, as Robert Knoll suggests, Surly provides the perfect embodiment of the third servant who buries his talent, since his singular purpose is avoiding any loss of his own—an obsessive care that lends genuine pathos to his realization that Dame Pliant has wed Lovewit: "How! Have I lost her, then?" (5.5.49).[85] He never gains anything, joining the ranks of gulls regardless, not on account of absurd fantasies but of a "want of putting forward" (5.5.55), as Lovewit explains. Surly indicts himself in similar terms, although he frames his own hesitancy as the consequence of honor, describing to Dame Pliant how she nearly lost her reputation (and nearly gained gonorrhea):

> Your honour was t'have catched a certain clap,
> Through your credulity, had I but been
> So punctually forward as place, time,
> And other circumstance would ha' made a man. (4.6.3–6)

The passage underscores Surly's constant worry over credulity, either Dame Pliant's or his own; he never offers credit to anyone but himself. He asserts his claim to a specific commodity, the wealthy widow of Jacobean drama, by virtue of what he has *not* done: "And where I might have wronged your honour, and have not, / I claim some interest in your love" (4.6.10–11).[86] Surly represents a certain type of London citizen who refuses to participate in the whirligig of early modern business, a system founded on informal exchange and mutual interest.[87] There is something about Surly's parsimonious behavior—as a rogue (which he is), as a merchant, or as a prospective husband—that Jonson refuses to endorse.

But Jonson never fully endorses Lovewit's triumph either, and Face, the true mastermind of the play, gets the last word of the epilogue. In characteristic fashion he engages the audience in a type of exchange supposedly based on goodwill but actually equivalent to judicial bribery: "this pelf, / Which I have got, if you do quit me, rests / To feast you often, and invite new guests" (5.5.163–65). Face marks a subtle correspondence between the audience and the rest of his gulls, since the money from their admission fees has ended up in his pockets as well, but he attempts to reassure spectators that they will receive ample compensation through future acts of hospitality—that is, more performances. It is a metatheatrical culmination of the play's entire plot, which repeatedly asks for charitable capital (in the form of consumer material and consumer behavior) intended to be alchemized into charitable uses, but which ultimately ends up as private profit.[88] As David Riggs notes, Jonson repeatedly gestures toward the play's "auspices of production," inviting spectators to note "that their situation was not just analogous, but identical, to that of their onstage counterparts."[89] In this case each guest in the audience has contributed to the commercial endeavor of Blackfriars, a theater that Jonson suggests treads its own fine line between morally suspect and morally approved business, diverting potential monies for charity to pleasurable uses. Indeed, Face's ambivalent comments register Jonson's possible discomfort with the theatrical phenomenon he has staged and in which he has participated.

Jonson repeatedly performs his own type of alchemical illusion for the gulls who frequent the theatre, and it becomes difficult to separate his work from the endeavors of Face and Subtle, who present their artful labors to a varied group of spectators:

> I should be sorry
> To see my labours now, e'en at perfection,
> Got by long watching and large patience,
> Not prosper where my love and zeal hath placed 'em—
> Which (heaven I call to witness, with yourself,
> To whom I have poured my thoughts) in all my ends
> Have looked no way but unto public good,
> To pious uses and dear charity,
> Now grown a prodigy with men. (2.3.10–18)

Subtle's rhetorical legerdemain here, a theatrical performance that claims to be intended for charitable uses, possesses uncanny resemblance to Jonson's various defenses of his dramatic work. Just as Subtle's art requires patience and long watching ("Heaven I call to witness, with your self"), the playwright describes his own efforts at composition in similar terms during the apologetical dialogue of *Poetaster*, stating, "If a free Mind had but the patience," he might damn "his long-watch'd Labours to the Fire." In his *Discoveries*, he endorses the crucial role performed by poets in behalf of the commonwealth. Of course Jonson, in the same work, describes how the artistic process involves a movement between public and private domains, one that acquires and appropriates material from a public storehouse of wit, "to convert the substance or riches of another poet to his own use." *The Alchemist*, which dramatizes the sheer fun of fraudulent exchange, potentially casts the playwright as just another cunning rogue, and it is tempting to wonder whether Jonson is gathering up literary material in order to sell his own theatrical commodity, much as Face commodifies the house's dole beer.[90]

Although both are putatively moral projects—Face and Subtle claim to be offering various services to their respective gulls, after all—there is a crucial difference between the "venture tripartite"'s criminal charade and Jonson's own mode of aesthetic production. Whereas the alchemical jargon used by the petty criminals aims to obscure their designs, Jonson repeatedly advertises in clear terms that deceptive language is hardwired into his dramatic enterprise. Placing his fictive mode at the forefront, he reminds readers in his preface, for example, to "beware at what hands thou receivest thy commodity; for thou wert never more fair in the way to be cozened (than in this age) in poetry, especially in plays" (2–4).[91] Here he ostensibly directs his critique at rival dramatists who traffic in hyperbole and popular romance, but the phrase, arriving in the prefatory epistle of a play that puts cozening center stage, serves as a kind of *caveat emptor* for his own audience who will be tempted by the machinations of Face and Subtle. But the deception can be productive as well. In *Eastward, Ho!,* for instance, the otherwise stolid Golding contrives a successful reconciliation between Touchstone and Quicksilver by feigning his own imprisonment and calling for his father-in-law to visit him in prison, where the goldsmith arrives just in time to hear Quicksilver deliver a self-composed penitential ballad. The scene's staging is elaborate, with Golding playing the role of chief dramatist, but Touchstone is untroubled by the ruse, claiming, "The deceit is welcome, especially from thee, whose charitable soul in this hath shown a high point of wisdom and honesty" (5.4.97).[92]

In *The Alchemist,* language is the primary means by which both characters and playwrights negotiate complex social exchanges—legitimate or otherwise—that advertise the possibility of marrying together charity and commerce. This is a fragile relationship that involves mutual trust and credit, as Jonson reminds Salisbury in his frantic letter from prison, when he complains that certain spectators "deal not charitably who are too witty in another man's works."[93] The process also requires an interpretive rigor to penetrate the illusions of self-interest and stabilize the dynamic of literary exchange. Jonson highlights this dilemma in his prefatory epistle to the readers of *The Alchemist,* whom he separates into two classes: "If thou be'st more, thou art an understander, and then I trust thee. If thou art one that takest up, and but a pretender, beware at what hands thou receivest thy commodity" (1–3). Note how the distinction, which centers on the issue of judgment, becomes felt at the level of social relations; an understander can be trusted, as a friend, as someone "more" than just a consumer of literary goods, whereas a pretender corrupts that relationship, and is in fact told to "beware" the theatrical commodities he purports to buy and judge.[94] He makes a similar distinction in the preface to *Catiline* between the "Reader in Ordinarie," for whom the book is a purchased product—"It is your owne"—and the reader extraordinary, to whom Jonson submits his work and life.[95] A commercial contract provides one kind of guarantor that stabilizes the literary exchange, as in the induction's articles of agreement in *Bartholomew Fair*, but in *The Alchemist's* prologue, Jonson suggests an alternative experience that can result in mutual success: "When the wholesome remedies are sweet, / And, in their working, gain and profit meet" (15–16). Assuming that Jonson does not intend "gain" and "profit" here as synonyms but rather as jointly beneficial outcomes—pleasure and edification, perhaps, or commercial and moral advantage—it seems the right combination of love and money can please both playwright and audience.

Of the various fantasies dramatized in *The Alchemist*, this notion of bringing together public gain and private profit is perhaps the most powerful, one that captured the collective imagination of the London marketplace. Although skeptical of the charitable work performed by merchants and other acquisitive individuals, and apparently ambivalent about his own participation in the enterprise of commercial theater, Jonson nevertheless thinks of his dramatic work in similar terms, as a kind of "pelf," if Face might stand in for Jonson, which "rests / To feast you often, and invite new guests" (5.2.164–65). Any kind of private gain is sublimated into public gifts of hospitality and liberality. Early on in his career Jonson suggested that the transformative powers of moral comedy might themselves galvanize charitable uses, such as the powerful conversion experienced by Sordido in *Every Man Out of his Humour*, whose "best Grain" will be "made alms-bread, to feed half-famished mouths" and whose "gather'd heaps being spread abroad, / Shall turn to better and more fruitful uses" (3.8.43–47). And near the end of his life, of course, Jonson famously used charity as a figure of literary scorn, likening Shakespeare's *Pericles* and other popular romances to "the shrieve's crusts," scraps "raked into the common tub," and "the alms-basket of wit" (21–30). But perhaps the figure suggested itself because he was already accustomed to thinking of his own productions as charitable gifts of a kind—not "plays" but instead a lifetime of good works.

Ad Aphilum.

Virg.8.Æneid.
Mortua quinetiam iun-
gebat corpora vius,
Componens manibusque
manus atque oribus era.

THE tyraunt vile MEZENTIVS, put in vre,
Amongſt the plagues, wherewith hee murthered men:
To binde the quicke, and dead, togeather ſure,
And then, to throwe them both into a denne.
   Whereas the quicke, ſhould ſtill the dead imbrace,
   Vntill with pine, hee turn'd into that caſe.

Thoſe wedding webbes, which ſome doe weaue with ruthe,
As when the one, with ſtraunge diſeaſe doth pine :
Or when as age, bee coupled vnto youthe,
And thoſe that hate, inforced are to ioyne,
   This repreſentes : and doth thoſe parentes ſhowe,
   Are tyrauntes meere, who ioyne their children ſoe.

Yet manie are, who not the cauſe regarde,
The birthe, the yeares, nor vertues of the minde :
For goulde is firſt, with greedie men prefer'de,
And loue is laſte, and likinge ſet behinde :
   But parentes harde, that matches make for goodes :
   Can not be free, from guilte of childrens bloodes.

Quàm malè inequales veniunt ad aratra iuuenci,
Tam premitur magno coniuge nupta minor.

Ouid. Epiſt.9.

FIGURE 7. Geffrey Whitney, *A Choice of Emblemes, and other devises* (Leiden, 1586), sig. N2.
Emblem 116: "Impar coniugium." The Rare Book & Manuscript Library, University of Illinois at
Urbana-Champaign.

CHAPTER 5

CHARITABLE SINGULARITY

Negotiations of Liberty in Civil War England

"The glue of the Spirit," "the Cement, that can joyne Hearts and Soules," "the lime and morter" of "the spirituall building," the bond of perfection: these related images figure forth one of the primary social, ecclesiastical, and political functions of charity during the early modern period, which was to bind together disparate persons into a unified community.[1] Charity was conceived as the primary guarantor of communal harmony. Even among individuals, such was the centripetal force of charity that John Donne could ascribe to it the power of collecting and fastening together the dispersed remains of spiritual identity—"the redintegration of a broken heart, the resuscitation of a buried soule, the re-consolidation of a scattered conscience."[2]

But for the Church of England, struggling to cleave to an imagined *via media* between Papism and Anabaptism, and for the country in general, the role of charity had become increasingly vexed by the 1630s, emerging as a problematic source of contention among the nation's various constituencies and disrupting the uneasy consensus that marked the earlier Jacobean church. And by the early 1640s, rival forms of charity had become entrenched in even sharper divisions, between supporters and opponents of prelacy, and between supporters and opponents of the king and his counselors, which left little room for moderation or temperance: "In the midst of these two, are a Remnant of sad lookers on."[3] What was supposed to bind together the people of England was contributing to the nation's fractured identity.

Historians debate the timing of this shift and attribute a variety of causal factors to the gradual polarization of the church, assigning significance to the strength of an emerging anti-Calvinist discourse (evident, for example, in Richard Montagu's work *A New Gagg for an Old Goose*), to an alteration of ecclesiastical policy and personality effected by the transition between monarchs, and to the appointment of William Laud to the archbishopric of Canterbury. These developments were profoundly disorienting for many in the Church of England, especially for Puritans of a more rigidly Calvinist disposition.[4] Whereas the conventional Puritan stance considered charity to be a crucial factor in separating the godly from the ungodly, and the Papist from the Protestant as a matter of course, Laudian practices were shaped by older notions of charity that emphasized social unity and communal ritual. This effort to reinstitute and reinforce native traditions was highlighted by the Book of Sports, which was reissued in 1633 and prompted spirited debates over sabbatarianism, as many Puritans found festive dances and other Sunday recreations to be redolent of England's Roman Catholic past.[5]

Perhaps none of these issues was new: one can trace a conciliatory attitude toward Roman Catholicism as far back as Richard Hooker, and conflict over double and absolute predestination was older still, while sabbatarianism had been a topic of debate throughout the latter half of the sixteenth century and Jacobean era.[6] But taken together with the apparent political influence at court of the Catholic queen Henrietta Maria and the rigorous application of Laudian policy, as well as the consolidation of ecclesiastical power among anti-Calvinist divines, all of these policies compelled a number of moderate and rigid Calvinists to worry that Laudian clerics were drawing England "neerer daily towards Popery, under shew of Antiquity, Uniformity, and Charity."[7] This form of charity, moreover, seemed to opponents to be reserved only for supporters of prelacy. Richard Crashaw's poem "On a Treatise of Charity," for instance, which was appended to Robert Shelford's *Five Pious and Learned Discourses,* used charity to defend even the pope from detractors: "O he is Antichrist: / Doubt this, and doubt (say they) that Christ is Christ. / Why, 'tis a point of Faith. What e're it be, / I'm sure it is no point of Charitie."[8]

Meanwhile, as Herbert Palmer notes, royalists and supporters of prelacy found it within their scruples to link Parliament and Puritans to the devil's party, a posture that "Rhetorizes so for charity on the one side, and wholly neglects it on the other."[9]

As in the previous century's Admonition Controversy, rival notions of charity now revealed fundamental differences in ecclesiastical discipline. Laudian clerics like Richard Watson aimed to preserve charity by placing a greater emphasis on uniformity, prompted by worries that the "knot of Christian charity" would be loosened too far by diversity of worship: "while there is a Congregation in the Church, there's a Conventicle in a chamber, a Meeting in a barn, and a Ring too it may be in the fields or woods; it's a hard matter to bind al these together."[10] This Laudian project culminated in the *Constitutions and canons ecclesiasticall* (1640), modeled after Elizabeth's 1559 *Injunctions* and the ecclesiastical canons instituted by James in 1604, and they explicitly invoked the "rule of charity" as a means of easing factional tension. Better known for its infamous *et caetera* oath, this collection included another important section on "some Rites and Ceremonies" (primarily concerned with the communion table) wherein the ecclesiastical authorities invoked the concept of *adiaphora* in order to defend the uniformity of worship: "we desire that the rule of Charity prescribed by the Apostle, may be observed, which is, That they which use this Rite despise not them who use it not, and that they who use it not, condemn not those that use it.[11] The chiastic expression embodies a message of accommodation and compromise, but its force is deflected by the rest of the document's rigid calls for compulsory uniformity. Opponents disagreed with the entire premise inherent to this form of charity. In a response to the canons, an anonymous commentator posited a rival interpretation of *adiaphora*, observing that the prelates abused the rule of charity by willfully appropriating the concept in order to put stumbling blocks in the way of honest Christians. As a consequence, so they claimed, the prelates had chosen to "prescribe to a whole Land a Rule of false Charity."[12]

Much of this contention had to do with the bonds of charity, which were too loose according to some, and too strictly enforced in the minds of others. The same clerics who insisted on preserving a loose contingency in their application of theological rigor or predestinarian logic, meanwhile, were often hardliners about uniformity of worship. Their opponents, frustrated by these ceremonial constraints, believed church authorities were too loose in countenancing ecclesiastical misgovernment and doctrinal error. These ironies are captured in John Winthrop's *Homily on Charity,* addressed to a small group of disaffected Puritans leaving England for Massachusetts on the ship *Arbella,* which enlists charity to their project and in fact insists that they should remain "all in each other, knit together by this bond of love."[13] Even as they crossed the vast space of the Atlantic Ocean to find freedom from the rigor of England's church authorities, Winthrop pictures his ideal Christian society as one united in charity. References to the knot or bond of charity often expose paradoxical commitments of this kind, particularly among contemporaries who wished to protect the liberty of individual conscience in a society bound together by stable communal norms.

At the same time, in debates between Caroline divines and Roman Catholic disputants, the role of charitable admonition continued to drive a wedge between religious factions. In 1630, the recusant knight Sir Tobie Mathew published an anonymous tract entitled *Charity Mistaken,* which responded to accusations by clergy in the Church of England, John Donne among them, that Roman Catholicism stood in violation of charity by willfully conferring damnation on all Protestants. Mathew's document is fascinating for a variety of reasons, but perhaps the most relevant feature is its general tone and attitude, evident in his dismissal of the motions toward toleration initiated by Charles and Laud, which he claims are incompatible with either confessional allegiance: "It will not be want of Charity in either of us, both to hold, and declare, the others Religion to be incompatible with salvation: nay it will be want of charity if we do it not."[14] Mathew's hard line may be a product of his suspicion that Caroline toleration was intended to convert recusants to the Church of England, but his work likewise refuses to align charity with the principles of accommodation, associating the virtue instead with a single, unified body of truth.[15] And in the spirit of fraternal correction, he declares it is his charitable obligation to rebuke the papacy's doctrinal opponents.

Mathew's treatise generated a number of Protestant responses, each demonstrating varying degrees of truculent partisanship, from the reputed Arminian Christopher Potter, the college head and later dean of Worcester, and the skeptical theologian William Chillingworth, to

Francis Rous, a strict Calvinist and John Pym's stepbrother.[16] These treatises reveal as many differences in English Protestant identity as they do
continuities. Potter's reply to Mathew, which adopts and only partially
upholds an irenic stance toward ecumenical charity, articulates a Laudian
exasperation with confessional polemic, and he might be referring to
Puritans as much as Catholics when he declares, "This angry unmercifull
passion they call Zeale to the holy cause, and that which is mere malice must passe for pure Charity."[17] On this point the Puritan Rous, who
refuses to cede the high ground of what he considers orthodox faith to
any project of charitable toleration, seems to have more in common with
Catholic controversialists like Mathew, John Floyd, and Matthew Wilson
(alias Edward Knott) than with his fellow Protestants—among whom
Chillingworth, in particular, expands the concept of *adiaphora* to accommodate the idiosyncrasies of personal disposition and conscience.[18]

Chillingworth wants to carve out room for an individual conscience
to negotiate spiritual perplexities, but Sir Kenelm Digby's response to
Chillingworth, in *A conference with a lady about choice of religion*, might
stand in for a range of religious and cultural constituencies anxious about
singularity: the main fault of Protestantism, for Digby, lies in its inherent subjectivity of faith, "euery particular man gouerning himselfe in this
matter by the collections of his owne braine."[19] English Protestants fretted about religious separatism as well: "Thus *quot homines, tot Sententiae*,
So many men, so many minds."[20] In his *Remonstrance*, the moderate
Calvinist Joseph Hall traces a similar ecclesiastical trajectory, worrying
over the perils of religious schism or separatism, and claiming "there will
be a division . . . until they come to very atoms."[21] Some voices welcomed
this flexibility and freedom, as in Thomas Carew's poem to Aurelian
Townshend that envisions love "made all spirit," his "corporeal mould
turn'd to atoms."[22] More often, however, the atom was invoked as an emblem of decay or chaos, a figure of the social, religious, and political fis-
sures that continued to widen in contemporary discourse.

In Caroline England "singularity" was conventionally associated with
religious nonconformity, in part because it refused to follow the rules of
the church: the Puritan Zeal-of-the-Land Busy, perhaps Jonson's most
memorable threat to the festive community of *Bartholomew Fair*, is characterized by the "violence of singularity in all he does"; Thomas Nashe

dubs singularity "the eldest childe of heresy"; and Richard Baxter, writing in the 1650s, laments how recent experience has taught the English to "imagine that private Meetings tend to schism or proud singularity."[23] At the beginning of *Histrio-mastix*, William Prynne feels obligated to disclaim any "factious Novalty, or puritanicall singularity"; Donne is even more direct: "God loves not singularity."[24] But the meanings attached to the term, despite its apparent opposition to the collective priorities of charity, bespeak a more fundamental ambivalence during the period. Although "singularity" often conveyed a sense of dissent, innovation, or self-aggrandizement, the word also could be used to describe an individual's deserved eminence or extraordinary skill. The singular voice, which was dangerous and prone to misjudgment, might nevertheless possess prophetic power and divine sanction. The intense factionalism of the 1630s and 1640s encouraged a number of writers to experiment with various inflections of "singularity": to find evidence of providential favor in the particularities of their own "singular" experience; to cultivate a rational skepticism opposed to the common errors of the multitude; to preserve the autonomy of individual freedom amid the contingencies of a shifting political and religious landscape.

This chapter discovers similar contradictions in Thomas Browne's *Religio Medici* and John Milton's divorce tracts, a series of treatises he composed in the 1640s that aimed to reform divorce law, especially the refined and expanded *The Doctrine and Discipline of Divorce* (1644). Both writers aimed to align the communal imperatives of charity with personal liberty, enlarging and protecting the scope of what they often refer to as "singularity." The project was a difficult one, however. Browne and Milton both promoted singularity during an era marked by worries that private imperatives were pulling apart England's social fabric. Milton's use of charity is especially surprising, because he invokes the concept, with all of its assumed power of binding, in support of divorce, severing the link between two spouses that is protected by divine power. (As Matthew 19 declares, "What therefore God hath joined together, let not man put asunder.") Browne's expressions of charity might seem more conventional, given his work's celebration of the Church of England, but he too employs the term to find space and sanction for "many things singular, and to the humour of [his] irregular selfe."[25]

These two writers might seem an odd pairing for this final chapter, given their apparent opposition in crucial matters of politics, religion, and, perhaps especially, temperament. Browne professes "to keepe the road," to "follow the great wheele of the Church," and so to "leave no gap for Heresies, Schismes, or Errors" (15), whereas Milton proudly aligns his own religious posture with heresy by observing of its etymology, "only the choise or following of any opinion good or bad in religion."[26] In his preface to *Religio Medici*, Browne delivers brief but decorous support of Charles and "the name of his Majesty defamed" (9); not long thereafter Milton writes in defense of regicide. Milton engaged in a polemical scrum with Joseph Hall, attacking the Bishop of Norwich with evident relish in his animadversions. Browne, meanwhile, was Hall's physician throughout the last two decades of the elderly divine's life, and he considered Hall to be "a person of singular humility, patience and pietie."[27] Browne claims in his preface to have composed *Religio Medici* merely for his own "private exercise and satisfaction" whereas Milton, in the second edition of his *Doctrine and Discipline of Divorce*, addresses Parliament and the Westminster Assembly. Even their memorable prose styles differ remarkably, with "the soft and flexible sense" (10) of Browne's writing contrasting Milton's forcefulness.

But in comparing Browne's *Religio* and Milton's divorce tracts, a number of relevant correspondences surface. These works were part of the same cultural moment and conversation, after all: Milton's first edition of the *Doctrine and Discipline* was published a few months after Browne's authorized version of *Religio Medici* appeared in 1643. More important to this book's premise, both of these texts directly engage the concept of charity in ways that are crucial to their respective projects and yet confounding to readers, then and now. In doing so they represent or embody certain principles and postures that have remained persistent concerns throughout this book—in particular the problematic role of charitable hermeneutics, interpreting the scriptural and somatic bodies, respectively—bringing nearly full circle a trajectory that began with More and Tyndale. Browne specifically discusses the problem of vagrancy and "those professed Eleemosynaries" (72), for instance, and his recent biographer makes a compelling case that Browne's notions of charity were influenced by a formative period in Halifax, a city that had gained proverbial renown for its reformed charitable institutions as well as its gibbet, a machine of execution that enacted a vivid intersection between private and public possessions and the criminal body: in order to regain their stolen goods, victims of theft were forced to cut the gibbet's cord themselves; otherwise the materials would be distributed to charitable uses.[28]

Meanwhile, Milton's depictions of charity throughout his divorce tracts regularly deploy an allegorical mode that remains fraught with many of the same bodily complications encountered in Spenser's *Faerie Queene*. Milton uses a range of celestial epithets to figure forth the concept: "the wing of charity," "the immaculate hands of charity" and "the now-only lawgiving mouth of charity"; "the all-interpreting voice of Charity her self" and "the divine and softning breath of charity."[29] By assigning corporeal (and female) dimensions to the virtue, envisioning feet, hands, a wing, a mouth, and a voice, the author comes perilously close to a composite picture of the Holy Spirit, with its tongues of flame, its breath of wind, and its associations with the dove. The Spirit was traditionally individualist and lay, opposed to clerical hierarchy, and associated with the dangers of religious enthusiasm and antinomian excess. Contemporaries, fairly or no, branded most religious thinkers who argued in behalf of the Holy Spirit as *"Anabaptisticall, Antinomian, Hereticall, Atheisticall"*—terms, in other words, of exactly the kind William Prynne attaches to Milton's first divorce treatise.[30] And yet Milton offsets this imagery by including in his *Doctrine and Discipline* a kind of rational ballast that links charity to natural law and equity—"the general and supreme rule of charity" (277), the "fundamental and superior laws of nature and charitie" (325), "that authentick precept of sovran charity" (343), or "charitie, the interpreter and guide of our faith" (236)—which gives his treatises a texture more in the style of learned commentaries by Hugo Grotius or John Selden than radical sectarians, and which prompt one scholar to suggest that Milton sacrifices "scriptural precept to reason."[31] So, Milton's contemporaries feared that his prose would usher in a Familist orgy fueled by religious enthusiasm; and now his scholars accuse him of privileging reason before revelation of any kind, including the Bible.

Browne's work elicited a range of responses, too, some of them heated in their opposition. In fact, his dispassionate emphasis on reason was a source of consternation for several of his earliest readers. Alexander Ross was displeased by Browne's restraint, which he suspected was the result of a tepid investment in the defense of true faith: "To suffer God to be wronged, and not to be moved, is not charity, but luke-warmnesse or stupidity."[32] Even Dean Christopher Wren, a conformist cleric of Windsor and the younger brother of Bishop Matthew Wren, expressed disappointment that Browne did not identify the pope as Antichrist, littering the margins of his copy of *Religio* with learned authorities who supported that claim. He seemed especially troubled by Browne's disinterested approach to charitable giving.[33] Wren took offense at Browne's claim that relieving misery is merely passionate and not reasonable (and so only "moral"): "But our natural affections and Passions Regulate by Divine Commaunds, transcend the highest Pitche and flight of Reason."[34]

Both Ross and Wren, as contemporary readers of *Religio Medici,* want to carve out a role for affection in their respective visions of charity, whereas Browne's seems cold by comparison. Scholars sometimes demonstrate a similar impulse, desiring more passion and controversy from Browne and less "university-educated, élitist contempt for the 'ignorance' of the clashing sects."[35] But recent work placing *Religio Medici* in the context of religious controversy has demonstrated how much Browne's otherwise idiosyncratic notions of charity engage relevant issues of ecclesiastical polity.[36] As Achsah Guibbory quite rightly notes, Browne cannot avoid the theological scrum of his period, and there is occasion to approach *Religio Medici,* which is apparently organized around the Christian virtues, through this sort of theological or ecclesiastical lens, treating the text as a relatively benign addition to contemporary religious controversy. But for Browne the usual dichotomies sometimes seem artificial, or at the very least only partially right.[37] While offering keen insight into the charged religious landscape of the moment, studies that emphasize the controversial aspects of *Religio Medici* rarely capture the fullness of Browne's work, reducing his notion of charity, for example, to questions of ritual and anti-Papal rhetoric. Or perhaps the problem is that these critiques imply a fullness in Browne's work that is actually fractured, since, as Guibbory notes, "Browne's 'singularity' and skepticism distance him from Laudian rigor and threaten to destabilize the Laudian ceremonialist order that Browne would defend."[38] Despite his promotion of singularity, however, Browne achieves a kind of equilibrium by enlisting charity to negotiate between solitary and communal imperatives, between God and man and nature, and between the worlds of spirit and physic.

Paradoxes abound throughout both Milton's and Browne's respective projects. In the *Religio*, charity is not merely the subject but also the vehicle of its discourse. Browne's treatise, both in its original and published form, was at least partially motivated by some aspect of charity (as a devotional meditation, for example, and as a curative for irresponsible publication), and various considerations of charity modulate the style and content of the work throughout, especially in his appreciation for the civil discourse that would enable the communal task of advancing learning.[39] That project was a vexed one for Browne, who uses charity in apparently contradictory fashion, sometimes to justify sharing knowledge in order to confute error and sometimes to encourage a safe silence that protects others from potentially contagious heresy or schism. In the second part of *Religio Medici*, Browne suggests that charity is enabled and enacted both by the acquisition of knowledge and the elimination of error, but earlier he claims that his own theological errors were prompted by "charitable inducements" (17). In similar fashion, when Milton declares that Parliament and the Westminster Assembly might open the "misattended words of Christ" with "the key of charity" (354), invoking a traditional metaphor for scriptural hermeneutics, he claims such an action will in fact discover and defend charity: charity is both the key that unlocks the box and the treasure inside. Dennis Danielson makes a similar point about Milton's theodicy, noting that its "conclusion is also its starting point."[40] In the divorce tracts, charity is both Milton's point of origin and his end, the virtue that prompts, governs, and validates the entire process of reading and interpretation.

A comparison of these two texts results in its own kind of paradox. Browne's desire for orthodox sanction, as well as his understanding of charity as a sign of communal sympathy, seems to gesture at Thomas More's position of a *sensis communis*. But this posture belies his repeated efforts throughout the *Religio* to difference himself and "draw into a lesser circle," to "play and expatiate with security" (18). Milton, meanwhile, deploys a mode of biblical hermeneutics inherited from William Tyndale and other reformers that privileges the individual conscience before custom and tradition, and his scriptural exegesis discovers a divinely sanctioned right to divorce. And yet Milton's charity repeatedly unites concepts of apparent opposition, traversing divisions between body and spirit, for example, and between reason and revelation, celebrating marriage even as he argues in behalf of divorce. Both Browne and Milton use charity to negotiate the tensions of binding and loosening, but their project of liberated selfhood is almost exactly inverted: Browne preserves his singularity by submitting to communal strictures, whereas Milton desires spiritual and civic autonomy before pursuing relational bonds.

Medicine, Morality, and the Charitable Physician

In the latter half of the 1630s and early 1640s, as Browne was composing and revising his *Religio Medici* amid an increasingly fractured religious culture, the discourse of medicine was similarly troubled by competing visions of charitable conduct for physicians. At the risk of oversimplification, these disputants might be separated into two camps: learned physicians, who relied on the study of complex Galenic humoral theory, and a rival assortment of alternative healers, who employed spiritual or herbal or distilled "chymicall" remedies. When Browne begins the first part of his treatise by mentioning "the generall scandall of my profession" (11), he is referring to the reputation for atheism among learned physicians, a specific complaint that was promulgated by Browne's rivals in the medical marketplace.[41] Later, when he shifts his focus from matters of faith to charity in the second part (although this division is a porous one), Browne continues to keep in mind "those sordid, and unchristian desires of my profession" (84). Physicians were vulnerable to a general perception that they profited from the pain and suffering of others, in addition to monopolizing medical practice and excluding outside access to learned physic, which was associated with paganism to boot. More specifically, the charitable imperative posed a thorny dilemma for contemporary doctors of physic: on the one hand, ministering to desperately ill patients placed a physician's reputation in danger if the disease proved incurable; on the other, refraining from treating dangerous cases confirmed for many contemporary observers that physicians lacked any Christian charity. Long before Stanley Fish declared that the author of *Religio Medici* was a "bad physician," Browne was accustomed to accusations of this kind; for many of his contemporaries, the adjective was redundant.[42]

Early modern doctors of physic responded to these accusations by deploying their own forms of charity to defend the profession. The most prevalent argument among physicians adopted something like the prescribed "order" of charity outlined in medieval canon law. That is, physicians posited a hierarchy of charitable obligations and skills in the sphere of medicine, and placed a primacy on their own authoritative knowledge, to which other practitioners should defer. As numerous theologians and social critics debated the possibly dangerous consequences of unregulated charitable giving, learned doctors of early modern England emphasized the medical hazards attending the administration of charitable physic. Well-meaning but insufficiently educated neighbors or ministers might do violence to the recipient's body. John Cotta, for example, after giving a slight nod to the benevolent intentions of some lay healers, delivers a scathing rebuke to unlicensed practitioners who dare attempt to displace the physician:

> And for those that herein make mercy and commiseration apologie for their rash violating the rules of wisedome, sobrietie and safe discretion in ignorant intermedling, I wish them consider how dangerous are the harmes and consequences of good intentions, and charitable indeauors, where they runne before knowledge and proprietie in the agent.[43]

Cotta employs the "rules" of wisdom and discretion to contrast the practice of physicians to the impassioned, rash response of ministerial charity, which runs too quickly ahead of the agent's actual capacities. The physical, pragmatic context of medicine, its constant specter of pain and mortality, makes the possible harm of "charitable indeauors" all the more relevant and apparent. There is nothing quite so uncharitable, Cotta implies, as irresponsible manslaughter by way of improperly applied physic. Providing several examples of cases in which patients suffered and even died as a result of "ignorant intermedling," he seems primarily concerned with the intrusion of ministers, who, "making themselues roome in others affaires, vnder pretence of loue and mercie," can sway prospective patients by asserting an authority that rivals the learned doctor.[44]

Nevertheless, there was a clear overlap between the vocation of physician and minister, one that was scripturally sanctioned by the example

of Christ, who performed miraculous cures. The distinction was especially porous in provincial areas where learned practitioners were scarce,
a pragmatic issue that prompts George Herbert's exhortation for country
parsons to study physic and surgery (or to marry a wife with skill in these
disciplines).[45] Robert Burton describes the phenomenon in less optimistic terms than Herbert, observing, "Many poore Countrey-Vicars, for
want of other meanes, are driven to their shifts; to turne Mountebanckes,
Quacksalvers, Empiricks."[46] A number of clerics, most notably William
Bullein, contributed to the vast body of vernacular medical literature in
the period.[47] Burton, for his defense, asserts a professional ethic of *quid
pro quo*, claiming ministers have their own grievances against physicians:
"I doe not otherwise by them, then they doe by us. If it be for their advantage, I know many of their Sect which have taken Orders, in hope of
a Benefice."[48] Moreover, cultural attitudes toward medicine during the
period were informed by Calvinist notions of providence, which often
viewed illness as an occasion for repentance and spiritual maturation,
lending additional authority to ministers who could offer spiritual as well
as corporeal healing.[49] Gabriel Plattes, in his utopian vision *Macaria* (1641),
a treatise explicitly derived from Bacon's *New Atlantis*, declares that ministers rather than physicians should provide medical care, with the clear im-
plication that clergy would practice medicine charitably instead of looking
for profit.[50] And the Neo-Platonism promulgated by Marsilio Ficino was
easily imported by Paracelsians who idealized the hermetic wisdom of a
priest-physician exercising his piety on the body as well as mind.[51]

  The learned physicians in early modern England hardly composed a
stable or monolithic community of adherents to Galenism, which was
itself extremely flexible in its adaptation to new medical developments.
Nevertheless, many physicians, concerned with the professional threat
posed by spiritual lay medicine and determined to oppose the heterodox
opinions associated with Paracelsianism or folk healing, developed concepts of charity that privileged the specific skills acquired by rigorous education. James Hart's *Klinike*, for example, suggests that charity needs to be
professionalized according to education and ability:

> Charitable workes, I confesse, are to be performed; but every person
> is not fit for the performance of every worke of charity. The ministers

charity is to have a care of his peoples soules, to visit and comfort them when they are sicke; and even to extend their charity to their bodies, according to their ability. As for the curing of their bodies, that exceedeth the compasse of their callings, and in so doing they break down hedges, and intrude upon another mans right.[52]

Hart's ideas of charity owe a great deal to Cotta's earlier writings, and both authors envision a division of charitable labor based on the giver's aptitudes, "according to their ability," a communal vision resonant of Paul's first epistle to the Corinthians, which discusses the charisms or gifts distributed to each individual by the Holy Spirit in order to stabilize the religious and social community.[53] But Hart's mention of hedges, which presumably distinguish the borders between various professions, embodies some of the tensions implicit in charity. Hedges were considered an emblem of legal and social order—it is unsurprising that William Laud invokes the hedge to illustrate the role of ecclesiastical ceremony—and in Hart's case, good hedges make good (and loving) neighbors.[54] The breaking down of hedges was conventionally associated with lawbreakers and popular uprisings, but hedges were also dubious metaphors for many contemporaries, symbolizing the private enclosure of land that had become a familiar illustration of uncharitable greed and a satirical commonplace of agrarian complaint.[55] In order to articulate his own notion of a charity that respects professional difference, Hart invokes a traditional opponent of communal charity.

The worst violators of charitable decorum, according to contemporary physicians, were the empirics, quacksalvers, astrologers, and wise women who employed charity as a plausible justification for mercenary motives. Here, too, there is an easy analogue to religious polemic, which often accused sectarian opponents of abusing the cloak of charity, or as Hart declares of physician-clerics: "I have heard some of them pretend a charity and love to their neighbours to helpe them in their need . . . But this is no new practice to cover vice with the mantle of vertue."[56] Richard Whitlock employs the same principle (though he tones down the rhetoric) to attack the supposed charity of cunning women: "It is generally believed they do use their little or no skill in meere *Charity* . . . Whereas on stricter Scrutiny, this Benevolent Practise will . . . end in *injuriousnesse,* and that to more than the *Patient*."[57] Much of this defensive posture is the result of insecurity among physicians, jealous of their privileged position in a varied landscape of medical practitioners that ranged from the traditional tripartite association of physicians, apothecaries, and barber-surgeons to an assortment of laypeople, from midwives and charitable gentlewomen to cunning men and, supposedly, witches.[58]

There was also widespread skepticism concerning the efficacy of learned physic—as Bacon claims, "We see [the] weakenesse and credulitie of men, is such, as they will often preferre a Montabanke or Witch, before a learned Phisitian"—which was placed in sharper relief by the recurring plagues during the early modern period, since Galenic medicine struggled to treat or theorize contagion.[59] And the reputation of physicians likewise suffered from their own conscious disavowal of the artisanal aspects of the profession, which were left to apothecaries and surgeons, as well as their absence during epidemics.[60] Nor was the learned physician's reputation helped by his apparently aloof attitude toward patients, which stood in contrast to the behavior of empirics, who participated more intimately in therapy and whose remedies were less expensive and sometimes more effective.[61]

More important, and in direct opposition to the notion of professional decorum expressed by Cotta and Hart, these competitors were often associated with charity. Many of them explicitly advertised their physic's elements of Christian mysticism or their own miraculous skill, invoking their apostolic inheritance of healing powers. Richard Bostocke, a Paracelsian, declared that the followers of the "Chymicall doctrine," unlike those heathenish Galenic practitioners, were "more paynefully, faythfully, sincerely, charitably and Christianlike for the certein helpe of his neighbor, and not for lucre or veine glory and pompe."[62] It is doubtful Bostocke intended that fantastic pun, "veine glory," but he clearly marked out his own territory of Christian healing in opposition to the atheist and blasphemous arts propagated by Aristotle and Galen. Charity was not merely associated with medical reform but also medical revelation; Sir Thomas Elyot compares contemporary physicians unfavorably to their Greek, Roman, and Arabic authorities, who "in this part of charity . . . far surmounted vs Christians, they that would not haue so necessary a knowledge as Phisick is, to be hid from them which would be studious

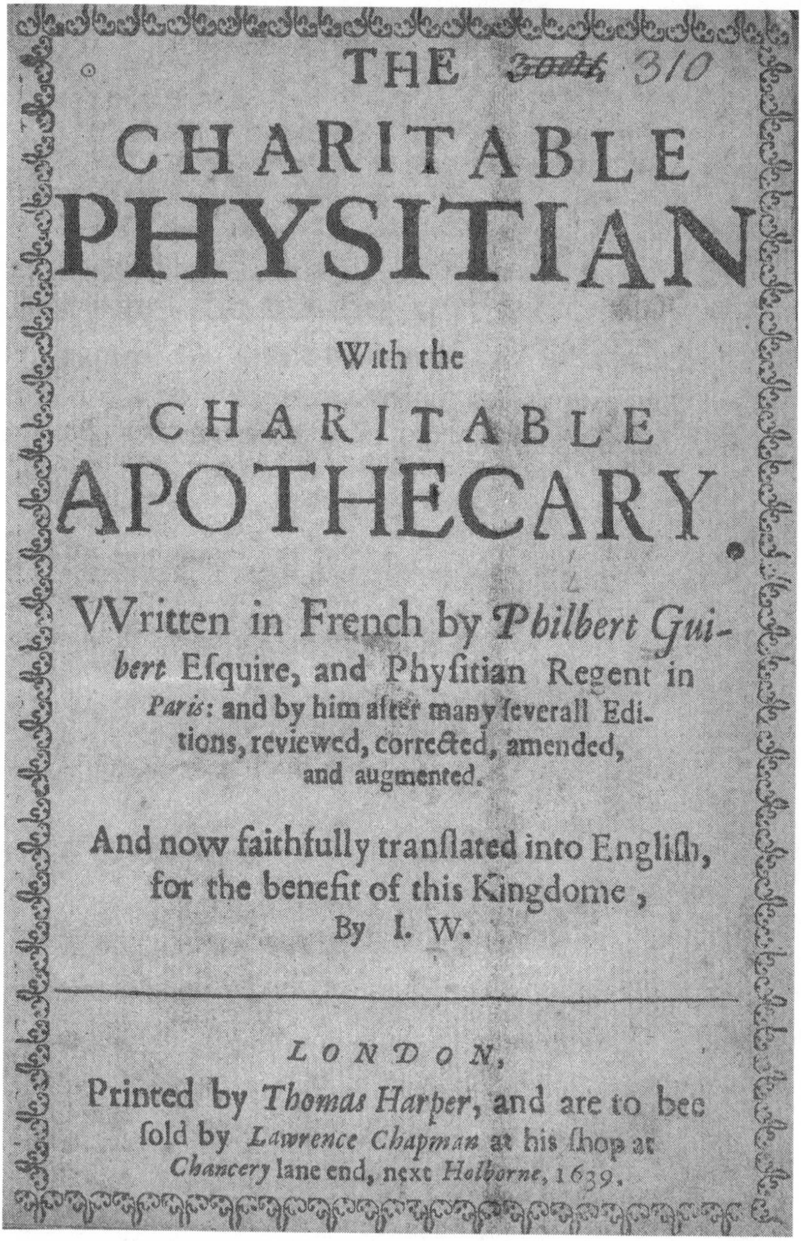

THE ~~South~~ 310

CHARITABLE
PHYSITIAN

With the

CHARITABLE
APOTHECARY.

Written in French by *Philbert Gui-
bert* Efquire, and Phyfitian Regent in
Paris: and by him after many feverall Edi-
tions, reviewed, corrected, amended,
and augmented.

And now faithfully tranflated into Englifh,
for the benefit of this Kingdome,
By I. W.

LONDON,

Printed by *Thomas Harper*, and are to bee
fold by *Lawrence Chapman* at his fhop at
Chancery lane end, next *Holborne*, 1639.

FIGURE 8. Philippe Guybert, *The Charitable Physitian* (London: 1639). Houghton Library, Harvard University.

about it."[63] Indeed, much like biblical translators providing vernacular access to the scriptures, promoters of Paracelsian medicine often advertised their work as a divulgation for the public benefit of secrets long hidden (in Latin and Greek) by the medical establishment, or as practical remedies intended to facilitate self-help or household healing.[64] In the preface to a treatise by John Hester, a noted distiller and Paracelsian, James Fourestier describes the content as "charitable learning or learned charitie, practised vpon and performed vnto those, which haue stood in neede."[65] Many Paracelsian treatises explicitly advertised the affordability and efficacy of their medicines.

Contemporary physicians did little to combat these perceptions. Cotta could, in a fit of hyperbole, describe the learned physician in rapturous terms—"What emploiments are more continuall workes of charitie? what vertue commeth nearer vnto God in goodnesse and mercie?"—but most advocates of learned medicine, Cotta included, more often appealed to the classical ethics of Hippocrates and Aristotle.[66] These tenets, though compatible with Christianity, clearly privileged acquired learning before spiritual revelation and seemed to place the imperative of charity in the context of professional reputation rather than as a good in itself. Municipal schemes of poor relief relied on a varied assortment of medical practitioners, and learned physicians participated with varying degrees of enthusiasm and often with the expectation of remuneration.[67] It is telling that the College of Physicians demonstrated no philanthropic activity of any kind, as was expected among London companies, and physicians rarely participated in any kind of civic role of office.[68] The college did not provide a charitable dispensary for the sick poor until the end of the seventeenth century.

Most damning, however, was the perceived "monopoly of physic" enjoyed and jealously guarded by learned practitioners, symbolically represented by the College of Physicians.[69] This was a theme expressed with greater vehemence after Browne published his *Religio*, when a substantial number of radical social critics would rail with articulate fury at the three professions of law, divinity, and physic. But resentment toward the college had been entrenched in the medical community practically since its founding in 1518.[70] Although its standards tightened under Laud's oversight, the ecclesiastical licensing system in place for the rest of England was relatively inclusive, and a medical license could be obtained by evidence of education and good reputation. In London, however, the College of Physicians exerted control over the city's apothecaries and barber-surgeons, and examined or prosecuted all "irregular practitioners," or those who did not possess a license, in addition to governing its small number of members. Rather than promoting education or participating in the civic fabric of parish and city institutions, the college's main function, it seems, was as a policing agency, and although its regulatory system was established ostensibly to guard against medical malpractice, it was equally effective in discouraging competition. By accusing learned physicians of forming a "monopoly," contemporaries were equating their professional conduct with the exploitation of royal prerogative, associating doctors with the Stuart regime's supposedly vast abuses of political corruption and promotion of special interest to the detriment of the public good.

Despite attempts by Cotta, Hart, and others to carve out a privileged position for physicians within the religious landscape, a stigma of atheism and avarice remained attached to Browne's profession. If his religiosity became a model for subsequent physicians, there is little evidence that Browne himself had the opportunity to draw on many conventional examples of the charitable physician.[71] These issues seem especially pertinent to his early years of practice in England, as he grew accustomed to the cultural peculiarities and practical exigencies of his chosen occupation. If Brooke Conti observes a "strangely defensive" tone at the beginning of *Religio Medici,* which she considers (rightly, I think) a mark of the author's genuine religious anxiety, such apprehension would likely have been exacerbated by the practical import of his profession's reputation, especially in a provincial and godly Yorkshire town like Halifax.[72] There are moments in the *Religio* when Browne distances himself from his fellow practitioners, but he often articulates a forceful defense of his medical profession. Like a number of learned physicians, Browne was sympathetic to elements of Paracelsian medicine, but his primary scholarly authorities were considered irreligious and medically suspect by a number of rival practitioners, and appeared to corroborate the learned physician's contemporary reputation as cold, aloof, and Latinate.

Perhaps Browne has these accusations in mind when he compliments the divinity of Aristotle and especially Galen, whose work compares favorably, he claims, to the Jesuit Suarez's work on metaphysics. Meanwhile, he alludes repeatedly to the boundaries between doctors of physic and divinity that distinguish their respective skills and professional contexts. Sometimes he apologizes (with irony) for his own breach of professional decorum, as when he claims, "I cannot goe to cure the body of my Patient, but I forget my profession, and call unto God for his soule" (79). But elsewhere he asserts a confident superiority to clerics, contrasting their authority and efficacy in treating spiritual maladies with his own: "I can cure the gout and stone in some, sooner than Divinity, Pride, or Avarice in others. I can cure vices by Physicke, when they remain incurable by Divinity, and shall obey my pils, when they contemne their precepts" (85). The poised syntax, its perfect balance of clauses, underscores the professional rivalry and suggestively heightens Browne's powers: the physician's pills can cure gout or stone as well as vices like avarice or pride, while the cleric's precepts fail at both. Finally, Browne admits that some physicians are guilty of avaricious conduct, but he does not retreat from the justice of a "worthy salary of our well intended endeavours" (85), suggesting, like those early modern English merchants from the last chapter, that private gain could be married to public good.

Religio Medici registers a sensitive awareness of the conflicting imperatives of medicine and divinity.[73] And yet the language of early modern medicine complemented many of the standard tropes employed in religious discourse, which were inherited from Old Testament imagery, in particular the Psalms and Proverbs, as well as extracanonical texts like the Vulgate's Book of Wisdom, which explicitly links illness with sin and declares that the Holy Spirit will only minister to a disciplined mind *and* body.[74] Moreover, the physician's reliance on a blend of conceptual theory and practical experience dovetails nicely with Browne's own treatment of the theological virtues, which emphasizes how abstract belief manifests itself in the concrete and physical domain of charity, "without which Faith is a meer notion, and of no existence" (70).

If Browne's medical profession made him vulnerable to claims of atheism, it nevertheless offered a paradigm through which he could examine crucial and vexed spiritual matters. He modifies his commitment to physic, moreover, with a "soft and flexible" discourse that accommodates a balance between the conventional bedrock of his natural philosophy and religion, and the rigorous skepticism with which he treats both disciplines. Throughout *Religio Medici,* Browne imports the learning acquired during rigorous medical preparation in order to dissect and diagnose contemporary religious illnesses as well as his own. He takes advantage of these medical tropes in order to facilitate his complicated negotiation of apparent conflicts of interest related to charity: between his own singularities in religion and a concern for "the common cause" (85), and between his desire for reforming error and his resistance to religious partisanship.

"The true Anatomy of my selfe": Browne's Charitable Constitution

Throughout the introspective project of *Religio Medici,* Browne searches for a constitutional balance in his own person while simultaneously glancing at disruptions to the larger social, political, and religious body in England. In assessing his own spiritual and ethical character, Browne often employs the language of anatomy, which was a conventional metaphor deployed by a number of social, religious, or intellectual critics during the period, but he takes seriously the link between spiritual and corporeal domains. At the beginning of the second part, for example, Browne appears to locate his charitable disposition in the stuff of physical matter: "And if I hold the true Anatomy of my selfe, I am delineated & naturally framed to such a piece of vertue: for I am of a constitution so generall, that it consorts and sympathizeth with all things" (70). Browne's medical training is immediately apparent in his peculiar logic of causation, which attributes his charitable impulses to a natural frame and constitution rather than any kind of education, habit, or willpower. At this moment in the text, Browne sounds very much like a physician, assessing both Galenic naturals and non-naturals, and finding "no antipathy, or rather Idio-syncrasie, in dyet, humour, ayre, any thing" (70). Charity can be the product of a physical disposition, it seems, and consequently might be subject to anatomical examination. Browne employs "anatomy" here in its figurative sense, of course, but the term refers more immediately to the physical realm, and Browne maintains this dialectic between moral virtue and its natural or bodily origins throughout *Religio Medici.*

Nor is such anatomical inspection an isolated enterprise, conducted out of curiosity or even narcissism. Instead the rigorous self-knowledge derived from this experience becomes essential to a healthy spiritual community. This type of empirical gaze, turned inward to assess one's own physical constitution and body or one's spiritual health, was a familiar principle of early modern medical regimens as well as in Calvinist manuals of pious living, since religious writers encouraged vigorous introspection so as to experience the influence of divine providence.[75] There was a pragmatic imperative at work as well. As Thomas Hill explains, medical diagnostics serve a crucial role because a knowledge of self allows you to love God and neighbor: "Seeyng it is true (gentle Reader) that the first and principallest poynt of wisedome is to know God, the second to knowe our selues, and the thirde to knowe our duties towardes our neighbors."[76] In other words, Hill notes, knowing yourself—and knowing your *body*—allows you to love yourself, God, and others as well. Thus the early modern period baptized the classical dictum *nosce te ipsum* ("know yourself") with medicine as well as religion. Browne's own attitudes toward charity are clearly shaped by this cultural commonplace, and his discussion of universal concepts often seem inflected by personal concerns, though he carefully frames his own remark in the conditional, "If I hold the true Anatomy," acknowledging the uncertainty of any diagnostic enterprise.

If he is careful to qualify his own capacity for self-knowledge, Browne appears less cautious in describing charity, which he considers to be a virtue comprehensive in its scope, one that "consorts, and sympathizeth with all things." It is easy to associate Browne's regard for the "diversitie" and "variety of nature" (73), as well as his professed conversation, which is "like the Sunne's with all men" (85), with contemporary appeals to religious toleration. In defending the Church of England from Catholic polemicists, for example, Christopher Potter uses a conventional musical metaphor, comparing the variety of doctrinal opinions afforded by charitable singularity to a textured song: "As in a musicall consort, a discord now and then . . . sweetens the harmony."[77] Browne's conception of charitable sympathy, meanwhile, envisions the human body interacting with the larger cosmos. Both of the verbs Browne uses, "consort" and "sympathize," when linked to charity, preserve the integrity of singular bodies or sounds even as they remain oriented toward a common good. Browne wants to sympathize with rather than be subsumed into all things, to find some correspondence that can produce harmony by consorting with dissimilarities. The passage embodies the notion of *concordia discors* even in its rhetorical fashioning, as Browne moves from a consideration of his individual constitution to matters of cosmic importance, but this interaction is knit together by paradoxical phrasing: Browne's own personality dilates outward into "a constitution so generall," whereas charity, which apparently creates universal harmony, becomes reduced to merely "a piece of vertue." As I will explain, this is typical of Browne's attitude toward charity, which tries to accommodate the concept's general imperatives to the particular contingencies of each individual.

A similar pattern emerges in Browne's discussion of heresy and schism, in which he deploys medical tropes to maintain a balance between individual and communal concerns. When he observes, "Those have not only depraved understandings but diseased affections, which cannot enjoy a singularity without a Heresie" (17), he suggests there is a medical as well as religious problem to solve, a disease as well as depravity, as with the French divine "so plunged and gravelled with three lines of Seneca, that all our Antidotes, drawne from both Scripture and Philosophy, could not expell the poyson of his errour" (31). Browne's curative rhetoric, which frames his arguments as "antidotes" intended to "expel" erroneous poison, was a conventional metaphor for describing heresy, but it becomes more relevant when employed by a physician. Indeed, Browne seems to employ a hybridized Galenic scheme to construct his understanding of heresy, with its attention to the correspondences between microcosm and macrocosm, and with its sensitivity to the disruption of every human individual's constitutional balance, which manifests itself in an infected singularity. He has few qualms in declaring his own penchant for various heresies, since all of these are prompted by "charitable inducements," a regard for the spiritual welfare of others—even, one might add, concern for the devil. That is, Browne's own heresies are brought on by his desire to participate in a universal framework, a clear contrast to Milton's equation of heresy with the choice of individual conscience.[78]

If Milton is proud of his singular interaction with the Holy Spirit, Browne is pleased that even his sins are neither rare nor exclusive:

I thanke the goodnesse of God I have no sinnes that want a name; I am not singular in offences, my transgressions are Epidemicall, and from the common breath of our corruption. For there are certaine tempers of body, which matcht with an humorous depravity of mind, doe hatch and produce viciosities, whose newness and monstrosity of nature admits no name. (81)

Browne, characteristically, expresses gratitude for his common sinfulness in idiosyncratic fashion. Moreover, in comparing moral corruption to contagion, he apparently reverses the etiological links between disease and immorality: rather than assuming that the pox was a divine penalty sent to punish depraved individuals and communities, a popular notion of the period dismissed by most learned physicians, Browne understands bodily constitution and disease ("humorous depravity") to be the origin of spiritual corruption. He looks to the material body as a landscape in which he can explore religious topics of dubious nature, using the mysterious intersections of human corporeality and spirituality to subvert common expectations. Elsewhere Browne explicitly mentions the consolation he derives from knowing that anatomical inquiry has yet to discover the seat of the rational soul (46–47), and in this case his initial expression of gratitude for his "common breath" of corruption allows him to move from the doctrine of original sin to complications of copulation between human and beast, and other singular depravities produced by humoral distempers.

So, while Browne desires to participate in the communal (if epidemical) social fabric, he engages in the topic with a pronounced sense of individuality. He never rejects singularity outright, even when he finds it dangerous, and in one celebrated passage reminiscent of Burton's digression of air in *The Anatomy of Melancholy,* he revels in the opportunity for speculation in "many things untouch'd, unimagined," as long as those explorations are restrained by sobriety, honesty, and orthodoxy:

'Tis true that men of singular parts and humors have not beene free from singular opinions and conceits in all ages; retaining something not onely beside the opinion of their own Church or any other, but also any particular Author: which notwithstanding a sober judgement may doe without offence or heresie; for there are yet after all the decrees of counsells and the niceties of the Schooles, many things untouch'd, unimagined, wherein the libertie of an honest reason may play and expatiate with security and farre without the circle of an heresie. (17–18)

For all of Browne's worry over the problem of singularity, this is a robust defense of individual liberty. It is a playful liberty, moreover, which, like the "liberty of reason" (88) he ascribes to the world of dreams, seems to accommodate his desire to humor his fancy. It is important to remember, then, that Browne intends for his vision of orthodox "security" to protect the private imagination. There is also a spiritual egalitarianism in this passage, which confidently declares the existence of "unimagined" spiritual matters that can be accessed by any singular individual. For someone who describes his own behavior as "full of rigour, sometimes not without morosity" (12), Browne carves out a remarkable space for his imagination to roam, but this recreative impulse first needs its limits defined by "a sober judgement."

Browne never seems fully capable of resolving this desire for playful expatiation with the more serious threats associated with singularity. Much of *Religio Medici* attempts to reconcile these competing impulses, and charity plays an important role in this effort. The impulse to break free of restraints imposed by the communal body often results in disruptive violence. Just after he explains that a melancholic disposition prompted his own temporary belief in apocatastasis, or Origen's belief in universal salvation, Browne invokes humoral pathology to describe and understand the problem of religious schism:

> For heads that are disposed unto Schisme, and complexionally pro-
> pense to innovation, are naturally indisposed for a community,
> nor will ever be confined unto the order or oeconomy of one body;
> and therefore when they separate from others they knit but loosely
> among themselves; nor contented with a generall breach or dichoto-
> mie with their Church, do subdivide and mince themselves almost
> into Atomes. (17)

It is difficult to tell whether Browne's mention of complexion here refers to the classic Galenic sense of humoral combination, or whether he is focusing on the skin, its color and texture, as if he were conducting a physiognomic study identifying the facial characteristics of the average schismatic. The phrase "heads . . . disposed unto Schisme" might refer to physical anatomy, the brain in particular, but it could also serve as a metonymic description of any kind of nonconformist thinker. A few sentences later, in a wonderful expression, Browne confides that religious subtleties never "stretched" his own *pia mater*. Regardless, a schismatic temperament is clearly a *natural* indisposition, and it seems to be a physical one as well, a medical malady that manifests itself in the social and religious community. The entire passage, with its concern for "the order or oeconomy of one body," conflates political, religious, and medical discourses, producing a confused mixture Browne uses to engage and explain the problem of singularity. In this case "innovation," a typical marker of complaint among religious reformers, results in bodily mutation or even a kind of willful atomism. In the course of Browne's description, schism ends up sounding like a flesh-eating disease.

In suggesting that schismatic complexion results from a humoral imbalance, Browne seems to point in particular to distempered bodies suffering from "adustion," a problem of overheating that was linked to madness. Even charity itself, a traditional opponent of schism, becomes vulnerable to overheating in this kind of affective discourse. Browne observes that the adage "Charity grows cold" is "most verified in those which most doe manifest the fires and flames of zeale; for it is a vertue that best agrees with coldest natures, and such as are complexioned for humility" (77). In this case the inherent warmth of charity is offset or even negated by the warmth of zeal, whereas a cooler disposition allows the heat of charity to thrive. A similar relationship between choler (or anger) and charity could be found in popular conceptions of Galenic medicine, such as Sir Thomas Elyot's *Castell of Health*, which claims that the natural heat engendered by ire results in "losse of charitie, amitie, credence, also forgetfulnes of benefite proceeding, and of obedience, dutie and reuerence."[79]

Elsewhere Browne employs this oppositional framework to envision a constitutional harmony in his own body that is mirrored by the universe:

It is no breach of charity to our selves to be at variance with our vices, nor to abhorre that part of us, which is an enemy to the ground of charity, our God; wherein wee doe but imitate our great selves, the world, whose divided Antipathies and contrary faces doe yet carry a charitable regard unto the whole, by their particular discords preserving the common harmony. (81)

Browne is appropriating humoral discourse to articulate a concept of stability in the physical and figurative body, gesturing at the problematic volatility of zealous reformers who upset the balance of various religious or political affections. Later, in *Christian Morals,* he will stress the moral limitations of Seneca and Epictetus, urging his readers not to be "Rocks unto the Cries of charitable Commiserators" (274), but here his medical vocabulary moves charity into an improvised (and slightly awkward) alignment with Stoicism, a "cold principle" (57) that Browne leans toward by privileging a "generall and indifferent temper" (71), declaring that "it is the method of charity to suffer without reaction" (14). It is worth noting again that Browne's indifference to Rome prompts Ross's accusation of a "luke-warm" and "stupid" charity, but the epithets only confirm what Browne has been laboring to demonstrate. Even as he tries to make space for singularity, Browne's own charitable ideal *is* lukewarm, *is* stupid, and consequently avoids the polarizing impact of the "hotter sort of protestants" and Roman Catholic controversialists.

"There is surely a physiognomy": Reading the Charitable Body

If Browne uses humoral theory to conceptualize a restrained, stable form of charity, his engagement with physiognomy, a relatively obscure discipline that studies bodily features and signs to predict a patient's future, reveals a similar fascination with the problem of singularity. Occult treatises of physiognomy during this period confidently declared their access to a secret wisdom, which, underwritten by a doctrine of corresponding signatures that were at once legible and essential, matched facial features with interior conditions (red hair always revealed a predisposition to ire, for example). This kind of attitude is evident in Helkiah Crooke's *Microcosmographia,* the most thorough anatomical treatise written in English during the period, which sneers at Momus for wanting windows into men's souls when the eyes will do just as well: "Do not all the passions of the minde appeare plainly characterized in the face, in the countenance, & in the eyes, so that he which runnes may reade them?"[80] The body was confounding but also crucial for early modern thinkers insofar as it offered potentially demonstrable evidence of spiritual or affective conditions, and the science of physiognomy provided a tantalizing opportunity to understand the relations between spiritual and physical discourses. Browne's entire literary career evinces a constant fascination with the subject of surfaces. He probes bodily exteriors for signs of human morality and divine purpose, attempting to discover a discipline whereby one might "acquire a Physiognomical intuitive Knowledge, Judge the interiors by the outside, and raise conjectures at first sight."[81] Browne's study of charity in *Religio Medici* repeatedly makes use of physiognomy, which provides a paradigm in which he can link together the singularities of each individual with the common features of humanity.

These habits of reading are evident in Browne's engagement with poor relief. Poverty remained an urgent social problem during the 1630s, but Browne nevertheless reserves a great deal of skepticism for projects of material charity, which he claims are complicated by self-interest and politics—and by greed, "the liberty to amasse & heape up riches" (71). Moreover, his own experience of witnessing Halifax's charitable schemes likely informed his reservations concerning the efficacy of poor relief, which, as we have seen, involved a problematic course of reading the poor and classifying them into categories of "deserving" or "able-bodied." Browne suggests the process is even more dynamic, that "those experienced and Master Mendicants" just as certainly read the bodily texts of their potential donors, targeting specific individuals in whom "they spy the signatures and markes of mercy" (72).[82] Here, in examining the circumstances and complications of poverty, the study of bodily appearance asserts itself as a troubled imperative. More generally, Browne's observation is emblematic of his tendency to use the vocabulary of learned physic and natural philosophy as a means of knitting together spiritual and material phenomena.[83]

Although he is vexed by the many counterfeits and problematic errors that confound "this great worke of charity," Browne remains fascinated by the opportunity to read in the physical body an enduring signature of divine love. Physiognomy might facilitate the exploitation of merciful dispositions, but the discipline can be marshaled (as Browne does in the same section) toward an appreciation of divine providence and the supreme handiwork of God. Indeed, he has already suggested that Christians, "who cast a more careless eye on these common Hieroglyphicks, and disdain to suck Divinity from the flowers of nature" (25), would do well to consider the mystical and hieroglyphic artifacts of divine creation. Later in his career, in *Christian Morals,* Browne reverses the interpretive dilemma and sets physiognomy in a positive light, claiming that "true Charity is sagacious" and urging readers to "Acquaint thy self with the Physiognomy of Want, and let the Dead colours and first lines of necessity suffise to tell thee there is an object for thy bounty" (419). His digression into physiognomy and chiromancy underscores the difficulty of reading the body's valuable but inscrutable text. At once holy—"The finger of God hath set an inscription upon all his workes" (72)—and also vulnerable to disease, violence, and disguise, the body figures as a complex work full of contradictions and interpretive challenges.

Browne invokes Aristotle as the classical precedent for this kind of intellectual inquiry, and though he clearly is thinking of Pseudo-Aristotle's *Physiognomica,* he might also have had in mind the *Prior Analytics,* which claims that "it is possible to infer character from physical features, if it is granted that the body and the soul are changed together by the natural affections."[84] However, as several early modern medical authorities emphasized in their own physiognomic studies, perhaps in an effort to distance their work from occult treatises, Aristotle acknowledged that the link between these signatures is probable rather than essential. Taking up the complicated meaning of a sign, medical writers considered the dilemma of encountering multivalent symptoms and attempted to design theories of probability that might stabilize the interpretive process.[85] That is, even as physiognomy was rooted in a tradition of hermetic wisdom, the discipline was gaining prominence in the medical field as a sophisticated mode of interpreting physical evidence.

This attitude toward physiognomy mirrors a more general trend in early modern culture noted by Richard Sugg with regard to the period's increased anatomical rigor and expertise: medical developments generated an intensified effort to discover the interplay between body and soul, an old notion now "vividly resituated in a new context of empiricism, sensuous exactitude, and interior complexity."[86] In other words, Browne could honor the mystical legacies he found so expressive of Christian piety even as he participated in the development of increasingly complex theories of probability in medical discourse. Learned physic provided its own form of charitable reading. More important, he repeatedly articulates his own brand of skepticism concerning the legibility of hieroglyphic signs, which are sometimes transparent and self-evident but often unreliably volatile, and are more likely, as Reid Barbour notes, "to reflect backwards on the human decipherer than outwards and upwards to the divine geometrician."[87] The interpretive flexibility of physiognomy allows Browne to engage charity without succumbing to the dichotomous logic plaguing contemporary disputes in England over social and religious policy.

Indeed, Browne is careful to protect his probabilistic logic from any kind of essentializing rigor that effaces individual difference. Consider his stern disposition toward those who quickly make generalizations after observing specific cases:

> There is another offence unto Charity, which no Author hath ever written of, and [as] few take notice of, and that's the reproach, not of whole professions, mysteries and conditions, but of whole nations, wherein by opprobrious Epithets wee miscall each other, and by an uncharitable Logicke from a disposition in a few conclude a habit in all. (75–76)

The statement is slightly disingenuous, of course, interjecting a bit of ironic humor to engage the polarized religious culture of early modern England; quite a few of Browne's contemporaries took notice of "opprobrious Epithets" like "Puritan," "Arminian," or "Papist." But the problem of erroneous classification is a serious one for Browne in that it reduces the various singularities of man or nature into rigid categories. Here Browne focuses on a reckless application of inductive reasoning or empiricism—he calls it an uncharitable *logic*—that moves up by induction from particular to general traits, whereby the behavior of individuals can be applied to a larger population. Motivated by and participating in the Baconian project, which makes clear the crucial importance of orderly method, Browne's statement stresses that this is a matter of social urgency as well.[88] Browne returns to this problem in *Pseudodoxia Epidemica,* itself a response to Bacon's call for a calendar of popular errors, by observing that this kind of mistaken logic is the most common: *"A dicto secundum quid ad dictum simpliciter . . .* This fallacy men commit when they argue from a particular to a general; as when we conclude the vices or qualities of a few, upon a whole Nation. Or from a part unto the whole."[89] Indeed, this frustration with fallacious logic might be a better context in which to understand Browne's aversion for the multitude, "that numerous piece of monstrosity" (71), which he explains in more detail in his examination of popular errors. In the *Pseudodoxia,* Browne describes this kind of fallacy as a "circle," linking the problem figuratively to his earlier discussion in *Religio Medici* of "the circle of an heresie" (18). But the main thrust of his argument, whether he intends to attack the multitude, religious controversialists, or natural philosophers, is to protect contingency, circumstance, and singularity. Even as he articulates a respectful orthodoxy, Browne remains careful to avoid anything that effaces individuality in the cause of essentialism, and he finds it particularly important to retain the probabilistic core of "charitable" logic.

Browne's own practice of semiotics was incredibly complex, often intersecting medical and moral imperatives. As he explains his prognosis in *A Letter to a Friend,* he mentions a consideration of his patient Robert Loveday's facial expression, the planetary motion during Loveday's nativity, peculiarities of the hand and ear, Loveday's record of previous illnesses, relative hairiness and dental records, diet, and even oneirocriticism.[90] Although Browne quickly rules out a number of factors as irrelevant or dubious, the scope and variety of his interest is dazzling. He reads nearly every aspect of his patient's life and illness. Loveday's skin and face—that is, his physiognomy—plays the most important role in this process, corroborating Browne's initial diagnosis and suggesting a mortal prognosis immediately confirmed by the patient's subsequent death. But the apparent fatality of the disease does not stop Browne from proceeding to a consideration of Loveday's interior condition, especially since so many patients exhibit "that stupid Symptom" of avarice near the end of their lives, a kind of spiritual sickness that joins the bodily disease. Browne clearly considers it important to mention that Loveday was charitable, ascribing something like material reality to the patient's generous but illusory desires to donate "publick and lasting Charities": "Surely where good Wishes and charitable Intentions exceed Abilities, Theorical Beneficency may be more than a Dream" (111). Browne assigns incredible vitality to the interior world of human desire. Here, in that wonderful phrase "theorical beneficency," we catch a quick glimpse at Browne's own permeable threshold between faith and charity, the two supposedly rival virtues of early modern theological discourse. Browne traces in his patient the ontological origins of charity, equating the start of good works to the onset of good wishes. Perhaps more important, Browne's description of Loveday's charitable intentions demonstrates his facility in moving between medical and ethical or spiritual matters, as his physiognomy does not conclude with a prognosis but continues into something like a eulogy. As Preston notes, the generic mixture of a "medical *consilium* which attends to the specifics of an individual case history, and *sententiae* which expound general truths" accounts for the odd push and pull of the work, blending together a focus on the singular disease of the patient with universal truths.[91]

This stylistic approach is typical for Browne, who deploys a similar pattern of logic throughout *Religio Medici,* especially in his treatment of charity. In the context of friendship, for example, charity generates an inverse movement. At times the virtue acts as an ideal bonding agent by uniting virtuous friends in a spiritual embrace. But charity also performs the crucial role of dividing friend's afflictions into an almost insensible quality, participating in the kind of intentional atomism Browne disparages elsewhere: "It is an act within the power of charity, to translate a passion out of one breast into another, and to divide a sorrow almost out of it selfe; for an affliction like a dimension may be so divided, as if not indivisible, at least to become insensible" (78). The end result is similar, since in both cases two bodies share aspects of one soul, but the pattern of movement initiated by charity is reversed in the latter. Regarding the topic of physiognomy, Browne makes a similar shift, moving from a discussion of natural hieroglyphs to a leisurely rumination on the singularity of each human being: "There is never any thing so like another, as in all points to concurre; there will ever some reserved difference slip in" (73). In this instance the observation seems potentially problematic to Browne, as if those differences might explode the hope of ever understanding the human body or soul, but he is also fascinated by the infinite variety of divine creation, and he quickly expresses optimism about the potential for charity to accommodate these distinctions.

Indeed, Browne's discussion of singularity near the beginning of the second part is not some mysterious digression that returns "from Philosophy to Charity" (74), but instead a crucial extension of his description of charity's paradoxical nature. If he is worried elsewhere over the threat posed by singularity, innovation, and schism, here he seems more optimistic about human difference: "I hold not so narrow a conceit of this virtue, as to conceive that to give alms, is onely to be Charitable, or thinke a piece of Liberality can comprehend the Totall of Charity" (74). Browne consistently returns to the problem of narrowing charity, a concern he revisits to in *A Letter to a Friend,* and it seems as if he is attempting to construct a multitudinous array of charitable acts to compensate for the particularities of each human: "Divinity hath wisely divided the acts thereof into many branches, and hath taught us in this narrow way, many paths unto goodnesse; as many ways as we may doe good, so many wayes we may be Charitable" (74).[92] Browne wants charity to accommodate the singularity of humankind. In other words, charity does not merely knit together society but also divides itself into as many fragments that exist in the world, a concept mirrored by "the discontinuousness of Browne's prose," especially in the second part, which partitions charity into so many independent pieces.[93]

Browne repeatedly uses charity as a means of facilitating this kind of "double movement," to use Barbour's apt phrase. He begins with an essential orthodoxy so that he might differentiate into particulars, remaining connected to the apostolic and patristic bedrock of Christianity but narrowing his own religious sphere to his nation's church, and constructing his own hybrid version of himself that can accommodate Puritan "morosity" with the accoutrement of Roman Catholic ceremony.[94] Indeed, Browne's paradoxical description of humankind—"that amphibious piece betweene a corporall and spirituall essence, that middle frame that . . . unites the incompatible distances by some middle and participating natures" (44)—becomes a fitting emblem of his idealized charity, with its link between the material and divine, between the corporate and singular.

Binding and Loosening:
Milton's Charity and Christian Liberty

If Browne worries over his religious singularities and feels compelled to explain his early attraction to heresy, Milton celebrates the power of singular beliefs in *The Doctrine and Discipline of Divorce*: "Many truths now of reverend esteem and credit, had their birth and beginning once from singular and private thoughts" (241). Addressing members of both Parliament and the Westminster Assembly, whom he styles "defenders of charity" (232), and describing a civic project aimed at national glory, Milton's expanded second edition of the treatise portrays the reformation of divorce law as an act of heroic defiance: "the agrieved person shall doe more manly, to be extraordinary and singular in claiming the due right whereof he is frustrated" (247). By shrugging off the tyrannical shackles of "Custom" and "Error" and canon law, Milton claims, England might liberate helpless Christian spouses, set free so many daughters of Israel, reclaim giddy sectarians for the true church, repair the institution of marriage to its original blessed intent, and restore humankind to its dignified state.

When Milton articulates a desire for liberty in his divorce tracts, there is a good chance that charity will be somewhere nearby, operating as a crucial guarantor of freedom. He deploys the virtue in a strenuous defense of the sufficiency and sovereignty of the self. The persistence with which Milton returns to the concept—he employs the word "charity" ninety-two times in these prose works, as Jason Rosenblatt has observed—demonstrates its crucial role in establishing and sustaining the link between individual and collective imperatives without relying on coercive power.[95] In this way Milton's project of divorce reform emulates the political economies embedded within the complicated legacies of both Christian liberty and classical *libertas*. The conventional Protestant conception of Christian liberty, for example, describes a freedom in Christ from bondage to the law of works, which, perhaps paradoxically, becomes essential to forming and sustaining Christian community by binding individuals together in mutual service. Although Milton seems to qualify its purpose in his divorce tracts, most notably by attempting to reinstate a particular feature of Mosaic divorce law, he uses Christian liberty as an exemplary vision of moral autonomy that forms the bedrock of a functioning state.[96]

Classical *libertas* functions in a similar capacity for Milton, who was a close reader and emulator of Cicero, Sallust, and other Roman exponents of republican ideals. If its simple definition merely distinguished between a free person (*liber*) and a slave (*servus*), protecting the individual's liberty to do as he pleases unless specifically prohibited by law, the Roman concept of *libertas* typically carried with it civic responsibilities and a movement back toward the collective sphere that ideally manifested in national glory. This is clearly in operation at a fundamental level in Milton's divorce tracts, as he envisions the legal reform of divorce producing patriotic engagement and civic leadership. His own rhetoric in the prefatory letter embodies this strategy. Even as he argues for his own heroic singularity and defends a particular set of domestic liberties, he frames his project in terms of the duty and service he owes to the entire British nation, claiming for himself such laurels as "to be reck'n'd among the publick benefactors of civill and humane life; above the inventors of wine and oil" (240).

In contrast to his vision of an ideal state, Milton describes in *Doctrine and Discipline* the trajectory of a spiritually decrepit community as a decline and fall in two steps—humans rely on legal bonds (as opposed to inner virtue), which cultivates moral looseness—a process he reiterates later in *Tetrachordon*: first, forgetting to obey inward virtue, men prefer to "live by the outward constraint of law," which results in the second step, "when law becomes now too straight for the secular manners, and those too loose for the cincture of law" (639). Milton directs his own spiritual republic in the opposite direction, envisioning charity as a liberating ethic that frees individuals to perform service in behalf of the state, resulting in the kind of virtuous conduct that he ascribes to Israel's patriarchs living in freedom before the inception of Mosaic law. The best kind of legal "bonds and ligaments of the Commonwealth," he claims, referencing Plato, are "unwritt'n, or at least unconstraining laws of virtuous education" (526).

Milton wants to loosen bonds—and banns—in order to ensure their binding power, declaring that divine charity endorses and enables divorce in order to protect and preserve the sanctity of marriage:

He who wisely would restrain the reasonable Soul of man within due bounds, must first himself know perfectly, how far the territory and dominion extends of just and honest liberty. As little must he offer to bind that which God hath loosn'd, as to loos'n that which he hath bound. (227)

Note, in this complicated quotation from Milton's prefatory address to Parliament and the Westminster Assembly, the general affect of Milton's chiastic phrase, which aims for a delicate equilibrium between the obligations of cultivating a holy community (binding) and protecting individual liberty (loosening), one might say between the desire for marriage and the need for divorce. Throughout the divorce tracts, Milton uses charity to bind these separate imperatives. (Indeed, charity often arrives in tandem with another abstract concept—"wisdom and charity" [248]; "God and charitie" [260]; "religion and charity" [310]; "somtimes with humanity, much lesse with charity" [355]—which underscores its capacity to couple with other related virtues.)

In this passage, the liberty inherent to the verb "loos'n" remains the heart of the matter, the moral imperative at the center of his chiasmus, but Milton takes care to show how such liberty radiates outward into tighter bonds than any produced by enforced conformity. That is, Milton suggests here what he makes even clearer elsewhere in his writing: the true measure of a commonwealth is not in the rigor of its statutory law, which cultivates so many fugitive and cloistered virtues, but in the free expression of "honest liberty" among its individual citizens. Compulsion in matters of love and marriage, in fact, results in frustrated spouses who become "unserviceable and spiritles" (347), and ultimately "dead to the Common-wealth" (632). He posits a different kind of civic economy than was traditionally associated with purely religious notions of charity, the proverbial "bond of perfection," which preachers and pamphleteers would invoke to prioritize communal and familial harmony at the expense of individual needs or desires.[97] Instead Milton privileges the one before the many, articulating a strenuous defense of individual freedoms. But his logic does not end there. By ensuring individual liberty he claims, paradoxically, to strengthen the bonds that tie together the rest of society, initiating a reformation that starts in the household and culminates in the perfection of state government.

The passage also demonstrates Milton's intimate and imaginative relationship with scripture, as he invokes Matthew 16:19 and 18:18, but with an important revision. Whereas the biblical texts confer on the disciples (and Peter in particular) a special prerogative—what they bind on earth will be bound by God in heaven—Milton transforms the passage into an admonition for ecclesiastical and political authorities to beware their exercise of power: do not bind on earth what has been loosened by God in heaven. This departs from his allusion to these scriptures in *The Reason of Church Government*, where he uses them to endorse ministerial (as opposed to prelatical) privilege.[98] Here Milton seems to be channeling the spirit of the larger context in which these quotations appear, Matthew 18 in particular, which expresses a theme of pastoral responsibility that prioritizes the one sheep before the ninety-nine.[99] In fact, the inherent balance of Milton's antimetabole is disingenuous, as he clearly focuses throughout the divorce tracts on the particular dangers of binding, preferring the dangers of Scylla's "abused libertie" to the "unmercifull restraint" of Charybdis (235). Better to empower a few libertines than to enslave even one misguided spouse. And yet, even as he celebrates personal liberty, Milton employs ambiguous syntax to underscore the importance of binding oneself from license: "[He] must first himself know perfectly, how far the territory and dominion extends of just and honest liberty." By gesturing toward the Delphic maxim in that pause before the subordinate clause arrives, Milton emphasizes the self-governance that is crucial to enacting fully the liberty he prioritizes throughout the divorce tracts.[100]

The importance of self-knowledge and self-restraint becomes more pronounced given Milton's preference for fewer legal constraints. He makes a pointed joke at the expense of reformed religion regarding its own peculiar superstitions, suggesting that the collective focus among Protestants on preserving binds is an offense to charity:

> The superstition of the Papist is, *touch not, taste not,* when God bids both; and ours is, *part not, separat not,* when God and charity both permits and commands. *Let all your things be done with charity,* saith St. Paul: and his Master saith, *Shee is the fulfilling of the Law.* Yet now a civil, an indifferent, a sometime diswaded Law of mariage, must be forc't upon us to fulfill, not onely without charity, but against her. (228–29)

Milton's tangled prepositions fail to obscure his principal assertion, that charity, as a divine command as well as divine gift, is the chief instrument for ensuring liberty, one in this case that liberates spouses otherwise confined by the strictures of canon law. By calling the law "indifferent," Milton gestures at the concept of *adiaphora,* but he avoids the typical arguments of this kind rehearsed throughout the early modern period by established authorities, who employed the sphere of religious indifference as an opportunity for political enforcement, as well as by religious dissenters, who claimed that nothing was indifferent to a sanctified Christian. Charity often became implicated in these arguments, but Milton ascribes to the virtue a power and influence in governing *adiaphora* that is remarkable. His charity demands that every single "thing indifferent" (and Milton applies the term "indifferent" broadly) should remain free of legislative and ecclesiastical jurisdiction. In his study of *Doctrine and Discipline,* Arthur Barker considers Milton's work to be orthodox in its treatment of *adiaphora*—merely heterodox in its consideration of divorce as a thing indifferent—but he also notes that charity serves as a vehicle for Milton's enlargement of Christian liberty in subsequent divorce tracts and other pamphlets.[101] That process is already under way in the prefatory letter to the second edition, as charity seems to overtake all other considerations civil and theological, heralded by that conjunction appearing to equate "God and charity," both of which are characterized by their permissive (and anti-Calvinist) natures.

In case he was not clear enough about binding and loosening at the beginning of *Doctrine and Discipline,* Milton repeats the scriptural reference in *Tetrachordon,* noting again in his exegesis of the passage "that the christian arbitrement of charity is supreme decider of all controversie, and supreme resolver of all Scripture" (637). Here he invokes Augustinian hermeneutics to negotiate ecclesiastical controversy, although this interpretive project likewise requires the cultivation of individual virtue and its concomitant ethical responsibilities. Charity for Milton not only preserves the sanctity of the individual conscience but also works as a catalyst that prompts that individual to perform strenuous moral interpretation, whether in biblical hermeneutics, marital relations, or civil society. This passage from *Tetrachordon* recalls the admonition Raphael delivers to Adam in Book 8 of *Paradise Lost:* "To stand or fall / Free in thine own arbitrament it lies" (640–41). It seems charity, much like reason, is but choosing, a liberating ethic but one that carries with it a set of political and intellectual obligations. In *The Judgment of Martin Bucer concerning*

Divorce, which he published a year before *Tetrachordon*, Milton reminded the reader of the "duties of true charity; which preferrs public honesty before private interest" (467).

A little over a decade after publishing his divorce tracts, Milton recycled his earlier riff on the passages from Matthew in *A Treatise of Civil Power*, admonishing civic magistrates who would engage in any kind of religious coercion: "As well may he loos'n that which God hath strait'nd or strait'n that which God hath loos'nd, as he may injoin those things in religion which God hath left free, and lay on that yoke which God hath taken off."[102] Here he reverses the constituent parts of his antimetabole, placing divine bonds at the center of his rhetorical figure, but the result is an even more vigorous defense of individual conscience. We are strictly bound by God, he seems to say, to keep and enjoy our liberty, and immediately after he adds references to Galatians 5 and 1 Corinthians, underscoring the scriptural link between love and liberty. Victoria Kahn notes that this passage, which blends together a doctrine of *adiaphora* with Machiavellian rhetorical politics, appears to endorse a republican form of government, since "republics are better able to preserve the realm of contingency in which individual conscience may be exercised and individual virtue may prosper."[103] The republican ideals of *Civil Power* already lay embedded in the arguments of the divorce tracts, which is one reason the Westminster Assembly took seriously the political implications of desacralizing divorce and severing bonds of any kind, whether they were related to marriage or the magistrate.[104]

Although he is not yet articulating comprehensive republican arguments in the early 1640s, Milton's preoccupation with cultivating individual virtue is one of the reasons he persistently expresses worry about excessive bonds in the divorce tracts and elsewhere in his prose works. In *Areopagitica*, in response to the Licensing Order of 1643, he declaims against magistrates trying "to bind books to their good behavior" (570), observing the crucial difference between two contrary attempts to discover Truth: the one, espoused by Presbyterian censors, employs force but results in a false show—"give her but room, & do not bind her when she sleeps, for then she speaks not true" (563)—whereas the other privileges "a little generous prudence, a little forbearance of one another, and som grain of charity," which "might win all these diligences to joyn, and unite into one generall and brotherly search after Truth" (554). One can discern in this latter description the general trajectory of Milton's charity, which begins by protecting individual liberties but inevitably results in fostering a larger communal enterprise. Even God cannot interfere in this process. In *Doctrine and Discipline*, he declares that no "Law or Cov'nant, how solemne or strait soever, either between God and man, or man and man, though of Gods joyning, should bind against a prime and principall scope of its own institution" (245), and at the beginning of *Tetrachordon*, he reminds his readers that "no ordinance human or from heav'n can binde against the good of man" (588). Milton's anxiety over bonds only intensifies after his divorce tracts. In *The Tenure of Kings and Magistrates*, he remarks ironically that certain Presbyterians "call it thir liberty to bind other mens consciences," and he reminds Cromwell in his sonnet addressed to the Lord General that "new foes arise, / Threatening to bind our souls with secular chains."[105]

"Those needful pores": Milton's Charitable Body

The preoccupation with binding and loosening helps distinguish between charity and its Miltonic philosophical corollary, "esteem," which he calls in *The Reason of Church-government* (1642) the second principle after the love of God in establishing pious virtue. As with charity, Milton's esteem does not rely on social or civic sympathies but rather derives its scope and power from a conscious sense of personal virtue, clear evidence that he was already shifting away from Calvinism. Both concepts are inwardly oriented for Milton, charity an "inward persuasion" according to *Civil Power* and esteem an "inward reverence," as he calls it in *Reason of Church-government*. In his study of early modern moderation, Joshua Scodel observes how Milton appropriates the notion of esteem as a more positive conception of self-love, and he notes the particularly Stoic resonances involved in a vision of self-respect that then produces self-restraint.[106] This commitment to self-governance embodies Ciceronian republican ideals crucial to Milton's own developing vision of politics, and he maintains a commitment to healthy esteem throughout his career, most notably in *Paradise Lost*, where Raphael intervenes in paradisal marriage: "Oft-times nothing profits more / Than self-esteem, grounded on just and right / Well managed" (571–73).

This apparently Stoic virtue, however, receives a kind of Epicurean counterbalance in Milton's recourse to charity throughout the divorce tracts, which express the necessity of fulfilling one's moderate desires, attempt to acquire freedom from spousal perturbation, and implicitly posit a fortuitous causality ruling over marital relations rather than perfect divine providence.[107] In his masque and anti-prelatical tracts, Milton admires the chaste self-restraint of esteem, which, according to Scodel, even combats the temptation to masturbate: "Yet is it not incontinent to bound it self, as humid things are, but hath in it a most restraining and powerfull abstinence to start back, and glob it self upward from the mixture of any ungenerous and unbeseeming motion."[108] But the threat of masturbation becomes replaced by the problem of congested menstruation in the divorce tracts, as Milton compares the restraint of lawful liberty to a menstruous body "where natures current hath been stopt, that the suffocation and upward forcing of some lower part, affects the head and inward sense with dotage and idle fancies" (278–79). In this somatic economy a careful degree of free external expression preserves the purity of "inward sense." In an anonymous pamphlet supporting toleration, *The ancient bounds, or Liberty of conscience,* the author (probably Francis Rous) employs a similar corporeal metaphor to describe healthy scriptural interpretation: "The Word of God, which requires this Libertie . . . for its better operation, as Physick doth require open weather, when the humors are stirring, not clung up nor restrained, for to purge them away."[109] The severe Stoic becomes a presiding image for Milton's conception of Presbyterian behavior during the civil war period, since Presbyterians initially opposed the joint prerogatives of prince and prelate but turned into "Malignant backsliders" when they refused to pursue genuine ecclesiastical or political reform, choosing instead to impose their own tyrannical rigor on sectarian opponents.[110] This preoccupation reinforces John Leonard's convincing reading of Sonnet 12 as an indictment of Presbyterians, which centers on a definition of "revolt" as "draw back or refrain [from one's duty]": they "bawl for freedom in their senseless mood, / And still revolt when truth would set them free. / Licence they mean when they cry Liberty; / For who loves that must first be wise and good."[111]

Milton probably has the rigor of Presbyterian opponents in mind when he nears the conclusion of *Doctrine and Discipline* and counters the severity of current divorce law with a remarkable invocation of Epicurean ideals:

Bee not righteous overmuch, is the counsel of Ecclesiastes; why shouldst thou destroy thyself? Let us not be thus over-curious to strain at atoms, and yet to stop every vent and cranny of permissive liberty: lest nature wanting those needful pores, and breathing places which God hath not debarr'd our weaknes, either suddenly break out into some wide rupture of open vice, and frantick heresy, or els inwardly fester with repining and blasphemous thoughts, under an unreasonable and fruitles rigor of unwarranted law. (354)

Using atoms as metaphors for individual spouses in a cosmology of marriage, Milton warns against those who prefer to strain, or bind, matter that prefers to be in motion. It is a fascinating defense of singularity. Note the inward effect of exterior rigor, how too much restraint produces "some wide rupture of open vice, and frantic heresy." Perfect righteousness is counterproductive, even dangerous, in this vision of Solomonic wisdom, and elsewhere too Milton employs the "Wise-man" and his ethics of honest pleasure to indict current divorce law.

Ecclesiastes was a controversial text during this period precisely because of its apparent support of Epicurean principles, and numerous early modern readers struggled to reconcile Solomonic hedonism and fortuity with a robust providentialism and Christian piety, a particularly vexed project for the Caroline church in the previous decade given the Stuart monarchs' identification with Solomon.[112] Milton, however, who was engaging Presbyterians at this point rather than Laudians, seems unconcerned by the association—indeed, he reinforces it by referring to atoms a mere sentence after quoting the scriptural verse, although his vision of deity is clearly in contrast to the Epicurean model and allows him to safely enlist Ecclesiastes in behalf of moderate pleasure. Far from removing himself from human affairs, in fact, Milton's God assumes the role of exemplary magistrate or lawgiver (Milton returns to this image throughout the divorce tracts), and the permissive liberty afforded by God to the Israelites should be replicated in the British state. Perhaps that is Milton's purpose for the "key of charity," which he mentions a few sentences later: to open up that space of "needful pores, and breathing places" in the commonwealth. The blend of legacies, both Stoic and Epicurean, illustrates the strain involved in Milton's project to cultivate self-governed virtue and pleasurable liberty.

Throughout *Doctrine and Discipline*, questions about divinely sanctioned pleasure become implicated in the realm of sexual ethics, especially since the topic of marriage elicits from Milton a noticeable ambivalence about the physical realities of matrimony—the conjugal debt owed to each spouse. In the midst of his project to redefine what constitutes marriage, Milton shifts the emphasis from a contractual arrangement designed to further procreation and to avoid sin, and focuses instead on a relationship born of spiritual love and the mutual desire for companionship, a concept of marriage he felt aligned better with the institution's scriptural origins in Genesis: "A meet and happy conversation is the chiefest and noblest end of mariage; for we find here no expression so necessarily implying carnall knowledg, as this prevention of loneliness to the mind and spirit of man" (246). Indeed, so careful is Milton to eliminate carnal intentions from marriage that he rereads Paul's injunction to the Corinthians—"It is better to marry than burn"—as a rational burning, a combustible lust for the company of a spiritual "help-meet" rather than a physical bedmate. Here is another likeness between Milton and Browne, whose *Religio* famously claims, "I could be content that we might procreate like trees, without conjunction" (83).

Milton's conspicuous sexual anxiety prompts Annabel Patterson to examine the treatise through a psychoanalytic lens, offering a persuasive reading of *Doctrine and Discipline* as a proto-domestic novel, a confession of the author's own unpreparedness for a heterosexual marital relationship.[113] Removing the carnal elements of matrimony assumes central importance in this treatise. Milton wants to replace marital *eros* with *caritas* and engender a safer form of loving community, but his project remains vexed on account of the pragmatics of marriage and the realities of human desire. James Grantham Turner captures the dilemma of the divorce tracts succinctly: Milton "ventures hesitantly into the complex implications of voluntary sexuality, only to take frequent refuge in the simplicities of dualism and ascetic denunciation of the flesh."[114] The anonymous writer of *An Answer to a book intituled, The doctrine and discipline of divorce* (1644) exploits this tension, mocking what he portrays as wondrous naiveté concerning sexual lust, and assuring Milton he need not worry about divorce since a poor marriage "will not endanger or stir up any other desires but to converse with the soules of other mens Wives; and this we allow you to do and keep your own still."[115] Indeed, the physical bonds of matrimony, knit closer than any filial relationship, impart a claustrophobia that jeopardizes Miltonic charity: "It will easily be true that a father or brother may be hated zealously, and lov'd civilly or naturally; for those duties may be perform'd at distance," Milton claims, but he cannot conceive how "all cohabitation of marriage be kept, how that benevolent and intimate communion of body can be held with one that must be hated with a most operative hatred" (263). The inherent physicality of marriage intensifies the binding rigor of the institution.

Several comments need to be added that partially qualify Milton's dualistic posture toward sexuality, which is complicated by his polemical language for one thing. Like a number of religious reformers before him, Milton employs Augustine's dualistic vocabulary of the flesh in *On Christian Doctrine* to articulate divergent motives in scriptural interpretation, between what Augustine called *caritas* and *concuspiscentia* or *cupiditas*, the former of which charitably privileges the spirit while the latter remains enslaved to an "alphabeticall servility" (280). This language acquires particular force in Milton's discussion of marriage and divorce, since scriptural interpretation becomes mapped over conjugal relations. To Milton, the emphasis in canon law on procreation and lust betrays its own carnal understanding of biblical marriage. And arguments used to bolster canon law by using obstinately literal interpretations of scripture serve "to bind our Saviour in the default of a down-right promise breaking, and to bind the disunions of complaining nature in chains together, and curb them with a canon bit" (334), merely demonstrating further evidence of carnality. Milton's sexual anxiety and scriptural hermeneutics are fused together by a discourse of charity.

Furthermore, as several scholars have noted, Milton's divorce tracts already reveal an emergent monism, not merely in his synergistic approach to law but also in his understanding of the overlap between spiritual and physical love.[116] Citing the divorce tracts, R. A. Shoaf makes a helpful distinction between dualism and duality in Milton's work, observing that "if Milton is so concerned with difference, distinction, separation, and severity, it is not because he subscribes to dualism, but because he is in search of unity and must therefore be ever on guard against 'unmeet consorts,' incompatible realities."[117] Milton desires charity to break the marital bonds shackling spouses to so many corporeal cases divested of any spiritual core. In fact, he characterizes sexuality of this kind as an affront to liberty, calling it "servil copulation" (258). The author constructs as his allegorical opponent in *Doctrine and Discipline* an image of anti-charity, referencing the maxim *scientia inflat* of 1 Corinthians 8 in deriding the "meer face" of Custom, "a swoln visage of counterfeit knowledge," which "puffs up unhealthily, a certain big face of pretended Learning" (223) and a "blown physiognomy" (232). It is perhaps his desire for the spiritual to gain authentic immanence in (and yet eminence over) fleshly communion that provokes his sternest denunciations of mere "bodily conjunction" (239–40), when an innocent (and apparently male) spouse "shall find himselfe bound fast to an uncomplying discord of nature, or, as it oft happens, to an image of earth and fleam" (254).

Here again the chiasmus of binding and loosening offers a helpful image of Milton's preferred sexual relations. He repeatedly emphasizes that increasing domestic liberty would have a strengthening influence on sexual morality: "The vigor of discipline they may then turn with better successe upon the prostitute loosenes of the times" (355). A perceptive reader of Spenser's *Faerie Queene*, Milton would have recognized one of the recurring paradoxes in its treatment of sexual behavior, as various characters (Redcrosse in particular) become entangled in chains born of loose eroticism, just as temperate restraint enables authentic freedom. My treatment of that phenomenon in Spenser's allegory locates one source of this convoluted imagery in Spenser's attention to the scriptural paradoxes associated with Christian liberty, but it is helpful to consider a number of other classical analogues that describe or metaphorize a lover enslaved by passion: Hercules in bondage to Omphale; the *servitium amoris* of Augustan elegists (Propertius in particular); Horace's Satire 2.7; and many others. Similar paradoxes abound in Milton. So, the heroic chastity and arduous intellectual effort endorsed by Milton throughout his prose career earns and even requires an honest recreative pleasure, "somtime slacking the cords of intense thought and labour" (596), whereas Samson deplores his own "foul effeminacy," which "held me yok't / Her Bond-slave" (410–11).

In Milton as in Spenser, however, distinctions between the bonds of *eros* and *agape* are difficult to perceive, particularly in the context of divorce. Further complicating matters, contemporary apologies for libertinism bore a nominal resemblance to Milton's arguments about liberty and divorce, as did many of the arguments promulgated by radical sectarians. In examining Milton's representations of sexuality, Turner notes that conservative contemporaries might be forgiven if they suspected Milton of radical sympathies, given his spiritual hermeneutics and censure of repressive ethics, even if they failed to recognize that "Milton's dialectic is meant to enhance moral distinctions, while Antinomianism seeks to soar beyond them."[118] Milton's anonymous answerer clearly associates the arguments for liberty in *Doctrine and Discipline,* as well as its apparent dismissal of the permanence of marital bonds, with Familist sympathies, declaring, "Fie, fie, blush for shame, and publish no more of this loose Divinitie."[119] Joseph Hall, too, uses Milton's own keyword to condemn the divorce treatise as "so loose a project."[120] Hall, Herbert Palmer, Ephraim Pagitt, Daniel Featley, and others heard in Milton's appeals for individual liberty echoes of the sexual libertinism associated with radical sects. In addition to privileging the inward conscience, as Milton does throughout the divorce tracts, sectarians often employed prophetic, paradoxical language to express spiritual and sexual freedoms.[121] Take one defense of pantheistic love, for example, which employs the same figures of antimetabole and parison to argue in behalf of transcending earthly bonds of marriage: "There is such a unity where there is this diversity, and such a diversity where there is this unity, that they cannot kisse one but kisse all, and love one but they love all."[122] It is worth noting that this logic results in its own kind of constraint that Milton would have resisted, regardless of any concern about sexual promiscuity—the participants of this orgiastic ritual must kiss *everybody* in order to embody the cosmic spirit. Whereas Milton's chiasmus emphasizes by scriptural warrant the equal need for binding as well as loosening, certain antinomians attempted to forestall anything that restricted their notion of liberty, disregarding any practical or moral distinction between sinful or righteous behavior.

Nevertheless, Milton seems to have felt a kind of sympathy for these radicals, and, if his divorce tracts are any indication, he probably considered many of them disappointed and unhappy spouses who suffer from "the restraint of some lawfull liberty, which ought to be giv'n men, and is deny'd them" (278).[123] This practical observation drives much of his argument, in fact, as he claims that an unfulfilling marriage exacerbates the natural desire for spiritual union, producing a melancholic despair and encouraging licentious behavior. After all, Milton really does desire to honor marital fidelity. It has become a commonplace assertion among scholars to note that Milton's divorce tracts, which declare the primacy of spiritual rather than copulative bonds, are actually less focused on divorce than on marriage. Even as he articulates a powerful defense of individual liberty, Milton likewise recognizes and celebrates the desire for human companionship.

This is an important reminder for readers of *Paradise Lost* who are tempted to map the divorce tracts onto the poem, who assume that Milton, were the narrative up to him, would have Adam divorce Eve rather than fall.[124] The vision of charitable singularity or liberty I have been tracing in Milton's divorce tracts can illuminate, I think, two separate episodes in *Paradise Lost*. The first is perhaps the most crucial moment related to binding in the poem (a poem that persistently figures forth bonds and links and chains of various kinds): when Eve presents the apple to Adam and he is apparently forced to choose between his allegiance to God or Eve. Numerous scholars have noted the echoes of Milton's divorce tracts in Book 9 of *Paradise Lost*, which reinstates several key concepts from the prose works and alludes to the scriptural words of institution in Genesis 2. Milton barely invokes the possibility of divorce, however, as an abhorrent prospect Adam mentions peremptorily, it seems, solely as a means of affirming his vows to Eve:

> How can I live without thee, how forego
> Thy sweet converse and love so dearly joined,
> To live again in these wild woods forlorn? (908–10)

Assuredly Milton intends for Adam's inability to envision paradise without the spiritual communion of Eve to elicit the reader's disapproval, but the scenario likewise reinforces a notion we first receive, oddly enough, from Satan when he first visits Eden in Book 4—namely, that this is a healthy and happy marriage, truly paradisal, at least as far as Adam is concerned. Rather than hypothesizing whether or not Milton would endorse an Edenic divorce, it seems more pertinent to observe that the author is dramatizing the other half of a phenomenon he had already explored in the divorce tracts: the intractable challenges marriage poses to liberty. In this case, a happy rather than disappointing marriage is the problem. Adam and Eve achieve that blissful height of matrimonial intercourse Milton prizes in the divorce tracts—sweet conversation—a characteristic of Edenic marriage that actually poses a threat to Adam's innocence, especially given his refusal to consider the prospect of enduring life without his spouse:

> Should God create another Eve, and I
> Another rib afford, yet loss of thee
> Would never from my heart; no no, I feel
> The link of nature draw me: flesh of flesh,
> Bone of my bone thou art, and from thy state
> Mine never shall be parted, bliss or woe. (911–16)

Shortly thereafter, in assuring Eve he will accept her offer of fruit, he echoes his earlier justification, claiming, "So forcible within my heart I feel / The bond of nature draw me to my own" (955–56). In making his choice, Adam abdicates moral autonomy, assigning to his fall a fatal necessity that does not exist. Even the closest marital union, Milton suggests, cannot absolve each spouse of his or her individual responsibilities to God and to the self.

As with several other principles championed by Milton, however, the charitable liberty he envisions governing ideal spousal relations is complicated by Eve, who appears to be confined to a marital domain constructed without her consent. A figure of "subjection" (4.308), the first woman "occupies a particularly problematic position in this universe," as David Norbrook puts it.[125] In her own account of her creation, Eve responds to divine instruction ("him thou shall enjoy / Inseparably thine") with something like coerced submission: "what could I do, / But follow strait, invisibly thus led" (4.472–76). Shortly after this, Adam's "gentle hand / seized" hers (489). There is a great deal of mutuality and equality in prelapsarian Eden, and elsewhere readers are reminded that Eve possesses "virtue and the conscience of her worth" (8.502), which she yields to Adam "with coy submission / And sweet reluctant amorous delay" (4.310–11), but all these

ironies and contradictions, however much they convey a complicated subjectivity, nevertheless struggle to add up to a convincing portrait of Eve's
spousal independence. Indeed, it is one of the great ironies of Milton's epic,
one that is difficult to square with his vision of marital relations, that Eve's
desire for autonomy at the start of Book 9 (born, it seems, from a rational
understanding of her own spiritual and ethical self-worth) becomes the
immediate catalyst for the fall. In a perceptive essay, Jared Kuzner has
suggested that the separation scene of *Paradise Lost* consciously modifies
Milton's earlier divorce tracts, which had not provided enough space for
domestic argument.[126] Whatever its relation to *Doctrine and Discipline*,
Milton's vision of Edenic marriage in the poem places his republican commitments under a great deal of strain.

The conditions of Eve's liberty remain murky, but it is clear that
Adam's decision to yoke himself to Eve (as well as her choice to eat the
fruit) results in a fracturing of self-identity which threatens to destroy
their marriage. Their sweet converse between body and soul immediately ruptures into an erotic sexuality, a devaluation of spiritual bonds
that quickly leads to Adam's violent misogyny. On the other hand, the
best guarantor of obedience is a loosening of those marital bonds—not
a temporary separation while working in the garden, nor an irrevocable
parting of spouses, but a healthy spiritual independence, which offers the
most reliable union. In this way singularity is less a threat than a guarantor of community. Reading this episode through the lens of charity,
Russell Hillier claims that Adam's invocation of the link or bond of nature satisfies only one half of what Hillier terms the double love, excluding
the love of God.[127] But even this perspective obscures the essential point
for Milton: social bonds always end up in idolatry of some kind if they are
not first invested in spiritual autonomy and obedience to divine prescription. Hillier prefaces his chapter by employing a passage from Herbert's
"Divinitie": "Love God, and love your neighbor . . . / . . . / O dark instructions; ev'n as dark as day! / Who can these Gordian knots undo?" It is
an apt epigraph for a consideration of Milton because it underscores the
unorthodox nature of his charity: the "immaculate hands of charity" become, for Milton, the instrument by which "tedious and Gordian difficulties" are dissolved. His charity is aimed at slackening or even untying the
knot that others celebrate.

Given this persistent desire to loosen bonds, one might get the impression that Milton is a spiritual and political and sexual claustrophobic, jealous of any infringement on his space.[128] Part of this stems from his desire for "negative liberty," as the inheritors of Milton's political philosophy would later call it, a near pathological resistance to state interference of any kind. But there are positive liberties at stake as well. Religious coercion negates the capacity for authentic worship and threatens to devolve into idolatry of various kinds. Consider the accusation he aims at opponents of divorce, who, despite stripping marriage of its sacramental power, nevertheless "invest it with such an awfull sanctity, and give such adamantine chains to bind with, as if it were to be worshipt like some Indian deity" (277). Milton attempts to invest the principle of charity with greater freedom by shifting the orientation of its discipline, both as social principle and as scriptural hermeneutic, asserting the virtue's spiritual and rational autonomy before it manifests a social presence in the world. This is one reason why his concept of charity almost always designates precedence to loving God and oneself before directing that charity into external society. Far from a selfless love, his charity requires rational choice and moral sovereignty as guarantors of authentic good works, or else they would undercut the individual's capacity to perform heroic labor.

Indeed, if Browne takes comfort in orthodoxy, communal binds that give him "the liberty of an honest reason [to] play and expatiate with security, and far without the circle of a heresy," Milton achieves liberty by inverting this trajectory. His is the harder road in many ways. Whereas Browne begins in a submissive posture that affords him the liberty of pleasurable recreation, Milton starts with autonomous liberty, which initiates a never-ending process of labor. The good works of charity are central to this enterprise, which Michael emphasizes to Adam at the epic's conclusion. Note the ethos of labor involved in Milton's description of human charity, appropriate for a poet who infuses georgic principles into his vision of prelapsarian paradise:

> . . . only add
> Deeds to thy knowledge answerable, add Faith,
> Add virtue, patience, temperance, add love,
> By name to come called charity, the soul

Of all the rest: then wilt thou not be loath
To leave this Paradise, but shalt possess
A paradise within thee, happier far. (12.581–87)

The obvious scriptural invocation of 2 Peter only partially dulls the immense labor involved in this supposed consolation offered by the archangel Michael. And it *is* a consolation to Milton, even if he takes seriously the willpower involved in responding to those imperatives with obedience. Milton suggests that Adam and Eve, after separate encounters with divine revelation, have acquired this internal resolve when "hand in hand with wand'ring steps and slow," they make "thir solitary way" out of Eden into the subjected plain. Even if Milton, publishing *Paradise Lost* in the wake of the Restoration, probably does not intend for Adam and Eve's reconciled marriage to adumbrate the civic potential of a commonwealth born of reformed divorce laws, he nevertheless concludes his epic with one final optimistic picture of binding and loosening: in responding to their respective falls, Adam and Eve have developed, at great cost, fully sufficient and solitary selves, each having implicitly added charity to their spiritual repertoire, departing paradise with clasped hands bound together.

CONCLUSION

"NOT A SINGLE CHARITY"

In April 1643, a few weeks after the publication of Browne's corrected edition of *Religio Medici*, and a few months before Milton's first divorce treatise appeared in the press, Herbert Palmer published *Scripture and reason pleaded for defensive armes,* a work of biblical exegesis articulating the scriptural grounds for legitimate political resistance and promoting a parliamentarian theory of government. The lengthy treatise was commissioned by the House of Commons in response to the assertions of Henry Ferne, a chaplain to the king whose 1642 work *The resolving of conscience* declared that armed resistance was prohibited even in the case of royal misconduct. Crucially, Ferne deployed charity in support of monarchical privilege, claiming that any opposition to the king was the sure mark of "a Conscience that wanted the Judgement of Charity."[1] Near the end of his work Palmer sets out to complicate this position, first by underscoring the volatility of charitable judgment and then by observing the contradictory obligations of charitable duty. He begins by invoking the problem of foolish pity. How easy it is to fall into "a pernitious Charity" or "a strange Charity," Palmer reminds his readers, and how dangerous it is for charity to "[drink] of the water of Lethe" and offer leniency that would make others "curse their Charity."[2] Palmer's line of argument culminates in a potent analogy that compares parliamentary charity toward the king's counselors, whom he accuses of gross abuse that placed the nation's safety in jeopardy, to a watchman giving "Charity towards Attempters against a City." There are echoes here of Piers's fable of the fox and kid in

Spenser's *May* eclogue, with similar anti-Catholic undertones reflecting Parliament's worry over Catholic influence at court.

Palmer's equivalence between royalists and intruders gestures at a range of communal obligations that further complicate matters of conscience, and he proceeds to give the imperatives of charity a political inflection. It is not enough, he suggests, for the general populace to offer charity to the king, as Ferne insists, since this ignores the mixed constitution at the heart of England's political governance: "And then for the People alone, have they not a charity to exercise toward the Parliament, as well as toward the Kings Followers?" Parliamentary representatives have a number of charitable duties themselves, meanwhile, perhaps most prominently a "Charity to ourselves," which "will not onely allow, but commend, and even command to suspect" any agents of royal policy, particularly when the parliamentary body must "Answer for Religion, Laws, and Liberties." Charity thus becomes in Palmer's treatise a principle of civic casuistry, which requires sifting a variety of communal commitments and political contingencies before reaching a position that approximates moral conviction. Having burdened his readers with such a laborious process of inquiry, he declares, "Let charity judge (if it dare, or can) the Parliament Fooles or Traytors." In that parenthetical Palmer seems almost ready to cede the virtue of charity to the royalist cause, defying its purpose and its power, but he quickly recalibrates his posture to accommodate his own political sympathies: "Take in then the Declarations and Protestations; on the one side and on the other, and remember is [*sic*] is not a single charity, whether I shall suspect the King."

Perhaps it is not a surprise that Palmer, a staunch supporter of Parliament, sees in charity a range of duties and faculties that ideally reach a consensus, whereas Ferne emphasizes the singular power of charity to resolve all contentions and disputes: in the royalist notion of charity, the virtue assumes the role of a monarch; in the parliamentarian vision, charity operates more like a republican state. But if Palmer's repeated jabs undercut Ferne's simple confidence in royal privilege—it is not enough to have "a single charity"—they nevertheless struggle to invest the parliamentary cause with anything like the moral ascendancy. His impassioned summary of the various perils and responsibilities of charity does not reject Ferne's position so much as it offers instead a rival understanding of conscientious love. Both parliamentarians and royalists appealed to charity in support of their respective powers, but each faction was enlisting to its aid a virtue that had in fact contributed to the emergence of partisan commitments that were strained to the breaking point.

More generally, in describing the several competing obligations of charity, its multiple contexts and audiences, and in illustrating the dangers of an incomplete understanding of these demands and potential outcomes, *Scripture and reason* provides an apt description of the interpretive complexity associated with discourses of charity throughout the early modern period. It was conventional for writers to invoke the Augustinian schema that divided the entirety of human motivation into two categories: properly ordered and disordered love, *caritas* and *cupiditas*. But the divisive conflicts of the era were not governed, as Palmer notes, by a single charity. In the world of religious polemic, charity was a resource and a threat. The concept could be marshaled by either side in nearly any debate, by a royalist like Ferne or a parliamentarian like Palmer, by a staunch defender of the Roman Catholic Church like Thomas More or by a reformist translator like William Tyndale, by a Puritan controversialist like Thomas Cartwright or a conformist archbishop like John Whitgift. To critics of mercantile expansion who preferred more traditional forms of sociability, supporters of emergent commercial networks could counter with their own visions of "charitable use" made manifest in a wide range of charitable trusts. Nor were these empty rhetorical gestures. All of these responses to the demands of charity reveal opposing priorities and commitments, a preference for purity above harmony, for instance, or for individual liberties before communal norms.

But these neat and tidy dichotomies forged in the heat of controversy often obscure overlaps and continuities between rival visions of charity, or they efface subtle but crucial distinctions in argument or strategy, and at their worst they can contribute to the "uncharitable logick" Browne deplores in *Religio Medici*. Here again the exchange between Palmer and Ferne is instructive. A year after their debate over conscience, in August 1644, Herbert Palmer preached a parliamentary fast sermon (later published as *The glasse of Gods providence*) that vilified Milton's *Doctrine and Discipline of Divorce* as "a wicked booke . . . deserving to be burnt," noting in particular that its author exploited the "pretence of liberty of conscience."[3]

Milton responded in *Tetrachordon*, with some justification, that he was applying the same logic of biblical exegesis to divorce reform that Palmer had used to support armed resistance against the king, since his claims of natural law were "drawn parallel from [Palmer's] own principal arguments in that of *Scripture and Reason*."[4] If their approaches to scripture were not different in kind, the difference in degree nevertheless mattered a great deal to Palmer, who could not imagine extending his argument so far as to unsettle the conventions of marriage.

Meanwhile the scriptural hermeneutic Milton advertises on the title page of his first divorce treatise, "the Rule of Charity" or *regula caritatis*, is referenced by Henry Ferne several times in *The resolving of conscience* to describe his own exegetical procedure in support of the king.[5] But Milton reimagines the rule of charity in order to raise, rather than settle, interpretive questions, exploding the proof-texting methods of Ferne and Palmer, both of whom would approvingly cite Matthew 19: 8–9 to prohibit divorce.[6] When placed in a larger conversation that includes nonconformists like Milton (or Roger Williams, one might add), Ferne and Palmer, whatever their differences, seem to reside in relatively close proximity, both in their application of scriptural hermeneutics as well as their political philosophy. The range of conclusions produced by these exegetical strategies, all of them ostensibly governed by a rule of charity, bring to mind the anarchy of lay interpretation More envisions in *Dialogue Against Heresies*, which serves as an early prototype of the many heresiographies published during the 1640s.

Milton's rule of charity, whatever its relation to Augustine's *regula*, does not rest with scripture but rather extends its evaluative gaze to the domestic world of marital relations. Although his divorce tracts met with resistance from contemporaries, Milton's mode of charitable reading, with its fretful energy and range of interpretive demands, remains characteristic of the period. The biblical mandates of loving God and neighbor, in addition to the various forms of love prescribed throughout the gospel narratives and New Testament epistles, implicated charity in a range of discourses that varied from medicine to mercantilism, cultivating dynamic reading practices of one kind or another. Perhaps no feature of early modern England demonstrates this more fully than the repeated efforts to expand and refine poor relief, which involved an elaborate and unwieldy system of inquiry, empowering municipal officers to assess and record (among other things) an individual's kinship network and access to alternative relief, as well as his or her disposition and relative fitness for labor and education, in addition to more typical matters of age, health, and estate. As additional legal measures appeared—begging badges, passports and licenses, earmarkings and brandings—bodies and texts merged into a complicated semiotics of poverty. The system of poor relief seemed to join together the traditions of equity and rhetoric, which bent their interpretive principles to accommodate context and circumstance, with a punitive rigor that was rooted in the logic of corrective discipline. For the vagrants and other members of the itinerant poor who threatened to destabilize this process, "punishment" was "all the Charitie that the Law affoordeth them."[7]

In their efforts to legislate against individual and spontaneous provision, parliamentary and municipal authorities attempted to keep the project of material charity rational, orderly, and governed by communal authorities. A similar emphasis compels More to strain his coercive powers in opposition to Tyndale's biblical translation and Whitgift to resist the ecclesiastical reforms of Elizabethan Puritans. But charity also empowered individuals to resist structural forces and entrenched interests, to articulate demands for moral reform, and to advocate for disenfranchised peoples. Many of these efforts were unruly, and often (as in the case of Tyndale) explicitly preferred the revelatory power of scripture and spirit before principles of custom and reason. But close attention to the work of early modern writers complicates an easy division between these rival imperatives: Browne, who was himself predisposed to suspect the logic of crowds, believed the best guarantor of individual liberty was an orthodox submission to communal authority; meanwhile, Milton's project of divorce quite clearly imagined freedom as the first step toward authentic union in a domestic, political, or spiritual economy. Others, like Spenser and Jonson, sought to evade simple dichotomies by way of irony or ambivalence.

In the midst of these charitable projects, whatever their inflection, various forms of duplicity emerge as potential threats to reading, further unsettling the cultural landscape. The vagrants apparently plaguing England's countryside and urban spaces stand in for a host of social and political developments undermining the process of charitable interpretation. Other threats come from within each individual's moral and spiritual interior, as Spenser memorably dramatizes in Redcrosse's journey through Faerie land, which provides a crucial reminder that loving conduct was vulnerable to misprision and required careful discipline. But there also seems to be something hardwired into charity itself that complicates the act of interpretation. In Erasmus's view, divine love, perhaps most fully evident in the act of incarnation, accommodates itself to human weakness, and human forms of charity require a similar flexibility. Throughout the early modern period a number of writers probe the limitations and strengths of this position. How then to distinguish between a vision of heavenly love or an alchemical delusion? Love itself could serve as a cloak keeping episcopal corruption from view, as Puritans repeatedly complained, just as the charity distributed by rich benefactors might obscure the avaricious means by which their wealth was generated. The adaptability of charity, its capacity to upset established norms and shift shape or policy, could make the conditions of loving action more difficult to decipher. In his polemic with William Tyndale, Thomas More (a great ironist in his own right) expresses worry over individual heretics, to be sure, but he seems equally concerned over the slippage in meaning of his culture's moral vocabulary, the "wordes of grete weight" that help make human experience legible and perhaps even bearable.

Back to words, which were the start of this book—not merely the "signes of fraternall loue" urged by Henry VIII to his parliament but also the "convicious words" deplored by Elizabeth's injunctions. Throughout the pages of *Love's Quarrels*, the one form of charitable speech often turns into the other, the consequence of misinterpretation or rivalry or zeal. But given the intensity and pressure of love's demands, it should be no surprise that so much passionate and contentious language radiated outward from the concept and practice of charity, as early modern society in England worked out its deepest held and most powerful convictions.

NOTES

Introduction: Charitable Signs and Tokens

1. Edward Hall, *Hall's Chronicle*, ed. H. Ellis (London: 1809), 865–66.

2. Peter Marshall, *Religious Identities in Henry VIII's England* (Aldershot, UK: Ashgate, 2006), 157.

3. John Stow, *A Survey of London*, ed. C. L. Kingsford (Oxford: 1908), 2:89.

4. Brinklow, who had urged the king three years earlier to seize clerical property "so that it maye be disposed to Godes glorye and the commone welthe," was the author, under the name of Roderigo Mors, of *The Lamentacion of a Christen Agaynst the Cytie of London* (1542).

5. Hall, *Hall's Chronicle*, 866.

6. Alan Kreider, *English Chantries: The Road to Dissolution* (Cambridge, MA: Harvard University Press, 1979), 165–85.

7. *A famous speech of King Henry the eighth* (London: 1642).

8. *The English Poems of George Herbert*, ed. Helen Wilcox (Cambridge: Cambridge University Press, 2007), 244.

9. See Mark 12:28–34, Matt. 22:35–40, and Luke 10:25–38. It was conventional during the period to use these twin mandates to divide the Ten Commandments neatly into two tables that ordered one's love of God and humankind, respectively.

10. *Oxford English Dictionary*, 2nd ed. (Oxford: Oxford University Press, 1989), s.v. "charitable."

11. Raymond Williams, *Keywords: A Vocabulary of Culture and Society* (New York: Oxford University Press, 1983), 55.

12. John Bossy, *Christianity in the West, 1400–1700* (Oxford: OPUS, 1985), 168.

13. Edward Pelling, *A practical discourse upon the blessed sacrament* (London: 1692), 143.

14. Samuel Collins, *A Sermon preached at Paules-Crosse* (London: 1607), 65; Christopher Potter, *Want of Charitie Justly Charged* (London: 1633), 8.

15. *The Jew of Malta*, 4.4.79–80, in *The Complete Works of Christopher Marlowe*, ed. Fredson Bowers (Cambridge: Cambridge University Press, 1973), 1:322.

16. *Love's Labor's Lost*, 4.3.360–62, in *The Riverside Shakespeare*, ed. G. Blakemore Evans, 2nd ed. (Boston: Houghton Mifflin, 1997), 233.

17. Two works are worth pointing out for their lucidity and insight regarding the conflicted epistemologies of poverty during the period: David Aers, *Sanctifying Signs: Making Christian Tradition in Late Medieval England* (Notre Dame, IN: Notre Dame University Press, 2004), esp. 99–156; and Kate Crassons, *The Claims of Poverty: Literature, Culture, and Ideology in Late Medieval England* (Notre Dame, IN: Notre Dame University Press, 2010).

18. Brian Tierney, *Medieval Poor Law: A Sketch of Canonical Theory and Its Application in England* (Berkeley: University of California Press, 1959). See also, among others, Miri Rubin, *Charity and Community in Medieval Cambridge* (Cambridge: Cambridge University Press, 1987); Christopher Dyer, *Standards of Living in the Later Middle Ages* (Cambridge: Cambridge University Press, 1998); and *Experiences of Poverty in Late Medieval and Early Modern England and France*, ed. Anne Scott (Burlington, VT: Ashgate, 2012).

19. See in particular Eamon Duffy's magisterial work *The Stripping of the Altars: Traditional Religion in England, c.1400–c.1580* (New Haven, CT: Yale University Press, 2005).

20. Alexandra Walsham, *Charitable Hatred: Tolerance and Intolerance in England, 1500–1700* (Manchester, UK: Manchester University Press, 2006); Debora Shuger, *Censorship and Cultural Sensibility: The Regulation of Language in Tudor-Stuart England* (Philadelphia: University of Pennsylvania Press, 2006); Katrin Ettenhuber, *Donne's Augustine: Renaissance Cultures of Interpretation* (Oxford: Oxford University Press, 2011); Reid Barbour, *Literature and Religious Culture in Seventeenth-Century England* (Cambridge: Cambridge University Press, 2002).

21. Thomas More, *A Dialogue Concerning Heresies*, in *Complete Works of St. Thomas More*, ed. Thomas Lawler, Germain Marc'hadour, and Richard Marius, vol. 6, part 1 (New Haven, CT: Yale University Press, 1981), 257.

22. Margaret Fell, *A testimonie of the touch-stone* (London: 1656), 7; *Certain Sermons or Homilies (1547)*, ed. Ronald Bond (Toronto: University of Toronto Press, 1987), 100.

23. Christopher Marsh, *The Family of Love in English Society, 1550–1630* (Cambridge: Cambridge University Press, 1993), 24.

24. See, among others, Patrick Collinson, *The Religion of Protestants: The Church in English Society, 1559–1625* (Oxford: Clarendon Press, 1982); Peter Lake, *Anglicans and Puritans?: Presbyterianism and English Conformist Thought from Whitgift to Hooker* (London: Unwin Hyman, 1988); and Alexandra Walsham, *Church Papists: Catholicism, Conformity, and Confessional Polemic in Early Modern England* (Woodbridge, UK: Boydell Press, 1993).

25. William Ames, *Conscience with the Power and Cases Thereof* (London: 1639), 174; Richard Hooker, *Of the Laws of Ecclesiastical Polity*, ed. Arthur Stephen McGrade, (Oxford: Oxford University Press, 2013), 1:192.

26. Gabriel Harvey, *Pierces supererogation* (London: 1593), 88; "A true puritan without disguise," Bodleian MS Malone 23, 215. For the original poem celebrating Puritans by Alexander Leighton, which was entitled "A Puritan: (So nicknamed: but indeed the sound Protestant)," see *The Interpreter* (Edinburgh: 1622), 3–7.

27. John Donne, *The Oxford Edition of the Sermons of John Donne*, ed. David Colclough, (Oxford: Oxford University Press, 2013), 3:9.

28. Recent work by social historians has greatly improved our understanding of the evolution of various systems of giving in England throughout the sixteenth and early seventeenth century. For a discussion of the national poor law, the seminal work of Paul Slack, *Poverty and Policy in Tudor and Stuart England* (London: Longman, 1988), remains a valuable resource. For a study of vagrancy, see A. L. Beier, *Masterless Men: The Vagrancy Problem in England, 1560–1640* (London: Methuen, 1985). See also, among many others, Marjorie McIntosh, *Poor Relief in England, 1350–1600* (Cambridge: Cambridge University Press, 2012); Steve Hindle, *On the Parish? The Micro-Politics of Poor Relief in Rural England, c. 1550–1750* (Oxford: Oxford University Press, 2004); Ian Archer, *The Pursuit of Stability* (Cambridge: Cambridge University Press, 1991); Paul Fideler, *Social Welfare in Pre-Industrial England* (Basingstoke: Palgrave, 2006); and Ilana Krausman Ben-Amos, *The Culture of Giving* (Cambridge: Cambridge University Press, 2008).

29. Keith Thomas, *Religion and the Decline of Magic* (New York: Charles Scribner's Sons, 1971), 563.

30. See Kathy Eden, *Hermeneutics and the Rhetorical Tradition* (New Haven, CT: Yale University Press, 1997).

31. Stephen Batman, *A christall glasse of christian reformation* (London: 1569), Oii.

32. Ettenhuber, *Donne's Augustine*, 155.

33. Thomas Browne, *The Works of Sir Thomas Browne*, ed. Geoffrey Keynes (Chicago: University of Chicago Press, 1964), 1:15.

34. *Measure for Measure*, 2.4.63–64, in *Riverside Shakespeare*, 597.

35. Alexandra Walsham, *Providence in Early Modern England* (Oxford: Oxford University Press, 1999).

36. Debora Shuger, *The Renaissance Bible: Scholarship, Sacrifice, and Subjectivity* (Berkeley: University of California Press, 1998), 3.

37. Brian Cummings, *The Literary Culture of the Reformation: Grammar and Grace* (Oxford: Oxford University Press, 2002), 11.

38. Thomas Floyd, *The picture of a perfit common wealth* (London: 1600), 186.

39. George Gifford, *A dialogue betweene a papist and Protestant* (London: 1599), 151.

40. Thomas Browne, *Religio Medici*, in *The Works of Thomas Browne*, ed. Geoffrey Keynes (Chicago: University of Chicago Press, 1964), 1:77.

41. *Pathomachia: Or, The Battell of Affections* (London: 1630), 28. The anonymous writer of *Pathomachia* might have been influenced by Robert Wilson's play *The Three Ladies of London*, in which Lady Love marries (and becomes disfigured by) Dissimulation.

42. B.N., *The True Character tending to Love* (London: 1547), A2.

43. William Langland, *The vision of Pierce Plowman,* ed. Robert Crowley (1550), Yii.

Chapter 1: Charitable Translation

1. Thomas More, *The Complete Works of St. Thomas More,* vol. 6, part 1, ed. Thomas Lawler, Germain Marc'hadour, and Richard Marius (New Haven, CT: Yale University Press, 1981), 285–86. There are several excellent studies that focus on Tyndale's translation of *agape* and the ensuing controversy with More. See in particular Allan Jenkins and Patrick Preston, *Biblical Scholarship and the Church: A Sixteenth-Century Crisis of Authority* (Aldershot, UK: Ashgate, 2007); and Germain Marc'hadour and Thomas Lawler, "Scripture in the *Dialogue,*" in More, *Complete Works,* vol. 6, part 2, 512–16.

2. Richard of St. Victor, "The Four Degrees of Violent Charity," in *The Essential Writings of Christian Mysticism,* ed. Bernard McGinn (New York: Modern Library, 2006), 156.

3. Brian Cummings, *Grammar and Grace* (Oxford: The Clarendon Press, 2002), 143.

4. Augustine, *On Christian Doctrine,* trans. D. W. Robertson (Upper Saddle River, NJ: Prentice Hall, 1997), 28.

5. For a fuller examination of these topics, see Augustine, *On Christian Doctrine* 1.36–37 and 2.12, in ibid., 30–31, 44–46.

6. See Augustine, *Confessions* 12.17–24, trans. R. S. Pine-Coffin (New York: Dorset Press, 1986), 294–301.

7. Augustine, *On Christian Doctrine,* 78.

8. Katrin Ettenhuber, *Donne's Augustine: Renaissance Cultures of Interpretation* (Oxford: Oxford University Press, 2011), 17.

9. Marjorie McIntosh offers a useful summary of recent scholarship in *Poor Relief in England, 1350–1600* (Cambridge: Cambridge University Press, 2012), 1–35. See also Miri Rubin, *Charity and Community in Medieval Cambridge* (Cambridge: Cambridge University Press, 1987); and Barbara Harvey, *Living and Dying in England, 110–1540* (Oxford: Oxford University Press, 1993).

10. David Lloyd, *Memoires of the lives, actions, sufferings & deaths of those noble, reverend and excellent personages* (1668), 275.

11. John Foxe, *The Acts and Monuments,* ed. George Townsend (London: 1846), 4:665; Alistair Fox, *Thomas More* (New Haven, CT: Yale University Press, 1982), 111.

12. More, *Complete Works,* vol. 6, part 1, 288.

13. The phrase is found in 1 Peter 4:8, which was itself referring to Proverbs 10:12.

14. See the first five entries for "lewd" in the *Oxford English Dictionary,* 2nd ed. (Oxford: Oxford University Press, 1989).

15. C.S. Lewis, *English Literature in the Sixteenth Century, Excluding Drama* (Oxford: Clarendon Press, 1954), 189.

16. James Simpson, *Burning to Read: English Fundamentalism and Its English Opponents* (Cambridge, MA: Belknap Press, 2007), 179.

17. Anders Nygren considers Christian *agape* to be in fundamental contradistinction to Platonic *eros*. See his *Agape and Eros*, trans. A. G. Hebert (London: Society for Promoting Christian Thought, 1932), part 1, 23–27.

18. See Matt. 22:37–39, Mark 12:29–31, and Luke 10:27.

19. C. Spicq, *Agape in the New Testament*, trans. M. A. McNamara and M. H. Richter (St. Louis: B. Herder Book Company, 1965), 2:77–125.

20. Ibid., 103–307. See Catherine Osborne's *Eros Unveiled: Plato and the God of Love* (Oxford: Clarendon Press, 1994), 26, for a helpful chart recording each use of *agape* in verb or noun form throughout the New Testament.

21. It does not seem probable that Jerome translated the Pauline epistles, but the unknown editor followed a similar formula when translating *agape*. See *The Cambridge History of the Bible* (Cambridge: Cambridge University Press, 1969), 2:108.

22. See Eugene Rice, *Saint Jerome in the Renaissance* (Baltimore, MD: Johns Hopkins University Press, 1985). 17.

23. *Constitution of the Provincial Council at Oxford*, in *Records of the English Bible*, ed. Alfred Pollard (Oxford: Oxford University Press, 1911), 80–81.

24. See entry 2.a. for "charity" in the *Oxford English Dictionary*, 2nd ed. Anne Hudson affirms the lack of controversy in Wycliffite translations (in contradistinction to Tyndale's work) in *The Premature Reformation: Wycliffite Texts and Lollard History* (Oxford: Clarendon Press, 1988), 24.

25. William Tyndale, *An Answere Vnto Sir Thomas Mores Dialoge*, ed. Anne M. O'Donnell and Jared Wicks (Washington, DC: The Catholic University of America Press, 2000), 19–20.

26. Quoted in David Daniell, *William Tyndale: A Biography* (New Haven, CT: Yale University Press, 1994), 120.

27. Stephen Greenblatt, *Renaissance Self-Fashioning* (Chicago: University of Chicago Press, 1980), 100.

28. *The Holy Bible: made from the Latin Vulgate by John Wycliffe and his followers*, ed. Josiah Forshall and Sir Frederic Madden (Oxford: 1850), 1:57.

29. More, *Complete Works*, vol. 8, part 1, 41.

30. See Benedek Péter Tóta, "The European Transmission of *Caritas* in More's *Dialogue of Comfort*," in *Travels and Translations in the Sixteenth Century: Selected Papers from the Second International Conferences of the Tudor Symposium (2000)*, ed. John Michael Pincombe (Aldershot, UK: Ashgate, 2004), 65–72.

31. *Tyndale's New Testament*, trans. David Daniell (New Haven, CT: Yale University Press, 1989), 257.

32. *Controversies: De Libero Arbitrio / Hyperaspistes 1*, in *The Collected Works of Erasmus*, ed. Charles Trinkaus (Toronto: University of Toronto Press, 1999), 76:17–20.

33. More, *Complete Works*, vol. 6, part 1, 337.

34. Ibid., vol. 5, part 1, 234–53. For more on this controversy, see Cummings, *Grammar and Grace*, 38–47.

35. More, *Complete Works*, vol. 6, part 1, 287.

36. Augustine, *The City of God* 19.7, trans. Henry Bettenson (New York: Penguin Books, 1972), 556–58; Thomas Aquinas, *Summa Theologiae*, vol. 19, trans. Eric D'Arcy (Cambridge: Cambridge University Press, 2006), 68–74.

37. William Tyndale, *The Obedience of a Christian Man*, ed. David Daniell (New York: Penguin Books, 2000), 19.

38. Tyndale, *Answere*, 19–20.

39. Spicq, *Agape*, 150.

40. *The Praise of Folly*, in *Collected Works of Erasmus*, 27:127.

41. Tyndale uses "concupiscence" in his translation of Romans 7, Thessalonians 4, and James 1.

42. *Tyndale's New Testament*, 3.

43. Tyndale, *Answere*, 20.

44. Cummings, *Grammar and Grace*, 198–99.

45. Paul Botley, *Latin Translation in the Renaissance* (Cambridge: Cambridge University Press, 2004), esp. 139–43. See also Jerry Bentley, *Humanists and Holy Writ* (Princeton, NJ: Princeton University Press, 1983), 52–53; Alistair Hamilton, "Humanists and the Bible," in *The Cambridge Companion to Renaissance Humanism*, ed. Jill Kraye (Cambridge: Cambridge University Press, 1996), 100–117; and G. R. Evans, *Problems of Authority in the Reformation Debates* (Cambridge: Cambridge University Press, 1992), 53. As Marc'hadour and Lawler note, however, More's critique of Tyndale likewise adheres to humanist principles. See "Scripture in the *Dialogue*," in More, *Complete Works*, vol. 6, part 2, 513.

46. *Collected Works of Erasmus*, 45:18. For Tyndale's mocking description of More's friendship with Erasmus, see Tyndale, *Answere*, 14.

47. Matthew DeCoursey notes Tyndale's independence from Erasmus in "Erasmus and Tyndale on Bible-reading," *Reformation* 1, no. 1 (1996): 157–64.

48. See Gerald Snare, "Reading Tyndale's Bible," *Journal of Medieval and Early Modern Studies* 35, no. 2 (2005): 289–326; and Douglas Parker, "Tyndale's Biblical Hermeneutics," in *Word, Church, and State*, ed. John Day, Eric Lund, and Anne O'Donnell (Washington, DC: Catholic University of America, 1998), 87–101.

49. Henry Wansbrough, "Tyndale," in *The Bible in the Renaissance*, ed. Richard Griffiths (Aldershot, UK: Ashgate, 2001), 129.

50. More, *Complete Works*, vol. 8, part 1, 199–200.

51. Ibid., 202.

52. Germain Marc'hadour and Thomas Lawler, "Scripture in the *Dialogue*," in ibid., vol. 6, part 2, 513.

53. As Jamie Ferguson notes, Tyndale did make revisions in response to some of More's critiques. See Ferguson, "Faith in the Language: Biblical Authority and

the Meaning of English in More-Tyndale Polemics," *Sixteenth Century Journal* 43, no. 4 (2012): 1004, n. 34.

54. Gerald Snare, in "Reading Tyndale's Bible," 289–325, likewise notes the importance and irony of Tyndale's indictment of Joye.

55. *Tyndale's New Testament*, 13.

56. Ibid., 14.

57. Ibid., 15.

58. Ibid., 13.

59. Thomas Lupset, *A Treatise of Charitie* (London: 1533), 28.

60. Ibid., 31.

61. Ibid., 32.

62. Ferguson, "Faith in the Language," 1010.

63. More, *Complete Works*, vol. 6, part 1, 28; vol. 9, 156–57.

64. *Ibid.*, vol. 8, part 1, 12.

65. For local responses to poverty and its associated problems in England, see among others McIntosh, *Poor Relief in England, 1350–1600;* and Steve Hindle, *On the Parish? The Micro-Politics of Poor Relief in Rural England c. 1550–1750* (Oxford: Clarendon Press, 2004).

66. Juan Luis Vives, *De Subventione Pauperum,* ed. C. Matheeussen and C. Fantazzi (Boston: Brill, 2002), xix.

67. Tyndale, *Expositions and notes on sundry portions of the Holy Scriptures,* ed. Rev. Henry Walter (Cambridge: Cambridge University Press, 1849), 73.

68. C. S. L. Davies, "Slavery and Protector Somerset: The Vagrancy Act of 1547," *Economic History Review,* 2nd ser., 19 (1966): 540.

69. Perhaps the clearest scriptural reference to this concept appears in Ephesians 4:15–16, which Tyndale translates: "But let us follow the truth in love, and in all things grow in him which is the head, that is to say Christ, in whom all the body is coupled and knit together in every joint."

70. *Some Early Tracts on Poor Relief,* ed. F.R. Salter (London: Methuen, 1926), 59.

71. Paul Slack, *From Reformation to Improvement: Public Welfare in Early Modern England* (Oxford: Oxford University Press, 1999), 9.

72. More, *Complete Works,* 7:166–67.

73. Brian Tierney, *Medieval Poor Law* (Berkeley: University of California Press, 1959), 44–67.

74. Ibid., 35. Tierney observes how separate quotations from Augustine in the *Decretum* complicated medieval understandings of charity: "Justititia est in subveniendo miseris"; "Eleemosyna opus est misericordiae."

75. *Some Early Tracts,* 47.

76. Michel Mollat, *The Poor in the Middle Ages: An Essay in Social History,* trans. Arthur Goldhammer (New Haven, CT: Yale University Press, 1986), 251.

77. *Statutes of the Realm: Printed by Command of His Majesty King George the Third* (London: Eyre and Strahan, 1817), 3:329.

78. Ibid., 330.

79. See *Tudor Royal Proclamations*, ed. Paul Hughes and James Larkin (New Haven, CT: Yale University Press, 1964), 1:352. Contemporary attitudes toward poverty and theater would have crucial implications for the future status of drama in early modern England. See, among others, Paola Pugliatti, *Beggary and the Theatre in Early Modern England* (Aldershot, UK: Ashgate, 2003); William C. Carroll, *Fat King, Lean Beggar: Representations of Poverty in the Age of Shakespeare* (Ithaca, NY: Cornell University Press, 1996); and Robert Henke, *Poverty and Charity in Early Modern Theater and Performance* (Iowa City: University of Iowa Press, 2015).

80. Robert Copland, *Selected Pieces of Early Popular Poetry*, ed. Edward Vernon Utterson (London: T. Davison, 1817), 2:55–57, 208–10.

81. Later poor laws show evidence they were influenced by rogue literature, as Linda Woodbridge has demonstrated in *Vagrancy, Homelessness, and English Renaissance Literature* (Urbana: University of Illinois Press, 2001), 41–43.

82. *Some Early Tracts*, 55–56.

83. See Margo Todd, *Christian Humanism and the Puritan Social Order* (Cambridge: Cambridge University Press, 1987), esp. 118–75; Natalie Zemon Davis, "Poor Relief, Humanism, and Heresy" in *Society and Culture in Early Modern France* (Stanford, CA: Stanford University Press, 1975), 17–64.

84. Kathy Eden, *Hermeneutics and the Rhetorical Tradition* (New Haven, CT: Yale University Press, 1997), 53–78.

85. Quoted in Cummings, *Grammar and Grace*, 137–38. See Mary Jane Barnett, "Erasmus and the Hermeneutics of Linguistic Praxis," *Renaissance Quarterly* 49, no. 3 (1996): 542–72.

86. See in particular his paraphrase on 1 Cor. 8: 1–2, in *Collected Works of Erasmus*, 43:110.

87. Marjorie O'Rourke Boyle, *Erasmus on Language and Method in Theology* (Toronto: University of Toronto Press, 1977), 83.

88. Erasmus, *Ratio Verae Theologiae*, in *Ausgewählte Werke*, ed. A. Holborn and H. Holborn (Munich: Beck, 1933), 282.

89. *Collected Works of Erasmus*, 61:77.

90. Ramie Targoff, *Common Prayer: The Language of Public Devotion in Early Modern England* (Chicago: University of Chicago Press, 2001), 7–9.

91. *Statutes of the Realm*, 3:330, 560. Marjorie McIntosh notes that various local communities had already begun punishing neighbors who performed acts of indiscriminate charity, but the "serious rhetorical campaign" against vagrancy began with the government's increased attention in the 1520s and 1530s. McIntosh, *Controlling Misbehavior in England, 1370–1600* (Cambridge: Cambridge University Press, 1998), 54–107.

92. Vives, *De Subventione*, 111.

93. *Some Early Tracts*, 54.

94. Thomas Elyot, *The Boke Named the Governour,* ed. Henry Herbert Stephen Croft (New York: Burt Franklin, 1967), 88.

95. *Dives and Pauper,* ed. Priscilla Heath Barnum, vol. 1, part 1 (London: Early English Text Society, 1976), 67. See Alexandra Walsham, *Charitable Hatred* (Manchester, UK: Manchester University Press, 2006), esp. 39–105.

96. Tierney, *Medieval Poor Law,* 58.

97. See Margaret Aston, *Lollards and Reformers: Images and Literacy in Late Medieval Religion* (London: Hambledon Press, 1984), 208–9; and James Simpson, *Reform and Cultural Revolution* (Oxford: Oxford University Press, 2002), 339–43.

98. Simon Fish, *A Supplicacyon for the Beggers,* in More, *Complete Works,* 7:419.

99. Hudson, *Premature Reformation,* 501–2.

100. More, *Complete Works,* 7:118–19.

101. See Susan Brigden, *London and the Reformation* (Oxford: Clarendon Press, 1989). Brigden examines the specific constraints on a person's private faith posed by the close urban communities of London.

102. Jesse Lander, *Inventing Polemic: Religion, Print, and Literary Culture in Early Modern England* (Cambridge: Cambridge University Press, 2006), esp. 1–55.

103. More, *Complete Works,* vol. 8, part 3, 1139.

104. See Craig D'Alton, "Charity or Fire? The Argument of Thomas More's 1529 'Dyaloge,'" *The Sixteenth Century Journal* 33, no. 1 (2002): 51–70.

105. David Loewenstein, *Treacherous Faith: The Specter of Heresy in Early Modern English Literature and Culture* (Oxford: Oxford University Press, 2014), 29.

106. More, *Complete Works,* vol. 6, part 1, 47.

107. The entire episode is found in More, *Complete Works,* vol. 6, part 1, 287–88.

108. Ibid., vol. 8, part 1, 44. Numerous scholars have noted how More fixates on Luther's marriage, which receives mention in all of his religious polemic with astonishing regularity, but none have done so with as much facetious wit as Rainer Pineas, who portrays the device as More's *deus ex machina,* in *Thomas More and Tudor Polemics* (Bloomington: Indiana University Press, 1968), 144.

109. More, *Complete Works,* vol. 8, part 1, 28.

110. Ibid., vol. 6, part 1, 409. See Walsham, *Charitable Hatred,* 41–42.

111. Tyndale, *Answere,* 148.

112. More, *Complete Works,* vol. 8, part 1, 51–55.

113. See Stanley Maveety, "Doctrine in Tyndale's New Testament: Translation as a Tendentious Art," *Studies in English Literature, 1500–1900* 6, no. 1 (1966): 151–58.

114. Tyndale, *Answere,* 166.

115. Ibid., 161.

116. Lorenzo Valla, *On the Donation of Constantine,* trans. G. W. Bowerstock (Cambridge, MA: Harvard University Press, 2007), 2; Martin Luther, *Prelude on the Babylonian Captivity of the Church,* in *First Principles of the Reformation,* ed. Henry Wace and C. A. Buchheim (London: John Murray, 1883), 221.

117. Tyndale, *Answere*, 14.

118. Ibid., 119 and 22.

119. Louis Schuster, "Reformation Polemic and Renaissance Values," *Moreana* 43 (1974): 47–54.

Chapter 2: Charitable Adminition

1. John Weever, *The Whipping of the Satyre*, in *The Whipper Pamphlets: Part 1*, ed. Arnold Davenport (Liverpool: University Press of Liverpool, 1951), 991–93. All forthcoming references to the Whipper pamphlets will include line numbers in parentheses.

2. For the Bishops' Ban, see *A Transcript of the Registers of the Company of Stationers of London 1554–1640 AD*, ed. Edward Arber (London: 1876), 3:677.

3. *Certain Sermons or Homilies (1547)*, ed. Ronald Bond (Toronto: University of Toronto Press, 1987), 125.

4. William Perkins, *A Golden Chaine* (1600), 502; Phineas Fletcher, *The way to blessednes* (1633), 122.

5. Debora Shuger, *Censorship and Cultural Sensibility: The Regulation of Language in Tudor-Stuart England* (Philadelphia: University of Pennsylvania Press, 2006).

6. Thomas Aquinas, *Summa Theologiae,* trans. R.J. Batten (New York: McGraw-Hill, 1975), 34:289. For a vision of fraternal correction that is even more emphatic, perhaps because it was formulated amid papal controversy, see William of Ockham's *Dialogus*, ably examined in A. S. McGrade, *The Political Thought of William of Ockham* (Cambridge: Cambridge University Press, 2002), 47–77.

7. *The Reports of Sir Edward Coke*, ed. John Henry Thomas (London: Butterworth and Son, 1826), 3:254–56.

8. *A Transcript of the Registers of the Company of Stationers of London*, ed. Edward Arber (Gloucester, Mass: Peter Smith, 1967), 1:247. In this case the wardens' worry over the "lewde attemptes" of printers is likely a matter of protecting their monopoly rights, but their comments likewise represent contemporary concerns about how "troublesome and daungerous" unregulated printers would be "bothe for matters of the state and religion."

9. Edwin Craun, *Ethics and Power in Medieval English Reformist Writing* (Cambridge: Cambridge University Press, 2010), 97.

10. Perkins, *Golden Chaine*, 502.

11. *Sions charity towards her foes in misery* (1641), 4–5.

12. Martin Parker, *The poet's blind mans bough* (London: 1641), A3r.

13. Francis Bacon, *A wise and moderate discourse, concerning church-affaires* (1641), 7. It is no coincidence that Bacon's comments on the Marprelate controversy, initially circulated in manuscript, were published in 1641 in the context of another ecclesiastical controversy, in this case the Smectymnuan exchange.

14. John Donne, *The Complete Poems of John Donne,* ed. Robin Robbins (New York: Routledge, 2010), 387.

15. Any use of terms to distinguish between various factions within the Church of England will inevitably obscure the complexities of sixteenth-century confessional identity and church discipline, so it is with some hesitation that I employ a binary between "conformists" and "Puritans." But these labels are helpful, especially as they relate to charity in this case, if they can gesture at loosely shared ecclesiastical priorities and disciplinary styles. I take "Puritans" in this period to mean those who argued for more thoroughgoing ecclesiastical reform and supported more stringent ethical criteria for church membership, demands articulated with particular vehemence by promoters of a Presbyterian polity, and I take "conformists" to mean those who supported the ecclesiastical regulations set forth, however contentiously, by the politico-religious establishment. There was some overlap between these positions, of course. For a thoughtful consideration of these questions, see Peter Lake and Michael Questier's introduction to *Conformity and Orthodoxy in the English Church, c. 1560–1660,* ed. Peter Lake and Michael Questier (Woodbridge, UK: Boydell Press, 2000), ix–xx; and for a helpful examination of relevant ecclesiastical politics during the period, see Peter Lake, *Anglicans and Puritans?: Presbyterianism and English Conformist Thought from Whitgift to Hooker* (London: Unwin Hyman, 1988).

16. Kenneth Fincham, "Clerical Conformity from Whitgift to Laud," in *Conformity and Orthodoxy in the English Church,* 127.

17. The phrase, coined by Robert Persons in *A Brief Discourse* (1580), elicited responses from William Fulke, Percival Wilborn, and John Field. Patrick Collinson adopts it as a useful governing conceit for Puritanism in *The Elizabethan Puritan Movement* (Berkeley: University of California Press, 1967), 26–27.

18. Ephesians 4:15–16. Unless otherwise noted in this chapter, all biblical quotations are from *The Geneva Bible: A Facsimile of the 1560 edition* (Madison: University of Wisconsin Press, 1969). See also the Geneva Bible's note to 1 Cor. 13, which claims, "Because loue is the fountaine and rule of edifying the Church, he setteth forthe the nature, office and praise thereof."

19. John Coolidge, *The Pauline Renaissance in England* (Oxford: Clarendon Press, 1970), 23–54.

20. John Field and Thomas Wilcox, *An admonition to the Parliament* (1572), B8r.

21. Ibid., D2r. The phrase is Theodore Beza's, from a letter to Edmund Grindal, which Field and Wilcox appended to the *Admonition.*

22. Thomas Cartwright, *A replye to an answere made of M. Doctor Whitgifte* (Hemel Hempstead: 1573), 176.

23. John Udall, *A demonstration of the trueth of that discipline* (East Molesey: 1588), 90.

24. William Fulke, *A brief and plaine declaration, concerning the desires of all those faithfull ministers* (London: 1584), 91.

25. Udall, *Demonstration*, 14.

26. *An exhortation to the byshops to deale brotherly with theyr brethren* (1572), B1v-B2r.

27. Martin Marprelate, *Hay Any Worke for Cooper*, in *The Martin Marprelate Tracts*, ed. Joseph Black (Cambridge: Cambridge University Press, 2008), 122.

28. James I, *His Maiesties declaration concerning his proceedings with the States generall of the Vnited Prouinces of the Low Countreys* (London: 1612), 6–7.

29. "The Elizabethan Injunctions, 1559," in *Documents of the English Reformation*, ed. Gerald Bray (Cambridge: James Clarke, 1994), 345.

30. Collinson, *Elizabethan Puritan Movement*, 346–55.

31. Claire McEachern makes a similar comment about the injunctions, claiming they were based "on the premise that social order wrought through the regulation of conduct cultivated spiritual correctness, rather than the other way round." "Spenser and Religion," in *The Oxford Handbook of Edmund Spenser*, ed. Richard McCabe (Oxford: Oxford University Press, 2010), 33.

32. Whitgift, *The defense of the aunswere to the Admonition against the replie of T.C.* (London: 1574), 22. Cartwright uses this trope in behalf of Puritans, adding further vehemence by employing a double negative: "And then where is charitie / which covereth the multitude of faultes / especially in brethren / when you do not only not cover them / but also take away their garments / whereby they are covered." *Replye to an Answere*, 9.

33. Richard Hooker, *Of the Laws of Ecclesiastical Polity*, ed. Arthur Stephen McGrade (Oxford: Oxford University Press, 2013), 1:192.

34. Henry Howard, *A Defense of the Ecclesiastical Regiment* (London: 1574), 40.

35. Thomas Cooper, *An admonition to the people of England* (London: 1589), 5.

36. Marprelate, *Martin Marprelate Tracts*, 129.

37. Joseph Hall, *A Defence* (London: 1641), 5; John Milton, *Complete Prose Works*, ed. Don Wolfe (New Haven, CT: Yale University Press, 1959), 1:62.

38. Michael Questier has shown that such tactics were rarely deployed in polemical disputes, although he notes that Robert Persons's *Christian Directory* was considered effective because it eschewed a polemical tone. *Conversion, Politics, and Religion in England, 1580–1625* (Cambridge: University of Cambridge Press, 1996), 37–38.

39. John Bridges, *A defence of the gouernment established in the Church of Englande* (London: 1587), 202.

40. Cartwright, *Replye*, 68.

41. Henry Barrow, *A briefe discoverie of the false church* (1590), 37.

42. Conformists came around to his way of thinking as well. Consider the following quote by Richard Bancroft: "Many others there be, who cover their malice more cunningly, nay more hypocritically, as though all they said proceeded of meere love and Christian charitie." *A sermon preached at Paules Crosse the 9. of Februarie 1588* (London: 1588), 92.

43. Whitgift, *Defense of the aunswere*, 56.

44. See Alexandra Walsham, *Charitable Hatred* (Manchester, UK: Manchester University Press, 2006), 39–105.

45. The quotation is from Robert Beale's letter to Burghley in 1584, found in Patrick Collinson, *Richard Bancroft and Elizabethan Anti-Puritanism* (Cambridge: Cambridge University Press, 2013), 44.

46. Cartwright, *Replye*, 79.

47. Bacon, *A wise and moderate discourse*, 46.

48. Edmund Spenser, *The Yale Edition of the Shorter Poems of Edmund Spenser*, ed. William Oram, Einar Bjorvand, Ronald Bond, Thomas Cain, Alexander Dunlop, and Richard Schell (New Haven, CT: Yale University Press, 1989), 87. All citations from the poem will include line numbers in parentheses.

49. For a hyperbolic example of this perspective, see James Jackson Higginson's declaration that "Piers manifestly expresses Spenser's own views," in *Spenser's Shepheard's Calender in Relation to Contemporary Affairs* (New York: Columbia University Press, 1912), 72. For the most convincing treatment of the poem, see John King's evenhanded *Spenser's Poetry and the Reformation Tradition* (Princeton, NJ: Princeton University Press, 1990), 35–42. See also Anthea Hume, *Edmund Spenser: Protestant Poet* (Cambridge: Cambridge University Press, 1984), 15–28; Nancy Jo Hoffman, *Spenser's Pastorals* (Baltimore, MD: Johns Hopkins University Press, 1977), 104–18; and Lynn Johnson, *The Shepheardes Calender: An Introduction* (University Park, PA: Penn State University Press, 1990), 77–82. All of these studies take E.K. more or less at his word, although they disagree as to whether Piers articulates Puritan or more moderate Protestant sympathies.

50. Harry Berger, Jr., *Revisionary Play: Studies in the Spenserian Dynamics* (Berkeley: University of California Press, 1988), 299.

51. Ibid., 294–306. See also Paul Alpers, *What Is Pastoral?* (Chicago: University of Chicago Press, 1996), 178; Roland Greene, *"The Shepheardes Calender, Dialogue, and Periphrasis," Spenser Studies* 8 (1987): 1–33; Patrick Cullen, *Spenser, Marvell, and Renaissance Pastoral* (Cambridge, MA: Harvard University Press, 1970); and Edward Armstrong, *A Ciceronian Sunburn* (Columbia: University of South Carolina Press, 2006), 82–84.

52. Patricia Berrahou Phillippy, *Love's Remedies: Recantation and Renaissance Lyric Poetry* (Lewisburg, PA: Bucknell University Press, 1995), 174–81.

53. Robert Lane, *Shepheards Devises: Edmund Spenser's Shepheardes Calender and the Institutions of Elizabethan Society* (Athens: University of Georgia Press, 1993), 101–14; and Gregory Kneidel, "'Mighty Simplenesse': Protestant Pastoral Rhetoric and Spenser's 'Shepheardes Calender,'" *Studies in Philology* 96, no. 3 (1999): 275–312.

54. See E.K.'s explanation of the emblems in *Spenser, Shorter Poems*, 105.

55. See S. K. Heninger, Jr., *"The Shepheardes Calender,"* in *The Spenser Encyclopedia* (Toronto: University of Toronto Press, 1990), 647.

56. Thomas Rogers, *The anatomie of the minde* (London: 1576), 46.

57. See "borrow, n., 3," *Oxford English Dictionary*, 2nd ed. (Oxford: Oxford University Press, 1989).

58. Cullen, *Spenser, Marvell, and Renaissance Pastoral*, 49.

59. Kneidel, "'Mighty Simplenesse,'" 300.

60. Walter Travers, *A Full and Plain Declaration of Ecclesiasticall Discipline*, trans. Thomas Cartwright (Heidelberg: 1574), 39.

61. *An admonition to the Parliament*, B6r.

62. Berger, *Revisionary Play*, 302.

63. Richard Chamberlain, *Radical Spenser: Pastoral, Poetics and the New Aestheticism* (Edinburgh: Edinburgh University Press, 2005), 49.

64. Spenser, *Shorter Poems*, 105.

65. Shuger, *Censorship and Cultural Sensibility*, 146–47.

66. *The returne of the knight of the poste from Hell with the diuels aunswere to the supplication of Pierce Penilesse* (London: 1606), B4v.

67. Robert Hayman, *Quodlibets* (London: 1628), 59.

68. Bryan Herek, "Reconsidering the 1599 Bishops' Ban on Satire," *Renaissance Papers 2011* (Rochester, NY: Camden House, 2012), 131–39.

69. Richard McCabe, *Joseph Hall: A Study in Satire and Meditation* (Oxford: Clarendon Press, 1982), 33–42.

70. Samuel Rowlands, *The letting of humours blood in the head-vaine* (London: 1600), E3.

71. Lawrence Manley, *Literature and Culture in Early Modern London* (Cambridge: Cambridge University Press, 1995), 378.

72. In addition to Shuger's *Censorship and Cultural Sensibility* and Clegg's *Press Censorship in Elizabethan England* (Cambridge: Cambridge University Press, 1997), see Christopher Hill, "Censorship and English Literature," in *The Collected Essays of Christopher Hill: Writing and Revolution in 17th-Century England* (Amherst: University of Massachusetts Press, 1985), 32–72; Annabel Patterson, *Censorship and Interpretation: The Conditions of Writing and Reading in Early Modern England* (Madison: University of Wisconsin Press, 1984); and Richard McCabe, "Elizabethan Satire and the Bishops' Ban of 1599," *Yearbook of English Studies* 11 (1981): 188–93.

73. Richard Niccols, *The Furies* (London: 1614).

74. John Marston, "Proemium in librum tertium," in *The scourge of villainie* (1599), F4v.

75. Thomas Lodge, *A Fig for Momus* (London: 1595), E3.

76. Donne, *Complete Poems*, 417.

77. Rowlands, *The letting of humours blood*, D2.

78. Joseph Hall, *The Poems of Joseph Hall*, ed. Arnold Davenport (Liverpool: Liverpool University Press, 1969), 47.

79. E. A. J. Honigmann, *John Weever: A Biography of a Literary Associate of Shakespeare and Jonson* (Manchester, UK: Manchester University Press, 1987),

17–20. See also William Jones, "'Say They Are Saints Although That Saints They Show Not': John Weever's 1599 Epigrams to Marston, Jonson, and Shakespeare," *Huntington Library Quarterly* 73, no. 1 (2010): 83–98.

80. Davenport notes the "odd image" of an ambry in *The Whipper Pamphlets: Part 2*, suggesting that it must possess special significance, though he does not offer a specific explanation. An "ambry" might refer to an "almory," or repository of alms, but it more properly refers to a church closet for housing sacramental vessels, vestments, books, and other features of ecclesiastical ceremony. See the *Oxford English Dictionary* for "ambry," second and third definitions.

Chapter 3: Charitable Allegory

1. Thomas Churchyard, *A musicall consort of heauenly harmonie (compounded out of manie parts of musicke) called Churchyards charitie* (1595), Ar–Av.

2. Allan Griffith Chester, "Thomas Churchyard's Pension," *PMLA* 50, no. 3 (1935): 902.

3. Richard Mulcaster's account has been reprinted in *The Queen's Majesty's Passage & Related Documents*, ed. Germaine Warkentin (Toronto: Centre for Reformation and Renaissance Studies, 2004), 93.

4. Ibid.

5. Susan Brigden, *London and the Reformation* (Oxford: Clarendon Press, 1989), 527. On the whole, however, Marian authorities supported hospitals, improving their administration and oversight, a legacy Elizabeth tried to continue. See Nicholas Orme and Margaret Webster, *The English Hospital: 1070–1570* (New Haven, CT: Yale University Press, 1995), 161–66.

6. *Queen's Majesty's Passage*, 124.

7. James Sutton, *Materializing Space at an Early Modern Prodigy House* (Aldershot, UK: Ashgate, 2004), 166–208.

8. John Savile, *King James his Entertainment at Theobalds* (London: 1606).

9. Sutton, *Materializing Space*, 188.

10. *The Progresses, Processions, and Magnificent Festivities, of King James the First*, ed. John Nichols (London: 1828), 2:72–73.

11. See Maurice Lee, *Great Britain's Solomon: James VI and I in His Three Kingdoms* (Urbana: University of Illinois Press, 1990), 130–31.

12. One wonders whether contemporary reports of the Theobalds entertainment suggested to Shakespeare a last-minute alteration to *Macbeth*, which was performed for King Christian during his visit, or whether Lady Macbeth's lines are simply a happy coincidence: "Was the hope drunk / Wherein you dress'd yourself?" (1.7.35–6). *The Riverside Shakespeare*, ed. G. Blakemore Evans, 2nd ed. (Boston: Houghton Mifflin, 1997), 1366.

13. Linda Gregerson, *The Reformation of the Subject: Spenser, Milton, and the English Protestant Epic* (Cambridge: Cambridge University Press, 1995), 55.

14. George Puttenham, *The Art of English Poesy*, ed. Frank Whigham and Wayne Rebhorn (Ithaca, NY: Cornell University Press, 2007), 272.

15. *Pascal's Pensées*, trans. Martin Turnell (New York: Harper and Brothers, 1962), 262.

16. Philip Sidney, *The Countess of Pembroke's Arcadia*, ed. Victor Skretkowicz (Oxford: Clarendon Press, 1987), 97; John Bunyan, *The Pilgrim's Progress*, ed. James Blanton Wharey, rev. Roger Sharrock (Oxford: Clarendon Press, 1975), 226.

17. Geoffrey Chaucer, *The Romaunt of the Rose*, in *The Riverside Chaucer*, ed. Larry Benson (Boston: Houghton Mifflin, 1987), 691.

18. William Langland, *The Vision of Pierce Plowman* (1550), U4v. I am using the Robert Crowley edition from the mid-sixteenth century, taken from the B-text, as this is what Spenser would likely have read. The C-text is slightly more sanguine, with Liberum Arbitrium noting, "Ac thorw werkes thow myhte wyte wher-forth he walketh." *Piers Plowman: A New Annotated Edition of the C-text*, ed. Derek Pearsall (Exeter, UK: University of Exeter Press, 2008), 280.

19. *Bernard of Clairvaux: On the Song of Songs*, trans. Kilian Walsh (Shannon, Ireland: Cistercian Publications, 1971), 1:7; Origen, *Prologue to the Commentary on the Song of Songs*, trans. R. A. Greer (New York: Paulist Press, 1979), 218.

20. Denys Turner, *Eros and Allegory: Medieval Exegesis of the Song of Songs* (Kalamazoo, MI: Cistercian Publications, 1995).

21. William Baldwin, "Christe to his spouse. Xxxiii," in *Canticles, or Balades of Salomon* (1549), F3v. See Noam Flinker, *The Song of Songs in English Renaissance Literature: Kisses of Their Mouths* (Cambridge: D.S. Brewer, 2000).

22. Cesare Ripa, *Iconologia*, trans. P. Tempest (London: 1709), 12; R. Freyhan, "The Evolution of the Caritas Figure in the Thirteenth and Fourteenth Centuries," *Journal of the Warburg and Courtauld Institutes* 11 (1948): 68–86. See also Edgar Wind, *Pagan Mysteries in the Renaissance* (New Haven, CT: Yale University Press, 1958).

23. Caecilie Weissert, "Personifications of Caritas as Reflexive Figures," in *Personification: Embodying Meaning and Emotion, ed. Walter Melion and Bart Ramakers* (Leiden: Brill, 2016), 491–517.

24. Sidney, *The Countess of Pembroke's Arcadia*, 14.

25. Thomas Adams, *The happines of the church, or, A description of those spirituall prerogatiues vvherewith Christ hath endowed her* (London: 1619), 429.

26. Robert Herrick, *The Complete Poetry of Robert Herrick*, ed. Tom Cain and Ruth Connolly (Oxford: Oxford University Press, 2013), 1:191–92.

27. Fulke Greville, "Sonnet L," in *Selected Poems of Fulke Greville*, ed. Thom Gunn (Chicago: University of Chicago Press, 2009), 79.

28. *Thomas Middleton: The Collected Works*, ed. Gary Taylor and John Lavagnino (Oxford: Oxford University Press, 2010), 801.

29. Richard Niccols, *The Furies* (London: 1614), C3.

30. *The Poems of Richard Lovelace,* ed. W. Carew Hazlitt (London: John Russell Smith, 1864), 137–38.

31. Gordon Williams, *Dictionary of Sexual Language and Imagery in Shakespearean and Stuart Literature* (Atlantic Highlands, NJ: Athlone Press, 1994), 1:230.

32. John Cleveland, "A Dialogue between two Zealots, upon the &c. in the Oath," in *The Poems of John Cleveland,* ed. Brian Morris and Eleanor Withington (Oxford: Clarendon Press, 1967), 4; Henry Tubbe, "Satyr. Debate Concerning the Engagement," in *Henry Tubbe, Oxford Historical and Literary Studies,* ed. G. C. Moore Smith (Oxford: Clarendon Press, 1915), 5:78.

33. Richard Brathwaite, *A strappado for the Diuell* (London: 1615), 204.

34. The description appears in a letter from Sir Richard Gresham to Henry VIII in August 1538, quoted in Brigden, *London and the Reformation,* 208.

35. John Foxe, *The Acts and Monuments of John Foxe* (New York: AMS, 1965), 7:559–60.

36. Thomas Cranmer, 29th Injunction, in *Documents of the English Reformation,* ed. Gerald Bray (Cambridge: James Clarke, 1994), 255, 341; Robert Persons, *An epistle of the persecution of Catholickes in Englande* (1582), 98.

37. Allen is quoted in William Fulke, *Two treatises written against the papists* (London: 1577), 239.

38. Ibid., 241.

39. Thomas Adams, *The Barren Tree* (London: 1623), A4v.

40. Nathaniel Shute, *Corona Charitatis* (London: 1626), 22–23.

41. Matthew Wilson, *Mercy and Truth. Or Charity Maintayned by Catholics* (1634), 284.

42. Paul Cefalu, *Moral Identity in Early Modern English Literature* (Cambridge: Cambridge University Press, 2004), 31; see also Theodore Dwight Bozeman, *The Precisionist Strain: Disciplinary Religion and Antinomian Backlash in Puritanism to 1638* (Chapel Hill: University of North Carolina Press, 2004), 121–45. For a contemporary discussion of the issue, see George Gifford, *Foure sermons vpon the seuen chiefe vertues or principall effectes of faith* (1584), esp. E6.

43. Thomas Cranmer, *Certain sermons or homilies (1547),* ed. Ronald Bond (Toronto: University of Toronto Press, 1987), 100.

44. Foxe, *Acts and Monuments,* 4:571.

45. Theodore Beza, *A booke of Christian questions and answers,* trans. Arthur Golding (1572), 85.

46. Cefalu, *Moral Identity,* 31.

47. William Perkins, *A case of conscience the greatest that euer was: how a man may know whether he be the child of God or no* (1592), 68.

48. Simonds D'Ewes, *The Journals of All The Parliaments During the Reign of Queen Elizabeth* (London: 1682), 683.

49. Francis Quarles, "On Faith, Love, and Charity," in *Divine fancies digested into epigrammes, meditations, and observations* (1633), 32.

50. Edmund Spenser, *The Faerie Queene*, ed. A. C. Hamilton, 2nd ed. (London: Routledge, 2013), 1.10.36–44. All forthcoming quotations are from this text and will include book, canto, and stanza numbers in parentheses.

51. Joseph Campana, *The Pain of Reformation: Spenser, Vulnerability, and the Ethics of Masculinity* (New York: Fordham University Press, 2012), 104.

52. C.S. Lewis, *The Allegory of Love* (Oxford: Clarendon Press, 1936), 322.

53. James Kearney, *The Incarnate Text: Imagining the Book in Reformation England* (Philadelphia: University of Pennsylvania Press, 2009), 134.

54. Ibid., 135.

55. Patrick Cullen, *Infernal Triad: The Flesh, the World, and the Devil in Spenser and Milton* (Princeton, NJ: Princeton University Press, 1974), 64.

56. Kenneth Gross, *Spenserian Poetics: Idolatry, Iconoclasm, and Magic* (Ithaca, NY: Cornell University Press, 1985), 17.

57. John King, *Spenser's Poetry and the Reformation Tradition* (Princeton, NJ: Princeton University Press, 1990), 62.

58. Foxe, *Acts and Monuments*, 4:560.

59. Cary is quoted in John Duncon, *The Returns of Spiritual Comfort and Grief in a Devout Soul* (London: 1648), 50. Interestingly, Cary replaces "hope" with "joy."

60. Heinrich Bullinger, *Questions of Religion*, trans. John Coxe (London: 1572), 48.

61. Alexander Nowell and William Day, *A true report of the disputation or rather priuate conference had in the Tower of London, with Ed. Campion Iesuite, the last of August* (London: 1583), D.d.iii.

62. George Withers, *A view of the marginal notes of the popish Testament* (London: 1588), 203. See also William Pemble, *Vindiciae fidei, or A treatise of iustification by faith* (1625), 217.

63. Kathryn Walls, *God's Only Daughter: Spenser's Una as the Invisible Church* (Manchester, UK: Manchester University Press, 2013), 160. See also Caroline McManus, *Spenser's "Faerie Queene" and the Reading of Women* (Newark, NJ: University of Delaware Press, 2002), 244–45.

64. Richard Younge, *A sovereign antidote against all grief* (1654), 207.

65. The phrase is also used to describe the steward Diet in the Castle of Alma (2.9.27), the Genius of the Bowre of Blisse (2.12.46), and, perhaps most ominously, the Squire of Dames who bears a "comely personage, / And louely face, made fit for to deceiue / Fraile Ladies hart with loues consuming rage" (3.7.46).

66. Robert Reid, "Holiness, House of," in *The Spenser Encyclopedia*, ed. A. C. Hamilton et al. (Toronto: University of Toronto Press, 1990), 373; James Nohrnberg, *The Analogy of The Faerie Queene* (Princeton, NJ: Princeton University Press, 1976), 453. Noam Flinker has discovered a similar balance of sacred and erotic imagery in *Amoretti*, which he notes is adapted from the Song of Songs tradition. Flinker, *Song of Songs*, 75.

67. Walls, *God's Only Daughter*, 160, n. 25.

68. Richard Brome suggestively inverts the role of Charissa even as he retains her erotic allure in *The Court Beggar*, as she becomes an attractive daughter used as amatory bait for her father Mendicant's courtly designs.

69. Sheila Cavanagh, *Wanton Eyes and Chaste Desires: Female Sexuality in the Faerie Queene* (Bloomington: Indiana University Press, 1994), 31–32; Gail Kern Paster, *The Body Embarrassed: Drama and the Disciplines of Shame in Early Modern England* (Ithaca, NY: Cornell University Press, 1993), 206.

70. The Longman edition of *The Faerie Queene* glosses the line as such: "By this: i.e. by this time."

71. Darryl Gless's discussion of Recrosse's need for self-love is particularly helpful in illuminating this episode. See Gless, *Interpretation and Theology in Spenser* (Cambridge: Cambridge University Press, 1994), 153.

72. William Perkins, *The whole treatise of the cases of conscience* (London: 1606), 168.

73. Lauren Silberman, *Transforming Desire: Erotic Knowledge in Books III and IV of the Faerie Queene* (Berkeley: University of California Press, 1995), 93.

74. See *A Catechism Written in Latin by Alexander Nowell*, ed. G. E. Corrie (Cambridge: Cambridge University Press, 1853), 49, 167. As for Milton, see God's question in Book 3 of *Paradise Lost*: "Dwells in all heaven charity so dear? (216). The phrase was often paired with "charity" as a means of reinforcing its sense. Consider Thomas More's claims in *The Supplication of Souls* that he is countering Fish's heresies "for the dere loue & cheryte that we bere to you," in *The Complete Works of Thomas More*, ed. Frank Manley et al. (New Haven, CT: Yale University Press, 1990), 7:112; or the English translation of Erasmus's first volume of *Paraphrases of the New Testament* (London: 1548), which describes divine charity as the "feruente burnyng fyre of his dere loue and charitie" (xxix).

75. *The Divine Comedy of Dante Alighieri*, ed. Robert Durling (Oxford: Oxford University Press, 2003), 2:383.

76. Although the passage was popular among contemporaries—Luther's commentary on Galatians was particularly influential in articulating a concept of Christian liberty—I do not mean to establish this as a specific biblical reference for Spenser (though it is cited by Hamilton in the Longman edition to gloss 1.10.6), but rather to describe the paradoxical logic of Christian liberty and its association with charity. Also of note is 1 Peter 2:16 and 2 Peter 2:19.

77. See the first and second entries for "sake, n.," *Oxford English Dictionary*, 2nd ed. (Oxford: Oxford University Press, 1989).

78. For a similarly positive reading of this episode—that Spenser intends for this gift exchange to illustrate the positive effects of cooperative mutuality—see Jessica Wolfe, *Homer and the Question of Strife from Erasmus to Hobbes* (Toronto: University of Toronto Press, 2015), 188–90. A number of scholars read this passage as a crucial misunderstanding by Redcrosse about the nature of gifts and grace. See

Kearney, *Incarnate Text*, 121–25; and Maureen Quilligan, *The Language of Allegory: Defining the Genre* (Ithaca, NY: Cornell University Press, 1979), 33–42.

79. Wolfe, *Homer and the Question of Strife*, 183.

80. See, among others, Maureen Quilligan, *Milton's Spenser: The Politics of Reading* (Ithaca, NY: Cornell University Press, 1983); McManus, *Spenser's "Faerie Queene,"* 234–35; and Elizabeth A. Spiller, "Poetic Parthenogenesis and Spenser's Idea of Creation in *The Faerie Queene*," *Studies in English Literature, 1500–1900* 40, no. 1 (2000): 63–79.

81. McManus, *Spenser's "Faerie Queene,"* 219.

82. Part of this recovery likewise stems from the simple fact that the speaker is Una, who has been associated with a higher kind of "dear love" throughout the narrative. Consider the speaker's description of Una in Canto 7: "Was neuer Ladie loued dearer day, / Then she did loue the knight of the *Redcrosse*; / For whose deare sake so many troubles her did tosse" (1.7.27).

83. Father Thomas Nelan, *Catholic Doctrines in Spenser's Poetry* (New York: New York University Press, 1946); Frederick Padelford, *The Political and Ecclesiastical Allegory of the First Book of The Faerie Queene* (Folcroft, PA: Folcroft Press, 1970); and Anthea Hume, *Edmund Spenser: Protestant Poet* (Cambridge: Cambridge University Press, 1984). For a more evenhanded approach, see Virgil Whitaker, *The Religious Basis of Spenser's Thought* (Stanford, CA: Stanford University Press, 1950); as well as John King, *Spenser's Poetry and the Reformation Tradition*; and for a convincing discussion of theosis, see Harold Weatherby, *Mirrors of Celestial Grace* (Toronto: University of Toronto Press, 1994). For a discussion of Spenser's sources for the episode, see Charles E. Mounts, "Spenser's Seven Bead-men and the Corporal Works of Mercy," *PMLA* 54 (1939): 974–80.

84. James Schiavoni, "Predestination and Free Will: The Crux of Canto Ten," *Spenser Studies* 10 (1992): 175–95; Gless, *Interpretation and Theology*; Carol Kaske, *Spenser and Biblical Poetics* (Ithaca, NY: Cornell University Press, 1999). See also Kearney, *Incarnate Text*, 128–35.

85. Thomas Herron, *Spenser's Irish Work: Poetry, Plantation and Colonial Reformation* (Aldershot, UK: Ashgate, 2007), 185–224.

86. Marjorie McIntosh, *Poor Relief in England, 1350–1600* (Cambridge: Cambridge University Press, 2012), 255–69.

87. William Carroll, *Fat King, Lean Beggar: Representations of Poverty in the Age of Shakespeare* (Ithaca, NY: Cornell University Press, 1996), 44–46.

88. *A Second Admonition to the Parliament* (1572), 52. Thomas Wilson is quoted in Paul Slack, *Poverty and Policy in Tudor and Stuart England* (London: Longman, 1988), 125.

89. Isabel MacCaffrey, *Spenser's Allegory: The Anatomy of Imagination* (Princeton, NJ: Princeton University Press, 1976), 189.

90. Rosamond Tuve, *Allegorical Imagery: Some Mediaeval Books and Their Posterity* (Princeton, NJ: Princeton University Press, 1966), 47.

91. St. Bartholomew's Hospital is perhaps the closest model. In 1544 the hospital "was reformed rather than repressed" and its clergy reduced from nine members to five, all of whom were charged with performing the seven corporal works of mercy. See *Letters and Papers, Foreign and Domestic, of the Reign of Henry VIII*, vol. 19, part 1, ed. James Gairdner and R. H. Brodie (London: 1903), 501; and Orme and Webster, *English Hospital*, 161.

92. Thomas Dekker, *The Dramatic Works of Thomas Dekker*, ed. Fredson Bowers (Cambridge: Cambridge University Press, 1964), 205.

93. I have written about this curious feature of Spenser's work in "Going Rogue: Spenser and the Vagrants," *Studies in Philology* 113, no. 3 (2016): 546–76.

94. Edmund Spenser, *The Yale Edition of the Shorter Poems of Edmund Spenser*, ed. William Oram et al. (New Haven, CT: Yale University Press, 1989), lines 83–86.

95. Naseeb Shaheen, *Biblical References in The Faerie Queene* (Memphis, TN: Memphis State University Press, 1976), 208.

96. Hugh Latimer, *The sermon that the reuerende father in Christ, Hugh Latimer, Byshop of Worcester, made to the clergie, in the conuocation, before the Parlyament began* (London: 1537).

97. This was a traditional means of "ordering" charity—love God first, and that will order one's love toward neighbors (see Augustine *De Doctrina Christiana* 1.4.4 and Aquinas *Summa Theologiae* 1.20.2)—which was retained by Calvinists like Thomas Playfere in his spital sermon *The Pathway to Perfection* (1593).

98. See Kathryn Walls, "Spenser's Kirkrapine and John Foxe's Attack on Rome," *Notes and Queries* 31, no. 2 (1984): 173–75; and Mother Mary Robert Falls, "Spenser's Kirkrapine and the Elizabethans," *Studies in Philology* 50, no. 3 (1953): 457–75. In *An almond for a parrat* (London: 1589), meanwhile, the pamphleteer, most likely Thomas Nashe, suggests that Presbyterians will use proceeds from the poor box to fund excursions to Geneva.

99. For an alternative reading of Envie, see King, *Spenser's Poetry*, 88, who refers to the emblem "Of Enuie" in Stephen Batman's *Christall Glasse of Christian Reformation* (1569), in which a friar and bishop forcibly remove a preacher of godly zeal from his pulpit.

100. Tobie Bland, *A Baite for Momus* (London, 1589), 17.

101. Thomas Cooper, *The Art of Giving* (London, 1615), 85.

102. See A. Bartlett Giamatti, "Proteus Unbound: Some Versions of the Sea God in the Renaissance," chap. 7 in *Exile and Change in Renaissance Literature* (New Haven, CT: Yale University Press, 1984), 115–50.

103. See King, *Spenser's Poetry*, 75–76; and A. Bartlett Giamatti, *Play of Double Senses: Spenser's Faerie Queene* (Englewood Cliffs, NJ: Prentice Hall, 1975), 118–34.

Chapter 4: Charitable Use

1. Francis Bacon, *The Advancement of Learning*, in *The Oxford Francis Bacon*, ed. Michael Kiernan (Oxford: Clarendon Press, 2000), 4:9.

2. Ibid., 7.

3. Ibid., 31.

4. Jeffrey Cordell, "Baconian Apologetics: Knowledge and Charity in *The Advancement of Learning*," *Studies in Philology* 108, no. 1 (Winter 2011): 86–107.

5. Francis Bacon, *The New Organon*, ed. Lisa Jardine and Michael Silverthorne (Cambridge: Cambridge University Press, 2000), 12.

6. Ibid., 12.

7. Bacon, *Advancement*, 37 and 38.

8. Ibid., 32 and xxii.

9. Ibid., 74.

10. See Stephen McKnight, *The Religious Foundations of Francis Bacon's Thought* (Columbia: University of Missouri Press, 2006); Steven Matthews, *Theology and Science in the Thought of Francis Bacon* (Burlington, VT: Ashgate, 2008); and Sarah Irving, "Rethinking Instrumentality: Natural Philosophy and Christian Charity in the Early Modern Atlantic World," *HOPOS: The Journal of the International Society for the History of Philosophy of Science* 2, no. 1 (2012): 55–76.

11. Hans Blumenberg, *The Legitimacy of the Modern Age*, trans. Robert Wallace (Boston: MIT Press, 1985), 383.

12. The phrase is Richard Kennington's, in "Bacon's Reform of Nature," *On Modern Origins: Essays in Early Modern Philosophy*, ed. Pamela Kraus and Frank Hunt (New York: Lexington Books, 2004), 13; but perhaps the foremost proponent of this attitude is Jerry Weinberger in *Science, Faith, and Politics: Francis Bacon and the Utopian Roots of the Modern Age* (Ithaca, NY: Cornell University Press, 1985). Their viewpoint is in some ways echoed by Denise Albanese, who claims that Christianity is "the code for an intellectual imperialism" in *New Science, New World* (Durham, NC: Duke University Press, 1996), 103.

13. The quotation is actually Stephen McKnight's in summarizing the general thrust of Howard B. White's *Peace among the Willows: The Political Philosophy of Francis Bacon* (The Hague: Martinus Nijhoff, 1968). See McKnight, *Religious Foundations*, 10.

14. Bacon himself offers an accessible definition of the term "use" as "a trust reposed by any person in the terre-tenant that he may suffer him to take the profits and that he will perform his intent." Bacon, *Reading of the Statute of Uses* (New York: Garland, 1979), 400–401.

15. Luther, "Sermon for the Third Sunday after Easter," in *The Complete Sermons of Martin Luther*, ed. John Nicholas Lenker (Grand Rapids, MI: Baker Books, 1983), 4:281–82. On Calvin, see David Little, *Religion, Order, and Law* (Chicago: University of Chicago Press, 1984), esp. 57–60.

16. Linda Gregerson, *The Reformation of the Subject: Spenser, Milton, and the English Protestant Epic* (Cambridge: Cambridge University Press, 1995), 53, n. 10. The intersection between charity and use was also bound up in crucial but vexed theories of natural rights. See Richard Tuck, *Natural Rights Theories* (Cambridge: Cambridge University Press, 1979).

17. Nicholas Heming, *A Godly Treatise concerning the lawfull use of ritches*, trans. Thomas Rogers (London: 1578), 14.

18. A quick EEBO search, admittedly an imprecise heuristic tool, shows eight uses of the terms "charitable uses" or "pious uses" from 1473 to 1597, the year of the first statute regulating charitable uses, and nearly eighty uses of either term from 1598 to 1625, when James died.

19. *A proclamation to redresse the mis-imployment of lands, goods, and other things giuen for charitable vses* (London: 1605).

20. 43 Eliz. I c. 4, *Statutes of the Realm: Printed by Command of His Majesty King George the Third*, vol. 4, part 2 (London: 1819), 969. For a cogent and thorough examination of the statutes, see Gareth Jones, *The History of the Law of Charity* (Cambridge: Cambridge University Press, 1969), 16–58.

21. Jones, *History of the Law of Charity*, 47–51.

22. 39 Eliz. I c. 6, *Statutes of the Realm*, vol. 4, part 2, 903.

23. George Wither, "Satyre 1," in Book 2, *Abuses stript, and whipt* (London: 1613), 137–38.

24. Lewis Bayly, *The Practice of Pietie* (London: 1613), 812.

25. Robert Burton, *The Anatomy of Melancholy*, ed. Thomas Faulkner, Nicolas Kiessling, and Rhonda Blair (Oxford: Clarendon Press, 1994), 3:35.

26. John Donne, *Pseudo-Martyr*, ed. Anthony Raspa (Montreal: McGill-Queen's University Press, 1993), 88.

27. Jones, *History of the Law of Charity*, 52.

28. Ibid., 53.

29. See Paul Slack, *Poverty and Policy in Tudor and Stuart England* (London: Longman, 1988), 169–73. Slack suggests that private donations provided an estimated two-thirds of the funding devoted to poor relief at the beginning of the seventeenth century.

30. Steve Hindle, "'Good, Godly and Charitable Uses': Endowed Charity and the Relief of Poverty in Rural England, c. 1550–1750," in *Institutional Culture in Early Modern Society*, ed. Anne Goldgar and Robert Frost (Leiden: Brill, 2004), 186.

31. *Statutes of the Realm*, vol. 4, part 2, 968–69.

32. Andrew Willet's catalog is appended to *Synopsis papismi, that is, A generall view of papistrie* (London: 1613), 1220–43.

33. Francis Bacon, *The essaies of Sr Francis Bacon Knight, the Kings Solliciter Generall* (London: 1612), 125–26.

34. Samuel Daniel, *The Complete Works in Verse and Prose of Samuel Daniel*, ed. Alexander Grosart (New York: Russell and Russell, 1963), 1:5.

35. Philip Massinger, *The City Madam,* ed. Cyrus Hoy (Lincoln: University of Nebraska Press, 1964), 73.

36. Craig Muldrew, *The Economy of Obligation: The Culture of Credit and Social Relations in Early Modern England* (Houndsmill, Basingstoke: Palgrave Macmillan, 1998). Among the (still important) studies promoting the earlier argument are Max Weber, *The Protestant Ethic and the Spirit of Capitalism,* trans. Talcott Parsons (New York: Scribner, 1958); R. H. Tawney, *Religion and the Rise of Capitalism* (New York: Harcourt, Brace, 1926); Christopher Hill, *Society and Puritanism in Pre-Revolutionary England* (London: Seeker and Warburg, 1964); Joyce Appleby, *Economic Thought and Ideology in Seventeenth-Century England* (Princeton, NJ: Princeton University Press, 1978); and, perhaps most relevant to this study because it explicitly and intelligently engages the subject of London theater, Jean-Christophe Agnew, *Worlds Apart: The Market and the Theater in Anglo-American Thought, 1550–1750* (Cambridge: Cambridge University Press, 1986).

37. See Theodore Leinwand, *Theatre, Finance and Society in Early Modern England* (Cambridge: Cambridge University Press, 1999); Ceri Sullivan, *The Rhetoric of Credit: Merchants in Early Modern Writing* (Madison, NJ: Fairleigh Dickinson University Press, 2002); Jill Phillips Ingram, *Idioms of Self-Interest: Credit, Identity, and Property in English Renaissance Literature* (New York: Routledge, 2006); Valerie Forman, *Tragicomic Redemptions: Global Economics and the Early Modern English Stage* (Philadelphia: University of Pennsylvania Press, 2008); *Global Traffic: Discourses and Practices of Trade in English Literature and Culture from 1550 to 1700,* ed. Barbara Sebek and Stephen Deng (New York: Palgrave Macmillan, 2008); and Aaron Kitch, *Political Economy and the States of Literature in Early Modern England* (Aldershot, UK: Ashgate, 2009).

38. Thomas Mun, *A discourse of trade, from England vnto the East-Indies* (London: 1621), 42.

39. Samuel Purchas, *Purchas his Pilgrimage* (London: 1625), 1:20. Thomas Middleton's 1617 pageant, *The Tryumphs of Honor and Industry,* rehearses a similar notion of commerce linking nations together in love when *"Traffic or Merchandise, who holds a globe in her hand, knits love and peace amongst all nations." Thomas Middleton: The Collected Works,* ed. Gary Taylor and John Lavagnino (Oxford: Oxford University Press, 2007), 1253.

40. *A petition to the Kings most excellent Maiestie* (London: 1622), F3v. See Leinwand, *Theatre, Finance and Society,* 42–80. François Rabelais, *The Complete Works,* trans. Donald Frame (Berkeley: University of California Press, 1999), 271.

41. Thomas Milles, *An Out-Port-Customer's Accompt* (1612), sig. L1v, found in Kitch, *Political Economy and the States of Literature,* 4.

42. Thomas Gainsford, *The Rich Cabinet* (London: 1616), 89v.

43. Laura Caroline Stevenson, *Praise and Paradox: Merchants and Craftsmen in Elizabethan Popular Literature* (Cambridge: Cambridge University Press, 1984), 26.

44. As Ian Archer notes, "The continual harping on the hospitality of yesteryear and the laments about the 'get-rich-quick mentality' of his own time convey

the impression that charity had waxed cold." "The Nostalgia of John Stow," in *The Theatrical City: Culture, Theatre, and Politics in London, 1576–1649*, ed. David Smith, Richard Strier, and David Bevington (Cambridge: Cambridge University Press, 1995), 27.

45. Ian Archer, *The Pursuit of Stability: Social Relations in Elizabethan London* (Cambridge: Cambridge University Press, 1991).

46. Helen Moore, "Succeeding Stow: Anthony Munday and the 1618 *Survey of London*," in *John Stow (1525–1605) and the Making of the English Past*, ed. Ian Gadd and Alexandra Gillespie (London: British Library, 2004), 101–2.

47. A number of studies have examined the relationship between city pageants and popular theatre. See Gail Kern Paster, *The Idea of the City in the Age of Shakespeare* (Athens: University of Georgia Press, 1985), 124–49; Leinwand, *The City Staged*, esp. 21–80; Janette Dillon, *Theatre, Court and City, 1595–1610: Drama and Social Space in London* (Cambridge: Cambridge University Press, 2000); Ian Munro, *The Figure of the Crowd in Early Modern London* (New York: Palgrave Macmillan, 2005), esp. 51–73; Jean Howard, *Theater of a City: The Places of London Comedy, 1598–1642* (Philadelphia: University of Pennsylvania Press, 2007); and Kitch, *Political Economy and the States of Literature*, 155–84.

48. Anthony Munday, *Chruso-thriambos. The Triumphes of Golde* (1611), C4r.

49. Paster, *Idea of the City*, 145.

50. Thomas Dekker, *The Dramatic Works of Thomas Dekker*, ed. Fredson Bowers (Cambridge: Cambridge University Press, 1958), 3:246.

51. Leinwand, *The City Staged*, 26.

52. *Thomas Middleton: The Collected Works*, 974.

53. See *The Ordre of my Lord Maior, the Aldermen* (1568), sigs. B2v–B3r; and John Stow, *A Survey of London*, ed. Charles Lethbridge Kingsford (Oxford: Clarendon Press, 1971), 167–68.

54. Jean Howard, "Afterword: Accommodating Change," in *Global Traffic*, 269. See Sullivan, *Rhetoric of Credit*, 178.

55. Andrew Willet, *Hexapla in Genesin & Exodum: that is, a sixfold commentary upon the two first bookes of Moses* (London: 1633), 250; Francis Quarles, "Of Pious Uses," in *The Complete Works in Prose and Verse of Francis Quarles*, ed. Alexander Grosart (1880), 2:240.

56. Robert Hayman, *Quodlibets* (London: 1628), 21; Samuel Butler, "A Ranter," in *Samuel Butler: Characters and Passages from Note-Books*, ed. A. R. Waller (Cambridge: University Press, 1908), 68.

57. The first quotation, from an anonymous army officer to Francis Walsingham in 1587, which proceeds to suggest levying a weekly tax on all playhouses, is printed in E. K. Chambers, *The Elizabethan Stage* (Oxford: Clarendon Press, 1923), 4:273–76. The second quotation is from *An Act of Common Council in London* (1574), from MS Lansdowne 20, printed in *Malone Society Collections* (Oxford: Oxford University Press, 1911), 1:175–78.

58. Consider the certificate sent to the Privy Council endorsing the license of the Fortune in 1600, which lists as the second reason for tolerating the playhouse's business, "Because the Erectors of the said house are contented to give a very liberal portion of the money weekly towards the relief of our Poor." See Chambers, *Elizabethan Stage*, 4:327–28.

59. *The Works of Francis Beaumont and John Fletcher*, ed. A. R. Waller (Cambridge: University Press, 1906), 3:199.

60. Ken Jackson, *Separate Theaters: Bethlem ("Bedlam") Hospital and the Shakespearean Stage* (Newark, NJ: University of Delaware Press, 2005), 222.

61. Ben Jonson, *The Cambridge Edition of the Works of Ben Jonson*, ed. David Bevington, Martin Butler, and Ian Donaldson (Cambridge: Cambridge University Press, 2012), 3:530. Further citations from this edition will identify act, scene, and line in parentheses.

62. Ibid., 355. See also Dillon, *Theatre, Court and City*, 109–123; and David Baker, "'The Allegory of a China Shop': Jonson's 'Entertainment at Britain's Burse,'" *ELH* 72, no. 1 (2005): 159–80.

63. *The Selected Plays of John Marston*, ed. MacDonald Jackson and Michael Neill (Cambridge: Cambridge University Press, 1986), 305.

64. Francis Bacon, "Of Usurie," in *The Essayes or Counsels, Civill and Morall*, ed. Michael Kiernan (Cambridge: Harvard University Press, 1985), 126.

65. See Jonathan Gil Harris, *Sick Economies: Drama, Mercantilism, and Disease in Shakespeare's England* (Philadelphia: University of Pennsylvania Press, 2004), 108–35.

66. The quote recalls a fascinating phrase from Robert Allen: "The one striving after a sort to overcome the other with kindnesse and benefites: according to the common saying which goeth concerning such: *There is no love lost betwixt them*. The which kind of strife hath bene always honourable, even among the nations of the heathen." *The Oderifferous Garden of Charitie* (London: 1603), 13.

67. Robert Wiltenburg, *Ben Jonson and Self-Love: The Subtlest Maze of All* (Columbia: University of Missouri Press, 1990), 30.

68. Philip Massinger was clearly taken with this scene, mimicking its irony in *The Parliament of Love*, when the physician Dinant pretends to offer his wife to an ailing philanderer as "a charitable, pious worke." See *The Plays of Philip Massinger*, ed. W. Gifford (New York: AMS, 1966), 2:287.

69. Alison Scott, "Censuring Indulgence: Volpone's 'Use of Riches' and the Problem of Luxury," *AUMLA* 110 (2008): 1–15.

70. *Measure for Measure* 2.4.68, in *The Riverside Shakespeare*, ed. G. Blakemore Evans, 2nd ed. (Boston: Houghton Mifflin, 1997), 597.

71. Robert Evans, *Jonson and the Contexts of His Time* (Cranbury, NJ: Associated University Presses, 1994), 61.

72. Ibid., 54.

73. Thomas Fuller, *The History of the Worthies of England* (London: 1662), 168.

74. Harriett Hawkins, "Folly, Incurable Disease, and *Volpone*," *Studies in English Literature, 1500–1900* 8, no. 2 (1968): 335–48.

75. John Creaser, "*Volpone:* The Mortifying of the Fox," *Essays in Criticism* 25, no. 3 (1975): 352.

76. This is my single qualification of the argument Susan Wells pursues in her discussion of the festive marketplace and its corrective influence on commercial ideology. Whereas Wells claims of *The Alchemist*, "The conventional answers—charity and contentment—press upon our attention less than the play's image of the lavish and carefree material life of the festive marketplace," I believe the play repeatedly points to charity as both a problem and a solution. Wells, "Jacobean City Comedy and the Ideology of the City," *ELH* 48, no. 1 (1981): 54.

77. See Alexander Leggatt, *Citizen Comedy in the Age of Shakespeare* (Toronto: University of Toronto Press, 1973), esp. 75–76; see also John Mebane, who claims that Mammon "masquerades as a prophet of humanitarian reform" in *Renaissance Magic and the Return of the Golden Age* (Lincoln: University of Nebraska Press, 1992), 151–52.

78. Ronald Huebert emphasizes this point in *The Performance of Pleasure in English Renaissance Drama* (Houndmills, Basingstoke: Palgrave Macmillan, 2003), 64–65.

79. Leggatt, *Citizen Comedy*, 76.

80. See in particular Jonathan Haynes, *The Social Relations of Jonson's Theatre* (Cambridge: Cambridge University Press, 1992), 99–118; and David Hawkes, *Idols of the Marketplace: Idolatry and Commodity Fetishism in English Literature, 1580–1680* (New York: Palgrave, 2001), 157–58.

81. See Rebecca Nivlin, "The Rogues' Paradox: Redefining Work in *The Alchemist*," in *Working Subjects in Early Modern English Drama* (Burlington, VT: Ashgate, 2011), 115–30.

82. See Peter Lake, with Michael Questier, *The Antichrist's Lewd Hat: Protestants, Papists and Players in Post-Reformation England* (New Haven: Yale University Press, 2002), 579.

83. Face and Subtle recycle a line from *Epicoene*, when the fashionable women hurry off to "Bedlam, to the china houses, and to the Exchange" (4.3.23).

84. Alan Dessen, *Jonson's Moral Comedy* (Evanston, IL: Northwestern University Press, 1971), 118.

85. Robert Knoll, "How to Read *The Alchemist*," *College English* 21, no. 8 (1960): 456–60.

86. Robert Watson notes that Surly mistakenly expects to triumph as a "morality-play Good Counsel figure." *Ben Jonson's Parodic Strategy: Literary Imperialism in the Comedies* (Cambridge, MA: Harvard University Press, 1987), 127–31.

87. Richard Grassby, *The Business Community of Seventeenth-Century England* (Cambridge: Cambridge University Press, 2002), 297–301.

88. Several scholars have expressed differing opinions of this aspect of Jonson's play. See, among others, David Riggs, *Ben Jonson: A Life* (Cambridge, MA: Harvard University Press, 1989), 170–73; Peter Womack, *Ben Jonson* (New York: Blackwell, 1986), 118–20; and Alexander Leggatt, *Ben Jonson, His Vision and Art* (New York: Methuen, 1981), 35.

89. Riggs, *Ben Jonson*, 171.

90. If Andrew Gurr's supposition is correct, that Lovewit is intended to represent Shakespeare, a housekeeper or shareholder of Blackfriars, the situation expresses an even deeper ambivalence about commercial theater for Jonson. Gurr, "Who is Lovewit? What is he?" in *Ben Jonson and Theatre*, ed. Richard Allan Cave and Brian Woolland (London: Routledge, 1999), 5–19.

91. Jonson, *Works*, 3:558.

92. See Howard, *Theater of a City*, 99–105.

93. Jonson, *Works*, 2:646.

94. Joseph Loewenstein describes this phenomenon as "the alienations of purchase, which divide producer and consumer," in *Ben Jonson and Possessive Authorship* (Cambridge: Cambridge University Press, 2002), 161.

95. Jonson, *Works*, 4:26.

Chapter 5: Charitable Singularity

1. William Laud, *A sermon preached on Munday, the seauenteenth of March, at Westminster at the opening of the Parliament* (London: 1628), 19; Thomas Foster, *Plouto-mastix: the scourge of covetousnesse* (London: 1631), 15; Francis Meres, *Wits Commonwealth The Second Part* (London: 1634), 168.

2. *The Oxford Edition of the Sermons of John Donne*, ed. David Colclough (Oxford: Oxford University Press, 2013), 3:131.

3. *Complaints concerning corruptions and grievances in church government* (1641), 3.

4. As with chapter 2, which employed a binary between "conformists" and "Puritans," I recognize that the terms used here—"Puritan," "Papist," "Laudian," and the more general "supporter of prelacy"—obscure the complexities of seventeenth-century confessional identity and church discipline. But these labels are helpful, especially as they relate to charity, if they can gesture at loosely shared ecclesiastical priorities, disciplinary styles, and political projects.

5. See Peter Lake, "The Laudian Style: Order, Uniformity and the Pursuit of the Beauty of Holiness in the 1630s," in *The Early Stuart Church, 1603–1642*, ed. Kenneth Fincham (Stanford, CA: Stanford University Press, 1993), 161–85.

6. The degree to which the Caroline church under Charles and Laud altered doctrinal and ecclesiastical policy is a matter of some debate. For a lucid summary of key principles, see Peter Lake, "Introduction: Puritanism, Arminianiam, and Nicholas Tyacke," in *Religious politics in Post-Reformation England*, ed. Kenneth Fincham and Peter Lake (Woodbridge, UK: The Boydell Press, 2006), 1–15.

7. [John Ley], *A discourse concerning Puritans* (London: 1641), 13.

8. Richard Crashaw, "Upon the ensuing Treatises," in Robert Shelford, *Five pious and learned discourses* (London: 1635), A1v.

9. Herbert Palmer, *Scripture and reason pleaded for defensive armes* (London: 1643), 79.

10. Richard Watson, *A sermon touching schism* (Cambridge: 1642), 33–34.

11. *Constitutions and canons ecclesiasticall* (1640), F1r.

12. *Englands complaint to Iesus Christ, against the bishops canons of the late sinfull synod* (1640), E5v.

13. John Winthrop, *Winthrop Papers*, ed. Stewart Mitchell (Boston: Massachusetts Historical Society, 1931), 2:293.

14. Sir Tobie Mathew, *Charity Mistaken, with the Want Wherof, Catholickes are Unjustly Charged* (Saint-Omer: 1630), 103.

15. See Anthony Milton, *Catholic and Reformed: The Roman and Protestant Churches in English Protestant Thought, 1600–1640* (Cambridge: Cambridge University Press, 1995), 60–92.

16. For more on the "charity debate," see Reid Barbour, *Literature and Religious Culture in Seventeenth-Century England* (Cambridge: Cambridge University Press, 2002), 236–44.

17. Christopher Potter, *Want of charitie iustly charged* (London: 1633), 8.

18. J. Sears McGee, "A 'Carkass' of 'Mere Dead paper': The Polemical Career of Francis Rous, Puritan MP," *The Huntington Library Quarterly* 72, no. 3 (2009): 347.

19. Kenelm Digby, *A conference with a lady about choice of religion* (Paris: 1638), 73.

20. [John Taylor], *The anatomy of the separatists, alias, Brownists* (London: 1642), 2.

21. Joseph Hall, *An Humble Remonstrance to the High Court of Parliament, by a dutifull sonne of the Church* (London: 1641), 40.

22. *The Poems of Thomas Carew, with His Masque "Coelum Britannicum,"* ed. Rhodes Dunlap (Oxford: Clarendon Press, 1949).

23. Ben Jonson, *Bartholomew Fair* (1.3.108–9), in *The Cambridge Edition of the Works of Ben Jonson*, ed. David Bevington, Martin Butler, and Ian Donaldson (Cambridge: Cambridge University Press, 2012), 4:293–94; Thomas Nashe, *An almond for a parrat* (1590), 10; Richard Baxter, *Certain disputations of right to sacraments and the true nature of visible Christianity* (London: 1658), 333.

24. William Prynne, *Histrio-mastix* (London: 1633), **1v; John Donne, *Sermons*, ed. George Potter and Evelyn Simpson (Berkeley: University of California Press, 1955), 2:279.

25. Thomas Browne, *The Works of Sir Thomas Browne*, ed. Geoffrey Keynes (Chicago: University of Chicago Press, 1964), 1:69; further citations from this edition appear in parentheses by page number.

26. John Milton, *The Complete Prose Works of John Milton*, vol. 7, ed. Robert Ayers (New Haven, CT: Yale University Press, 1959), 246.

27. Browne, *Works*, 3:134.

28. Reid Barbour, *Sir Thomas Browne: A Life* (Oxford: Oxford University Press, 2013), 219–55.

29. Milton, *Complete Prose Works*, vol. 2, ed. Ernest Sirluck, 309, 340, 591, 604–5, and 669. Further citations from this edition are parenthetical by page number.

30. William Prynne, *Twelve Considerable Serious Questions Touching Church Government* (1644), 7.

31. R. Kenneth Kirby, "Milton's Biblical Hermeneutics in *The Doctrine and Discipline of Divorce*," *Milton Quarterly* 18, no. 4 (1984): 118.

32. Alexander Ross, *Medicus Medicatus* (1645), 7.

33. See Reid Barbour, "Dean Wren's *Religio Medici*: Reading in Civil War England," *The Huntington Library Quarterly* 73, no. 2 (2010): 263–73.

34. *Christopher Wren's 'Religio Medici,'* Cardiff MS 1.160.

35. Michael Wilding, *Dragons Teeth: Literature in the English Revolution* (Oxford: Oxford University Press, 1987), 93. See also Stanley Fish, *Self-Consuming Artifacts* (Berkeley: University of California Press, 1972), 353–73; and Joan Webber, *The Eloquent "I": Style and Self in Seventeenth-Century Prose* (Madison: University of Wisconsin Press, 1968), 165.

36. See Raymond Waddington, "The Two Tables in *Religio Medici*," in *Approaches to Sir Thomas Browne*, ed. C.A. Patrides (Columbia: University of Missouri Press, 1982), 81–99; Achsah Guibbory, *Ceremony and Community from Herbert to Milton* (Cambridge: Cambridge University Press, 1998), 119–46; Ingo Berensmeyer, "Rhetoric, Religion, and Politics in Sir Thomas Browne's *Religio Medici*," *Studies in English Literature, 1500–1900* 46, no. 1 (2006): 113–34.

37. It is likely for this reason that two of the most perceptive studies of Browne's religion resist conventional categories, characterizing him instead as a "liberal" or "lay" theologian. See Victoria Silver, "Liberal Theology and Sir Thomas Browne's 'Soft and Flexible' Discourse," *ELR* 20, no. 1 (1990): 69–105; and Debora Shuger, "The Laudian Idiot," in *Sir Thomas Browne: The World Proposed*, ed. Reid Barbour and Claire Preston (Oxford: Oxford University Press, 2008), 36–62.

38. Guibbory, *Ceremony and Community*, 119.

39. Claire Preston discusses Browne's civility in the context of Bacon's project in *Thomas Browne and the Writing of Early Modern Science* (Cambridge: Cambridge University Press, 2005), 10–41.

40. Dennis Danielson, *Milton's Good God: A Study in Literary Theodicy* (Cambridge: Cambridge University Press, 1982), 229.

41. Margaret Pelling rightly takes issue with the manner in which the term "medical marketplace" has been employed anachronistically by historians of medicine. *Medical Conflicts in Early Modern London* (Oxford: Clarendon Press, 2003), 342–43. When I mention the term I do not mean to suggest a laissez-faire economic model, but I do take it for granted that questions of religion were implicated in the decisions of potential patients when engaging in contractual medicine.

42. Browne failed to convince every reader of his Christian belief. Consider physician John Collop's poem *"On Doctor Browne,"* which celebrates *Religio Medici* and simultaneously acknowledges its reputed irreligion: *"Religio Medici* though th'wor[l]d Atheism call, / The wou[r]ld shows none, and the Physitian all. / More zeal and charity *Brown* in twelve sheets shows, / Then twelve past ages writ, or th'present knows" (lines 1–4), quoted in Browne, *Works,* 3:181.

43. John Cotta, *A short discouerie of the vnobserued dangers of seuerall sorts of ignorant and vnconsiderate practisers of physicke in England* (London: 1612), 24. See also Securis, *A Detection and Querimonie of the Dailie Enormities and Abuses Committed in Physicke* (London: 1566).

44. Cotta, *A short discouerie,* 86.

45. *The Works of George Herbert,* ed. F. E. Hutchinson (Oxford: Clarendon Press, 1941), 259–63.

46. Robert Burton, *The Anatomy of Melancholy,* ed. Thomas Faulkner, Nicolas Kiessling, and Rhonda Blair (Oxford: Clarendon Press, 1989), 1:22. It is worth noting, however, that Burton, despite his defensive remarks aimed at learned physicians, nevertheless apologizes for divulging *"secreta Minervae"* (16).

47. See Paul Slack, "Mirrors of Health and Treasures of Poor Men: The Uses of the Vernacular Medical Literature of Tudor England," in *Health, Medicine, and Mortality in the Sixteenth Century,* ed. Charles Webster (Cambridge: Cambridge University Press, 1979), 237–74. Even the Presbyterian reformer Thomas Cartwright might have contributed to this genre, if he is indeed the "T.C." who gathered the various remedies of *An hospitall for the diseased* (London: 1579).

48. Burton, *Anatomy,* 21–22.

49. See David Harley, "Spiritual Physic, Providence and English Medicine, 1560–1640," in *Medicine and the Reformation,* ed. Ole Peter Grell and Andrew Cunningham (London: Routledge, 1993), 101–17.

50. Gabriel Plattes, *A Description of the Famous Kingdome of Macaria* (London: 1641), 5–7.

51. Ficino explicitly invokes charity to defend his marriage of divinity and medicine in the *Apologia* to his *Three Books on Life,* trans. Carol Kaske and John Clark (Binghamton, NY: Center for Medieval and Early Renaissance Studies, 1989), 397.

52. James Hart, *Klinike, or The diet of the diseased* (London: 1633), 403.

53. Juan Huarte employs this scriptural reference in "The second Proeme to the Reader" of *The Examination of mens Wits,* trans. M. Camillo Camili and R. C. Esquire (London: 1594), when he suggests that professional distinctions are the result of physical complexion.

54. William Laud, *A relation of the conference betweene William Lawd, then, Lrd. Bishop of St. Davids; now, Lord Arch-Bishop of Canterbury: and Mr. Fisher the Jesuite* (London: 1639), sig.*3v.

55. See Andrew McRae, *God Speed the Plough: The Representation of Agrarian England, 1500–1660* (Cambridge: Cambridge University Press, 1996).

56. Hart, *Klinike*, 403.

57. Richard Whitlock, *Zootomia* (London: 1654), 54.

58. For an excellent overview of the varied medical profession in Norwich, see Margaret Pelling, *The Common Lot: Sickness, Medical Occupations and the Urban Poor in Early Modern England* (London: Longman, 1998), 203–29.

59. Bacon, *The Advancement of Learning*, ed. Michael Kiernan (Oxford: Clarendon Press, 2000), 97. The responses to plague by early modern physicians did not merely recycle features of Galenic theory, but rather incorporated their own experience of what was generally regarded to be a new type of disease. They nevertheless struggled to find a framework to understand plagues. See Andrew Wear, *Knowledge and Practice in English Medicine, 1550–1680* (Cambridge: Cambridge University Press, 2000), 275–313.

60. With regard to medical practitioners leaving the city during epidemics, see Margaret Pelling, "Skirting the City?: Disease, Social Change and Divided Households in the Seventeenth Century," in *Londinopolis: Essays in the Cultural and Social History of Early Modern London,* ed. Paul Griffiths (Manchester, UK: Manchester University Press, 2000), 154–75.

61. Several explanations for the poor reputation of physicians were put forward by contemporaries. See, in addition to Bacon's *Advancement*, Thomas Powell, *Tom of all trades. Or The plaine path-way to preferment* (London: 1631), 29.

62. Richard Bostocke, *The difference betwene the auncient phisicke* (London: 1585), sig., Fiiiv. See also the apologetical preface by B.G. a Portu Aquitanu [Penotus] in *A hundred and fouretene experiments and cures of the famous physitian Philippus Aureolus Theophrastus Paracelsus,* trans. John Hester (London: 1596), sig. A3.

63. Thomas Elyot, *The castell of health, corrected, and in some places augmented by the first author thereof* (London: 1595), sig. Av. Burton similarly indicts contemporary physicians by comparing them to their classical pagan counterparts who served patients out of charity (*Anatomy*, 2:211).

64. See William Eamon, *Science and the Secrets of Nature: Books of Secrets in Medieval and Early Modern Culture* (Princeton, NJ: Princeton University Press, 1994), 138–39.

65. See James Fourestier, "Epistle Dedicatorie," in John Hester, *The pearle of practise,* (London: 1594), iir.

66. Cotta, *Short discouerie,* 122. For the early modern physician's relative silence on the topic of charity, see Andrew Wear, "Medical Ethics in Early Modern England," in *Doctors and Ethics: The Earlier Historical Setting of Professional Ethics,* ed. Andrew Wear, Johanna Geyer-Kordesch, and Roger French (Amsterdam: Rodopi, 1993), 98–130.

67. See Margaret Pelling, *Common Lot,* 79–104; and Andrew Wear, "Caring for the Sick Poor in St Bartholomew Exchange," in *Living and Dying in London,* ed. W. F. Bynum and Roy Porter (London: Wellcome Institute, 1991), 41–60.

68. Pelling, *Medical Conflicts*, 18–21.

69. The quote is from Gerard Boate, in Pelling, *Medical Conflicts*, 179–84.

70. Charles Webster, "English Medical Reformers of the Puritan Revolution," *Ambix* 14, no. 1 (1967): 16–41; Webster, *The Great Instauration: Science, Medicine and Reform, 1626–1660* (New York: Holmes and Meier, 1975), 246–323; Christopher Hill, *Change and Continuity in Seventeenth-Century England* (Cambridge, MA: Harvard University Press, 1975), 157–78; Pelling, *Common Lot*, 230–58.

71. One potential model is Thomas Clayton, the Regius Professor of Physic during Browne's time at Oxford, as Mary Ann Lund has explored in "The Christian Physician: Thomas Browne and the Role of Religion in Medical Practice," in *"A man very well studyed": New Contexts for Thomas Browne*, ed. Kathryn Murphy and Richard Todd (Leiden: Brill, 2008), 229–46.

72. Brooke Conti, "*Religio Medici's* Profession of Faith," in *Sir Thomas Browne: The World Proposed*, 154.

73. Browne already had witnessed conflict between medical and ecclesiastical authorities in Padua, which had experienced a plague in 1630–31 that aggravated tensions between the two communities. See Barbour, "Atheists, Monsters, Plagues, and Jews: Tares in the Garden of Thomas Browne's Padua, 1632," in *Writing and Religion in England, 1558–1689: Studies in Community-Making and Cultural Memory*, ed. Roger Sell and Anthony Johnson (Farnham, Surrey: Ashgate, 2009), 328–29.

74. See Levinus Lemnius, *The Touchstone of Complexions*, trans. Thomas Newton (London: 1576), 24. See also Margaret Healy's discussion of the overlap in medical and religious discourse during the period in *Fictions of Disease in Early Modern England: Bodies, Plagues, and Politics* (New York: Palgrave, 2001), esp. 42–45. For a discussion more specifically focused on Browne, see Lund, "The Christian Physician," 229–46.

75. As Celsus states in *De Medicina*, "Above all things everyone should be acquainted with the nature of his own body." Celsus, *De Medicina*, trans. W.G. Spencer (Cambridge, MA: Harvard University Press, 1971), 57. For more on the overlap between medical practice and Calvinist spiritual experience, see Harley, "Spiritual Physic, Providence and English Medicine," 101–17.

76. Thomas Hill, *The contemplation of mankind* (London: 1571), sig. v.

77. Potter, *Want of charitie iustly charged*, 40.

78. For the clearest description of Milton's understanding of heresy, see the preface of *A Treatise of Civil Power*, in *Complete Prose Works*, 7:647.

79. Elyot, *Castell of health*, 96. Juan Huarte makes a similar claim in *Examination of mens wits*, 147.

80. Helkiah Crooke, *Microcosmographia: a description of the body of man* (London: 1615), 8.

81. Browne, *Works*, 3:285.

82. Although Browne claims to have been unfamiliar with Montaigne's *Essays*

when he wrote *Religio Medici*, this sentence bears a remarkable similarity to a passage in John Florio's translation of the essay "Of Physiognomy": "There are some favourable Physiognomies; For in a throng of victorious enemies you shall presently amiddest a multitude of vnknowne faces, make choise of one man more than of others, to yeeld your selfe vnto, and trust your life." Montaigne, *The essayes or morall, politike and millitarie discourses of Lo: Michaell de Montaigne*, trans. John Florio (London: 1603), 630.

83. The subject continued to fascinate Browne, who included a more complete discussion of gypsies, or "counterfeit Egyptians," in *Pseudodoxia Epidemica*. Browne, *Works*, 2:481–82.

84. *The Complete Works of Aristotle: The Revised Oxford Translation,* ed. Jonathan Barnes (Princeton, NJ: Princeton University Press, 1984), 1:113.

85. See Ian Maclean, *Logic, Signs and Nature in the Renaissance* (Cambridge: Cambridge University Press, 2002), esp. chap. 5.

86. Richard Sugg, *Murder after Death: Literature and Anatomy in Early Modern England* (Ithaca, NY: Cornell University Press, 2007), 89.

87. Reid Barbour, "The Hieroglyphics of Skin," in *Sir Thomas Browne: The World Proposed*, 295.

88. For a comparison of the inductive methods of Bacon and Browne, see Egon Merton, *Science and Imagination in Sir Thomas Browne* (New York: Octagon, 1969).

89. Browne, *Works*, 2:35. For Bacon's appeal for a calendar of errors, see *Advancement of Learning*, 91.

90. I am following Frank Huntley in using Loveday's name, although I acknowledge the identification is dubious, for reasons most recently outlined in Kathryn Murphy's essay "The Christian Physician: Thomas Browne and the Role of Religion in Medical Practice," in *"A man very well studied,"* 240.

91. Claire Preston, "'An Incomium of Consumptions': *A Letter to a Friend* as Medical Narrative," in *Sir Thomas Browne: The World Proposed*, 209.

92. As Seth Lobis notes, Sir Kenelm Digby appears to misunderstand Browne when he critiques the "narrow view of charity" in the *Religio*. Lobis, *The Virtue of Sympathy: Magic, Philosophy, and Literature in Seventeenth-Century England* (New Haven, CT: Yale University Press, 2015), 63.

93. Webber, *The Eloquent "I,"* 154. The manuscripts of *Religio Medici* are even further fragmented, as Reid Barbour notes in "The Power of the Broken: Sir Thomas Browne's *Religio Medici* and Aphoristic Writing," *Huntington Library Quarterly*, 79, no. 4 (2016): 591–610.

94. Barbour, *Literature and Religious Culture*, 190–91.

95. Jason Rosenblatt, *Torah and Law in "Paradise Lost"* (Princeton, NJ: Princeton University Press, 1994), 103. Barbara Lewalski briefly notes the relation between charity and liberty in the divorce tracts in "Milton, Liberty, Servility, and the

Paradise Within," in *Milton, Rights and Liberties*, ed. Christophe Tournu and Neil Forsyth (Bern: Peter Lang, 2007), 35–36.

96. Arthur Barker discusses the divorce tracts and the role of charity in shaping Milton's notion of Christian liberty in *Milton and the Puritan Dilemma, 1641–1660* (Toronto: University of Toronto Press, 1942).

97. Consider the position of Smectymnuan Edmund Calamy, who appropriates the charity of Colossians 3:14 as a defense against divisions of any kinds, "whether they be Ecclesiasticall, or Politicall, in Kingdomes, Cities, and Families," claiming that "Whatsoever is divisible, is corruptible." *An indictment against England because of her selfe-murdering divisions* (London: 1645), 4–7. A member of the Westminster Assembly, Calamy was an active participant in its discussion of marriage throughout 1644.

98. Catherine Gimelli Martin suggests that Milton's preoccupation with this biblical topos predates even his anti-prelatical tracts. She attributes this early fixation to Milton's interest in Bacon's *Advertisement Touching the Controversies of the Church of England* (later printed as *A Wise and Moderate Discourse*), reading the "two-handed engine" of *Lycidas* as the scriptural word that binds and loosens. Gimelli Martin, *Milton among the Puritans* (Aldershot, UK: Ashgate, 2010), 136–38.

99. This same chapter of Matthew includes the famous reference to the millstone hanging from the offender's neck, and it is interesting that Milton turns to a scriptural chapter so popular among earlier English reformers to admonish potential abuses of excessive power among Presbyterians.

100. Thomas Hobbes later underscores the hermeneutics embedded in the dictum when he translates the phrase as "Read thyself" in *The Leviathan* (London: 1651), 2.

101. Barker, *Milton and the Puritan Dilemma*, 98–120.

102. Milton, *Complete Prose Works*, 7:263. Rather than referencing Milton's earlier allusions to Matthew 16 and 18, the Yale edition considers this passage an allusion to Job 38:31.

103. Victoria Kahn, *Machiavellian Rhetoric: From the Counter-Reformation to Milton* (Princeton, NJ: Princeton University Press, 1994), 182.

104. See Diane Purkiss, "Whose Liberty? The Rhetoric of Milton's Divorce Tracts," in *The Oxford Handbook of Milton*, ed. Nicholas McDowell and Nigel Smith (Oxford: Oxford University Press, 2009), 186–99. See also Mary Lyndon Shanley, "Marriage Contract and Social Contract in Seventeenth-Century English Thought," in *Western Political Quarterly* 32, no. 1 (1979): 79–91.

105. Milton, *Complete Prose Works*, vol. 4, part 1, 239; *Milton: The Complete Shorter Poems*, ed. John Carey (New York: Longman, 2007), 329.

106. Joshua Scodel, *Excess and the Mean in Early Modern English Literature* (Princeton, NJ: Princeton University Press, 2002), 271.

107. Milton seems opportunistic in his appropriation of Stoic and Epicurean cosmologies in behalf of divorce. At times he gestures at anti-providentialism by underscoring the problem of marital accidents, declaiming the "most unchristian mischance of mariage" (311). Elsewhere, however, he adopts a fatalism in suggesting that some spouses are by their natural complexion incompatible.

108. Milton, *Complete Prose Works*, 1:841–42.

109. [Francis Rous?], *The ancient bounds, or Liberty of conscience* (London: 1645), A3.

110. Milton, *Complete Prose Works*, 3:222.

111. Milton, *Complete Shorter Poems*, 297. John Leonard, "The Troubled, Quiet Endings of Milton's Sonnets," in *Oxford Handbook of Milton*, 136–54.

112. See Reid Barbour, *English Epicures and Stoics* (Amherst: University of Massachusetts Press, 1998), 105–11.

113. Annabel Patterson, "No Meer Amatorious Novel?," in *John Milton*, ed. Annabel Patterson (London: Longman, 1992), 87–101.

114. James Grantham Turner, *One Flesh: Paradisal Marriage and Sexual Relations in the Age of Milton* (Oxford: Clarendon Press, 1987), 204.

115. *An Answer to a book intituled, The doctrine and discipline of divorce*, (London: 1644), 32.

116. Stephen Fallon, *Milton among the Philosophers* (Ithaca, NY: Cornell University Press, 1991), esp. 79–110. See also Catherine Gimelli Martin, "Dalila, Misogyny, and Milton's Christian Liberty of Divorce," in *Milton and Gender*, ed. Catherine Gimelli Martin (Cambridge: Cambridge University Press, 2004), 53–74.

117. R. A. Shoaf, *Milton, Poet of Duality* (New Haven, CT: Yale University Press, 1985), 26

118. Turner, *One Flesh*, 93.

119. *An Answer*, 37. Milton responded to this misunderstanding of liberty by characterizing the answerer as "a Servingman both by nature and by function" (741).

120. Joseph Hall, *Cases of conscience practically resolved* (London: 1654), 298.

121. There are similarities in imagery as well. Consider the likeness of Milton's "key of charity" to the Ranters' "key of liberty, whereby he [God] authorizes us to fulfil our own lusts." See *The Ranters declaration* (1650), 2.

122. *A justification of the mad crew in their waies and principles* (1650), 15.

123. David Loewenstein, "Milton among the Religious Radicals and Sects: Polemical Engagements and Silences," *Milton Studies* 40 (2001): 222–47.

124. See, for example, Northrop Frye, *Five Essays on Milton's Epics* (London: Routledge, 1966), 69 and 83–84, as well as Philip Gallagher, *Milton, the Bible, and Misogyny*, ed. Eugene Cunnar and Gail Mortimer (Columbia: University of Missouri Press, 1990), 104 and 127. This argument receives a thorough critique from both Russell Hillier, *Milton's Messiah: The Son of God in the Works of John Milton* (Oxford: Oxford University Press, 2011), 140–41, and Dennis Danielson, "Through the Telescope of Typology: What Adam Should Have Done," *Milton Quarterly* 23, no. 3 (1989): 124.

125. David Norbrook, *Writing the English Republic: Poetry, Rhetoric and Politics, 1627–1660* (Cambridge: Cambridge University Press, 2000), 482–89.

126. Jared Kuzner, "Habermas Goes to Hell: Pleasure, Public Reason, and the Republicanism of *Paradise Lost*," *Criticism* 51, no. 1 (2009): 105–45. See also Norbrook, *Writing the English Republic*, 482–89.

127. Hillier, *Milton's Messiah*, 140.

128. Milton is less worried about binding if it is scripturally sanctioned, as expressed by the Chorus in *Samson Agonistes:* "Who made our Laws to bind us, not himself" (309).

Conclusion: "Not a Single Charity"

1. Henry Ferne, *The Resolving of Conscience* (York: 1642), 50. Ferne's use of charity to support political quietism became a model for royalists like Henry Hammond, in *The Scriptures plea for magistrates* (Oxford: 1643), 8, and Thomas Warmstry, in *An answer to certain observations of W. Bridges* (Oxford: 1643), 25–26.

2. Herbert Palmer, *Scripture and reason pleaded for defensive armes* (London: 1643), 69–70. All other quotations from this text are found on these pages.

3. Palmer, *The glasse of Gods providence* (London: 1644), 55–57.

4. *The Complete Prose Works of John Milton*, ed. Ernest Sirluck (New Haven: Yale University Press, 1959), 2:582.

5. See Ferne, *Resolving of Conscience*, 47.

6. For more on Milton's "rule of charity," see Dayton Haskin, *Milton's Burden of Interpretation* (Philadelphia: University of Pennsylvania Press, 1994), 54–83.

7. Michael Dalton, *The Countrey Justice* (London: 1655), 130. The quotation is attributed to the Assize judge Francis Harvey.

INDEX

Page numbers in italics refer to illustrations.

EVAN GURNEY is assistant professor of English at the University of North Carolina at Asheville. Educated at the University of North Carolina at Chapel Hill, where he specialized in the literature of early modern England, he has published articles on Thomas More, Edmund Spenser, William Shakespeare, Ben Jonson, and John Milton. He lives in Asheville with his wife and three children.